Prehistoric Ceramics Research
Occasional Publication 3

Prehistoric Britain
The Ceramic Basis

Edited by
Ann Woodward and J. D. Hill

Oxbow Books

Published by
Oxbow Books, Park End Place, Oxford OX1 1HN

© Oxbow Books and the individual authors, 2002

ISBN 1 84217 071 6

A CIP record for this book is available from The British Library

This book is available direct from
Oxbow Books, Park End Place, Oxford, OX1 1HN
(Phone: 01865–241249; Fax: 01865–794449)

and

The David Brown Book Company
PO Box 511, Oakville, CT 06779, USA
(Phone: 860–945–9329; Fax: 860–945–9468)

and

via our website
www.oxbowbooks.com

Printed in Great Britain at
The Short Run Press
Exeter

Contents

Foreword iv

1. Introduction *(Ann Woodward and J. D. Hill)* 1

2. A Date with the Past: Late Bronze and Iron Age Pottery and Chronology
   (Steven Willis) 4

3. The Nature of Archaeological Deposits and Finds Assemblages *(Joshua Pollard)* 22

4. Aspects of Manufacture and Ceramic Technology *(Alex Gibson)* 34

5. Between Ritual and Routine: Interpreting British Prehistoric Pottery Production
   and Distribution *(Sue Hamilton)* 38

6. Staying Alive: The Function and Use of Prehistoric Ceramics *(Elaine L. Morris)* 54

7. Sherds in Space: Pottery and the Analysis of Site Organisation *(Ann Woodward)* 62

8. Pottery and the Expression of Society, Economy and Culture *(J. D. Hill)* 75

9. Ceramic Lives *(Alistair Barclay)* 85

10. Pots as Categories: British Beakers *(Robin Boast)* 96

11. Inclusions, Impressions and Interpretation *(Ann Woodward)* 106

12. A Regional Ceramic Sequence: Pottery of the First Millennium BC
    between the Humber and the Nene *(David Knight)* 119

13. Just About the Potter's Wheel? Using, Making and Depositing Middle
    and Later Iron Age Pots in East Anglia *(J. D. Hill)* 143

14. Roman Pottery in Iron Age Britain *(Andrew Fitzpatrick and Jane Timby)* 161

Bibliography 173

Contributors 196

Foreword
The human clay

Studies of prehistoric pottery have changed dramatically, and many of the more exciting developments are considered in this book. A few years ago one might be forgiven for thinking that the main purpose of archaeological fieldwork was to recover pottery and that the only point of publishing that material was because, like Everest, it was 'there'.

Not any more. With a new generation of studies of material culture – studies that seek to locate it at the heart of a modern archaeology – artefact analysis has been rejuvenated. Although aretfacts can, and should be used to investigate questions of chronology, now they have other, equally important roles to fulfil. It is not for me to spell these out as this is done most effectively by the contributors to this volume.

But why pottery rather than other kinds of artefact? These essays mount a powerful case that ancient ceramics were central to many aspects of prehistoric social life. They are no longer considered important just because they were common. It is clear that pottery, and the clay from which it is made, has a powerful metaphorical role in many societies. This is well argued here, but I had not realised quite how powerful those links might be until I was looking for a title for this piece. I wanted to check whether 'The human clay' had been used before. In the course of my search I discovered innumerable book titles that play on the same association between people and ceramics. Here is a small selection:

Brothers in Clay; Children of Clay; The Healing Power of Clay; I am the Clay; Impassioned Clay; Living Clay; Of Blood and Clay; Singing the Clay; The Spirit of the Clay; Talking with the Clay; When the Clay Sings; Talking Pots; Ceramic Gestures; Communicating Vessels; Vessels of Honour; Vessels of Faith; and (even) *Vessels of Evil.*

There are other titles that are more eccentric but they seem to be making the same point: the processes of potting are fundamental to human understanding of the world. These are a few of my favourites:

The Clay Machine Gun; I Know What Red Clay Looks Like; God Uses Cracked Pots; and, strangest of all, *I Been in Sorrow's Kitchen and Licked Out All the Pots.*

'The human clay', my own title, carries the same emphasis. Ceramics are no longer a specialist preserve, cut off from the main currents of contemporary archaeology. They are central to the whole enterprise. This interesting book tells us why.

Richard Bradley

1 Introduction

Ann Woodward and J. D. Hill

Pots are very closely related to people. Across the world, the terms applied to different parts of baked clay vessels are derived from descriptions of parts of the human body (Fig. 1.1). Nigel Barley has stated that 'Pots lend themselves to thinking about the human form' and observes that in West Africa this rich imagery recurs as a major cultural theme (Barley 1994, 85). But we need to ask why this should be so. One possible answer is that in many societies, both ancient and modern, it is pots that form the vehicle whereby two of the essential requirements of human life – food and water – are introduced into the human body itself. The other crucial human requirement is heat and warmth, and it is this property that is engaged to make the pots in the first place. The transformation of clay, part of the living earth, by fire, creates an entirely novel and man-made material – a medium which is both malleable, plastic and highly versatile becomes, when fired, a hard, rigid and highly fragile category of material culture. However the theme can be developed even further, because it is through the application of heat to the finished pots that liquids may be heated, and

foodstuffs cooked. So, the beverage passes from the lip and mouth of the cup to the human lips and mouth, and warm food from the belly of the jar enters the human stomach.

This fundamental and close connection between pottery vessels and the human body suggests that pottery might be a powerful indicator for many of the things that we wish to know about people in prehistory. For instance, we need to investigate how people lived, worked and subsisted on a daily basis, how their activities varied by the seasons, how they celebrated festivals and rites of passage at home and with other people, how they interrelated and socialised with their neighbours at local and regional levels, and how they related to the world around them. We believe that the enlightened study of pots can go a long way to inform many of these lines of enquiry. This is partly due to the close corporeal symbolism outlined above, but also to some key aspects of ceramic technology and usage.

Firstly, fragments of pottery survive well in the soil. Amongst the wide-ranging categories of raw material used during prehistory – metals, bone and

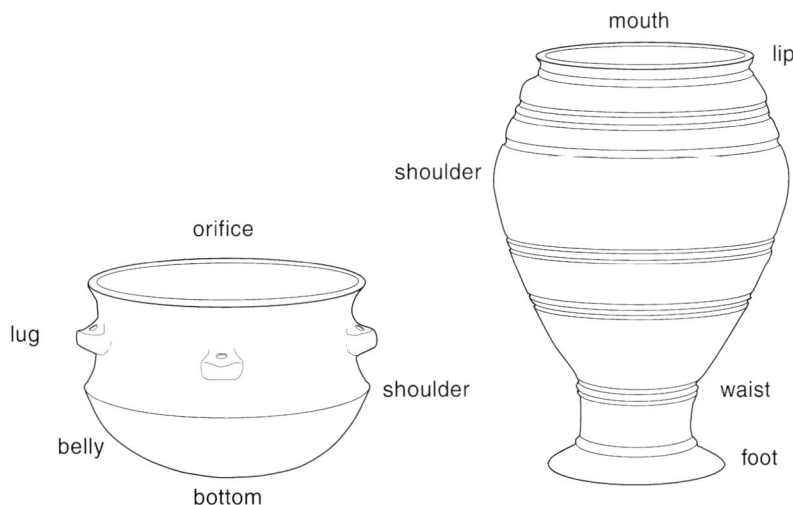

Fig. 1.1. Pots as bodies.

antler, flint and stone, fur, leather, reeds/withies, wood and bark, lithic items are the only artefacts that survive as well as potsherds. Therefore there are substantial quantities of pottery to be discovered and studied. Secondly, due to its exceptional plastic qualities, clay can be crafted in a multitude of ways – it is conducive to the production of vessels of widely ranging size, shape and style which may be adorned with surface treatments and decoration executed in myriad techniques. The subtle changes of these parameters through time and space mean that pottery provides a powerful tool for the analysis of chronological change and for the study of changing style within individual homesteads and larger settlements, as well as across neighbourhoods and regions. Thirdly, clay pots form versatile and convenient containers. Whilst baked clay was used for other purposes, notably for ovens, hearths, walling, whorls and perforated weights and (though not in Britain) to mould anthropomorphic or animal figurines, its prime usage appears to have been in the production of vessels.

This brings us back to our first topic, as vessels were involved primarily with the manipulation of food and drink. The multifarious functions of pottery in this realm can be divided into three main areas of activity: storage of commodities, heating and cooking, and finally, the presentation and serving of foodstuffs and beverages. The invention and adoption of pot making and a more home-based existence (Ian Hodder's *domus* – 1990a) from the Neolithic onwards allowed the art of cooking to be developed in far-reaching and exciting ways. Previously many wild plant foods would have been consumed in a raw state, as may some animal products, although there is evidence for the roasting of meat, and some may have been boiled in animal skin containers. However, clay pots immediately allowed the opportunities to cook food in many more ways: boiling, simmering and stewing probably were the mainstays of the possible new techniques, but the methods of poaching, frying and steaming no doubt also were employed. Prehistoric societies were able to enter new realms of food preparation – truly a prototypical nouvelle cuisine. At the same time the potential to manufacture vessels of many different sizes, shapes and styles meant that customs of presenting food, drink and drugs, both at the domestic and communal levels could be elaborated to a high degree. The shapes, colour, texture and decoration of pottery vessels could be developed to signify kinship or status, and

Fig. 1.2. Gussage All Saints: distribution of imported ceramics in the Late Iron Age phase (after Hill 1995a, Fig 9.21).

to act as symbolic markers relating to many spheres of social and spiritual life. These are the sorts of connections that this book is intended to address.

The Prehistoric Ceramics Research Group is an independent body of about a hundred ceramic specialists who meet biennially to discuss aspects of prehistoric pottery in England. We do two main things: the handling and viewing of large, usually newly discovered, assemblages of prehistoric pottery around the regions, and the discussion of theoretical and practical approaches to the study of such pottery. Initially, the Group confined its scope to pottery of Iron Age date, but in recent years coverage has been extended to include Neolithic and Bronze Age pottery also. In 1991, the Group produced its first Occasional Paper which comprised a brief presentation of a set of general policies, and this was followed in 1992 by the *Guidelines for Analysis and Publication.* These related to pottery of Late Bronze Age and Iron Age date only, but such has been the demand, that they have been reprinted in 1995 and 1997. The *General Policies* define a set of seven academic issues for consideration. These are deposition, chronology, manufacture and technology, production and exchange, function, settlement organisation and cultural expression.

It is these issues that provide the format for the first section of this book. However, since the formulation of the seven issues in 1991, much has happened, both within pottery studies and in the study of British prehistory in general. The divisions between such definite themes have become blurred, and certain more wide-ranging and far-reaching goals are being attempted. Such goals include in particular the analysis of structured deposition in features and on sites of all kinds (Fig. 1.2) and the interpretation of style, colour and decoration in relation to social and cultural expression. The inevitable result of all this is that the reader will be able to detect a considerable degree of overlap between the content of several of the papers in the first section of the book.

Also, in the second section, which includes a series of detailed case studies, the themes of style and symbolic function will be seen to loom large. However plenty of hard facts and practical information will also be found. The case studies vary from a detailed regional study of later prehistoric ceramics in the East Midlands, intended to counter the common concentration on the better known sequences of southern England, through studies of form and function in varying periods (the Late Neolithic and Early Bronze Age of the Thames Valley, Beaker pottery, the later Iron Age of East Anglia and the theme of Roman pottery found in Iron Age Britain) to a more general consideration of the potentially symbolic significance of decorative techniques and motifs from the Neolithic to the Early Iron Age periods. Most of the papers have been contributed by past or present officers and committee members of the Group.

We are extremely grateful to all our contributors, who worked cooperatively within the confines of the original design set for the volume. Many of the papers were submitted in 1996 and 1997, but a few were not completed until 1999 or 2000. minor updating has been undertaken in 2002. For this reason most papers do not contain references to publications appearing after 1997. We also thank the University of Southampton, The British Museum and Robert Read for assistance in the preparation of the illustrations. Many people have acted as academic readers. These included Niall Sharples, Elaine Morris, Steven Willis, Bill Sillar, Colin Haselgrove and Sue Hamilton. We would also like to thank The Prehistoric Society, The University of Oxford Committee for Archaeology, Oxbow Books, Wessex Archaeology and many individual authors for permission to use or redraw many of the illustrations in the volume. Our aim has been to produce a book about pottery which is primarily about people, not pots, and which is illustrated not by drawings of pots, but by diagrams, plans and drawings which show why pottery is of paramount importance to prehistorians, both in Britain and around the world.

2   A Date with the Past: Late Bronze and Iron Age Pottery and Chronology

Steven Willis

"The identification, recovery and detailed analysis of sufficiently diagnostic groups in stratigraphic sequences is of fundamental importance ... In view of the problems with Carbon 14 calibration there is a need for greater use of other scientific dating methods to provide an absolute timescale ... Secure associations, particularly with dateable imports and metalwork, remain important" (PCRG 1991, 4).

Introduction

The chronological framework for much of Britain during the first millennium BC is still largely reliant upon pottery remains (cf. Barrett 1980, 297). This paper examines a range of issues relating to the dating of later prehistoric pottery and the use of this pottery as dating evidence. It does not attempt to present a purely chronology centred perspective nor an all-encompassing survey of the development of later prehistoric pottery chronology over the past century. Rather the aim is to offer a review of the 'state of the art' and to set this within the context of later prehistoric studies. In the first sections of the paper the importance of dating for later prehistory, and its inherent difficulties, are set out. This is followed by assessments of the various means by which we are able to sequence and date this key material. The focus of the later sections is upon substantive problems and themes and explores how later prehistoric pottery chronology relates to the wider aspects of the period. I have endeavoured to make this a relevant discussion for those already working in first millennium BC studies, but also an accessible essay for readers who are non-specialists or new to this field.

Though never out of fashion, dating has rarely been as central a theme in Britain as it has in later prehistoric research on the continent. This fact must explain why, surprisingly, there has been no specific synthetic literature dealing with the dating of later prehistoric pottery in Britain in recent years. Examination of the dating of Late Bronze Age and Iron Age pottery and related issues is timely since this has recently excited heightened attention for various reasons. Not least amongst these are recent initiatives such as the luminescence dating research project being conducted at Durham University by Sarah Barnett and the *English Heritage Later Prehistoric Pottery Register* co-ordinated by Elaine Morris, the collated results of which will surely provide some totally new perspectives on the chronological distributions of this material. Further, the dating of the Late Iron Age and its pottery in Britain and in northern France and Belgium has received special attention during recent years.

Why is Dating Important?

To address this question it may be of value to begin by reflecting upon the fundamental contrast between the vast existing temporal knowledge of our contemporary world and its recent past and the limited framework that we operate within when approaching later prehistory. Considering our own Western culture, its astonishingly well documented and accessible record of historical dates and series of events is a defining characteristic, and the utility of being able to locate or place an object or event within a temporal sequence is readily apparent. The temporal reference points, temporal structures and temporal data of our culture form an immensely rich chronological milieu by means of which we make sense of the world and which we draw upon in order to deepen our awareness of both it and of human being.[1] An absence or limitation of temporal information restricts our potential to understand and interpret the past. First millennium BC studies, by contrast, operate within a framework of restricted chronological information and certainty, and hence require particular approaches.

Establishing chronological frameworks is a fundamental aspect of the archaeological project. Archaeological 'dates' and chronologies constitute our attempts to impose form upon the otherwise temporally undifferentiated past in order to make it interpretable (cf. Simmel 1971, 353–431). They are conceptual and methodological tools for understanding finds and 'what was happening'. Dating and the establishment of chronologies enables us to place artefacts and assemblages, and in turn sites and processes, within a temporal context. This is one of the first steps towards being able to say something meaningful about ancient evidence, facilitating ordering, comparison and assessment of rates of change. The quality of our dating frameworks imposes itself upon the type of archaeology we can construct on the basis of it. In other words the degree to which we are able to place material (in this case pottery groups) within a reliable sequence, and in particular the tightness of the date brackets we can assign it, has deep implications for what we can then use this material and information for. Moreover, since 'the date' of recovered pottery may well be the principal dating evidence available for an excavated context, site phase, or, indeed, a site as a whole, the same constraint applies to the use of these tiers of evidence as well: if pottery dating is vague so too may be the dating of sites. Our current ability to date material and sites within the first millennium BC requires improvement since it is relatively imprecise and thus limiting. Whilst this situation has not precluded expanding interest and new research into various aspects of the archaeology of the period it must hinder its scope.

To the experienced archaeological practitioner reference to the limiting nature of comparatively broad brush dating schema will be familiar. However, there are qualifications that may be made to this picture. First, the importance of dating is not fixed and absolute. Individual archaeologists will differ in perspective over how important dating, and precision in dating, may be to their archaeologies. Its importance will depend on the nature of the material (e.g. pottery) being assessed and on the sort of archaeological questions being addressed. Secondly, though little typological change in pottery over long time-periods may hinder attempts at chronological differentiation this continuity is in itself of no small interest; as has been pointed out (cf. Haselgrove 1989, 1–3), later prehistorians have tended to focus differentially upon periods of overt change, to the detriment of the study of those timespans with seemingly little apparent change. Third, if dating frameworks are less than precise this may well affect archaeological research agendas in a way

that is not negative, by leading to concentration upon different sorts of questions, such as examining long term developments, relative sequences or the study of processes and activities for which comparatively close dating may not be crucial, for example spatial analyses. In this way the character of our dating frameworks can profoundly influence what sort of archaeology the study of the British Late Bronze Age and Iron Age is and can be.

It would be a misconception to believe that an unequivocal 'black and white' chronology for the period somehow exists within the archaeological record awaiting discovery. Chronology will invariably have interpretative and contested elements. Just as Julian Thomas has observed in the case of human identities, the chronology of the past is something which must be assembled from fragments which: 'may have to be juggled and played off against each other if we are to construct a story which is coherent' (Thomas 1996, 54).

The Problem of Dating Later Prehistoric Pottery

The dating of later prehistoric pottery from the British Isles is far from straightforward. As with most ceramics later prehistoric pottery is not intrinsically datable (the exception being dating via the luminescence techniques). Few pottery types can be dated reliably to within 50 year time-blocks by any means and, as a general rule, the earlier the material within the first millennium BC the greater the imprecision may be when using typological criteria for dating. There are particular characteristics associated with this pottery in Britain which hamper its dating, especially precision in dating:

- the considerable typological variability manifest across space and time.
- the fact that types do not develop in clear linear sequences.
- that in some regions pottery styles altered very little or only slowly over centuries.
- the problem that whilst excavated sites of the period can produce quantities of pottery there are often few other cultural finds (critically metalwork items such as brooches, weaponry and fittings) recovered which might assist dating. Coins, of course, do not appear until towards the end of the period and are in any case not frequent within settlement layers.[2]
- there is a conspicuous absence of any widely occurring artefact type with firmly understood and differentiated chronology (as with samian in the Roman period).
- the fact that stratification on Late Bronze Age

and Iron Age sites is usually meagre or comparatively thin (especially when considered against subsequent periods), meaning that context sequences will be short, thus limiting the scope for building relative sequences from excavated pottery groups.

– the division between the Bronze and Iron Ages cannot be readily discerned ceramically (Hill 1995b; cf. Vyner 1988, 76–7).

– additionally in some regions, such as the south-west peninsula, Dorset, East Sussex and north-eastern England, pottery which is technologically and stylistically of Iron Age tradition continued in currency well into the Roman period (cf. Elsdon 1978, 397; Saunders and Harris 1982, 134–8; Quinnell 1986, 113–4 and 119–20; Bidwell and Silvester 1981; Cunliffe and Brown 1987, 207 and 289; Green 1980; Vyner 1988, 76).

– finally, whilst the distinction between handmade and turned pottery is in many ways significant it does not represent a clear chronological threshold for there is often little certainty as to the date when this change occurred. Turning and the use of the wheel were not universally adopted innovations during the Late Iron Age. They occurred at different places at different times, often with the continued currency of some handmade pottery. Hence in this case, as others, technological difference is not an assured dating index.

The consequence of this range of factors is that there may be few convenient dating certainties to hand for later prehistorians when approaching new assemblages, and establishing the chronology of types, styles and traditions is often a problematic task. This is equally true in the case of suggesting dates for individual vessels or sherds. Later prehistorians may justifiably envy the comparatively sharp chronologies of the succeeding Roman period when contrasted to their own unrobust dating. The sophistication of our dating, and its potential, is fundamentally bound up with the nature of the pottery and archaeology of the period.

Reliable pottery sequences and chronological understanding are predicated upon methodologies that pay close attention to the context of the material, to site formation processes, and which involve an assemblage and/or stratified group level approach. Selective concentration on particular items, such as decorated sherds or 'recognized' rim styles is a discredited procedure. Quantification of pottery variables, such as form and fabric, can, as discussed below, provide information important for chronological interpretation, as well as for addressing other questions.

Methods: How we arrive at Dates and Pottery Chronologies

The circumstances facing later prehistorians outlined above have been tackled using a variety of methodologies and options. None of these approaches are exclusive to later prehistory, but all are particularly important for it. Since they are all methods which will be familiar to later prehistorians (and which those new to the subject will find covered in the general introductory texts (e.g. Renfrew and Bahn 1996)) it is not necessary to rehearse the history of their development nor technical details. In this section they are considered in terms of our period. Though each is discussed in turn below, how we arrive at dates for pottery and sites will in practice frequently be the outcome of a critical consideration of the evidence derived from several of these approaches, with comparative assessment of other assemblages from the wider region usually being a key element.

Strictly speaking the date brackets which we arrive at for later prehistoric pottery traditions and types are 'archaeological dates'. Ideally they should be the result of an amalgam of information as to the date of contexts in which this material was most commonly deposited. If this information was plotted as a distribution curve the 'date' would define the time-span around the peak of the curve. Hence the date brackets that we quote for pottery traditions and types are really calibrations, referring to their normal date of deposition.

Typology and Stratification

The study of types, being one of the principal characteristics of the archaeological discipline, is crucial for attempts to comprehend the chronology of later prehistoric pottery. In combination with other categories of evidence, especially stratigraphic information and stratigraphic association, it constitutes the staple means of assigning a 'date' to pottery of the period. This section considers the importance of the typological approach and how this is combined with stratigraphic information, often via seriation and 'ceramic phases', to arrive at relative sequences for pottery groups. It will also look at how pottery groups are 'dated' by the occurrence of other artefacts with which they are found stratified.

Typology

Examination and recording of intrinsic typological attributes of pottery (in this case especially those of form) have long been central to endeavours to place material into sequences and to date it relatively or absolutely. For our period rim forms are usually the part of the pot most likely to vary over time, and even slight differences may be sensitive indicators of relative date. Fabrics and decoration are, of course, other typological characteristics which may alter with time and they too may be used, possibly in combination with the study of form details, to suggest sequences.

For the typological approach to be valid and reliable requires (i) some consistently recognizable degree of variability or change in pottery forms over time, and (ii) significantly, that this has some coherence and identifiable order. It cannot be assumed that consistent characteristics observed in pottery assemblages from across a region are necessarily contemporary; this is a matter for investigation. The greater the degree of change and development in the pottery from a site or region the more precise our understanding of its sequence of

change can be, and in turn the better our potential accuracy in dating. Little or no typological development in a pottery tradition over long periods means that (in the absence of other indicators) its pots may only be assignable to an appropriately broad dating bracket, perhaps several hundred years. As outlined above this situation may profoundly inhibit the archaeological interrogation of such periods. A case in point is the north east of England where, as noted above, Late Bronze Age and Iron Age tradition pottery alters little during the first millennium. This means that at sites like Burradon (Jobey 1970) and Thorpe Thewles (Heslop 1987), which have clear multiple-phase occupation, little chronological differentiation is possible on the basis of the typology of the pottery sample. Figure 2.1 shows the changing typology of pottery from Maiden Castle, Dorset.

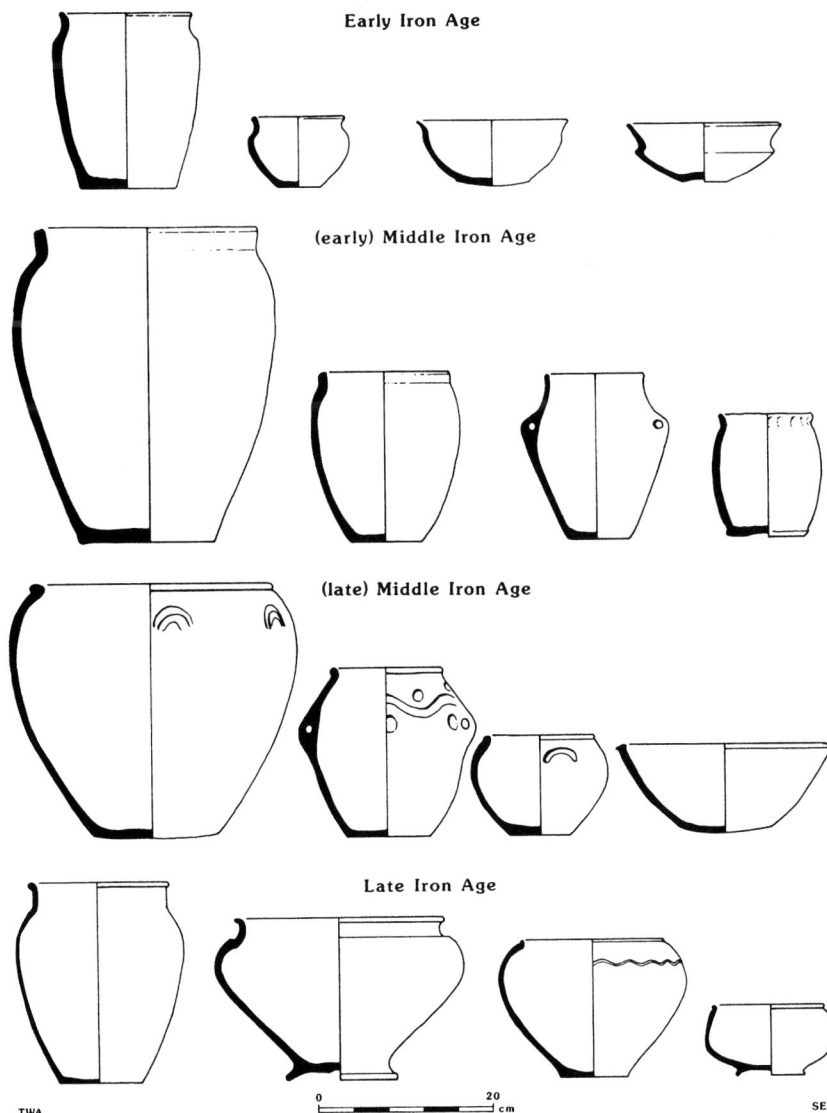

Fig. 2.1. The changing typology of pottery from Maiden Castle, Dorset, 1985–6 (after Sharples 1991, Fig. 200).

Seriation

Seriation is one means by which typological differences may be employed to place site pottery groups into a relative temporal series. This is usually done on the basis of form or fabric, or more rarely decoration. It is only possible where there is a reasonable degree of standardization in the pottery. It is not a common practice but can be especially useful at sites where a number of sizeable pottery groups have been recovered from discrete deposits but where (not infrequently for prehistoric sites) stratigraphic associations and other dating information is limited (e.g. Morris 1988, 41–5). Alternatively the comparison may be between assemblages from different parts of the same site. Seriation may also be employed to test phasing arrived at by other means, as at Old Down Farm, Hampshire (Shennan 1981).

Normally seriation is conducted using either basic fabric types or the rims and/or profiles of vessels, with the incidence of these variables being approached on the basis of either (i) an hypothesized sequential development of such characteristics, (ii) informed judgement by specified criteria (e.g. Morris 1983, 18–9; 1988, 42), or (iii) using a statistical method quantifying attributes (e.g. Doran and Hodson 1975, chapter 10; cf. Millett 1979; Millett and Graham 1986). Effectively the approach aims to seriate groups in terms of the presence/absence of a type or the changing proportions of different types present, and thereby identify a temporal sequence. In theory groups containing a high frequency of similar types should have a similar date range. Potentially groups may be ordered according to how these proportions for specific types 'best fit' with a normal distribution curve (cf. Millett 1987, Fig.1; Tyers 1996, 37–8); alternatively data may be expressed as a seriograph (e.g. Morris 1983, Fig.11; Campbell 1991, Illus.13; cf. Rice 1987, Fig.14.5). Seriations can be 'tested' and adjusted as evidence comes to hand; for instance, they can be considered in the light of any newly available information regarding the phasing, association or matrix location of pottery groups. Ideally groups being seriated should cover a comparatively short duration, have a low residual component, be of some size and not encompass a great typological diversity.

Since the composition of pottery groups will be the result of a range of variables it is necessary to determine that the seriation does indeed reflect temporal change rather than other sources of variation such as spatial factors (cf. Shennan 1981, 159). The considerable typological variability within some later prehistoric pottery traditions makes them less than suitable for this approach; material from southern Britain is likely to be most conducive to this method.[3]

Stratified Sequences

Frequently sites yielding large groups of pottery have an amount of stratification, even if this sequence is in some cases simple. In these instances variability in pottery types may be identifiable and with study may be related to site stratification. Hence site stratification possesses a potential framework by which to establish the relative temporal sequence of pottery styles. Attempts to use stratified groups in this way are, of course, standard practice. With some excavations this results in the site stratification and phasing providing the main framework for assessing the typology and sequence of the pottery. This is so, for instance, with the assemblages from Maiden Castle, 1985–6 (Brown, L 1991a), Danebury (see below) and Cadbury Castle, where the rampart sequences cover periods from the Late Bronze Age through to the Roman, and indeed, post-Roman era (Barrett *et al.* 2000). The identification of ceramic phases for sites (cf. below) is often predicated upon assessment of stratified groups, as was the case at Dragonby (Elsdon and May 1996). Figure 2.2 illustrates the relationship between the pottery typology and stratification at Ashville Trading Estate, Oxfordshire.

In principle the longer a site was occupied the more chance there should be of establishing pottery sequences on the basis of stratified deposits. Hence the question of settlement continuity through time (or lack of it) for the period is a key factor. However, our knowledge of general regional patterns in settlement continuity and how they may affect the construction of pottery sequences is deficient. Whilst this question has often been considered in local and sub-regional studies (e.g. Hawkes 1995) little synthetic analysis has been undertaken. We do not have a clear and robust picture of the proportions of sites within regions which show continuity through from the Late Bronze Age to the Middle Iron Age, for instance, or from the Middle to the Late Iron Age. Examples of continuous settlement at a site, or at the same location within a complex, for more than few hundred years seem rare. Moreover, sustained use of a site is not synonymous with continuity in the nature of its use and identity; changes in the use of a site may have consequences for the types of pottery present.

Ceramic Phases

A related approach with stratified groups is to establish the relative chronology of site pottery in terms of 'ceramic phases'. Perhaps the most prominent example of this approach for the period is manifest in the Danebury reports representing the work of Cunliffe and Brown (e.g. Cunliffe 1984b, 231–331; Brown, L 1991b). Here the very large quantities of recovered pottery have been processed

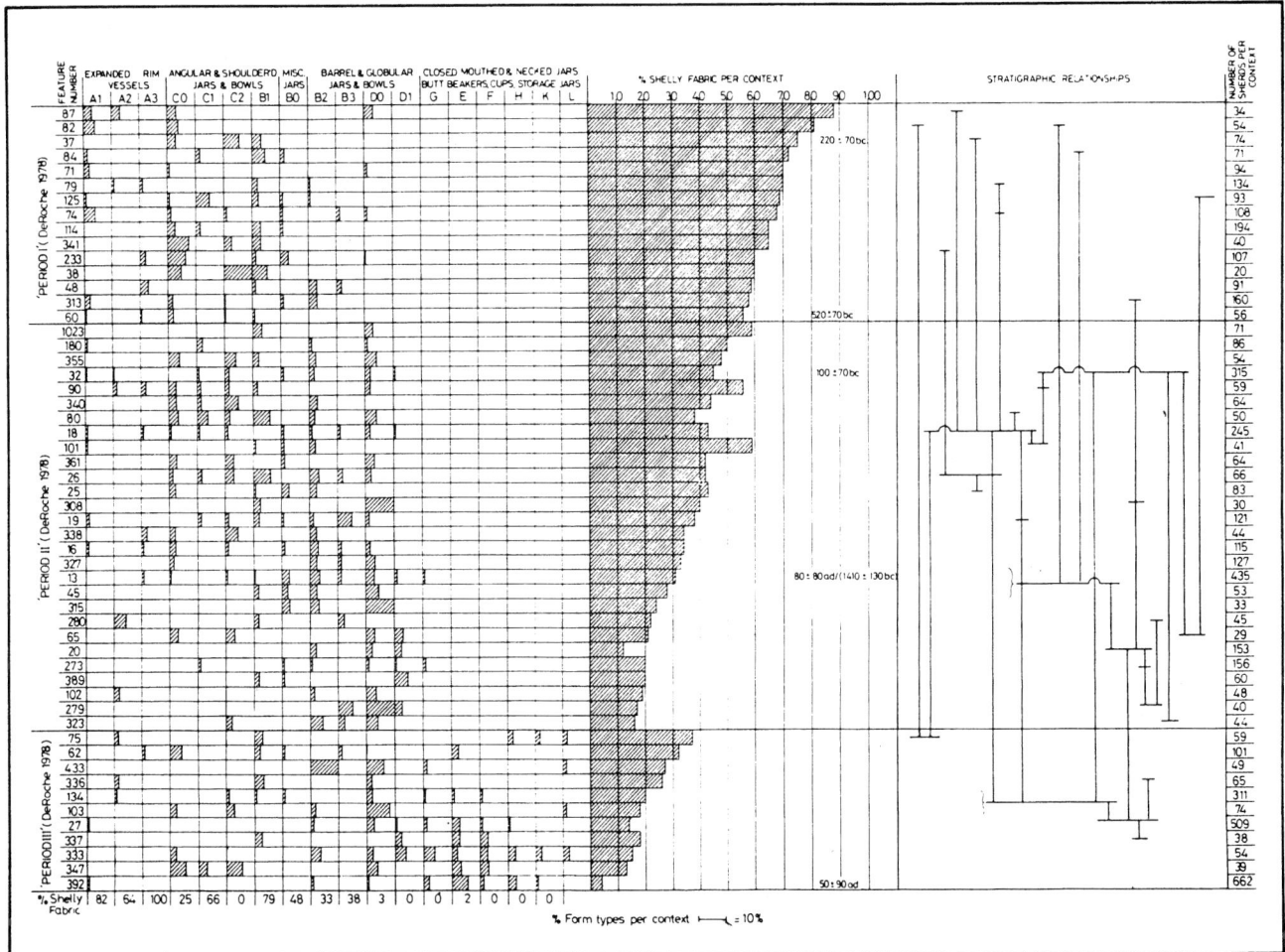

Fig. 2.2. The relationship between the pottery typology and stratification at Ashville Trading Estate, Abingdon, Oxfordshire, 1974–6 (after Lambrick 1984, Fig. 11.6).

using a tiered scheme based on typological elements ("basic class", "type", "form", "variety", plus fabric and surface treatment (Cunliffe 1984b, Section 6.2; Appendix 1)). On this basis, together with assessment of regional comparisons, the pottery was ordered into stylistic ceramic phases.

With the ceramic phases approach distinctive pottery styles and repertoires may be characterized and, when assessed in the light of their stratified occurrence, may be seen to represent sequential ceramic episodes or phases. They may span site stratigraphic periods and phases or lie within them. In turn it may be possible to bracket groups from other site features into these 'ceramic phases'. Groups from other sites might also be interpretable within these phases (cf. Elsdon 1992a, 52). Ideally a matrix of regional parallels, sequences and knowledge can be brought together to identify reliable ceramic phases which are not site specific.

The ceramic phases method has been adopted for a number of larger assemblages in addition to Danebury, for instance, Dragonby (Elsdon and May 1996), where equivalent regional parallels were lacking, and Weekley, Northants (Jackson and Dix 1988); it has also been employed for the study of pottery assemblages from Roman sites (e.g. Going 1987).

At Danebury seriation was used to 'test' the hypothesized ceramic phases (cf. Lock 1984a; 1984b). Subsequent analysis for the later Danebury volumes identified a high percentage of disagreement between the preferred ceramic phasing of groups (on the basis of their pottery) and their stratified phasing (Lock 1991; 1995). As Lock's discussions make clear this is not to the detriment of the method, rather it was almost entirely a function of the decision to assign all undiagnostic body sherds to site ceramic phase 3 and the common problem of residuality (cf. below). Lock's conclusion is pertinent: such anomalies can only be detected and corrected in situations where there are well stratified contexts (1991, 284).

Colin Haselgrove (*pers comm.*) has noted that there

is a tendency to assume that decoration and form changed at the same time, resulting in a discernment of discrete packages (ceramic phases). However, such simultaneous change in attributes is far from being universally true, hence considerable care is required in discriminating ceramic phases.

Associated Artefacts

Ancient pottery has long been 'dated' via its association with other cultural material, such as metal artefacts recovered at the same find-sites, for which a firmer chronology exists. In some cases types can be matched with continental parallels with fairly secure established sequences. Often this associated material can provide highly significant chronological information, and for many later prehistoric assemblages this might be one of the few (or indeed the only) guide to site and pottery date. Hence both the dating of site phases and pottery, via associated material is a standard practice (e.g. Tait 1965, 26; Wainwright 1967, 39; Armit 1991; Stead 1991a, cf. Figs 73 and 74; Fitzpatrick 1997a, 203–4).

When the associated material (e.g. brooches) is relatively plentiful and has itself a reasonably well understood chronology, site and pottery 'dating' should be unproblematic. Potential for problems exists when associated finds are few in number. It might also be recalled that most artefact types too, are subject to periodic redating and refinement. Occasionally reassessments have shown that the use of ostensibly more chronologically diagnostic finds to date pottery and/or sites is fraught with danger (cf. Guido 1974). In the past excavators in search of dates for their pottery sequences and sites can be seen to have focused upon any exotic or unusual finds types recovered alongside their pottery which tend to have seemingly well defined chronologies based on finds from other regions. However, as Clarke (1971) and Topping (1987) have pointed out in the case of class 8 yellow beads from the Hebrides, because of their very character the special and exotic items which are often taken as chronological guides, may actually have longer and complex biographies within the regions to which they were imported or novel than in their places of origin. Such items should, in principle, be approached with caution rather than assumption. Similarly Armit (1991, 196–8) has noted that where finds of Roman material culture have been recovered at sites in Atlantic Scotland, the dating of these sites has been strongly influenced by the relatively close dating of this material. This he argues has mislead understanding of the chronology of these sites. This is a clear example of the tendency for dates assigned to sites to cluster around convenient dating handles (as for instance with Wheeler's (1954) dating of the Stanwick complex, North Yorkshire (see below)).

Confidence in dating by association can only begin to be forthcoming when by association one means close stratified association and/or where caveats are appended in which dating implications are discussed.

An example of the considered use of associated finds is May's discussion of the evidence from the Iron Age settlement site at Ancaster Quarry in south Lincolnshire (May 1976a, 133–41). Dating evidence for the occupation was limited, not least because so few sites of this period have been investigated in this area and since the recovered pottery was of Ancaster-Breedon ('Scored ware') type which seems to span the Iron Age of the East Midlands. The evidence of associated objects, in particular two stratified brooches, was consequently evoked to tentatively propose a Middle Iron Age date for the site (1976a, 140), albeit with provisos. At the other end of the county the dating of pottery groups and features at the later Iron Age site at Dragonby is likewise assisted by associated items (cf. Elsdon and May 1996). Similarly the importance of such material for dating the later phases at Maiden Castle is apparent in the site report (Sharples 1991, 241–2), despite the fact that the Iron Age pottery sequence for the site is comparatively well established.

More chronologically diagnostic artefacts, such as brooches and other metalwork generally, often have a more refined dating due to their quicker rates of development and through the incidence of type parallels on the continent, where they may be more frequent (especially as grave goods), and where their sequence is often reasonably well established. Hence continental imports at later prehistoric sites in Britain are often chronologically helpful. This is particularly so for the later Iron Age when they are more common and in fact include pottery such as Armorican vessels, amphorae and Central Gaulish and Gallo-Belgic *terra rubra* and *terra nigra* (e.g. Partridge 1981; Cunliffe 1987). These items can at least provide a *terminus post quem* for material stratified with them. Haselgrove (1997, Appendix 1) provides a list of Iron Age bow brooches by type from Britain, that are associated with pottery in settlement contexts.

Discussion

The typological approach to dating, in its widest definition, is in principle a logical procedure employing objective criteria. Combined with the principles of stratification it is a highly useful tool for placing pottery into relative sequences. In theory this is straightforward. However, the character of later prehistoric ceramics, and, moreover, site formation processes can manifestly frustrate its use. The results of Lock's study of the Danebury material are a case in point. On the face of it this appears discouraging for if this is the case with large stratified samples what are the prospects for establishing reliability in less favourable circumstances where stratigraphic control is weaker? On a more positive note the 'problem' was identified and this and other cases should improve awareness of the difficulties facing prehistorians when constructing ceramic phases and sequences, particularly the potentially serious problems resulting from the nature of site formation processes (cf. below).

Finally, the impact of the 'style zones' typology of Cunliffe's *Iron Age Communities* volumes (1974; 1978; 1991) warrants discussion. This has proved a useful introductory tool for Iron Age researchers, presenting in succinct form a guide or flavour of regional pottery styles and variations, with a view to chronological progression. In terms of the present discussion it readily conveys the disparate traditions and sturdy regionalism manifest in British later prehistoric ceramics. It confirms that pottery production was neither following nor gravitating towards a unilinear progression through the British Iron Age; clearly the various traditions are not simply explained as expressions at different stages along a continuum. The wide accessibility and utility of this typology has resulted in it taking on a formal identity and solidity within the consciousness of many later prehistorians. This consequence was not its author's original intention and we may now be at a stage wherein perception of the style zones of *Iron Age Communities* begins to represent a *de facto* typological 'fossilization' which is questionable. It may potentially be detrimental to the advancement of different and new chronological understandings of Iron Age ceramics. An evaluation of these 'style zones' from the point of view of chronology, using the latest data, is desirable if they are to remain helpful.

It is now apparent that reasonably reliable pottery sequences and chronologies will only be forthcoming when typology is linked to the context of finds and associations in a systematic and critical manner. Such chronologies can be strengthened by seriation and other quantitative measures, supplemented, where possible and appropriate, by absolute dating techniques.

Absolute Dating Methods

The methods outlined in the previous section essentially provide means for ordering groups into relative sequences. Such sequences ideally need to be anchored with an absolute date or guide. A range of techniques are used in archaeology which yield absolute dates in terms of calendar years. Radiocarbon and thermoluminescence dating are particularly important for establishing and testing dates for

pottery chronologies in later prehistory and they are discussed below. The prospect of dating pottery via dendrochronology and archaeomagnetic dating is also considered.

Radiocarbon Dating[4]

Radiocarbon dating has been highly significant for first millennium BC studies. From around 1960 the dating of excavated organic material by this means has had a direct and dramatic impact upon British pottery chronologies. The method is not however a panacea for the dating of the period or its pottery. Not least this is because the dates suggested by the method come with attached qualifications. A distinction may be usefully made between the value of C14 in (i) dating sites and phases for which chronological information based on pottery and other indices is weak and (ii) for dating pottery associated with C14 samples.

Taking (i) first, C14 has had special impact where other dating guidance is poor, particularly for regions and periods which witnessed apparently little or slow typological change in pottery. One such region is north east England/southern Scotland where the impact of C14 can be readily gauged by two examples. In writing up his 1950s excavations at Huckhoe, Northumberland, Jobey (1959) was unable to give a confident date for the initial settlement phase; that the later prehistoric tradition sherds recovered were not chronologically specific was a major contributing factor. Instead he had to rely upon parallels drawn with other sites, themselves not well dated.[5] These parallels suggested a first century AD date (1959, 251). When a radiocarbon date was subsequently obtained this indicated a date some 600–700 years earlier, pointing to an Early Iron Age or even Late Bronze Age cultural association (Jobey 1968); (from the perspective of the 1990s this association appears entirely probable). A second example relates to the Stanwick complex, North Yorkshire. Here, influenced by the historical texts, Wheeler (1954) interpreted his extensive excavations as indicating that the site began no earlier than the mid first century AD. In fact four C14 accelerator dates associated with the earliest phase encountered during the work of the 1980s, represented by qualitatively similar features and finds to those encountered by Wheeler, have a centre date tightly clustering around 100 BC (Haselgrove *et al.* forthcoming). Had similar C14 dates been available to Wheeler he would have had to construct a different account of the development of the site to that which he published (1954). Although our knowledge of the later prehistoric pottery of this region has expanded greatly in recent years (e.g. Swain 1987; Evans 1995), its slow typological change means that C14 remains important here and is a standard resource (e.g. Hill

1982, Appendix 2; Jobey and Jobey 1987; Vyner 1988; Smith 2000). In such circumstances C14, at least, places some dating anchors upon long lived or slowly developing ceramic traditions.

Turning to (ii), since it is assumed that pottery recovered in association with C14 dated samples must have an approximately contemporary date (of deposition) C14 has been employed to test existing hypothesised chronologies for the period. As is well known during the early and middle decades of this century these had been largely inferred on an intuitive basis, in some cases from the interpretation of pottery sequences and any associated items, though often from unstratified finds. The advent of C14 lead to the re-evaluation of these chronologies and now supplies a means for constructing new, more reliable, ones.

In the case of the Danebury project the opportunity of obtaining a large sample of C14 dates was taken during the initial decade of excavation at that site. The overt intention was that these be closely tied to pottery groups so that the chronology of the ceramic sequence was associated with absolute dates (Cunliffe and Orton 1984). This planned strategy was appropriate for such a large scale research project in which the excavation of great numbers of features could be anticipated, and where pottery was bound to play a crucial role *apropos* dating. It is easy to overlook the fact that many modern excavations have lacked such a specific reasoned strategy (or the resources to implement it) and hence the principle of the Danebury approach is commendable.

From the first ten years of excavation (1969–78) a sample of 65 usable dates were available for analysis, constituting a luxuriously high number by any comparison within the British and indeed European Iron Age. These dates, and how they have been worked with and discussed, are significant not only for the Danebury reports but also more widely in that they comprise a uniquely large sample relating to such a prominent excavation project. For the initial report the dates were submitted to a range of analyses allowing differing interpretative perspectives; the approach necessarily contained a speculative and experimental element (Cunliffe and Orton 1984). Ultimately these C14 determinations were used to suggest absolute dates for the site ceramic phases on a best fit basis (1984, 193–8; cf. Haselgrove 1986[6]). Subsequently the Danebury date-list has been re-analysed using more recent methods, though still with the intent that this provides absolute dates for the ceramic phasing (Cunliffe 1995, 17–8; Orton 1995). As an examination of the relevant literature testifies the biography of this dating project encompasses many aspects of the journey to a greater awareness of the C14 resource which has taken place since the 1970s. In fact the career of this dating project may not yet be over.

Presently where the chronology of Late Bronze Age and Iron Age pottery forms, types and repertoires is not well known radiocarbon dating at best (ie, via high-precision calibration (see below)) can provide only a rough guide to date. C14 does not constitute a means for constructing a particularly fine chronological framework for our period since it yields fairly broad dating probability brackets. Indeed, same-sample control tests have shown that dates may not necessarily be replicated. Two significant points follow from this. Firstly, such broad dating may be adequate (at present?) for earlier prehistory where long tracks of time may be being grappled with; however, such dating may seem less satisfactory for the first millennium BC wherein processes appear to have been unfolding comparatively quickly, and where we would like to date both pottery and site phases, with assurance, to within 50 years or less. What is a short period in terms of C14 years is actually of long duration in terms of the Iron Age. There is a regional dimension here too. Lambrick (1994) has observed that in some cases the dating suggested by C14 may actually be less precise than that based on existing knowledge of particular pottery sequences. Where Lambrick's point is valid C14 might constitute independent confirmation of the sequence but, he points out, it is otherwise unnecessary. No doubt this is true of Wessex and the upper Thames valley but is not the case over much of the rest of Britain.

In theory a reasonably robust dating scheme for a later prehistoric pottery tradition or type might be attained through the acquisition of a sizeable sample of dates for contexts in which it occurs and from a range of sites. Dates can be plotted together in graph form spreadout across their probability (Cunliffe and Orton 1984, fig. 5.1), with centre dates specified. In this way a picture of the behaviour of a type (and of the method) in a series of dated circumstances would emerge, suggesting (ideally) the 'lifespan' of the tradition/type (cf. Millett 1987, 99–101, fig. 1). Haselgrove (1997, 58) advocates a similar approach and is optimistic. He references the preliminary study by Duncan Jackson (1995) of c.60 calibrated radiocarbon dates from contexts containing Middle Iron Age pottery which detected a significant degree of chronological structure. The advent of accelerator C14 dating (Bowman 1990), often referred to as AMS, is further grounds for positive expectation.

The prospect of isolating the 'lifespan' of styles needs to be set within its context and is some way from being realized. Currently, the number of radiocarbon dated contexts for the Late Bronze Age and Iron Age in Scotland, Wales and England is around 1200 (*pers comm*. Colin Haselgrove) and the regional coverage is highly varied. Of these dates only about 170 (excluding Danebury) come from the ceramically rich area of England. More dates are desirable and will become available. Their acquisition is unlikely to expand rapidly for later prehistory in the near future, unless a common agreement towards this end emerges. The variability of later prehistoric pottery traditions means that progress in this area will be incremental. C14 dates are not inexpensive but their real cost is less than it once was. Whether the shift to developer funding is having an impact upon budgets for C14 sampling will be clearer in several years time.

Two further problematic areas with C14 which have broad implications for pottery chronologies concern carbon sampling strategy and calibration. The need to calibrate Carbon 14 dates is established (e.g. Brown, L 1991a; Cunliffe 1991, 591–2; Jordan *et al*. 1994; Renfrew and Bahn 1996, 134–6). Unfortunately older published C14 dates used to develop or inform pottery chronologies can now be seen to lack accuracy as they are not well calibrated (e.g. Topping 1987; Lane 1990; Jordan *et al*. 1994). Understandings based on these earlier dates will have permeated pottery dating frameworks. The extent of the influence of these older C14 dates upon existing ceramic chronologies is not adequately mapped. The cautionary implication is that technical improvements leading to periodic redating should be anticipated. A second substantive difficulty in this area concerns the calibration of radiocarbon dates falling in the 800 to 400 BC period and at other intervals in the first millennium BC. As is well known, the C14 calibration curve for this period is flat (cf. Baillie and Pilcher 1983, 58–60); dates for this time-span are therefore vaguer. Unfortunately this coincides with a period of comparatively slow typological development in pottery traditions generally in Britain meaning that our chronological understanding of the Early Iron Age is especially weak. Foster (1992), assessing C14 dates for the Scottish Iron Age, has pointed up related difficulties, not least the fact that in the process of producing dates the curves result in certain periods being artificially underrepresented in the collection of dates. Clearly this has implications for the dating of artefacts; paradoxically, Foster notes that, the dating of artefacts arrived at by separate means might be compared with C14 dates and used to 'correct' the impression of C14 curves.

There are grounds for greater confidence with regard to the Late Bronze Age in so far as the problems of the shape of the calibration curve are less severe. An accumulation of dates for the period is improving understanding and for several sites programmes have dated a series of samples. In the case of Rams Hill, Oxfordshire, a reassessment by Needham and Ambers (1994) has brought forth an important set of dates. Determinations from Brean Down, Somerset, Unit 4, are of interest (Bell 1990, chapters 9 and 11, and p.113). Two of the three dates seem to be too early. They contrast with established thinking and indicate that our perception of a unilinear progression from Middle to Late Bronze Age ceramic styles may be incorrect.

Growing awareness of the problems surrounding the selection of material for C14 dating casts doubt on some erstwhile sampling strategies. In principle caution is necessary when building, testing and using chronological frameworks involving C14 dates since, as Haselgrove (1986; 1992) has stressed, the contemporaneity of ceramics and organic material present within contexts should not be unquestionably assumed, as both they and their date of deposition are independent variables. Until recently items selected for C14 dating have commonly included burnt wood or bone fragments with care taken to establish that the sample was 'securely stratified'. Latterly there has been a widening awareness of the problem of residuality and its potential impact, resulting, in the case of C14 samples, in earlier dates being ascertained for the deposition of the context than the actual date. One means of counter-acting this possibility is to date carbonized grains (via AMS) from samples recovered for environmental analysis since these are comparatively fragile remains, less likely to survive the re-working of site deposits as wood fragments appear to. This approach has been used in the case of a number of sites from north east England, principally as part of Van der Veen's analysis of botanical assemblages (1992), including Rock Castle (Fitts *et al*. 1994, esp. 22–3) and Stanwick (Haselgrove *et al*. forthcoming).[7]

To this author's knowledge there has been no C14 dating attempted for the carbonized residues which not infrequently occur on the surfaces of later prehistoric pottery. These are often extensive and thick (frequently >1mm). Might this be the consequence of a wide failure to appreciate the potential of these deposits? Conceivably there may be technical problems with such substances, for instance, low signals. C14 dating of such residues has been undertaken in the case of some pottery from Uganda which was also subject to luminescence dating; the results of both methods were in excellent agreement (*pers comm*. Sarah Barnett).

Luminescence dating
The application of luminescence dating to later prehistoric pottery is a comparatively recent development, with thermoluminescence (TL) dating being the main technique used to date. Its potential for testing and establishing pottery chronologies holds promise since it effectively suggests a date (like C14, within probability margins) for the production of

vessels on the basis of intrinsic properties (cf. Renfrew and Bahn 1996, 145–7; Aitken 1985). Whilst C14 can result in an evaluation of the date of pottery deposition, albeit indirectly through association, TL suggests a direct date for the original firing of pottery (or when it was last heated to a temperature of around 500°C). Consequently if one's objective is to date pottery, perhaps to establish the chronology of a type, the context of sherds being dated via the technique is not of great significance; residual sherds may be used. Similarly if sherds dated by the technique are residual they might nonetheless be useful for establishing site chronologies.

Radiocarbon dating has generally been more popular with archaeologists over recent decades than thermoluminescence, with the latter employed for our period when carbon samples are unavailable or unsuitable. Given the difficulties of establishing chronologies for later prehistory by other means though it has been a welcome alternative. It is conceivable that sampling for luminescence dates may become more common than C14 in the future. Yet, as with C14, luminescence does not offer straightforward answers to archaeological dating problems. Precision of ±7% is now routinely achievable, dependent upon sample characteristics. Residuality again may be a potentially serious complication (Bailiff 1987) if one's objective is to employ the pottery to date individual site phases.[8] Other problems associated with the technique are summarized by Rice (1987, 440–3). As with C14, luminescence dating holds the prospect of more reliable and accurate dates as both the technique and sampling strategies are refined.

The Luminescence Dating Laboratory at Durham University has played an important role in recent years in advancing the technique and a major part in its application to dating later prehistoric ceramics. Pottery of this age from a variety of sites and contexts has been dated. The method has been especially useful for obtaining dates for pottery from the English Midlands, north eastern England and southern Scotland where typologies are less chronologically specific than further south. Figure 2.3 shows the TL dates obtained for pottery from Thorpe Thewles and Wasperton (see below), using the quartz inclusion technique. Dr S. Barnett has conducted a research project at Durham aimed at obtaining a reliable set of dates for later prehistoric pottery traditions from this broad area based upon a systematic sampling procedure (Barnett 1996; 1998).

A programme of TL dating was undertaken for the Iron Age site at Thorpe Thewles in the Tees Lowlands (Heslop 1987). In the absence of other evidence this was crucial in providing a window upon the site chronology and indicated a sequence virtually spanning the Iron Age (Bailiff 1987; Heslop

1987, 111–2). The dating of the samples was in accord with the stratigraphic sequence. Publication of the Thorpe Thewles dates was especially significant since previously the later prehistoric tradition pottery from the region lacked corroborative absolute dating. Dates for other pottery samples from northern England have strengthened the framework, some notable examples being the rim sherd from within the Hasholme logboat, East Yorkshire (Millett and McGrail 1987), pottery from the wetland site at Winestead, Holderness (Smith 1995; Van de Noort and Ellis 1995, 284–5), and Iron Age tradition pottery from Catcote, Hartlepool (Vyner and Daniels 1989; Bailiff and Larsen 1989; Barnett 1998); the current dating programme for pottery from the Easingwold bypass in the Vale of York also seems likely to shed light upon the chronology of pottery of this tradition.

Turning to the English Midlands, luminescence research may also help to clarify the early chronology of Ancaster-Breedon ('Scored ware') pottery (Elsdon 1992b). The 'start date' for this widespread and long-lived tradition is unclear. A set of survey dates, however, obtained from examples of this tradition from the recently excavated settlement site at Wanlip, Leicestershire (Wainwright 1993, 12–4; Beamish 1998) have an average date of 690 BC ± 43 (precision) ± 199 (overall potential error including systematic and random errors) at 68% confidence (Barnett and Bailiff 1993). This date is perhaps older than would have been anticipated, while not being improbable. If supported by further sampling or other indices of date from other sites it will mean that existing dating conventions will once more have been challenged by scientific dating techniques. (Now see Barnett 2000.)

A further significant contribution has been made through the dating of a sample of material from a multi-phased complex of unenclosed and enclosed occupation foci at Wasperton, Warwickshire. A series of 12 TL dates (Bailiff 1988; Barnett 1998) and a single radiocarbon determination were obtained. The TL dates appeared to span a long period of activity, from the later Bronze Age (1300 ± 275 BC) through to the Late Iron Age (latest TL date: 100 ± 225 BC). However, the standard deviations are large, varying between ± 120 and ± 400 years. A single general context dated by both methods gave results of 440 ± 195 BC (TL) against 260 ± 80 bc BC (radiocarbon). The sequence of absolute dates is in general accord with the typology of the associated pottery, although this observation is based upon the analysis of context groups containing relatively small numbers of diagnostic sherds (*pers comm.* Ann Woodward).

Luminescence dating has, in the past, proceeded with what can now be seen to have been inadequate sampling strategies. Frequently it was undertaken

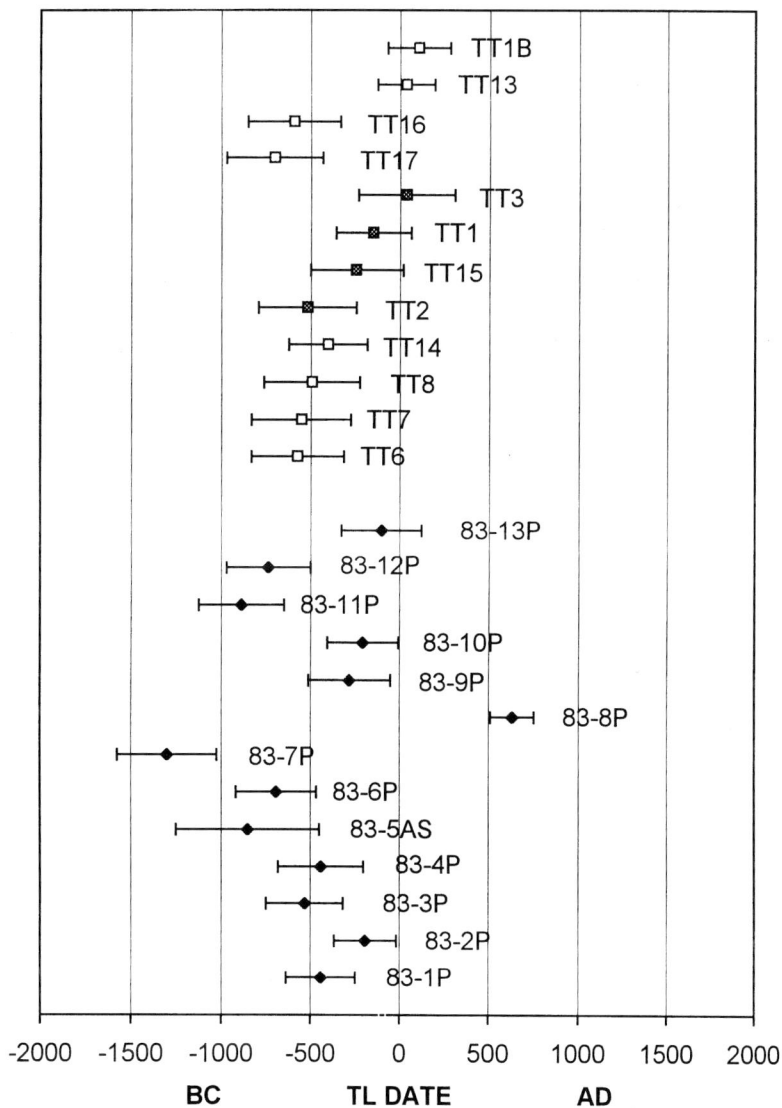

Fig. 2.3. Thermoluminescence dates for pottery from Thorpe Thewles (TT) and Wasperton (P), using the quartz inclusion technique (after Barnett 1998, Fig. 1a).

after the completion of excavation, which is far from ideal. The most effective sampling will be the product of planning. It is in the excavator's interests to consider the prospect of luminescence dating before, or at least during excavation, not least so that the background radiation and water levels of the immediate soil environment can be measured. These are important variables to be incorporated in the dating procedure.

Thermoluminescence dating was twice employed for the assemblage from Dragonby, north Lincolnshire (May 1996), where excavation during the 1960s and early 1970s had recovered stratified pottery groups of crucial regional importance. The aim was to secure a clearer idea of the early chronology of the sequence, for which there was little

other guidance. The first work was initiated during the excavations at an early stage in the evolution of the technique (May 1996, 438); subsequently a further programme was conducted in 1994 (Stoneham *et al.* 1996). Unfortunately the dates forthcoming were of limited assistance for establishing the chronology, perhaps due largely to the unfavourable sampling circumstances.

A TL date was obtained for a sherd of later prehistoric tradition pottery from Ian Smith's work at The Dod, Roxburghshire (Willis 2000). It was only possible to date one sample from these excavations. Whilst unsatisfactory in sampling terms, the single date ascertained was in agreement with the results of C14, the site phasing and the cultural association of the finds. Solitary dates must be treated with much caution, unless there are supporting indices (as there were with The Dod and the Hasholme boat). Crucially, advances in our understanding of the behaviour of the method, as well as greater precision and assurance in dating are likely to come from controlled and systematic sampling (cf. Barnett 1996). Barnett's recent work on pottery from Fordham, Cambridgeshire, and Willington Hill Farm, Derbyshire, has indicated that the calculation of a weighted mean date for contexts or groups of features can provide greater precision than that of the individual TL dates contributing to it. Research has also included investigation of the optical stimulation technique (OSL), the first results of which have suggested that the method has the potential to determine precise dates for individual sherds (Barnett In press).

More analysis of how luminescence dates compare with C14 or dendrochronological dates obtained from the same later prehistoric sites is likely to be of no small interest as these become available in the future. Presently there are few published luminescence dates for later prehistoric pottery in Britain and it is important that sherds and sites dated by this means are fully published.

Dendrochronology
Dendrochronology has yet to make a significant contribution to the dating of the pottery of the period in Britain. An impact in the future may, however, be anticipated as the wetland archaeology of later prehistory is further explored. On the continent the method has been successfully pursued to give 'direct' dating for ceramic assemblages (e.g. Kaenel 1990). Wood samples have been taken at the Glastonbury Lake Village and at Meare East and Meare West, Somerset, in recent years but no certain matches have been made to date with established dendrochronologies (Morgan 1988; Coles and Minnitt 1995, 175). Similarly samples from Dragonby could not be matched with the existing chronologies (May 1996, 214 and 623). Preserved mature timbers which have not been heavily worked are the desired raw material. Hence the method may prove important for areas where such timbers are more likely to be preserved associated with pottery, as for instance with the Somerset Levels, Holderness, The Fens, parts of Humberside and loch/lake environments (though established local tree-ring chronologies might be necessary). Since prehistoric timber platforms serving various functions (domestic, religious, access, etc) are known from across the British Isles there is a wide potential for the association of pottery with dendro dated wood.

Archaeomagnetic Dating
Archaeomagnetic dating has been infrequently used to date later prehistoric site features and horizons, for instance at Maiden Castle (Clark 1991) where C14 was not employed. Although it is inexpensive the method has not had a direct influence on the dating of pottery of our period. Whilst it provides relatively precise dates it can only date specific contexts (burned areas) and therefore dates pottery indirectly through association.

Summary: Arriving at a Date
This section has outlined the various methods by which the chronology of later prehistoric pottery may be established. For different sites different types of information may be available and often, as noted above, dates are arrived at by considering a combination of evidence and through comparison with other sites. Armit's model (1991) prioritizing the various types of chronological information available to the archaeologist (in a particular case) is an attractive one in principle. In different regions and for different circumstances the priority order might be re-arranged as appropriate. In some cases pottery will provide the best (or perhaps significant) evidence for the dating of site phases; at others it may be less helpful for this purpose than other methods (such as C14, or dating from say metalwork finds). In the latter instances these other indices will perhaps suggest firmer dates for the pottery than can be arrived at from knowledge of the pottery itself. In practice prioritization of available dating evidence occurs in a *de facto* manner and in most contemporary excavation reports this will be explicit or implicit in the relevant discussion of dating. It is important that reports state why a particular type of dating evidence was accorded a more valued status than others.

Some Substantive Issues
Residuality

Residuality, as we have seen, is a major problem which can complicate both attempts to date pottery and the use of pottery as dating evidence.[9] Residual material comprises artefacts and ecofacts which are significantly older than the archaeological deposits from which they are recovered; they have been incorporated within their host deposits through various site formation processes that are common place. We can anticipate that at most sites at which occupation was of some duration an amount of material which was associated with earlier phases or originally contained within earlier deposits is likely to have been disturbed by subsequent activity leading to its redeposition within a later group. Residual charcoal can produce anomalous C14 dates, residual pottery can do likewise with TL (cf. Bailiff 1987, 72; Heslop 1987, 111) and also frustrate seriation, phasing, ceramic phasing and a basic typological approach. Brown and Lock have outlined the impact of residuality on attempts to ascertain the chronology of the pottery from stratified deposits at Maiden Castle and Danebury where intensive activity has clearly resulted in high degrees of redeposition (Brown, L 1991a, 191; Lock 1991).

Although residuality is endemic the archaeological community was until recently slow to comprehend the potential consequences of this phenomenon. Despite growing awareness and recognition (e.g. Elsdon and May 1996; Darling 1988, 9) little analytical exploration of the problem has taken place; notable exceptions are Lambrick's examination of Iron Age groups from Manor Farm, Dorchester (1984, 165–7), Lock's studies of the Danebury assemblage (1991) and the paper by Evans and Millett (1992). Recognition of how residuality has markedly affected the Danebury sample will surely raise consciousness of the phenomenon. The limited investigation of residuality to date may be due to the wide appreciation that the presence of residual elements in a site group will depend upon a range of circumstances quite probably unique to that group, including the previous history of the site, particularly the nature of pottery supply, consumption and site forming processes (cf. Lambrick 1984; Evans and Millett 1992). Hence residuality has to be engaged on a site-by-site, context-by-context basis. Since residuality may not only confuse dating but also obscure or distort other trends in pottery which we are interested in, an inability to identify residual items systematically is an Achilles Heel. This area is unequivocally one of the greatest challenges facing later prehistoric ceramic studies in the years ahead.

The identification of residuality, and indeed quantitative assessment of the proportion of a group which residual sherds comprise, are dependent upon the degree to which pottery can be chronologically distinguished. For our period the longevity of ceramic traditions and our relatively vague dating brackets for many types limit ability to recognize residual material. By comparison, for instance, the identification of such items amongst Roman assemblages is facilitated by the fact that the life spans of Roman pottery types are better known and frequently of circumscribed currency; (indeed, software now exists which readily assists the identification of proportions of residual sherds within Roman phase assemblages). There is an attendant complication in attempts to use particular types such as decorated or exotic vessels, which are often supposed to be more reliably dated, as indices of residuality since being different and perhaps more valued these pots

may have differing life spans in certain situations than more mundane types. Lambrick's conclusion that the proportion of redeposited/residual pottery within a group can seldom be firmly established for later prehistoric groups remains cogent (1984, 167); though Lock's concentration upon rim sherds alone (1991) proved a satisfactory proxy. Lambrick's discussion of residuality (1984, 164–7) remains a significant statement on the problem.

Deposition and Context

The nature of any excavated pottery group is the outcome of numerous variables (cf. Millett 1987, fig. 4) many of which will have implications *vis-à-vis* dating. The processes lying behind the formation of deposits are, however, especially significant and it is important that archaeologists endeavour to understand both these and their associated consequences. One sphere in particular warrants attention.

The expanding evidence from various parts of the British Isles that a proportion of deposits excavated on Iron Age sites are the apparent product of symbolic or ritual acts (e.g. Campbell 1991; Hingley 1990c, 1992; Hill 1994; 1995a; Gwilt 1997; Willis 1999) has potentially important implications. So too does the probability that the disposal/deposition of 'rubbish' was influenced by ideologically informed normative rules. In the former case such deposits are often (or potentially) identifiable as not comprising 'normal rubbish' deposits. (Hence they are the antithesis of what are regarded as desirable groups to study when we wish to engage other questions involving pottery (cf. Lambrick 1984; Millett 1987)). Factors lying behind the inclusion of pottery and other material in these deposits are likely to result in 'chronological distortions'. It is clear, for instance, that the items included in such deposits were often intentionally selected. Hence they may include old, long curated, pottery (and other artefacts) which are unrepresentative of the contemporary everyday material culture. The chronology of the pottery recovered from a site with ritual deposits might therefore not match well with the actual date of occupation or activity.

Similarly, if rubbish was systematically removed from activity areas and deposited outside site bounds this may result in occupation phases being under or un-represented in the artefact record. This may be one reason why Iron Age sites in the north east of England and Atlantic Scotland, for instance, which have demonstrably long occupation sequences (e.g. Burradon (Jobey 1970) and Crosskirk (cf. Armit 1991, 196)) yield comparatively meagre pottery samples. The consequences of such past actions from the point of view of using excavated pottery as dating evidence have yet to be fully studied.

The Uneven Nature of the Later Prehistoric Archaeological Record

Dyer has observed how history does not lie uniformly over the past (1995, 6). Equally archaeological remains, archaeological attention and archaeological 'dates' are not spread evenly over the ancient past and its landscapes. Here and there (to paraphrase Dyer) drifts have formed. For the later prehistoric period in Britain the drifts are at their deepest during the later Iron Age and in southern Britain (cf. below). This temporal and spatial drifting has implications for both the dating of later prehistoric pottery and its use as a dating index.

Temporal Contrasts

The archaeological record is evidently thicker for the Late Iron Age than for earlier stages within the first millennium BC. Although this pattern has yet to be demonstrated in a systematic quantitative manner the strong impression, gained from numerous excavations, is that later Iron Age phases commonly yield much greater quantities of pottery and other finds than previous periods. This development is most clearly seen in south eastern England but is also detectable elsewhere, and certainly through eastern England generally. It warrants further investigation (cf. Willis 1997).

That our period has a quantitatively uneven ceramic record through time carries implications for dating. The occurrence of greater quantities of pottery and of other finds (significantly often found in variety and association) available for study from the Late Iron Age goes hand in hand with the generally more refined dating for this period. Not surprisingly it is when and where the archaeological record is thinnest (both in terms of artefactual remains and/or stratification) that our chronological understanding is least sophisticated. This is generally apparent with sites of the earlier and middle millennium, as well as upland sites.

Regional Contrasts

These are manifest at a number of levels. As is well characterized, significant regional differences exist in: the amount of archaeological attention and research input that areas have received; in ceramic traditions; in the pace of typological change in pottery styles; and in the surety of ceramic sequences and dating. These marked regional contrasts complicate and frustrate attempts at inter-regional comparison and generalization. The consequences of differences from the point of view of establishing chronologies are significant.

(i) Research Input. The outcome of unequal research input is predictable: some traditions have been subject to more study than others and so are better understood. In some regions and sub-regions comparatively little fieldwork has been undertaken, hence there are less groups to study. Later prehistorians are acutely aware of this imbalance and indeed that regions hitherto less well explored, such as Herefordshire and Worcestershire, Leicestershire and Nottinghamshire, the Vale of York and Holderness, have more complex and interesting archaeological records than used to be assumed. For less well studied areas chronological trends may be discernible in pottery groups as more material is now becoming available for study, and indeed, because more field research is being undertaken. It used to be assumed, for example, that throughout its long currency Ancaster-Breedon pottery was more or less a homogeneous tradition. Yet this thinking was based upon little systematic work. Elsdon's considered study of the recently expanded corpus of this tradition (1992b), however, suggests that some stylistic changes seem identifiable.

Concerted (and quantitative) examination of 'unpromising' traditions may result in improved chronological resolution. This cannot though be presumed in all instances. With some traditions it may be that there is no typological development over centuries. Additionally, it seems likely that the typology of some traditions may simply be unconducive to establishing firm ceramic sequences. Topping (1987) has suggested, for example, that the typological differences of assemblages from the Western Isles cannot be related to chronology (though see Campbell 1991).

(ii) Temporally Distinct Traditions and Concurrent Traditions. Whilst some areas have a distinct Late Iron Age ceramic phase, as for instance in Wessex and parts of Lincolnshire, in others, such as East Yorkshire, pottery traditions current in the Middle Iron Age evidently endured up to the time of the Roman conquest with little change. At some sites, if not regions, it appears that traditions which we normally regard as temporally distinct were actually in use at the same time: for instance, at Werrington, and, probably, Cat's Water (Fengate) in Cambridgeshire, where Ancaster-Breedon type Scored wares occur alongside Late Iron Age (so-called 'Belgic') style vessels (Rollo 1988, 116; Pryor 1984, 155) – and seemingly not as residual material. Similarly an overlap in the currency of Middle Iron Age and stylistically later tradition pottery was believed to occur at Hengistbury Head (Cunliffe and Brown 1987, 289). Whilst this may not have been problematic for the consumers of the pottery it raises, to use the parlance of Max Weber, 'awkward questions' for the typological approach to chronology.

The Late Iron Age

The Late Iron Age, particularly in lowland Britain and Atlantic Scotland, from around 100 BC, is characterized by numerous changes, many however, representing manifestations of processes with earlier roots (cf. Haselgrove 1989; Hill 1995b). In lowland Britain these changes extend to pottery where often increasing use of the wheel went hand in hand with greater diversity of forms, the introduction and development of which mark useful if vague horizons for developing sequences. In particular the increased quantities of pottery and other artefacts being incorporated into site deposits at this time assists dating through the stratified association of pottery and better dated metalwork and imports. The latter should help date the pottery, the sequences of which, for parts of the south and south east of Britain at least are better understood and dated than for any preceding prehistoric phase.

Dissatisfaction, however, exists with our dating of the Late Iron Age at several levels. One is an on-going implicit belief that our chronologies for this period *should* be more subtle and more secure. This evaluation is seemingly based on the relatively advantageous nature of the archaeological evidence, and is perhaps influenced by the spatial proximity of the late La Tène continent, where the equivalent period can be divided into blocks of decades (Miron 1986; 1991; Metzler 1995), and the temporal proximity of the Roman era to the British Late Iron Age, which again has comparatively closely dated horizons. One may surmise that also at play is a strong belief that an evidently dynamic Late Iron Age warrants finer dating and is in need of it if our understanding is to improve. At a second level there is a complication associated with the apparent 'Gallo-Romanization' of pottery production which gives rise to typologically transitional wares which are sometimes difficult to classify or closely date. Further, for the majority of (non-military) sites it is impossible to identify the Roman conquest within pottery assemblages (Willis 1996; Pollard 1988; Hill 1996). In addition there are now serious doubts over the reliability of the established chronology of the period for southern Britain, especially whether we are dating horizons too late. Pottery dating is at the centre of these concerns which are currently being discussed.[10] Haselgrove, in a recent paper (1997) has cogently argued that the dating framework of the later Iron Age in southern Britain may be some 50 years too late!

The lack of clarity in our understanding of the chronology of the Late Iron Age, however, can be seen as the product of four factors:

(i) The archaeology of the period is complex with variations in the record reflecting complex social changes, often regionally, sub-regionally and locally specific.

(ii) Insufficient numbers of sites of the period have been investigated to any scale, particularly examples with comparatively long occupation through the Late Iron Age.

(iii) Hence we are over-dependent upon a small number of sites (including Aylesford (Evans 1890), Swarling (Bushe-Fox 1925), Camulodunum (Hawkes and Hull 1947), the Welwyn burials (Stead 1967), Skeleton Green (Partridge 1981) and King Harry Lane (Stead and Rigby 1989)), some of which were either dug prior to modern techniques and/or consist of burial groups not yielding artefact assemblages representative of settlements.[11]

(iv) The problems of dating the period can be seen as the outcome of our conceptual approaches to it. We have to some extent been asking the wrong questions and expecting too much of our data, particularly in terms of precision which might turn out to be illusive. A current dilemma, for instance, exists over the dating of King Harry Lane. Inconsistency exists between the pottery specialist's preferred dates for the pots and the dates for the brooches preferred by Don Mackreth. However, there are inherent problems in comparing the 'dates' of different types of material culture for they might be expected to have differing durations of use and deposition, and these might not be expected to match. In principle context and phase dating should be established via evaluations of whole finds assemblages. By their very nature pottery groups do not provide exact dates and greater satisfaction should be forthcoming by other measures such as mapping trends and social processes comparatively and over periods of time. This resonates with Hill's observation that later prehistoric pottery should not be approached as an indicator primarily of chronology but of social practice and identity (1995b, 75; Chapter 13 This volume).

A major review of the dating of Late Iron Age pottery in southern Britain using up to date methods seems due. Haselgrove's work on coinage (1987) and brooches (1997) provides a strong platform for this and emphasizes the importance of integrating typological, contextual and quantitative data.

Dating, Chronology and Research Directions

Clearly pottery of the first millennium BC constitutes an often limited form of dating evidence, and in turn the dating of pottery is not straightforward. The 'downside' is that this inevitably circumscribes our ability to observe Late Bronze and Iron Age social practices with subtlety. Given the amount of work directed throughout the past 100 years towards establishing chronologies for the period, plus the technical advances of recent decades, it is perhaps disenchanting to realise that most of the work of the early and middle 20th century must be discarded as invalid and that the existing product is a measured sense of the limiting scope of the chronological framework for the period.

Practicalities mean that the expectations of those working in the field of later prehistoric studies must adjust to these perimeters. Accordingly, on the 'upside', the existing unsophisticated dating framework has not precluded the dramatic flowering of research into a diversity of aspects of the period which has taken place over the last decade or so. Pottery study has played an important role in these advances. An emphasis away from the study of pottery as a dating index has been bound up with other broader changes in perspective within studies of the period. Pottery is proving one of our best means for exploring a range of other dimensions, including many of those highlighted in the 1980s (e.g. Lambrick 1984; Millett 1987; cf. papers in this volume) and our chronological structures have been adequate to facilitate this. There is no shortage of research questions which can be addressed within existing chronological awareness. We are, as a cumulative product, making sense of the world of the Late Bronze and Iron Age without more refined dating and in ways that are in some respects richly nuanced. Whilst then our chronological knowledge is limited, it would seem that the effect of this has not been entirely deleterious for research.

An obvious tension exists as to whether it would be fruitful to encourage a greater emphasis in our subject upon research into chronology, thus potentially producing more robust and precise dating frameworks, or at least better defining the perimeters. There is unquestionably large potential for new work in this area (e.g. Jackson 1995; Haselgrove 1997). At present chronological research on later prehistoric Britain proceeds in a largely piecemeal manner with those systematically pursuing questions of chronology being few in number. There is no agreed policy regarding dating priorities within first millennium BC studies; C14, TL and other dates are obtained on a site-by-site/project-by-project basis. Readers will have their own opinions regarding this situation.

Conclusions and Outlook

More absolute dates, more accurate dating tools, and refined ceramic chronologies are unquestionably desirable (cf. Davies 1996, 67). They can provide a potentially subtle temporal framework assisting our central goals of characterizing and interpreting later prehistoric evidence and for conceiving what people did, and how they did it. C14 (AMS) dates are becoming more precise and are accumulating but, as observed, their aggregate total for first millennium Britain is modest, and there have been problems associated with both sampling and the employment of dates. If TL becomes established as a regularly employed technique in which archaeologists have well placed faith, this will mark a new revolution in the dating of our period. In the case of dendrochronology a single new site with a good oak sample could make a dramatic impact at any time. Otherwise, in the immediate future, refinements of pottery sequences and in turn the chronology of the period will be gradual and incremental, relying on an amalgam of various dating indices as at present. Typology and stratification will remain key elements of future pottery chronologies and analysis must involve close attention to context, stratified groups, associations and quantitative measures. Our chronological frameworks will inevitably include comparative, interpretative and subjective components (though the latter are unlikely to be permitted the degree of reign which lead research in this field astray in the past). Above all a flexible attitude should be adopted, one open to the evidence of different measures and the probability of the periodic redating of archaeological data. The chronological framework should inform but not inhibit evolving perceptions of the period.

Notes

1   These realms do not, of course, exist free from questions of interpretation and power.

2   Some qualification is appropriate here though, for coins are not absolutely rare in Late Iron Age settlement deposits in southern and eastern Britain. On the other hand they are often associated with Gallo-Belgic imported pottery which is often taken to date the deposits. Study of the typologically earlier British potin coinage has played a significant role in enhancing our dating frameworks for the later Iron Age (Haselgrove 1988; 1995).

3   For further reading see Robinson 1951; Robinson and Brainerd 1952; Kendall 1971; Cowgill 1972; Graham *et al.* 1976; and Tyers 1996, 37–9.

4   Radiocarbon dating is only absolute when calibrated.

5   In the 1950s the cost of C14 had been prohibitively expensive (Jobey 1968, 293).

6   The radiocarbon programme at Danebury was not pursued into the second decade of excavation, 1979–

88 (Cunliffe and Poole 1991a, 239). Anyone interested in C14 dating and pottery and the historiography of Iron Age studies should read the relevant section of the 1984 Danebury report. The discussion there might be considered in the light of reviewers' comments (Collis 1985, 349; Haselgrove 1986).

7　It is of interest that in all three cases from Danebury in which grain samples were dated alongside bone and charcoal samples from the same contexts the grain yielded a younger date (Cunliffe and Orton 1984, Table 18). This does not mean that the bone and charcoal in these instances was residual, simply that the results are consistent with this possibility.

8　Luminescence can identify residuality (cf. Barnett In press).

9　Whilst artefact residuality can obstruct chronological understanding its identification has a positive side in so far as it can (i) shed light upon site activity and development and (ii) assist estimations as to the extent of residuality amongst material which cannot be chronologically differentiated on the basis of its own taxonomy such as faunal remains.

10　Pottery and the dating of the Late Iron Age was a central theme at three conferences in 1996: the annual conference of the *Study Group for Roman Pottery* (University of Hull), the AGM of the *Prehistoric Ceramics Research Group* (Oxford) and the Table Ronde held at Arras entitled *La Céramique Precoce en Gaule Belgique et dans les regions Voisines: De la Poterie Gauloise à la Céramique Gallo-Romaine.*

11　Skeleton Green is a comparatively recent excavation though it is as yet without contemporary parallel and its interpretation remains somewhat uncertain.

Acknowledgements
I am most grateful to Sarah Barnett, Colin Haselgrove, J.D. Hill and Ann Woodward for reading an earlier version of this contribution and for their helpful comments and kind assistance.

3   The Nature of Archaeological Deposits and Finds Assemblages

Joshua Pollard

"The elucidation of deposit formation processes can also have considerable implications for specialist studies of material and wider issues of archaeological interpretation" (PCRG 1991, 4)

The issue of how pottery entered the archaeological record is rarely identified as problematic. Form, fabric and function, techniques of manufacture, sourcing, chronology, distribution and associations, remain central concerns in ceramic research. Whilst it is to be acknowledged that much 'basic' work of this kind remains to be done on British and Irish prehistoric pottery (cf. Longworth 1990), there is a danger of resorting to empirical study at the expense of understanding past social processes, and of forgetting to ask why such material should be available in the archaeological record in the form it is in (Thomas 1991a; Hill 1995a). It is readily accepted that pottery assemblages vary qualitatively and quantitatively according to type, period, site and context. The serried ranks of Bronze Age funerary urns in many museum collections contrast with often sparse and fragmentary assemblages of Neolithic sherds, for instance, but we rarely reflect in any depth on why this should be so. Clearly, such variation in the representation of the ceramic record cannot be explained wholly as a result of selective excavation, nor of post-depositional survival, though these factors are significant. Rather, it is a reflection of the depositional practices engaged in by past social agents. A critical understanding of depositional practices, and by implication the archaeological record in general, is essential not only from the perspective of coming to terms with how the record is constituted, but as part of a broader enquiry into the relationship between social relations, the maintenance and transformation of cultural values, and material culture.

This paper is therefore largely concerned with outlining cultural processes behind pottery deposition in British prehistory. Although post-depositional processes and refuse maintenance strategies are examined in brief in the first part of the paper, the bulk of the discussion will focus on the form and interpretation of deliberate (so-called 'structured') pottery deposits.

Understanding the Archaeological Record

Interpreting the archaeological record is an inherently complex, almost preposterous, process. The archaeological record is not a direct window onto the past, but is contemporary, existing as a residue of activity that has been transformed by subsequent human and natural agencies, including the processes of archaeological investigation itself (Binford 1983; Schiffer 1987). It can only be given contemporary reality and meaning through the act of interpretation, which itself involves the imposition of intellectual values and agendas specific to ourselves as archaeologists (Barrett 1987). The past does not speak for itself, and the questions we ask of it are those of our own choosing.

The archaeological record is patterned and structured as a result of the organisation of activity functionally and across space, the attritional/transformative effects of post-depositional processes (what happens to material once discarded) and, more importantly, the practices surrounding artefact deposition. Such patterning needs explanation. This is more difficult than first appears, since we cannot assume a direct correlation between the discard of material and the spatial presence and organisation of productive activities; nor can we be sure that deposition operated within the same realms of cultural value and categorisation as those of our own. Therefore, it is misleading to construct all-encompassing laws relating to depositional 'behaviour' as a means to interpret the archaeological record (*contra* Schiffer 1976), simply because the variety and eclecticism of human culture, which is the outcome and condition for all forms of action, cannot be reduced to such a generalising level.

There are two issues which deserve attention. First, we should recognise that 'rubbish' (unwanted material, often considered dirty or unpleasant) forms a category that is not universal, but culturally specific (Hodder 1982; Moore 1982, 1986), relating to conceptualisations of purity and impurity/dirtiness that vary from one cultural context to another (Douglas 1966). Furthermore, such categorisations of the material world are a product of and help to sustain relations of cultural order and domestic power (Moore 1986). As a consequence, what may appear to ourselves as unclean, repellent and of no value may to others have favourable qualities and associations. Acknowledging this goes some way to explaining why middens were allowed to accumulate around domestic structures on Neolithic settlements at Runnymede, Berkshire (Needham 1991), and Skara Brae, Orkney (Childe 1931), for example. Rather than reflecting a lack of concern for hygiene and tidiness, in such contexts domestic refuse may have been deliberately accumulated around houses because it was perceived as a neutral or even favourable substance. To interpret a deposit as 'rubbish' simply because that is how it appears to ourselves is to impose a part of our value system on the past. Archaeological interpretation should always be contextually specific in that it should involve an awareness, if not understanding, of the position of action in relation to varied and different systems of value.

Secondly, we also need to be aware that the patterning and process that we identify in archaeological deposits need not simply represent the routine, and largely unconsidered, playing-out of culturally specific values relating to refuse. The presence of objects in graves and special, so-called 'placed' or 'structured', deposits (Richards and Thomas 1984; Hill 1995a), provides illustration that the deposition of artefacts was occasionally a more overtly conscious practice engaged in as a part of social strategies, ritual included. In such contexts we see clear evidence of the way in which material culture meanings were actively involved in the construction, maintenance and transformation of social values and identities. Through the processes of metaphoric, metonymic and connotational reference, the deposition of material was occasionally engaged in to situate or 'presence' meanings and

references in particular locations and contexts (Edmonds 1992, 187). It would, however, be unwise to classify or define the intentions behind depositional practices too strictly. What we see in the archaeological record are a range of practices varying in intentionality and context, from the largely unconsidered disposal of domestic refuse (still structured by culturally specific classifications) to set-piece acts of overtly symbolic deposition as a part of ritual (grave assemblages included).

Post-Depositional Processes

Following burial, artefact assemblages can be substantially transformed by natural processes, such as physical and chemical weathering and biological and faunal action, along with anthropogenic action including subsequent disturbance and re-burial, ploughing, trampling and the vagaries of excavation and differential recovery (Clarke 1978). In the case of ceramics we must also consider immediate post-breakage uses that can shape the form and content of assemblages. Pottery is after all a potentially useful material even when broken, and sherds may undergo temporary storage or 'provisional discard' with the intention of being reused at a subsequent date (Sullivan 1989). Sherds may be broken down as grog for use in pottery production, might be directly reused as utensils such as scrapers, scoops or new vessel forms, used to line pits, or serve as infill for hollows or consolidation for damp ground (Needham and Sørensen 1988, 125; Sullivan 1989).

Relatively little work has been done on the post-depositional attrition of pottery, although it is generally acknowledged that the material we recover from excavation and surface collection represents a tiny fraction of an original total ceramic 'population'. Hill, for example, gives estimates for pottery survival of 1–10% on Iron Age sites in Wessex (Hill 1995a, 22). Any familiarity with prehistoric ceramics makes it immediately evident that they are not stable materials, being susceptible to destruction through a variety of attritional processes related to factors both intrinsic and extrinsic to the pottery itself (Shepard 1985; Skibo and Schiffer 1987). Survival is primarily dependent upon intrinsic factors that condition the physical strength of a vessel's fabric, and therefore its resilience to chemical and mechanical breakdown; strength being dependent not just on firing temperature, but on differences in the composition of clays used and the mode of vessel manufacture. Some fabrics, for example the soft grog tempered types typical of later Neolithic Grooved Ware, are more susceptible to decay than others, and so in certain contexts the representation of different ceramic types can be markedly transformed by post-depositional attrition. We tend to be more aware of extrinsic processes, human and natural, that lead to pottery destruction, such as trampling, ploughing, weathering and the action of roots. In this respect, the context of burial is all important. Pottery survival will always be greatest in the protected environment of a pit or ditch fill, particularly if rapidly backfilled. In contrast, most prehistoric and early medieval pottery is in fabrics that will not withstand the attritional effects of ploughing, repeated trampling or exposure to the extremes of weather (Schofield 1989). Its survival in the ploughsoil very much represents the exception rather than the rule, being dependent upon past and present land-use, as illustrated by the remarkable dearth of prehistoric pottery from major programmes of surface collection like the Stonehenge Environs Project (Richards 1990, 25).

Discard and post-depositional treatment can be complex processes (Hill 1995a; Lambrick 1984). Final deposition in a feature or surface deposit may represent the end of a complex chain of processes, beginning with overt refuse management, but being followed by the deliberate or incidental reworking and reincorporation of deposits (Needham and Sørensen 1988, 125; Needham and Spence 1997). For example, pottery may undergo a cycle that includes provisional deposition with the intention of reuse, subsequently followed by 'ultimate' discard in a midden or feature fill, which is in turn subject to movement as part of the reorganisation of settlement space, or its use in intentionally symbolic practices. Sherd size analysis (Bradley and Fulford 1980) and refitting provide means by which the depositional and post-depositional history of a deposit might be traced, though recognising the complexity of formation processes and the cultural specifics of refuse disposal strategies mentioned above, caution should be applied in their application to the reconstruction of the spatial organisation of activity areas within settlements.

Depositional Practices and the Ceramic Record in British Prehistory

What follows is a brief review of major themes relating to the deposition of pottery from the Neolithic to the end of the Iron Age. It is intended more as a summary statement and introduction to recent interpretations of depositional activity, and inevitably represents a particular (and very incomplete) perspective on the archaeological record.

1. The Fourth to Mid-Third Millennia BC

The appearance of ceramic technology in the British Isles was inextricably linked to the ideology of being and becoming Neolithic (Thomas 1988). Ceramic containers are associated with the adoption of novel ways of preparing, presenting and consuming foodstuffs that were fundamentally different to those engaged in by Mesolithic communities (Herne 1988). Furthermore, pottery required the employment of new technologies surrounding the transformation of natural substances (clay in the case of manufacture, raw food in the case of cooking) into culturally specific material categories. It is not, therefore, surprising that the earliest ceramics, particular carinated bowls in the Grimston tradition, should have acquired and sustained distinct symbolic value (Herne 1988).

One of the most striking features is the diverse range of contexts within which pottery was used and deposited during the 4th millennium BC. This in itself suggests that the categorisation of pottery as a material item was not necessarily associated with a restricted range of practices, and that its value as a material symbol was actively altered and manipulated according to specific circumstances. Plain and decorated bowl assemblages are known from contexts regarded (albeit with occasional ambiguity) as domestic, in surface middens, houses and pits, for instance. They also feature amongst finds from enclosures, chambered tombs, earthen long barrows, cursus monuments, flint extraction sites; along with exceptional contexts like the Somerset Levels Sweet Track (Coles *et al.* 1973), and a range of natural locations such as rivers, bogs and caves (Thomas 1991a, 73).

The domestic arena must have provided the dominant environment within which pottery was used and discarded. However, identifying the full range of functions and depositional practices for pottery is hindered by the transient nature of much Neolithic settlement, which generally left few durable traces, and by consequent post-depositional survival. Neolithic pottery is generally only recovered from the protected environments of cut features such as pits and ditches, where, as will be seen below, assemblages often comprise the residue of intentionally structured and overtly symbolic acts of deposition. On only a very few occupation sites do intact surface deposits survive, for example those at Runnymede, Berkshire, sealed by alluvium (Needham 1991), and on the unique 'crannog' site of Eilean Domhnuill, North Uist (Armit 1992). But because such instances of preservation are exceptional, it is difficult to define the status of activity and process represented on these sites in relation to those with poorer survival, and consequently they cannot provide general models for Neolithic settlement and domestic depositional practice.

Pits probably provide the single most frequent context from which earlier Neolithic pottery is recovered. Whilst there is little doubt that these features relate to settlement events, their status needs consideration in view of claims that many were dug specifically to receive deposits of selected material (Thomas 1991a, 59–60). Intentional selections of objects, for example querns, axes and particular animal remains, are clearly present in some, but the contents of most take the form of seemingly undifferentiated assemblages of domestic debris, principally flint, pottery and animal bone within organic matrices. The debates surrounding the status of such deposits reflect our own cultural perspectives in relation to the past, and it is perhaps because such deposits appear simply as rubbish, that there is a tendency to view pit assemblages as unproblematic, without paying attention to the detail of the practices surrounding and including deposition. Where detailed analysis of ceramic, lithic and faunal assemblages from early Neolithic pits has been undertaken, the material sometimes appears to have been curated, probably from surface deposits.

The pottery from the so-called Coneybury Anomaly, for example, showed signs of slight weathering, and all vessels were incompletely represented, suggesting prior accumulation on a temporary midden (Cleal, in Richards 1990) (Fig. 3.1). However, that many sherds occurred as nested groups within the fill indicates a degree of care expended in deposition – that is the material was not casually dumped or thrown into the pit.

That assemblages from early Neolithic pits rarely take the form of primary refuse, and that most pits were backfilled in a single operation, is itself interesting, and contrasts markedly with the accumulative character of Roman and Medieval rubbish pits. It indicates that pit depositions were temporally specific acts (a sort of 'spring clean'). It also bespeaks of a particular attitude to rubbish, in that refuse was allowed to accumulate in middens and surface spreads around living areas, but at a certain stage it was considered necessary to bury the material, apparently with some formality. Here, it is undoubtedly the symbolic qualities of refuse which were being brought to the fore and manipulated. Thomas has suggested that within a lifestyle of high settlement mobility pit depositions may have served

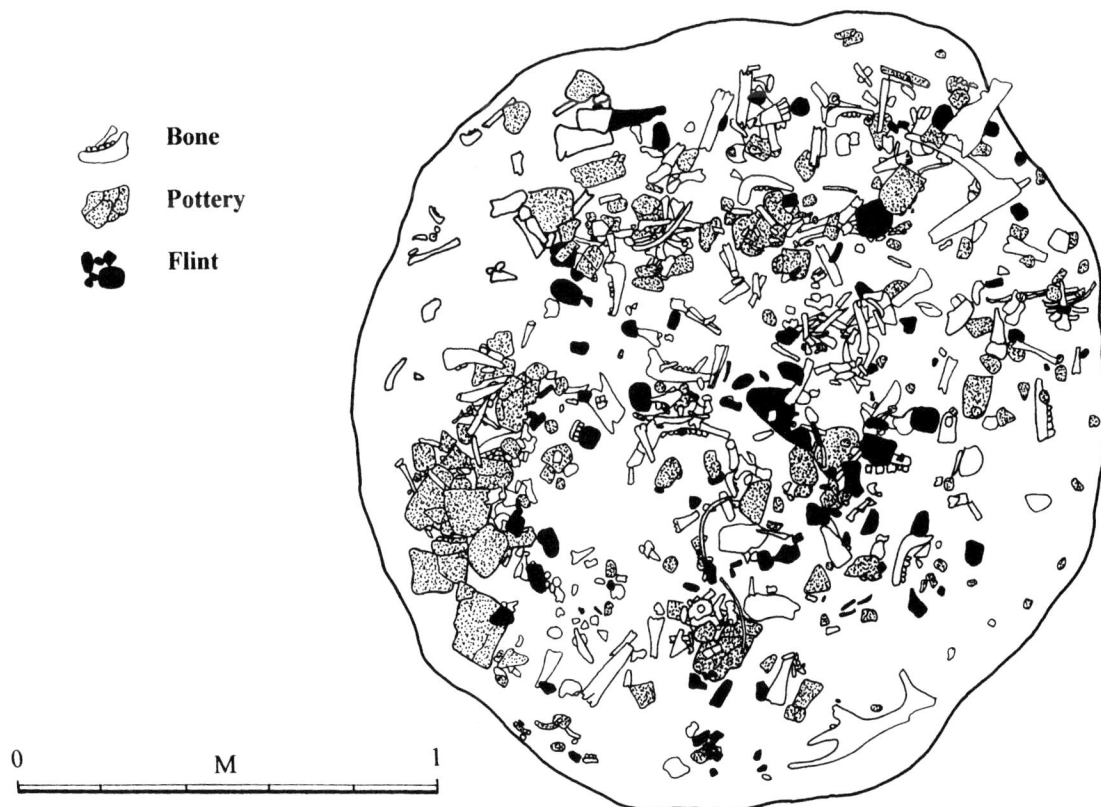

Bone

Pottery

Flint

0   M   1

Fig. 3.1. The primary deposits within the early Neolithic 'Coneybury Anomaly', a substantial pit deposit containing pottery, flint and bone, near Stonehenge, Wiltshire (after Richards 1990). (Redrawn by the author).

to 'fix' evidence of domesticity at particular locales (Thomas 1991a, 76), symbolically locating and commemorating the associations of people, events and significant practices within the landscape. The process of transformation of refuse, involving primary discard (the 'death' of objects), its incorporation in middens (essentially a liminal state), then deliberate reburial in a pit (reincorporation), perhaps stressed metaphoric connections between the transformation of the material world and that of the human dead.

There is in fact considerable variation in the form, and presumably actions and intentions, behind pit depositions, and this warns that interpretation should always be specific to individual deposits. Illustration of such is provided by the occasional burial of complete pots in pits, either upright and intact, as at Hurst Fen, Cambridgeshire (Clark *et al.* 1960), or smashed, as at Hemp Knoll, Wiltshire (Robertson-Mackay 1980). A prosaic, and valid, explanation is that pots were inserted into the ground as storage containers, though the ethnographic record suggests a range of other possibilities, including the use of vessels in domestic settings as containers for personal souls and spirits (Sterner 1989).

Formal pit depositions remain a feature of the latest 4th and 3rd millennia BC, associated with Peterborough Wares, Grooved Ware and sometimes Beaker pottery. There is undeniably greater complexity and formality surrounding pit deposits associated with Grooved Ware. This is seen in processes of selection and, in some instances, evidence for the careful arrangement of material within pit fill sequences. Much of the material used in pit depositions again seems to have been collected from midden sources, seen in curated collections of animal bone (Legge 1991) and lithics (Brown, A 1991), as well as pottery. Other elements, such as intact stone axes and elaborate flint tools, occasional pieces of human bone, entire animals, and placed skulls, could represent ritual paraphernalia and/or votive deposits. Interestingly, the range of 'exotics' occasionally found in Grooved Ware associated pits – polished stone tools, boar's tusk blades, bone pins, and so forth – very much mirrors assemblages from contemporary individual burials (Kinnes 1979).

Although ceramic assemblages from these features often appear relatively undifferentiated, in many there is evidence for preferential selection of large and/or highly decorated sherds. Fragments of Woodlands sub-style vessels in particular frequently occur as large crocks, despite their fragility (e.g. Hope-Taylor 1977, 348–9; Cleal 1991, 146). Note can also be made of massive slabs of Grooved Ware found lining a pit at the Ashville Trading Estate, Abingdon (Parrington 1978), and of the assemblage from Pit 6, Puddlehill, Bedfordshire, which was dominated by

large and highly decorated sherds (Matthews 1976, 6). Intentional arrangement of pottery in these pits also appears to be a frequent feature, seen at Puddlehill with horizontal spreads of bone and pot sherds sealing layers of charcoal-rich loam, and with slabs of Grooved Ware acting as a 'lining' between the basal and upper fills of the Ashville pit.

Grooved Ware associated pit depositions seem to represent more prescriptive and formalised acts than those associated with earlier ceramic styles, and perhaps with it more restricted contexts of action and meaning. Although often associated with settlement, they are unlikely to relate to everyday routine. The frequent presence of objects that would normally be associated with individual or sectional identities may provide one context for understanding. One interpretation sees pit depositions as employed in the maintenance and negotiation of the gender-related division of space within settlements (Brown, A 1991, 120–1). Alternatively, deposits were perhaps linked to the creation and maintenance of specific social identities as a part of mortuary rituals or those surrounding initiation. The employment of objects within ritual practice could itself have led to their being "ritually 'charged' and dangerous", and in need of carefully prescribed control through burial (Richards 1993, 192).

With evidence that later Neolithic pit depositions increase with frequency and complexity with proximity to ceremonial monuments (Barrett *et al.* 1991, 83–4), the identification of patterns of formal deposition within monuments should occasion no surprise. These are after all contexts associated with ceremonial and ritual, where explicit material symbolism was an integral component of special practices. It is not without interest that the clearest evidence for intentional, and overtly symbolic, compositional and spatial structuring in deposition has been identified within the most 'complex' of monuments, namely henges and timber circles of the 3rd millennium BC (Richards and Thomas 1984; Barrett *et al.* 1991, 96–105; Pollard 1995); though similar practices are known from earlier enclosures and long mounds (Thomas 1991a, 65–70). Again, we may be seeing a general trend towards more prescriptive and formalised depositional practices from the 4th to the 3rd millennia BC. On the one hand, deposition within henges and timber circles was structured by and served to reproduce complex classifications of space, themselves related to principles of cosmology, and the control of bodily movement and visual evaluation (Thomas 1993, Pollard 1995). Secondly, through metaphor and metonym, objects (ceramics included) were seemingly brought in to such arenas as a means to situate values and references relating to the social world at large.

There is evidence for processes of vessel use, breakage, and deliberate sherd selection for deposition at henge monuments. Grooved Ware dominates, and the special status of this ceramic is evident not simply from its context of deposition, but also through careful curation and repair (Cleal 1988), and the presence on some vessels of design elements that have links with passage-grave art and 'non-utilitarian' objects such as maceheads and stone balls (Cleal 1991). Individual design elements on vessels were apparently significant in their own right because of the associations/meanings they held, and these meanings were drawn upon in the act of deposition. Cleal has drawn attention to the restricted distribution of sherds with circular and spiral motifs around the entrance to the Southern Circle at Durrington Walls, and to similar distributions at Woodhenge, Wiltshire, and Wyke Down, Dorset (Cleal 1991, 141–2). On a more general level, Richards and Thomas have convincingly argued that a relationship exists between categories of vessel decoration and different contexts of deposition at Durrington Walls, illustrating an active manipulation of ceramic style in relation to constructed monumental space, and presumably sequence and position within carefully orchestrated ritual practices (Richards and Thomas 1984).

Although frequent within a range of special contexts, from pit depositions to henges, pottery rarely occurs in direct association with funerary deposits during the Neolithic. Associations with human remains in earlier Neolithic long barrows and chambered tombs are not frequent, and in instances where pottery does occur, as both intact vessels and sherds (for example at Fussell's Lodge (Ashbee 1966) and Norton Bavant, on Salisbury Plain), it is usually associated with collective burial deposits rather than individual corpses (Kinnes 1992, chapter 6). The very nature of a collective burial tradition may have negated the need for formal grave goods. However, it would be misleading to ignore potential regional and chronological variability in practice, as seen for example in the presence of sometimes sizeable assemblages of Unstan and Grooved Ware from Orcadian chambered tombs (Davidson and Henshall 1989). Nor are pottery vessels commonly part of the repertoire of items found with the early individual burials of eastern Yorkshire and the Thames Valley. Occasional plain, Towthorpe and Mildenhall bowls were included with some 4th millennium BC single burials (of Kinnes' stages B and C: Kinnes 1979), but later traditions (stages D and C) show an increasing emphasis on the incorporation of decorative and dress fittings and a virtual absence of ceramics. Furthermore, vessels that do occur with middle and late stage burials can sometimes be rather peculiar, such as the miniature Mortlake (?) bowl from Liff's

Low, Derbyshire (Kinnes 1979). Unlike the situation in the earlier Bronze Age, it appears that ceramics were not being employed as a part of strategies to signal or create specific personal identities in funerary ritual.

Pottery is nonetheless frequently encountered in contexts external or secondary to mortuary deposits; occurring in the proximal or forecourt areas of earthen and chambered long barrows, and in flanking ditches and quarry pits (Thomas 1991a, 68–70; Kinnes 1992, 108–12). Its presence can perhaps be equated with feasting and rites surrounding the veneration of the ancestral dead, though in some circumstances material may have been generated elsewhere and brought on to these sites specifically for deposition. Whatever its origin, there is recurrent evidence for deliberate spatial and compositional structuring in deposition. This is most obvious with finds of Peterborough Ware in the secondary silts of long barrow ditches, such as those at Thickthorn Down, Dorset (Barrett *et al.* 1991, 37–8), and Badshot, Surrey (Keiller and Piggott 1939). Substantial portions of vessels were present at the latter site, and at Thickthorn Down, sherds were exclusively restricted to the terminals of the flanking ditches (Barrett *et al.* 1991, fig. 2.11). Significantly, such secondary depositional activity is recurrently associated with woodland and scrub regrowth (Evans 1990). With reference to a deposit of Mortlake sherds at the Ash Hill long barrow, Lincolnshire, Phillips and Thomas (1987) have suggested that such a practice was intended to 're-animate' what was an already ancient monument. Exceptional contexts include the large-scale, and apparently long-term, episodic deposition of pottery (Peterborough Wares, Grooved Ware and Beaker) and other materials in the secondary chamber filling of the West Kennet long barrow (Thomas and Whittle 1986). Spatial variation in the representation of sherds according to decorative motifs was noted, and could be related to age and gender distinctions articulated through the ordering of human bone evident in the primary burial deposits. The West Kennet chamber deposits are also unusual in containing deliberate deposits of Grooved Ware, which was otherwise seemingly excluded from earlier funerary monuments in southern Britain.

2. Mid-Third to Later Second Millennia BC

Whilst traditions of settlement in the earlier Bronze Age may have differed little from those of the Neolithic, ideological change is represented by the widespread adoption of individual burial, the increasing importance of lineage and genealogy created through specific personal identities, and the consequent abandonment of many ritual practices associated with large-scale communal monuments. It is not without interest that these changes are frequently linked with the appearance of a novel ceramic style, that of Beaker pottery. On the one hand, the move towards single burial with accompanying grave furniture has implications for understanding the ceramic record. For the first time in British prehistory pottery was routinely deposited as a part of funerary ritual, either accompanying burials as personal grave goods, or as containers for cremated remains. This, combined with long traditions of antiquarian and archaeological exploration of funerary monuments, has resulted in an imbalance in the ceramic record – a dominance of pots from funerary deposits and impoverished domestic assemblages. This has had an unfortunate effect of reinforcing impressions that certain ceramics had purely funerary associations.

The fact that pottery occurs in earlier Bronze Age burials with such frequency is so readily accepted that we rarely ask why this should be so. The study of Beaker pottery neatly exemplifies this. It is no doubt because so many Beakers have been recovered intact, due to burial in graves, that they have been the subject of numerous typological studies, themselves linked to chronological stages in evolutionary progression, or pseudo-historical events (e.g. Clarke 1970). These have never resolved themselves into an acceptable and workable scheme, and recently both the idea of strict formal typology, and that of stylistic succession have been seriously questioned. The results of the British Museum radiocarbon dating programme suggest the absence of any restricted chronological currency to particular styles (Kinnes *et al.* 1991). Furthermore, the realisation that traditional classificatory schemes have been constructed around the identification of intuitively defined archetypes, which ignore enormous variability in shape, decoration and finish, calls into question the validity of constructing formal classificatory schemes in the first place (Boast 1995 and Chapter 10 this volume). As a consequence, more emphasis is being placed on interpreting Beaker style in relation to contexts of use and deposition, following an understanding that through the medium of style Beakers were employed as meaningful material categories. This is seen in claims that Beakers, along with other components of grave assemblages (the body and coffin included), were used in funerary ritual to signify specific social identities for the deceased (Thomas 1991b; Mizoguchi 1995). The form and decoration of such vessels seems to have been explicitly linked to the status of the deceased, in terms of their age, (occasionally) gender and/or their position within a burial sequence (Mizoguchi 1995). Significantly, it appears that Beakers from burial contexts were produced specifically for grave de-

position, and differ in terms of fabric quality and decoration from those produced for domestic use (Boast 1995).

Beakers are unusual in having a very specific relationship to a particular mode of burial (single inhumation), and in being intimately linked to practices surrounding the creation or presentation of individual social identities. A range of ceramic styles – Beakers, Collared Urns, Food Vessels and Food Vessel Urns – appear to have been in concurrent currency during the early 2nd millennium BC; all being employed in funerary ritual as well as domestic use. However, unlike the situation with Beakers, there is more sense of theme and variation (some of it working at regional levels) when the associations between various urn styles and particular funerary practices are considered. Whilst particular ceramic styles have dominant associations with certain forms of burial, these associations are evidently not part of a playing-out of fixed and immutable cultural 'rules'. Collared Urns, for example, frequently occur with cremations, but were also used to accompany inhumation and mixed rite burials, as well as occasionally serving as accessory vessels (Longworth 1984, 47). Much the same variability in context and practice can be identified with other styles, such as Food Vessels in the north of England (Gibson 1978, 27). Pots served as caskets/containers, holding cremations, as ceramic burial chambers and as grave goods ('incense cups' and other accessory vessels). Very occasionally, all three functions occurred in single contexts, seen for example with a burial on Gallibury Down, Isle of Wight (Fig. 3.2), comprising a Food Vessel Urn containing a cremation and a worn and repaired Amorican vase (presumably an heirloom), both of which were themselves contained within a second Food Vessel Urn (Tomalin 1988, fig. 5). As Barrett has stressed, in interpreting the role of ceramics and other materials in funerary deposits it is important to distinguish between inhumation and cremation burials, and items placed with the body and those separate from it, since such represent distinct and fundamentally different stages in the process of mortuary ritual (Barrett 1988, 32).

Ceramics were still being employed in funerary contexts into the latter half of the second millennium BC, as containers for cremations interred in flat cemeteries and existing or sometimes newly created barrows (e.g. White 1982); though such practices decrease in frequency towards and into the first millennium BC. A number of Deverel-Rimbury urns show signs of repair suggesting the use of pots curated from domestic contexts. Direct evidence for a link between settlement and cemetery occurs at Itford Hill, Sussex, where a portion of a handled globular urn from the well-known settlement was found to have come from a vessel excavated in an

Fig. 3.2. Ceramic cist, container and grave-good in one. An Early Bronze Age cremation burial from Gallibury Down, Isle of Wight (after Tomalin 1988). (Redrawn by the author).

adjacent cremation cemetery (Ellison, in Holden 1972, 110). Reuse may imply that vessel style, as a potentially active medium of social discourse, had now become secondary to the function of vessels as convenient ceramic containers.

Finally, whilst much attention has been paid to funerary ceramics, more critical evaluation and interpretation of earlier Bronze Age domestic assemblages is overdue, especially since special pit depositions in apparently domestic contexts are being recognised (Rawlings and Fitzpatrick 1996, 37). In the case of pits backfilled with soil containing 'fresh' Beaker pottery excavated at Fengate, Cambridgeshire, which were spatially related to junctions and butt-ends of the (later?) field- and droveway system, Pryor has suggested their digging and filling as a part of boundary maintenance rituals (Pryor 1992, 519). However, the intentions behind such acts were probably various and contextually particular, as illustrated by the great dissimilarity in the form and composition of pit depositions at sites such as Dean Bottom, on the Marlborough Downs (Gingell 1992, 27), and adjacent to, and possibly reflecting the continuing importance of, the Dorset Cursus at Firtree Field on Cranborne Chase (Barrett *et al.* 1991, 118–20).

3. Later Bronze Age and Iron Age Settlements

The mid-late second millennium BC is recognised as a watershed in British prehistory, representing a

change from an archaeological record dominated by funerary and ceremonial monuments to one in which permanent/semi-permanent settlements and agrarian landscapes take on a higher profile (Burgess 1980). Necessarily, such changes in representation are themselves an outcome of a broader re-alignment of social values, seen in new forms of occupation practice, tenurial and economic relationships, and social authority (Barrett 1994). Such changes are complicated, sometimes long drawn-out, and vary greatly in detail according to region. As such, their explanation cannot be reduced to simple cause-and-effect scenarios, making a study of their consequences more profitable than a search for their 'origins'. At a broad level, we seem to be witnessing a change from structures where rights and identities were created with reference to the dead and lineage succession, to ones where the household and routines of agricultural production became central arenas for the maintenance and creation of social roles. With an emphasis on the routine of the everyday, ideologies and ritual practices centred on agricultural and social fertility (Barrett 1994). This was to remain the dominant theme into the Iron Age. With regard to the ceramic record, such changes focus attention, because that is where the social action lay, on a different range of depositional contexts to those described for the Neolithic and earlier Bronze Age. Settlements now become the main category of site from which pottery is recovered. The production of permanently defined settlement space through the construction of houses, permanent middens, and occasionally settlement enclosures, produced a physical environment which affected the way material culture was produced, used and discarded. In addition to their situation in domestic routine, it was also the house and the margins of settlements which became places of religious concern (Barrett 1994, 147). We therefore have evidence for a range of practices affecting the way in which pottery was treated in deposition, from routine and largely unconsidered use and disposal to special acts as a part of ritual.

The immense range of activities and processes taking place on settlements inevitably makes interpretation of finds assemblages difficult. Nonetheless, there have been several interesting studies of intra-site spatial organisation and deposition on Middle and Late Bronze Age settlements (eg. Drewett 1982; Ellison 1987; Bradley *et al.* 1980; Barrett *et al.* 1991). Drawing on the work of Schiffer (1976), Drewett's analysis of the Deverel-Rimbury settlement at Black Patch, Sussex, presents an explicit attempt at reconstructing the spatial organisation of activities through patterning in artefact distribution. At both this and the analogous site of Itford Hill (Burstow and Holleyman 1957) it was recognised that artefactual material (including quantities of pottery) did not form a general scatter across the sites, but was concentrated in specific locations, principally on hut floors. Drewett interpreted this material as *de facto* refuse, relating to activities that took place within these buildings, but which was left upon abandonment (Drewett 1982, 333). This, like a number of similar functionalist studies, has been criticised for making a one-to-one correlation between refuse and the prior location of activities (Barrett and Needham 1988). Barrett and Needham point out that the finds from the hut floors of these settlements are unlikely to represent material that accumulated during the routine use of domestic space, but rather 'the casual discard and the deliberate deposition of material within the buildings at the period of their abandonment' (Barrett and Needham 1988, 136). In understanding deposition the biographies of buildings and settlement space need to be taken into account; as in fact noted by Drewett (1982, 338). Construction involved the incorporation of foundation deposits. During the functional life of a house small refuse might accumulate along wall lines and around hearths and other permanent fittings. Earthen floors would also act as traps for material trodden into them. At a later stage a building might be abandoned as a dwelling, though could serve a secondary function whilst still standing, including as a repository for secondary refuse. Certain items were removed and others left or deliberately deposited upon abandonment. Of particular significance in relation to Black Patch and Itford Hill is the suggestion that the highly incomplete nature of pottery vessels resulted from the removal of much refuse for manuring, with midden material being reworked and spread over the settlements' fields (Burstow and Holleyman 1957, 199; Drewett 1982, 329). Manuring, however, is a manifestation of particular attitudes and values ascribed to rubbish, which themselves may be bound into ideological concepts of agricultural fertility. Furthermore, the demonstration of such a practice in one particular prehistoric context cannot be taken to imply its universal presence. As previously illustrated in relation to Neolithic pit depositions, middens were often put to other uses.

The functional structuring of settlement space itself represents a continual reproduction of historically constituted cultural values incorporating cosmological and symbolic principles (Parker Pearson and Richards 1994b). This is clearly displayed in the archaeological record of the Later Bronze Age and Iron Age by the consistent orientation of roundhouse and enclosure entrances to the east, and more precisely equinoctial and midwinter sunrises (Parker Pearson and Richards 1994a, 47) – a fusion of time, space and routine. The deposition of material within settlements often served to reinforce such forms of

spatial classification, with special deposits around entrances to houses and enclosures reinstating significant divisions/classifications of space (Hill 1995a). This can be seen in the location of deposits of pottery and other materials on the right-hand side of entrances into early Iron Age double ring roundhouses in Wessex (Fitzpatrick 1994). In other instances, as at the Late Bronze Age enclosures of Mucking North Ring (Bond 1988) and Lofts Farm, Essex (Brown, N 1988), and the Iron Age settlement at Winnall Down, Hampshire (Fasham 1985), a spatial association has been observed between main residential houses and deposits of fine-ware, perhaps reflecting the importance attached to communal eating as a strategy of social cohesion (Fig. 3.3).

A sense of the complex range of processes and actions behind the formation of deposits is illustrated by several later Bronze Age and Early Iron Age settlements in Wessex and the Thames Valley where large scale consumption led to the rapid accumulation of sizeable midden deposits. Detailed analysis has been undertaken of the formation of midden deposits on one of these settlements, fronting the Thames at Runnymede Bridge, Berkshire (Needham 1991; Needham and Sørensen 1988). Occupied during the first two centuries of the first millennium BC, a later build-up of alluvium over the site protected surface midden deposits and artefact spreads from normal attritional processes. The scale of deposition here was large, illustrated by the recovery of 72kg (around 9,000 sherds) of pottery from a single area of 13m^2. Three types of depositional activity were recognised within a single midden: the incorporation of substantial parts of single vessels; dumps of large fragments from several pots; and the very occasional deposition of whole single vessels (Needham and Sørensen 1988, 120). Perhaps the most important observation was that variability in depositional practices occurred through the sequence of accumulation – essentially that middens changed their content and configuration with time, perhaps due to changes in the internal structuring of settlement space, and the rise and decline of certain forms of activity. Routine deposition was not undifferentiated. Broken tableware (bowls, fine-ware and decorated vessels) were being preferentially deposited along the river channel edge of the settlement (Needham 1991, 381). An association between the deposits containing fine pottery bowls and horse remains also seems to exist (Needham 1991, 382), demonstrating again how deposition was inextricably related to specific cultural orderings of the world. Whole pots occurred in primary levels adjacent to the river channel and, given the spatially and temporally specific nature of this practice, along with the occurrence of a cremated lamb in one (Needham and Sørensen 1988,

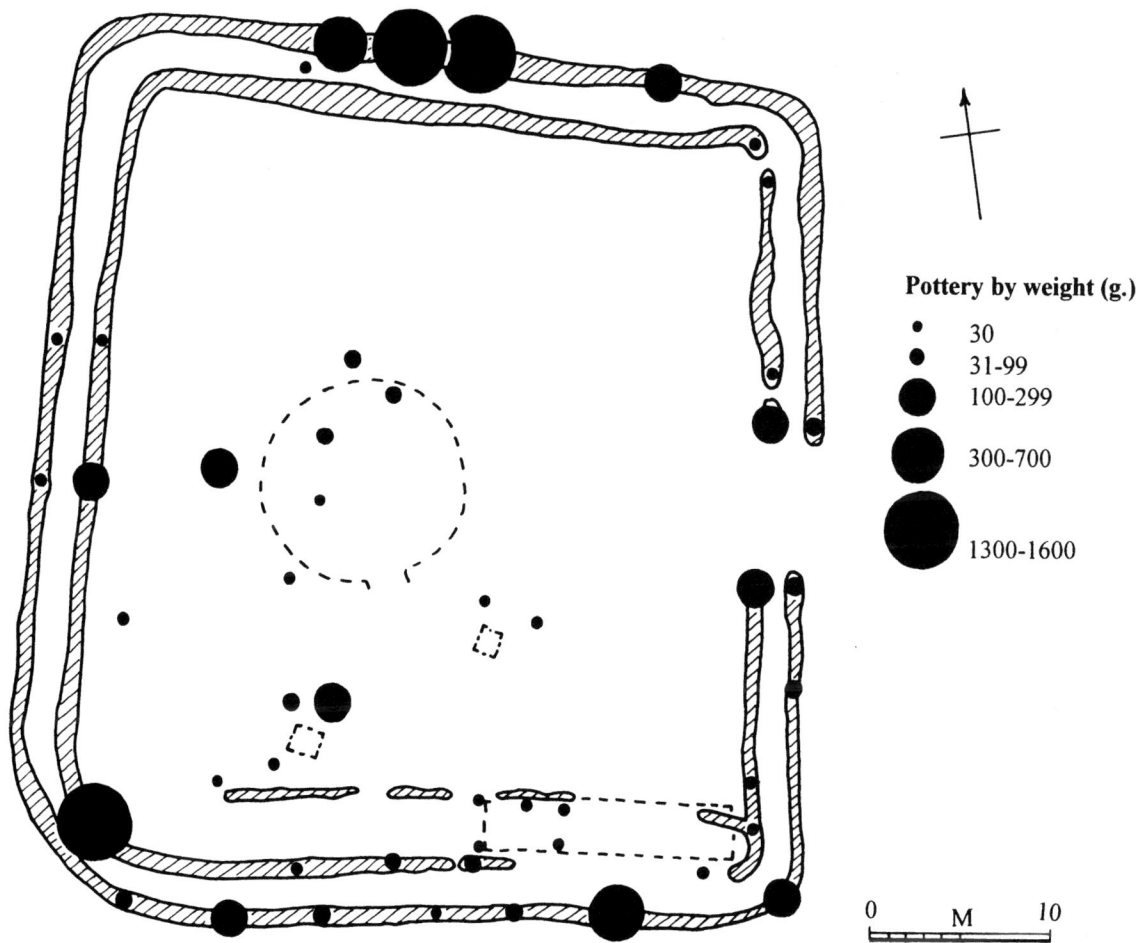

Fig. 3.3. The distribution of pottery within the Late Bronze Age enclosure at Lofts Farm, Essex (after Brown, N 1988). (Redrawn by the author).

124), might be associated with boundary-mainten-ance rituals surrounding the early stages of the settlement's history (cf. Hingley 1990a).

Not too distant in date from Runnymede are a series of distinctive sites in Wiltshire which span the Later Bronze Age – Early Iron Age transition (McOmish 1996). All (of which eight have so far been identified) are located in or along the Vale of Pewsey, and appear to represent a distinct regional phenomenon. Each is defined by vast accumulations of occupational debris up to 2m deep, and covering anything up to 3.5–5.0 ha in the case of those at Potterne (Gingell and Lawson 1984) and East Chisenbury (McOmish 1996). Where excavated, these sites have revealed structural features at their bases, over which middens have rapidly formed, perhaps within a century or two at most. The precise nature of the activity that generated such vast quantities of material still seems poorly understood, whether *in situ* occupation, feasting, or the dumping of material brought from occupations nearby. In the case of East Chisenbury, it has been suggested that much of the pottery was incorporated (and occasion-ally carefully placed) during a small number of major depositional events. Linked with the presence of sizeable numbers of fine-ware bowls suited for serving food rather than storage or cooking, there is a strong suggestion of large scale consumption, even feasting, with little attempt at repairing or curating pottery vessels. Sherds from East Chisenbury were large and unabraded, and had not been subject to attritional processes, implying rapid burial (McOmish 1996, 70). In some instances they formed a component of intentionally 'structured' deposits; one comprising a fragment of human skull sur-rounded by sherds from a single vessel and a small block of sarsen (McOmish 1996, 73). Here is a case of 'rubbish' as monumental landscape expression, perhaps linked to other forms of display within an increasingly competitive social environment which saw the emergence of new forms of authority (McOmish 1996, 74–5).

Clearly, archaeological deposits from settlement contexts cannot be taken as a direct reflection of the functional organisation of activity. Not only should the 'life-cycle' of rubbish be considered, but also the symbolic structuring of routine depositional practices, and the deployment of artefactual and faunal material in ritual. Nowhere has this been more dramatically illustrated than in the interpretation of material from Iron Age storage pits. Whilst finds from pits and enclosure ditches have traditionally, and often uncritically, been regarded as undifferentiated rubbish, there is growing recognition of the selective, highly structured, and 'ritualized' nature of many of these deposits (Cunliffe 1993; Hill 1995a). Hill's work on assemblages from Iron Age settlements in Wessex has stressed the recurrent and deliberately ordered association between selected types of finds, providing a structure that can only be fully understood relationally, with respect to all categories of material (Hill 1993, 1994, 1995a). Thus, at sites such as Winklebury, Winnall Down and Easton Lane in Hampshire there are consistent associations through deposition between decorated pottery and human bone, small finds and articulated animal bone groups (Hill 1995a, 68). Pottery deposits are seen to form a continuum, from the occasional deposition of complete vessels to mixed collections of sherds, perhaps metaphorically mirroring the treatment of other material categories such as animal bone, with an element of deliberate sacrifice or 'killing' also being represented (Hill 1995a, 109).

4. Late Iron Age Assemblages in South Eastern England

Major social changes in south east England during the 1st centuries BC and AD reflect both decreasingly insularity, and the increasing influence of Roman imperialism. Processes of political affiliation or subjugation seem to have led to the emergence of systems of centralised and competitive tribal kingship, within which regional identity was expressed through the adoption and use of new forms of material culture, economic practice (including the use of coinage), and settlement (for example oppida) (Cunliffe 1991, chapter 6). A greater distinction between spheres of practice defined as sacred or profane is seen in the separation of ritual away from settlement, involving the construction of shrines and formal cremation cemeteries (Hill 1995a, chapter 12). Arguably, this is also the first point in British prehistory where we can confidently identify rigid institutionalised social hierarchy. The adoption of Romanizing practices became one of the main arenas for social competition and the articulation of status relationships, within which eating and drinking continued to play a central role. The appearance of imported pottery (luxury tablewares and amphorae) and other specialised ceramic and metal containers, was a part of new Romanized culinary practices employed in particular forms of social discourse (Hill 1995a, 121). As a readily identifiable symbol of status and social affectation, it is not surprising that imported and so-called 'Belgic' pottery was often afforded special treatment in deposition. Pottery forms the most frequent component of grave assemblages from the period, ranging in quantity and form from single jars acting as cremation urns, to complete sets of eating and drinking equipment, as in the 'Welwyn' burials from Snailwell, Cambridgeshire (Lethbridge 1953) and the type-site itself (Stead 1967) (Fig. 3.4). Selection for grave deposition is evident from the rarity of traditional 'Middle Iron Age' forms, and the ubiquity of new types such as flagons, cups, beakers and platters (e.g. Stead and Rigby 1989), perhaps reflecting the non-traditional nature of such burial practices themselves. Although not fully explored, a hint of other forms of specialised treatment is given by the occurrence of large-scale, single episode, Late Iron Age and early Roman pottery depositions at sites like Baldock, Hertfordshire (Stead and Rigby 1986, part III). The complete or near-complete condition of many vessels from these groups implies wasteful, if not deliberate, consumption at single events, perhaps during episodes of feasting (See Chapter 13 this volume).

Concluding Comments

If anything is evident from the above discussion it is the complexity surrounding the interpretation of the archaeological record and finds assemblages. An understanding of the context of pottery deposition, and of the range of practices, intentions and cultural values that lay behind deposition, is an essential first step before questions of functional association, the intra-site organisation of activity, and even ceramic sequence can be addressed. The fact that depositional practices were structured by culturally specific values, and that much of the material from contexts such as pits, ditches and burials related to special activities (including ritual), is an issue in need of study in its own right. Through deposition, we are seeing the active use of ceramics in social strategies that were an integral part of past political and economic realities. This is hardly surprising when it is remembered that pottery functioned as containers for the storage, preparation, serving and consumption of that most valuable and socially circumscribed material, food.

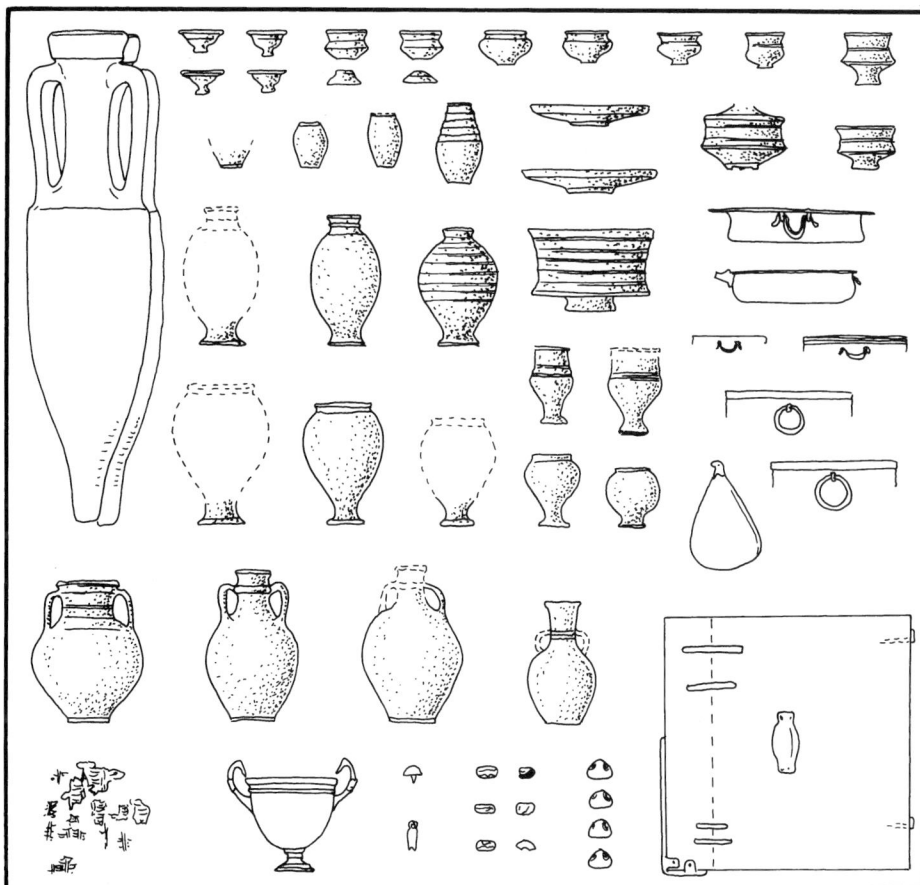

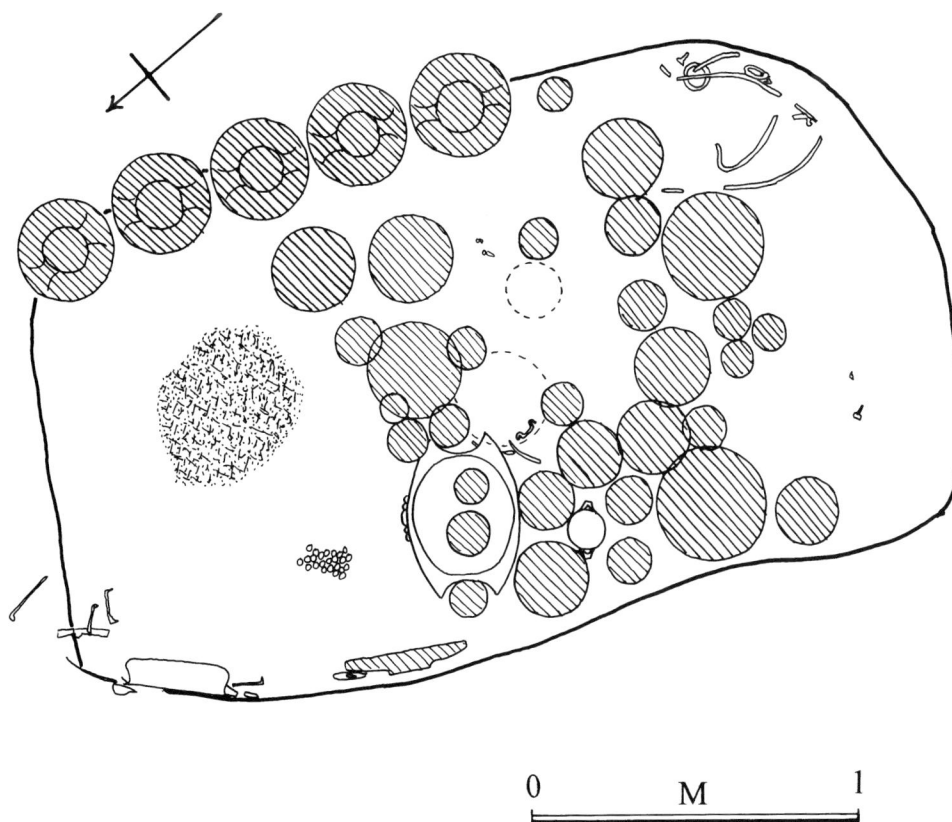

Fig. 3.4. Late Iron Age burial from Welwyn, Hertfordshire, containing imported and locally manufactured fine wares (after Stead 1967). (Redrawn by the author).

4 Aspects of Manufacture and Ceramic Technology

Alex Gibson

The clarification of ceramic manufacturing methods for a range of different quality wares is an important requirement. The identification of raw material sources, wasters and structures potentially associated with firing pottery would be of value. Experimental studies deserve a higher priority (PCRG 1991, 4)

At the outset it must be stressed that, from the ceramics point of view, the writer's area of research is confined to the Neolithic and Bronze Age. While doubtless much ceramic technology is relevant to all prehistoric periods and, indeed, often to the historic period too, it is chiefly earlier prehistoric ceramics that have been studied. Secondly, this chapter is intended as an introduction to a broad topic which has already been dealt with in more detail (*inter alia* Gibson and Woods 1997) and the more inquisitive reader is directed towards those sources and their references to greater explore the subject.

Ceramics are broadly clay items, usually vessels, which have passed through the ceramic change so that when in contact with water they will not revert to a clay state. The ceramic change involves driving off the water of chemical composition in the clay molecules by means of heating to around 600°C.

Clay

Clay, the raw material of pottery, takes two basic forms, residual (or primary) and sedimentary (Gibson and Woods 1997). The residual clay is one that has not moved from its site of geological formation such as the Cornish china clays. They are generally pure, have few organic inclusions and have a large particle size making them less plastic and generally less suitable for potting than the sedimentary clays. The prehistoric populations of the south-west peninsula were certainly aware of these clays and even exploited them, using them as linings for cracked earth-set vessels (Baring-Gould 1896) but no evidence has been found to suggest that they were used for potting. Sedimentary clays, in contrast, have been transported by geological action such as water, wind or glacial action, from their place of formation and are correspondingly less pure than the primary clays. They are better suited to the rigours of open firing and were exploited by prehistoric potters.

Inclusions

Once excavated, a sedimentary clay can generally be worked to a sufficient standard with little preparation. If the clay is coarse, then excessive naturally occurring inclusions may be removed and, if fine, then other inclusions may be added. These inclusions give prehistoric pottery its coarse appearance and they can vary in size from less than 1mm to several centimetres across; the writer has seen Early Bronze Age vessels whose fabric is so thick that it has accommodated river pebbles several centimetres in diameter.

Ann Woods (Gibson and Woods 1997) has outlined the two main types of inclusion, naturally occurring and deliberately added, and how they may be recognised in thin section. The naturally occurring inclusions are better indicators for the provenancing of a clay while the deliberately added inclusions are interesting in their own right from the point of view of the choice of material used. Any non-clay material may be added to the clay and have the effect of reducing plasticity and making the clay easier to work and to form. However, some inclusions are better suited than others are. The most suitable is grog, crushed pottery, which has already gone through the ceramic change and which also absorbs some of the water of plasticity from the clay being worked. Hard igneous rocks are also suitable such as are found in the dolerite tempered ware of the Welsh Marches (Gibson 1997). Organic inclusions such as grass or chaff may also be used but they often have a high moisture content that may cause problems in the firing.

At first sight, these inclusions are a mixed blessing since they strengthen the wet clay and facilitate the formation of the pot but when fired they have a weakening effect on the vessel walls. However they are essential for the firing of prehistoric ceramics. Firstly they allow the water of plasticity (the water which lubricates the clay particles allowing the clay to be moulded) to escape during drying and secondly, during firing, they provide escape corridors at their junctions with the clay body for the water of chemical composition to escape as steam. Accordingly, Woods has recommended that these fillers be termed 'opening materials' since this best describes their function (Gibson and Woods 1997, 32) and that distinction be made between deliberately added and naturally occurring inclusions. Unfortunately this plea had been largely ignored by 'archaeoceramicists' and less specific terms such as 'temper', 'filler', 'backing' and even 'grits' (!) continue to be used with no distinction between natural and artificial elements.

The deliberately added opening materials, while not necessarily of any use for provenance studies, can often be interesting in their own right. Flint, for example, is frequently added to clay, particularly in southern Britain, yet is not really a best-suited substance since, like the clay, it contains water of chemical composition which, on contact with fire, can turn to steam, expand and explode with potentially devastating results. However this problem is often overcome by the use of calcined flint, that is flint which has already been burnt to force out the water of chemical composition. So far so good, but it is still a wonder why this material is used because crushed burnt flint can often have razor sharp edges and must have presented prehistoric potters with painful experiences.

Quartz also contains water of chemical composition, albeit in small quantities, and can spall when heated and cause dunting when cooled. Yet this also seems to have been deliberately chosen by the Peterborough Ware potters of Wales and the Marches (Gibson 1995a). However, quartz also occurs at ritual sites of the Neolithic and Bronze Age (Burl 1976) where its reflective qualities are thought to have given it some special (magical?) qualities. Could this be the reason for its selection in Peterborough Ware? Perhaps the rock gives an added symbolism to the vessel in which it is contained.

A similar argument has been proposed for the selection of dolerite in the Bronze Age Cordoned Urn pottery from Glanfeinion, Powys (Gibson 1997). In this case doloritic and rhyolitic inclusions were added to the vessels made from a local clay in which dolerite and rhyolite fragments were not naturally occurring and in an area where these two rocks could only have been found as rare river pebbles. Again there is an element of deliberate selection of material. In this case the material selected is better known for its use in the manufacture of battle-axes. Are these broken axes or axe fragments which are being crushed for use in potting, the symbolism of the rock giving greater significance to the ceramics? In Anglesey, rock fragments from the Graig Lwyd outcrop appear in pottery yet mainland ceramics are devoid of these inclusions (David Jenkins *pers comm.*). Is there deliberate selection of an nonindigenous material? These examples are clearly hypotheses that require further study, but the deliberate selection of material for use as an opening agent is becoming increasingly recognised (Cleal *et al.* 1994).

Manufacture

Once the clay has been prepared, the pot can be fashioned. The most common techniques used in British prehistory are ring building or coil building. The two techniques involve building up the pot walls in layers either with elongated cylinders of clay or with flattened straps and differ in that coil building comprises the addition of clay in a spiral arrangement while ring building consists of adding 'doughnuts' of clay in distinct layers. It is often impossible to differentiate between these two closely related techniques in archaeological material and 'ring building' is often used to refer to either technique.

The joins between rings present obvious points of weakness in the vessel walls where the rings have not been properly bonded. Vessels frequently break along these weak points giving characteristically round edged sherds, often called 'false rims' for obvious reason. This problem was clearly understood by prehistoric potters who took care in the joining of the clay rings, often bonding them at angles to provide greater surface areas and even using a form of tongue and groove to again increase the surface areas to be joined (see Gibson and Woods 1997, 37ff for a greater discussion of this). The imperfectly bonded rings can often be seen in the fabric of sherds and study of these may give insights into the method of manufacture. For example the direction of joins may change midway up the height of a vessel suggesting that it was made in two sections which were subsequently joined together.

Pinching was another technique probably used by prehistoric potters. This is the simplest of all potting techniques and involves the squeezing out of a small vessel from a ball of clay using the thumb and forefinger. Initially small pots result but these may be used as the bases for larger coiled vessels. Pinching is a difficult technique to identify if the potter has been competent and the small size of a pot alone should not be used as evidence (Rye 1981). Moulding and slab construction are other manufacturing techniques that are difficult to detect in a finished product. The former involves moulding the plastic clay around a template and is not suited to vessels with abrupt changes in direction though it may have been used for simple round-based bowls. Like pinching, however, a moulded pot may form the basis for a vessel finished in another technique. Slab building is in effect pottery prefabrication joining slabs of clay together to form a whole. Again this is difficult to identify but there is no unequivocal evidence for the use of this technique in British Neolithic or Bronze Age pottery.

All these techniques, when practised by competent potters, may produce pots of excellent quality whose finish shows no traits for their method of manufacture. They may also be supplemented by secondary techniques such as paddle (or beater) and anvil where the vessel walls may be beaten externally with a wooden paddle against a hard object (anvil) such as a stone held on the inner surface. This further thins, expands and bonds the clay rings and can turn a straight walled vessel into a bulbous one (Dumont 1952; Woods 1984).

Firing

Firing is necessary to drive off the water of chemical composition and convert the clay body to ceramic. This is a chemical change which, once achieved, will mean that the vessel will be water-resistant, even if absorbent. This stage is usually achieved when the temperature of 600°C is reached throughout the thickness of the vessel. This stage is critical in the process since the water of plasticity expands and escapes as steam and, if unable to escape through voids in the fabric, it will cause the pot to spall: this process may be violent.

Despite the use in the archaeological literature of the terms 'kiln' and 'clamp', there is no evidence for the use of either structure in the British Neolithic or Bronze Age. The former implies a built structure in which to control the firing environment while the latter is a temporary structure used for the firing of bricks (Peacock 1982). Temporary structures may

well have been used in the British Neolithic, but there is no direct archaeological evidence for it. Indeed, there is little direct archaeological evidence for firing sites of any sort, largely resulting from the flimsiness of the surviving evidence and the ambiguity inherent in the interpretation of archaeopyrotechnic data (Gibson 1986); for example, is it a hearth, a cooking pit, a firing site or, indeed, all three? Nevertheless, tell-tale traces on the vessels themselves indicate that Neolithic and Bronze Age pottery appears to have been open fired in bonfires or in pits with no or little control of the firing environment.

Once the vessel has been formed, the clay is dried to let excessive water evaporate. It is impossible in a climate such as ours to dry clay completely. This is because the hygroscopic nature of clay will be affected by the ambient atmosphere but instead a low heat will raise the temperature of the clay to 100°C and effectively boil off the water of plasticity – the water lubricant between the clay particles. This is known as the water smoking stage and is usually preparatory to, or part of the firing process. It can be a crucial stage of firing for if the water is dried off too rapidly, it can turn to steam, expand and, being unable to find a sufficiently large escape corridor, can blow up and damage or destroy the vessel. Even after this water has been driven off, however, and despite the hardness and dryness of the pot, the vessel will still revert to a plastic state on contact with water since it has not passed through the ceramic change.

British prehistoric pottery was open-fired either in a bonfire or a pit. Evidence for this comes from the ceramics themselves and not from manufacture sites since the latter are unlikely to have left much trace on the ground. Experimental work on a pit-firing site at Leicester University showed that, despite repeated use, the heat affects on the sides of the pit were minimal (Gibson 1986). Rather the pots themselves exhibit the characteristic traces of open firing.

Firstly, prehistoric ceramics, when first unearthed, have often the consistency of wet cardboard. This is indicative of imperfect firing since the surfaces of the vessel have gone through the ceramic change but the firing has not been hot or long enough to sufficiently affect the fabric core. Subsequently the outer surfaces are ceramic but the vessel core has reverted to its former plastic state.

Secondly, where firing has been complete, the fabric may frequently have a black core which is also indicative of short term firing since this results from the incomplete combustion of the organic materials naturally occurring in the clay. In the archaeological literature, this effect is frequently described as 'a reduced core' but this is incorrect and shows an ignorance of the firing processes.

Thirdly, Neolithic and Bronze Age pottery frequently has a patchy or blotchy coloured surface and anyone who has undertaken pottery analysis knows that, when trying to match sherds to vessels, colour can be an unreliable criterion. This is due to the variability of the firing atmosphere that is difficult to control in rapid open firings. Fully oxidised ceramics may be various shades of pink or brown while other areas of the surface may be dark or black. These black patches, or fire clouds, are usually the result of sooting whereby carbonaceous matter is absorbed into the surface of the pot as a result of it being in contact with a flame or smoking ember. Rarely is the black area reduced since reduction, or the firing of a pot in an anaerobic atmosphere, is virtually impossible in an open fire due to the difficulties of controlling the firing environment. Even firing one vessel inside another upturned pot rarely achieves complete reduction. Areas of pots may, however, be reduced if, for example they have been starved of oxygen by being buried in ash or by some other accident of firing.

Some prehistoric vessels exhibit spalling which is a sign that the water content of the clay has escaped violently. These spalls are frequently discs of clay that have blown off the vessel wall. Sometimes these spalls can be catastrophic causing the vessel to collapse, other times they may only affect the surface of the pot in which case the vessel will still have been usable, almost as a 'second'. Such spalls have been noted in Neolithic assemblages such as, *inter alia* the material from Eilean Domhnuill, Uist and Allt Chrisal, Barra (Gibson 1995b).

Dunting is also a product of an unsuccessful firing being the cracking of a vessel wall caused when the vessel cools too quickly and resulting from the change in volume of free silica as it cools. Traces of dunting may be difficult to detect in sherd material, being difficult to differentiate between breakages and dunting cracks. Nevertheless, the occurrence of repair holes in prehistoric ceramics may well result from an attempt to bind together dunting cracks since, as in spalling, the damage to the vessel need not be complete and mild dunting need not render the vessel useless.

Conclusion

This brief and simplified introduction to often complex and variable processes has tried to stress that the evidence for the manufacture of earlier prehistoric ceramics generally comes from the vessels themselves both as technological indicators in the fabric of vessels and as tell-tale traces of the firing process. It is also partly a plea that as archaeologists, we should strive towards a better comprehension of ceramic processes and avoid the use of inappropriate terminology in our descriptions of material. Thus, through combining a better understanding of the manufacturing techniques, the limitations and properties of the natural resource and the processes involved in firing we may be able to present a fuller picture of this aspect of prehistoric technology.

5   Between Ritual and Routine: Interpreting British Prehistoric Pottery Production and Distribution

Sue Hamilton

"Further work elucidating the social and economic context of production, distribution and exchange mechanisms (including comparisons for wares of different quality) is needed, based on regional studies. Distribution and exchange of pottery and its contents should be studied within the context of wider economic considerations" (PCRG 1992, 4).

Introduction

Pottery is central to our understanding of the nature of production and distribution in later prehistoric Britain. It is the commonest item of manufactured material culture remaining from the period. This is particularly so for the Late Bronze and Iron Ages of southern Britain. This chapter aims to highlight some key interpretative issues concerning British prehistoric pottery production and distribution. In order to properly address many of these issues we now need a *'bottom-up'* approach to British prehistoric pottery studies. By concentrating on large constructs we potentially introduce 'high order' presumptions into our analyses which may mask the real mechanisms of socio-economic articulation. The chapter therefore concludes with a 'micro' study of one area of southern Britain (East and West Sussex) over a restricted time span (the first millennium BC) of pottery production.

Ceramic Building Blocks?

To effectively consider how pottery production was organised, and exchange articulated, several levels of information need to be brought together. These include:

1   Identification of the raw materials used in production.
2   Isolation of the source(s) of the raw materials exploited for production.
3   Recognition of the locales of production.
4   Determination of how particular categories/ types of pots were made.

5   Consideration of the ideological and socio-economic meaning(s) involved in the choice(s) of specific raw materials and modes of production.
6   Isolation of the scale(s) of production.
7   Consideration of the contexts in which the use and circulation of pots took place.

Points 1–4 are empirical, pragmatic 'building blocks' of information about the *mechanics of production,* and much of this information can be extracted from extant pottery reports and site archives. Without several of these blocks in place our ability to assess points 5–7 is curtailed. Points 5 and 7 both govern, and impact upon, the mechanics of production *and* the scale of production (point 6).

Identifying Sources

Over the last 25 years it has become standard practice in prehistoric pottery reports to define fabrics at least in terms of their characteristic macroscopic inclusions, and to suggest the sources of the raw materials used. We now have vast quantities of text describing fabrics in terms of inclusion types, inclusion frequencies, inclusion size grade range, and the like. These descriptions are an important resource for identifying patterns of raw material exploitation (clays and tempers) and production.

Characterisation and sourcing studies have concentrated on pottery comprising clays and inclusions with distinctive mineralogies – a particular characteristic of British upland zones. The Lizard peninsula is, for example, a pre-eminent area for ceramic petrology. Here, the restricted location of gabbro and serpentine, and the presence of easily identifiable rocks such as granites, sandstone and greenstones facilitates sourcing of potting clays and fillers (Parker Pearson 1995, 92). By comparison, the geology of lowland Britain comprises common sedimentary rocks and deposits, and a general absence of mineralogically discrete outcrops. Broad investigation of the organisation of pottery production and exchange in prehistoric Britain is severely hampered by this, since lowland Britain still provides the greater part of our British prehistoric pottery collections.

Methods of textural analysis of pottery fabrics which specifically address the problem of common sedimentary minerals (e.g. Ellison 1975; Hamilton 1977, 1993) need to be more widely used for assemblages from lowland Britain. Textural analysis has the potential to separate inclusions of the *same* mineralogy into source subgroups based on their morphological (e.g. roundness, angularity) and frequency characteristics.

Access to Sources and Raw Materials

Without any indication of where production actually took place, the geological sourcing of clays and tempers merely provides information on the places of resource exploitation, rather than the loci of production, or the place(s) of exchange. To some extent, the sources of potting raw materials would have been set apart from contemporary settlement. Few British prehistoric sites are actually on a clay source. The extent to which potting raw materials were brought back to settlement sites *versus* production taking place at source is an essential consideration. Basic questions relating to this include:

1   Who travelled to the raw material sources – specialist, itinerant potters, or members of the settlement community?
2   Did several communities share the same source, perhaps coming together to work on cooperative-operative tasks?
3   Was the exploitation of specific sources unique or privileged to individual communities?

It has been suggested (on the basis of discrete hammerstone distributions) that particular parts of the Cumbrian rock outcrops used for Neolithic axe production may have been controlled by different communities living in the surrounding landscape (Bradley and Suthren 1990). Such questions remain strikingly absent for prehistoric pottery production, yet are fundamental to any understanding of the social fabric of production.

Both trade in raw materials, and the use of the same geological outcrops by potters from several communities, are evidenced by the ethnographic literature (e.g. Miller 1985, Tobert 1984). Although ethnological observation (Peacock 1979) suggests that *long distance* transport of clays and tempers is atypical, there are examples of local clays being avoided in favour of 'more suitable', non-local, resources (Arnold 1985, 58). The use of pack animals or boats would also affect the viability of exploiting non-local resources. Acquisition of non-proximate clays and tempers may have been part of a wider strategy of periodically acquiring multiple geological materials from specific resource zones for a range of uses (e.g. for querns, rubbers, whetstones, and hearthstones). The parable distribution patterns of Neolithic greenstone axes and Hembury Style pots of gabbroic clay (both comprising raw materials acquired from the Cornish Lizard) is clearly one such example (Peacock 1969). Another example, from Cumbria, is the concurrent use of the same rocks for tempering Early Bronze Age Collared Urns and Food Vessels, and as raw material for stone implements (Freestone 1992).

The Choice of Raw Materials and the 'Meaning' of Source

It is easy to forward practical, 'technical logics' as to why particular raw materials and their sources were exploited for potting. Such explanations include: i) ease of access to the sources; ii) availability of raw materials; iii) the behavioural characteristics of particular clays and tempers in manufacture (e.g. aiding plasticity; increasing refractory powers); and the use-properties of the raw materials (e.g. using calcareous or organic inclusions to produce porous fabrics resistant to thermal shock). However, we need to also consider *how people choose* raw materials and production techniques (van der Leeuw 1989, 241), together with the cognitive context within which the choices are made (Barrett 1991, 203; Mahias 1993, 162). Concepts may have been more pre-eminent than practical concerns in making these choices. As has been argued for Neolithic stone axes (Bradley and Ford 1986; Patton 1991), specific raw materials and their sources may have had a conceptual significance beyond utility. The establishment and maintenance of group identity may have been dependent on the acquisition of resources from ideologically meaningful places. For pots this might be envisualised, for example, as the use of alluvial clays from *special* rivers, or the acquisition of clays and tempers from prominent landforms – hills, valleys, and outcrops, relating to a *particular* totemic geography. Indeed, sources which were difficult to access may have had a heightened cachet.

Where the tempers or inclusions are visually distinctive by shape, structure, or colour, they will have provided a recognisable origin biography or authentication for a pot, potentially acting as signifiers for wider structures of beliefs and connections with places. The fact that pottery breaks is clearly important in ritual. Arguably, one of the most significant developments of British later prehistoric archaeology from the 1980s has been the recognition of intentional, structured depositional practices involving sherds, as well as whole and part-complete pots and other artefactual material. Be it relating to Neolithic causewayed enclosures and henges (Barrett *et al.* 1991; Richards and Thomas 1984, Thomas 1991a), or Iron Age pits (Hill 1995a), such depositional practices would have relied on sherds being distinctive. Complex decoration, form attributes, and fired-colour are part of this 'distinctiveness', but fabric must have been a key component – fabric being the one recognisable attribute that *all* sherds possess.

Examples of British prehistoric pottery with visually distinctive inclusions are numerous. These inclusions often break through the surfaces of the vessels with no attempt to cover them up. Examples of pottery fabrics with potentially ideologically significant inclusion sources might include:

1. Wiltshire, Early Neolithic, Hembury Style oolitic wares.
The fabric contains grey-white, granular oolites (derived from shelly clays originating from the Jurassic limestone of the Bath-Frome area). The fact that blocks of oolitic limestone were also brought into the Avebury area and incorporated into funerary monuments suggests that oolite-rich material may have had a wider symbolic significance (Cleal 1995; Smith 1974; Whittle 1977).

2. Welsh, Late Neolithic Peterborough Ware with quartz temper.
The quartz temper in Welsh Peterborough Ware is highly conspicuous, being bright white with individual pieces measuring up to 6mm across. Quartz is not an ideal filler, and its selection as temper may have had a non-functional aspect (Gibson 1995a, 29). Quartz pieces and blocks are regularly associated with Late Neolithic/Early Bronze Age ritual sites in the region (Ashbee 1960; Burl 1976; Fox 1959), for example in bounding barrows, and the incorporation of quartz in pottery may have been within the framework of these ritual associations.

3. Shropshire, Middle Bronze Age urns with dolerite temper.
The temper comprises coarse grits up to 4mm across and is sourced to the Clee Hills, two spectacularly dramatic (and mythologically empowered?) outcrops, around the base of which Bronze Age cemeteries are positioned (Stanford 1982). Such sources may have had an ideological significance of considerable longevity. The same source was still being exploited *c.* a millennium later in the Middle Iron Age (Morris 1981).

Production: Where Were Pots Made?

Pottery is a synthetic material whose production involves a mosaic of practical activities. These spheres of action are based around choosing/locating, collecting and processing clays and tempers, and the forming, finishing, drying and firing of pots – yet any real sense of these 'taskscapes' or production loci of British prehistoric pottery are distinctly absent from the literature. A generally perceived view is that evidence for prehistoric pottery production loci, such as traces of kilns, wasters or potter's tools, is rarely encountered and unlikely to provide fertile ground for reconstruction. Perhaps we should not be so pessimistic. Case (1995, 64) in discussing British Beakers, for example, summarises the evidence for potter's tools, remains of clay bricks used in open firing clamps, and concentrations of prepared temper. A broad literature search of sites producing first millennium BC ceramics likewise indicates that a range of evidence does in fact exist for the structures, tools, and places of pottery production (Hamilton 1993). The data are widely scattered through individual excavation reports (e.g. Curwen 1941; Needham and Sorensen 1988; Needham and Spense 1996), but collectively suggest a database which includes: clay quarry pits; clay settling vats; caches of unfired clay (sometimes prepared with temper); hammerstones and stores of prepared temper; unfired pots; tools for modelling and decorating pottery; burnishing tools; tournettes (Jones 1975, 408–9); bonfire firing debris; clay fittings from pit kilns (e.g. clay bars and columns); and wasters/firing cripples (Figures 5.1–5.3).

Catalogue of selected illustrated finds potentially evidencing the presence of on-site prehistoric pottery production, and specific production technologies Figures 5.1–5.3).

Figure 5.1

1. Flint pebble pounder, Runnymede, Surrey. Late Bronze Age. Suggested use: for crushing flint for temper. From Needham and Spencer 1996, fig. 94: S213.
2. Flint pebble pounder, Runnymede, Surrey. Late Bronze Age. Suggested use: for crushing flint for temper. From Needham and Spencer 1996, fig. 94: S212.
3. Clay test piece (testing plasticity for pot manufacture?), Runnymede, Surrey, Late Bronze Age. From Needham and Spense 1996, fig. 98: C19.
4. Antler tool, for modelling or ornamenting pottery (?), Meare, Somerset, Middle Iron Age. Gray and Cotton 1966, pl. LV: H174.
5. Antler tool, for modelling pottery (?), Meare, Somerset, Middle Iron Age. Gray and Cotton 1966, 343, pl. LXI: H230.
6. Bone tool, for modelling pottery (?), Meare, Somerset, Middle Iron Age. Gray and Cotton 1966, 303, pl. LV: B126.
7. Bone tool, for modelling pottery (?), Meare, Somerset, Middle Iron Age. Gray and Cotton 1966, 303, pl. LV: B105.
8. Bone tool, for modelling pottery, Meare, Somerset, Middle Iron Age. Gray and Cotton 1966, pl. LV: B104.
9. Antler potter's stamp, Meare, Somerset, Middle Iron Age. Gray and Cotton 1966, 343, pl. LV: H206.
10. Small pottery bowl, Runnymede, Surrey. Late Bronze Age. Suggested use: water pot for finger-dipping to wet pottery during forming and finishing procedures. From Needham and Spense 1996, fig. 60: P652.
11. Small pottery bowl, Runnymede, Surrey. Late Bronze Age. Suggested use: water pot for finger-dipping to wet pottery during forming and finishing procedures. From Needham and Spense 1996, fig. 60: P651.

Figure 5.2

12. Bone spatula, Runnymede, Surrey. Late Bronze Age. Suggested use: for smoothing or burnishing pottery. From Needham and Spense 1996, fig. 101: B20.
13. Bone spatula, Runnymede, Surrey. Late Bronze Age. Suggested use: for burnishing pottery. From Needham and Spense 1996, fig. 102: B21.
14. Bone spatula, Runnymede, Surrey. Late Bronze Age. Suggested use: for burnishing pottery. From Needham and Spense 1996, fig. 101: B19.
15. Pebble burnisher, Bishopstone, Sussex. Late Bronze Age/Iron Age. Suggested use: for burnishing pottery. From Bell 1977, fig. 62:20.
16. Pebble burnisher with iron oxide staining, Bishopstone, Sussex. Late Bronze Age/Iron Age. Suggested use: for burnishing pottery (iron oxide rich fabric). From Bell 1977, fig. 61:17.
17. Sherd from an angular bowl evidencing a slab join, Ashville trading estate, Abingdon, Oxfordshire. Early Iron Age. From Parringdon 1978, fig. 33:28.

Figure 5.3

18. Fired clay bar, Bishopstone, Sussex. Late Bronze Age/Early Iron Age. Suggested use: kiln bar from a pit or bonfire kiln (alternative interpretation: briquetage from salt boiling). From Bell 1977, fig. 58, C24.
19. Fired clay bar, Bishopstone, Sussex. Late Bronze Age/Early Iron Age. Suggested use: kiln bar from a pit or bonfire kiln (alternative interpretation: briquetage from salt boiling). From Bell 1977, fig. 58, C21.
20. Clay 'thumb pot', Thorpe Thewles, Cleveland. Iron Age. Suggested use: test piece (to monitor kiln temperature and firing process). From Heslop 1987, fig. 46:171.
21. Clay 'thumb pot', Thorpe Thewles, Cleveland. Iron Age. Suggested use: test piece (to monitor kiln temperature and firing process). From Heslop 1987, fig. 44, 104.
22. Pot with spalling (flaking of vessel surface due to thermal fracture during firing), Runnymede, Surrey. Late Bronze Age. From Needham and Spense 1996, fig. 70:P703.
23. Pit filled with potting and kiln debris, Bishopstone, Sussex, Early Iron Age. From Bell 1977, fig. 31: pit 790.
24. Pit (clay vat?) filled with possible potting (unfired clay) and kiln debris, Aldermaston, Berkshire, Late Bronze Age. From Bradley *et al.* 1980, 224, fig. 5: pit 7.
25. Reconstruction drawing of a Late Iron Age kiln, with clay fire bars and supports, and separate fire area (stoke-hole), Hanborough, Oxfordshire. From Harding 1972, fig. 9.

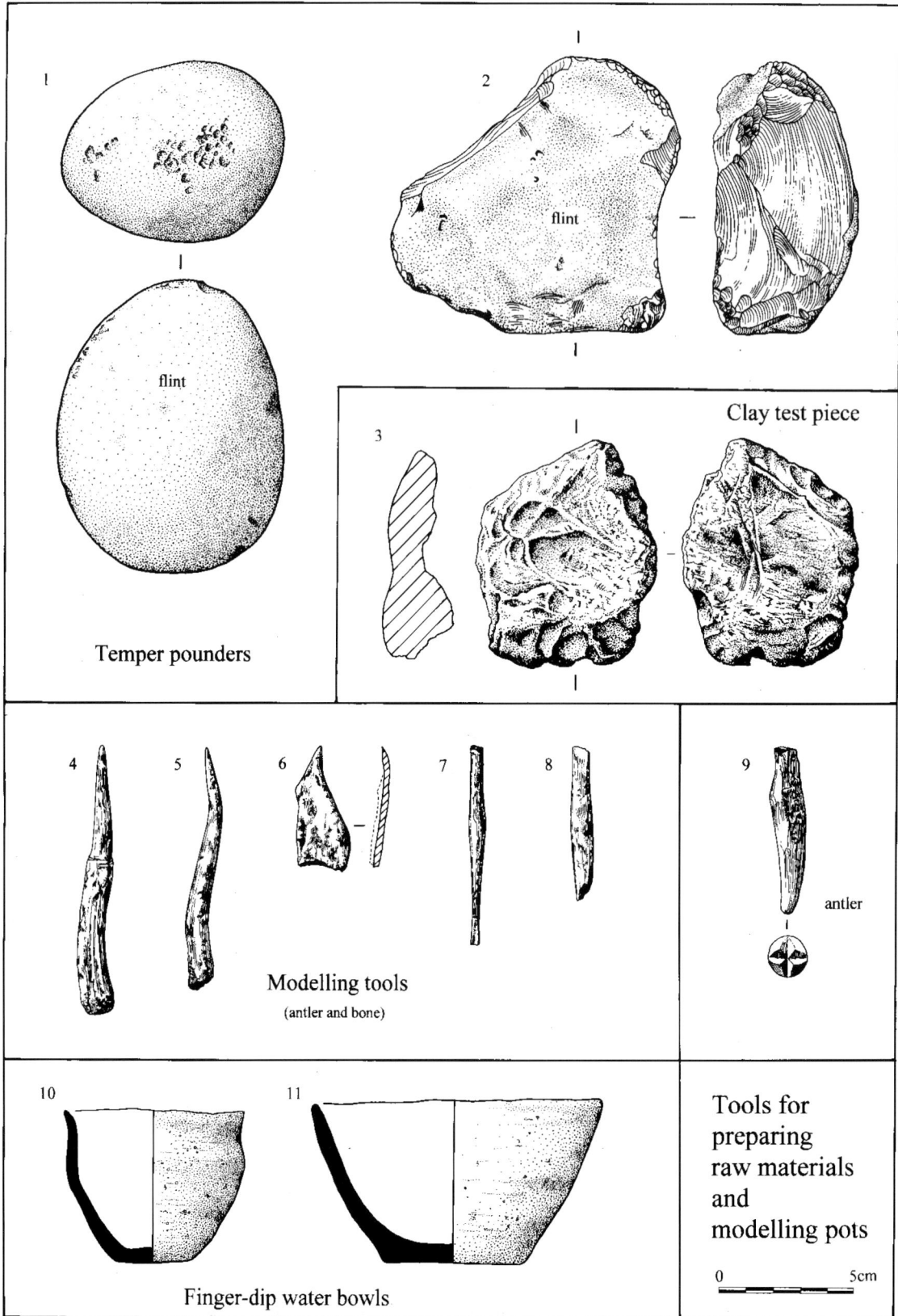

Fig. 5.1. Examples of tools and debris associated with preparing raw materials and modelling British prehistoric pots. See main text catalogue for sources.

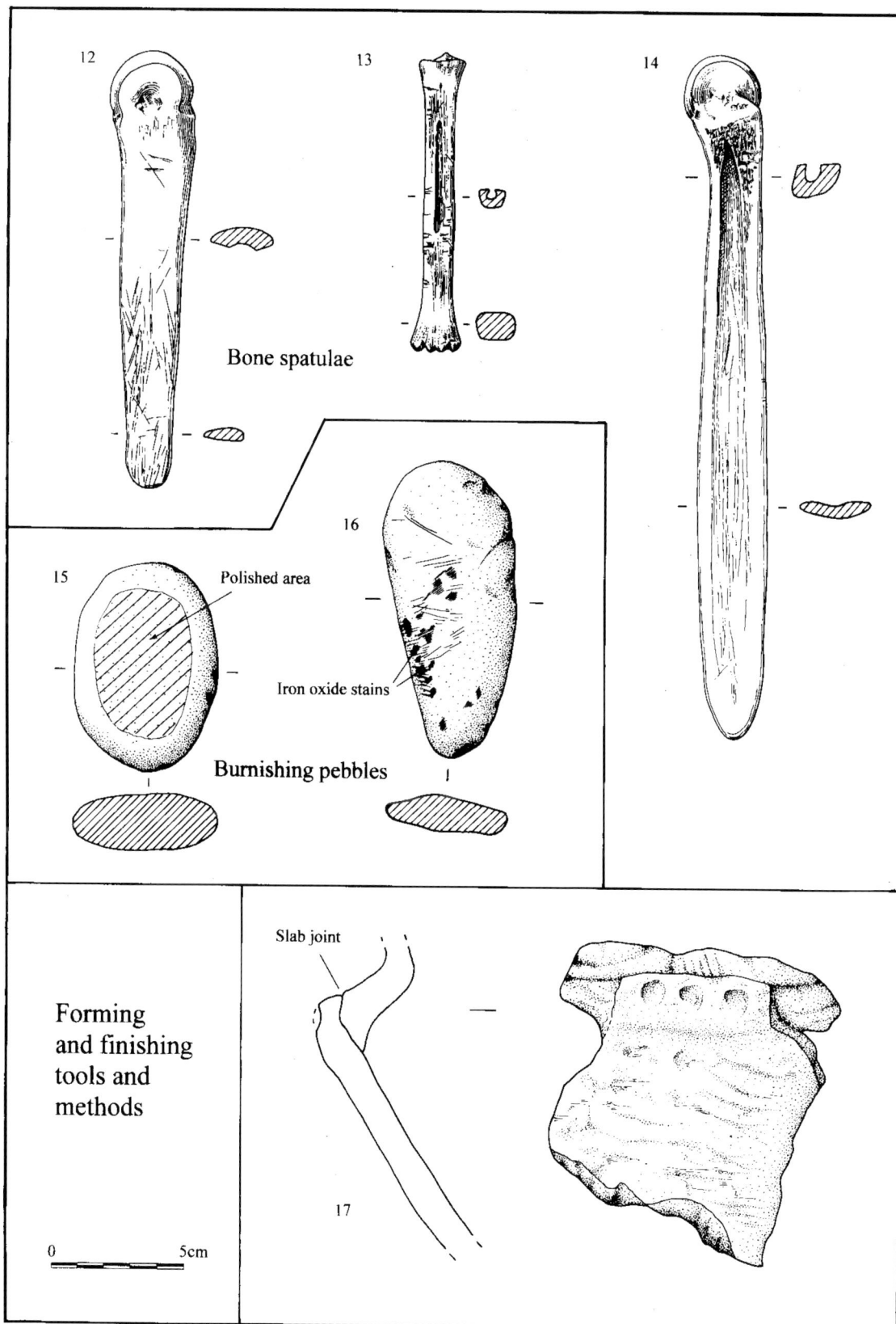

12

13

14

Bone spatulae

15 Polished area

16

Iron oxide stains

Burnishing pebbles

Forming
and finishing
tools and
methods

Slab joint

17

0   5cm

Fig. 5.2. Examples of tools associated with finishing British prehistoric pots, and evidence of pottery forming technology. See main text catalogue for sources.

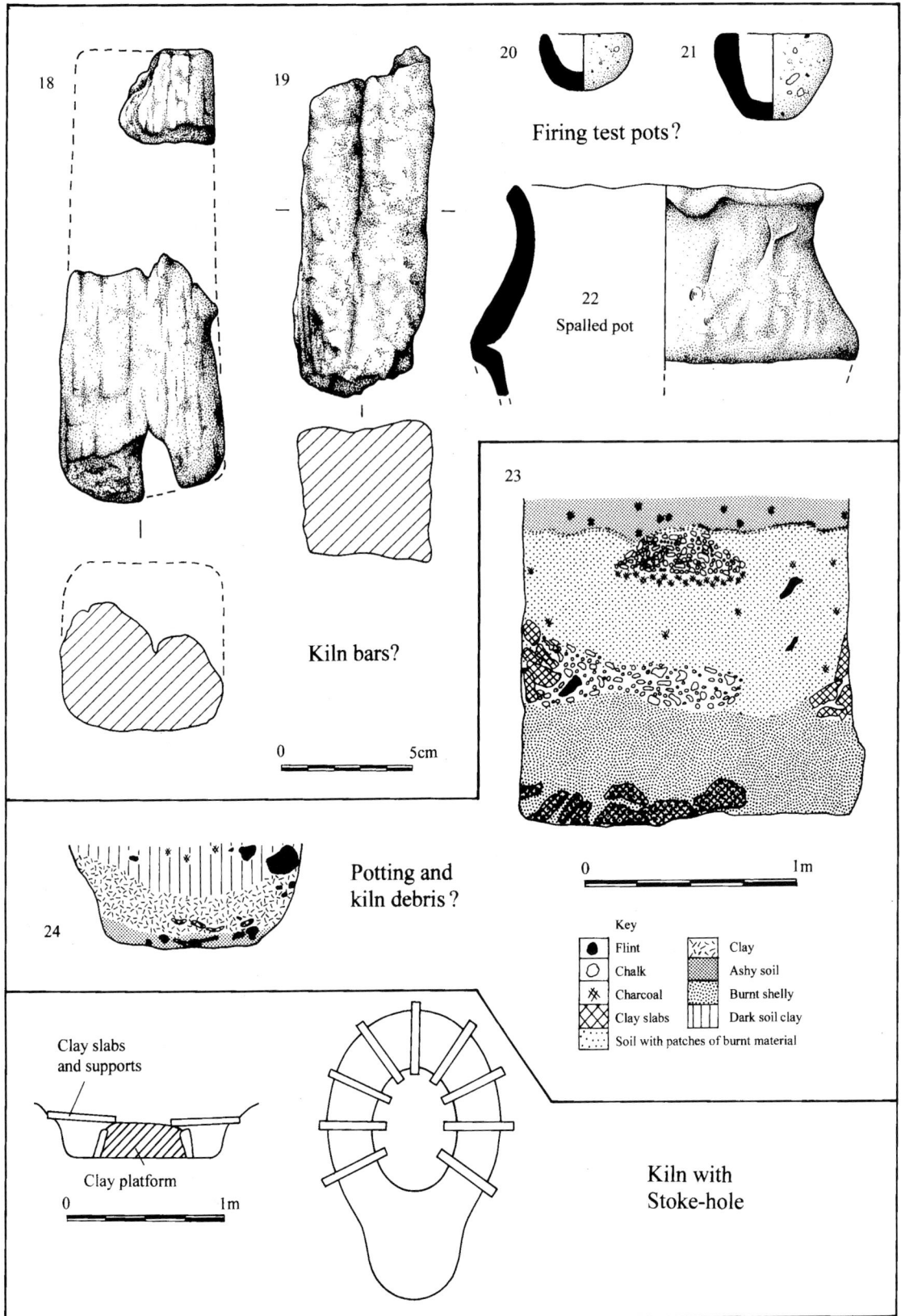

18
19
20
21

Firing test pots?

22
Spalled pot

Kiln bars?

0   5cm

23

Potting and
kiln debris?

24

0   1m

Key

●	Flint		Clay
○	Chalk		Ashy soil
✳	Charcoal		Burnt shelly
	Clay slabs		Dark soil clay
	Soil with patches of burnt material		

Clay slabs
and supports

Clay platform

0   1m

Kiln with
Stoke-hole

Fig. 5.3 Examples of British prehistoric potting and kiln debris and structures. See main text catalogue for sources.

Was Production Seasonal?

This question of possible seasonal production is often posed, but never really answered! Particularly in the context of domestic production, geological prospecting for clays and tempers, together with pottery manufacture, may have fitted into a periodic routine. The British winter months are clearly less suitable for adequate drying of pre-fired pot, although this could have been overcome by indoor drying with fires. The pressure of other tasks within the agricultural cycle may have, however, necessitated seasonal production of pots. Occasional examples of fired-out non-storable, seasonal, vegetable matter in pots suggests autumn firings (e.g. hawberries accidentally incorporated into Essex Iron Age pottery – Hamilton 1988), but this is a largely uninvestigated topic.

Vessel Repair:
The Implications for Production

The existence of a normative tradition of vessel repair both reflects *and effects* the nature of pottery production and exchange. Repair would have reduced demand for new pots, and impacted upon the frequency and scale of production.

Repair holes occur on British prehistoric pottery of all periods (Neolithic: Cleal 1988, Smith 1965; Early Bronze Age Cordoned Urns and Food Vessels: Briggs *et al* 1990, 177; Middle Bronze Age Deverel-Rimbury traditions: Ellison 1972; Late Bronze Age: Hamilton 1997; Middle Iron Age: Peacock 1968a; 1968b). While some of the repairs may have been associated with drying cracks (Briggs *et al.* 1990, 177), many more relate to use-damage. The holes have generally been bored post-firing, and often occur in 'pairs'; one each side of a crack/break in the vessel wall. It is presumed that the cracks were held together using sinew or leather thongs (Ellison 1972). Iron rivets occur on some Iron Age examples (Peacock 1968b, 421, 1969, 52).

Repair is notably characteristic of some pottery traditions more than others. In some cases, repair might simply be indicative of the fact that the time spent on vessel production would have been significantly greater than the task of repair. The latter could be an explanation for the recurrence of repair holes on Middle Bronze Age Deverel-Rimbury urns (Dacre and Ellison 1981; Ellison 1972, 111–2). Many of these urns are large and heavily flint-gritted, and would have required time-consuming preparation of huge quantities of clay and temper. Difficulty of acquiring replacement pots due to periodic, or non-local production, provides another potential reason for repair. Peacock (1968a, 1968b) suggests the latter as

explanation for iron repair rivets on Middle Iron Age pottery from western England (linear tooled and stamped ware, and Glastonbury ware). The use-patterns of vessels also would affect frequency of damage and the need for repair.

The *relevance* of repair must also have been determined by the social or ritual contexts within which specific pots were used. Certain use-contexts may have heightened the intrinsic importance of the vessel as an *integral unit*. Repair holes are a recurrent feature of Late Neolithic Grooved Ware assemblages, but are notably infrequent in concurrent Beaker and Peterborough traditions (Cleal 1988, Table 1, 1991, 147). Cleal (1988) suggests that the symbolic content of Grooved Ware's complex decorative schemes, together with the pottery's importance in deposition ritual (e.g. in henges), made the vessels worth repairing in their own right.

Innovation in Production

There are several points at which British prehistoric pottery production is significantly reconfigured at an inter-regional level. These reconfigurations stand out on the basis of at least one of the following: i) the use of new raw materials; ii) the introduction of new methods of manufacture; iii) the appearance of new vessel forms; and iv) changes in the scale of production.

We have barely begun to address how decision making occurs with regard to changing pottery production methods and changing products (Torrence and van der Leeuw 1989, 7–8). Analyses tend to concentrate *either* on the effects of technology on social organisation, *or* the isolation of the social contexts required for the uptake of specific technologies and production modes (van der Leeuw 1989, 240). It is important to take on board the complex interfaces *between* these factors. Major changes in pottery production must have variously emerged out of significantly altered demands of the recipient communities, both in terms of the quantity of pots required, *and* in terms of new arenas of social interaction - with pots taking on/being ascribed new roles in domestic and/or ritual discourse. Three examples of broad-scale changes in pottery production in later British prehistory are considered below in a wider socio-ideological framework:

1. The Appearance of Grog as a Major Inclusion in the Late Neolithic and Early Bronze Age.

Cleal (1995) has drawn attention to the fact that grog (crushed pottery) temper first appears in the Late Neolithic with Grooved Ware, and that its introduction is mirrored by a general avoidance of previously prevalent shell-tempering. Subsequently, grog temper is extensively used in Beakers, Biconical Urns, Collared Urns and Food Vessels (e.g. Tomalin 1983 for a consideration of the tradition of grog temper in British Biconical Urns). Grog temper is markedly less common in the succeeding Middle Bronze Age.

Grog is certainly a very effective temper. It has similar properties to the clay matrix with which it is mixed and is stable both during, and post-, firing. It is therefore notable that its regular use as a temper is restricted to specific periods of British prehistory. The absence, or presence, of grog as a filler might simply reflect a dislocation, or concurrence, between the contexts of production and the contexts of disposal of pottery. Ideological factors, rather than practical considerations, may have however governed its use. Several authors have commented on the obvious symbolism of grog-tempering – the transformation or perpetuation of one pot into another (Bewley *et al.* 1992; Brown 1995, 127). Grog may have been incorporated into pottery specifically because the donor sherds/pots had a 'special' status (e.g. Grooved Ware). Conversely, grog could have been rejected as a temper due to a taboo on incorporating 'old pots' into new vessels, as a result of the meaning(s) attached to functioning or broken pottery (Cleal 1995).

Within the Late Neolithic and Early Bronze Age practice of grog-tempering, specific pottery traditions are distinguished by unique combinations of technological, and style, traits. For instance, novel aspects of Beaker pottery technology are; i) that the pots are finer and thinner than other Late Neolithic/ Early Bronze Age ceramics; ii) that Beakers are often oxidised red, (indicative of free-air firing); *and* iii) that they often have prevalent grog tempering (Case 1995). This unique combination of technological and vessel traits seems to have emerged out of what the Beaker represented, and how it was used (Boast 1995, Boast this volume Chapter 10). Thus, while the use of grog in Beakers was part of a contemporary 'macro-language' of pottery production, the forms, decorative schemes, and emphasis on red-coloured finishes distinguished Beakers as being different from other coeval pots (possibly relating to their initial ritual use for burials).

2. Widening of the Vessel Size Repertoires in the Middle and Late Bronze Ages.

Studies of vessel size indicate a distinct widening in the vessel size repertoire by the beginning of the Middle Bronze Age (Woodward 1995; Woodward and Cane 1991) and, again, in the Late Bronze Age (Barrett 1980). Multiple size groupings first occur in the Middle Bronze Age urns compared to a simple small/large dichotomy in preceding Early Bronze Age and Neolithic pottery. Subsequently, Late Bronze Age assemblages are particularly distinguished by the introduction of bowls and cups. This increased range of vessels reflects the growing role food preparation and consumption i) *in the division of household tasks* during the Middle Bronze Age (Woodward 1995); and ii) *as a enabler of social discourse (drinking and feasting)* during the Late Bronze Age (Barrett 1980; Barrett, *et al.* 1991, 239; Rowlands 1980).

Cooking pots and tableware are generally broken and replaced more frequently than pots used for storage. As a consequence, ethnographic studies indicate that vessels for preparing and serving food are available in much larger quantities in markets than storage vessels (Okpoko 1987, 453). It is likely that changes in the social role of pottery during the Bronze Age created an increased demand, particularly for fine wares, making specialisation and innovation in pottery production more viable. In the Late Bronze Age this techno-dynamism is evidenced by: i) : *the selection of finer clays* (e.g. iron oxide clays) and round-grained tempers (e.g. quartz sand); ii) *the production of superior finishes* (evenly-fired, and burnished, surfaces); and iii) *the development of new forming technologies* (regular use of slab-building; rims joined as a separate strip at the vessel shoulder; dense temper on the bottom of bases; and bases joined to the bottom of pots by finger-pinching), (Adkins and Needham 1985; Brown 1988; Hamilton 1997).

3. Changes in Manufacturing Technique and the Scale of Production: Late Iron Age wheel-turned and wheel-thrown traditions.

During the Late Iron Age in parts of southern, and eastern, England, there are marked changes in vessel form, fabric (new quartz-sand-tempered, and grog-tempered wares), and manufacturing techniques (introduction of the potter's fast wheel). The technological innovations have long been considered to have emerged within the establishment of larger-scale centralised production (discussed below). The introduction of the fast wheel is particularly associated with Aylesford-Swarling pottery of south east England. In other cases, in West Sussex, Hampshire and Wiltshire (Southern Atrebatic and Northern Atrebatic pottery, Cunliffe 1991), and Dorset (Durotrigian pottery, Cunliffe 1991), the new forms are recurrently described as wheel-turned rather than wheel-thrown. It is often stated that the introduction of the potter's fast wheel (rapid rotation allowing the potter to use centrifugal force to shape the clay in a continuous movement) enabled more sinuous forms to be produced, thus allowing emulation/

copying of continental forms. However, it would be dangerous to see these changes purely in terms of tool determinism. Hill (1995a, this volume chapter 13) has importantly emphasised that these innovative regional production traditions are variously associated with novel *social* forms of tableware. These notably include Mediterranean-style drinking vessels, and food-serving platters and cordoned bowls (e.g. Aylesford-Swarling and Durotrigian tazzae; Aylesford-Swarling platters; Durotrigian, Southern Atrebatic, and Aylesford-Swarling cordoned bowls). These novel vessel types *and* their methods of production might however be considered to be by-products, rather than initiators, of the new social matrixes associated with the uptake of novel eating and drinking customs.

The Organisation of Pottery Production and Distribution

Since the late 1960s, the view that prehistoric pottery-making was a largely domestic activity has required re-evaluation – to accommodate the petrological evidence suggesting the existence of specialist workshops from the Neolithic onwards (Peacock 1968a, 1968b, 1969b). Ethnographic studies (e.g. Balfet 1962; van der Leeuw 1976; Tobert 1984) allow a range of production modes to be distinguished on

the criteria of i) the intensity of labour investment in production, ii) the complexity of the technology involved, and iii) the accessibility of raw materials utilised (Morris 1994; Peacock 1982). The modes or typologies of production most recurrently isolated in considerations of British prehistoric pottery are summarised in Figure 5.4. Such typologies are best seen as starting points, and generalised concepts, around which to consider the archaeological database (Costin 1991, 9). The evidence for later prehistoric Britain indicates that a great variability, and multiplicity, of pottery production strategies pertained either concurrently, or individually, at different periods and associated with different regions. This means that the scattered data are taxing to interpret, but pivotal to understanding the nature of regional diversity and general trends through *c.* four millennia of British prehistory.

The Archaeological Evidence for Modes of Production

Neolithic and Early Bronze Age modes of pottery production are ill-understood. The lack of evidence for substantial domestic sites and ceramic assemblages before the second millennium BC, and the restricted size-range of vessels produced, suggests that pottery production may have been primarily

Production mode and market	Commonly presumed archaeological characteristics
Household production. Household-based production for domestic consumption.	Site assemblages with pottery made from local clays and inclusions
Household industry. Production by household-based specialists for the settlement in which the specialists are based, and/or for proximate communities.	Site assemblages with pottery made from local or relatively local clays and inclusions, and/or the presence of vessels of the same fabric and typology on several sites in a region.
Workshop industry. Specialist production which is not domestically based, which has permanent workshops, and involves a greater intensity of production than household production and household industries. Production may be for the region within which the workshop(s) is based, and/or for communities at some distance from location of the workshop(s).	Pottery often of non-local clays and inclusions, evidencing high technological investment, uniform wares and vessel styles, and forming all or part of site assemblages. Regional or inter-regional pottery distributions.
Itinerant specialists. Mobile, specialist potters servicing several sites/communities and using resources local to each community.	Difficult to isolate: pottery with shared production techniques but variable site traditions, and 'customised' style traits may result. The pottery fabrics for individual sites will likely comprise local raw materials.

Fig. 5.4. The range of production modes commonly proposed for British prehistoric pottery.

for special social and ritual activities (Woodward 1995). The first large domestic assemblages occur in the Middle Bronze Age. From this period onwards pottery manufacture was one of the major production industries over much of prehistoric Britain. The archaeological evidence for these variable and changing modes of British prehistoric pottery production can be outlined as follows:

1. Neolithic Production: Hembury Style, Windmill Hill Style, Peterborough Ware, and Grooved Ware

The existence of at least some Early Neolithic specialist pottery production, involving workshops located at sources non-local to the pottery find-sites, has been recognised since Peacock's (1969) work on Hembury Style pottery. Cleal's (1995; Cleal *et al.* 1994)) consideration of the inclusions (predominantly shelly) which characterise Wessex Neolithic pottery (Windmill Hill Style, Hembury Style, Peterborough Ware, and Grooved Ware) suggests the acquisition of inclusions (marine shells, and glauconitic sands and/or clay), shelly clays, or finished pots from non-local sources/production locales up to 50km from the pottery finds-spots. Gibson's (1995a) study of Welsh Middle Neolithic pottery (Peterborough Ware) indicates that while local manufacture predominates, both Ebbsfleet and Mortlake vessels occur in non-local fabrics (e.g. at the Breiddin, and Gwernvale). These few examples suggest a wealth of complexity in Neolithic pottery production and exchange patterns. They also emphasise the essential importance of ceramic studies to our understanding of the social and economic framework within which Neolithic communities operated.

2. Early Bronze Age Production: Beakers, Collared Urns, Biconical Urns, and Food Vessels

A striking aspect of Late Neolithic and Early Bronze Age pottery production is the suggestion that Beakers were made in distinctly different contexts to other preceding and contemporary pottery traditions. Although Beaker ware adheres to a general technological tradition (grog tempering, see above), Beaker fabrics regionally exhibit a wide variety of mineral inclusions derived from local lithologies (Case 1995; Parker Pearson 1990). This implies decentralised, locally-based production. The time and energy needed for the manufacture of highly decorated Beaker pots further suggest that they were made by specialists, perhaps within individual settlements. Interestingly, there are qualitative distinctions between domestic Beakers and those used in burial. Less work is evident in the processing of the fabric for Beakers recovered from burials, but

with more effort being placed on the surface treatment and decoration (Boast 1995). This suggests, on the part of the producer, a specific knowledge of the ultimate context of use and disposal of the vessel being made. It points to Beakers being customised items, involving a direct relationship between the producer and the 'customer' (Parker Pearson 1995, 98).

Analyses of other Early Bronze Age pottery traditions (Food Vessels, Collared Urns) suggests the partial existence of two-tier production comprising i) workshops; and ii) localized small-scale production centres (household workshops?). These two tiers are particularly evident in the south western Early Bronze Age. Here the evidence indicates the existence of workshops exploiting raw materials on or near the Lizard gabbro (Parker Pearson 1990), alongside local manufacture. By contrast in other areas, such as Cumbria, Lancashire, south west Scotland, and Wessex wholly local manufacture can be surmised (Bewley *et al.* 1992, 340; Olivier 1987, 149; Russell-White *et al.* 1992, 318; Parker Pearson 1995).

3. Middle Bronze Age Production: Deverel-Rimbury Traditions

The Middle Bronze Age Deverel-Rimbury pottery traditions of central southern Britain indicate the emergence a more formalised, and widespread, three-tier operation of production (Ellison 1981a). The large thick-walled storage vessels ('heavy duty wares') have considerable intra-regional variation in their fabrics, suggesting that they were made on, or near, the sites where they were used. The presence of repair holes suggests *seasonal household production*, or *small-scale household industries*. The medium-sized vessels comprising medium-coarse fabrics ('everyday wares') have distribution areas ranging from 10–20km radius, and are considered to be indicative of *household industry production*. The fine ware, decorated, globular urns have more homogenous fabrics and distributions over larger geographic areas, suggesting *workshop production*, or seasonal industries executed by part-time specialists. These three distinct levels of production and distribution mirror the evidence for contemporary bronze products from southern Britain (Rowlands 1976) and indicate the incorporation of Middle Bronze Age pottery production into a wider system of small-scale interlocking exchange networks. Outside southern Britain, this tri-partite structure of production is less evident. Middle Bronze Age assemblages from, for example, the East Midlands and Shropshire are dominated by locally manufactured vessels (Allen *et al.* 1987, 219; Ellison 1976–77, 19).

4. Late Bronze Age (Post Deverel-Rimbury) and Iron Age Production

Several aspects of Late Bronze Age pottery traditions from lowland Britain suggest specialist production. These include the selection of finer clays and tempers, the appearance of more even finishes, and the increasing uptake of new production techniques. These innovations, the possible social contexts which generated them, and the likelihood of increased craft specialisaton have been discussed earlier in the chapter. The level at which this specialisation took place is ill-understood. Where fabric studies have been undertaken, evidence of the exploitation of non-local resources is quite rare, but does comes from the west Midlands, the south west, the Wessex area of central-southern Britain, and Sussex (Morris 1994, 374; Hamilton 1993). Inter-site distributions of vessels with common fabric, technological and style/decorative traits have not yet been isolated, and in general the situation suggests specialisation at a household level.

Throughout the first millennium BC specialist *versus* non-specialist pottery production, or local *versus* non-local, centralised production cannot straightforwardly be linked with specific levels of social complexity which are suggested by settlement patterns and types (Hill 1995b; Morris 1994). This begs the wider question of what factors affected the nature and extent of craft-specialisation. By the Early Iron Age the total output of pottery production was considerable. Much of this production is characterised by well-defined regional styles which might be thought to reflect ethnic division and/or imply some degree of centralised specialist production. While regional distributions and fabric standardisation characterise some traditions, the relationship between stylistic traits and individual production centres (recognised by mineralogical analysis of fabric) are not however exclusive (e.g. Middle Iron Age Glastonbury wares: Avery 1973). The latter subject needs further detailed work if we are to isolated the nature of production *and* interpret the distribution of pottery style traits.

Morris (1994) has importantly pieced together the published data on first millennium BC pottery assemblages with particular respect to the spatial distributions of pottery fabrics and their associated vessel forms and styles. She has identified broad patterns of local, and non-local intra-regional, production and distribution. Using Arnold (1981; 1985), her definition of non-local is where tempers and clays identified in the pottery fabrics are demonstrated to have come from more than 10km from the location where the pottery was utilised.

The pottery evidence no longer supports the traditional view of increasing centralisation of production through the period of first millennium BC Britain. Throughout the millennium there is a dominance of local production systems everywhere (Morris 1994). The development of specialised production only takes place in *some* areas, and is not specific to the latter part of the period. For example, while the majority of early first millennium BC pottery appears to have been made locally, small-scale specialist production of decorated fine wares is certainly present in south west and central-southern Britain. The latter are distinguished by clays and inclusions from sources up to 40km from the vessel finds-spots (e.g. Sussex iron oxide wares and some of the Wessex 'haematite-coated' wares).

During the Middle Iron Age a marked increase in specialist production occurs, but again only in *some* regions. Peacock's (1968a, 1968b, 1979) seminal analyses of two distinct Middle Iron Age pottery styles from western, and south western Britain (stamped and linear tooled ware, and Glastonbury ware) first suggested the existence of specialist potters working from a limited number of production centres/household industries, and serving communities within *c.*80–130km of the sources of the raw materials used. More recent work allows us to surmise the nature of regional production systems, as opposed to isolating the production context of single pottery traditions. Multi-tiered production was extant in the Middle and Later Iron Age in central-southern, south western, south eastern Britain, and the Severn Valley and West Midlands (Morris 1994, tables 3 and 4). For the Severn Valley and West Midlands, Morris (1981; 1982; 1983; 1991) has identified the existence of a three-tier production system by the later Iron Age comprising i) the *regional distribution* of plain and decorated wares 50–80km from raw material sources; ii) *small-scale specialist production* and distribution, up to 30km from raw material sources; and iii) *household production* using proximate resources. In other areas, such as eastern lowland Britain, assemblages predominantly comprise fabrics made from local resources, suggesting that household production was the standard pattern.

During the latest pre-Roman Iron Age there were major typological and technological changes in pottery manufacture in a restricted number of areas, notably Cornwall (Cunliffe 1991, 181–2), central-southern Britain (Brailsford 1958; Brown 1991; Hamilton 1985), south east Britain (Thompson 1982), and parts of eastern England (May 1996). For these areas, it is traditionally suggested that centralised workshop industries emerged, identifiable by new production techniques (wheel-turned, and wheel-thrown, products) and new standardised fabrics (using raw materials non-local to the vessel finds sites). These new regional pottery traditions have been characterised as being internally highly uniform, having great coherence of design, and evidencing considerable technical proficiency (e.g. the Aylesford-Swarling wheel-thrown corrugated vessels, Thompson 1982). Standardisation is traditionally regarded as a by-product, and/or indicator of centralised or professional production and larger scale output. Costin (1991, 33–39), and Welbourn (1985) have however highlighted the need to critically assess the relationship between production, scale of output, and standardisation. There is, for instance, the problem of identifying *actual* standardisation, as opposed to dispersed potting communities working to a common production and vessel-style templates. These issues need to be particularly investigated with respect to the supposed centralised workshop pottery traditions of Late Iron Age lowland Britain. Brown (1991), for example, has noted that as new assemblages of Late Iron Age, 'Durotrigian' pottery from Dorset are examined and old assemblages are reassessed, it has become apparent that the typological standardisation is not as great as previously thought.

The Long View

The major shifts summarised above clearly relate to the varying role of pottery as a whole, and specific categories of vessel in particular, in social discourse. Where detailed regional studies of some time-depth have been undertaken, it is possible to isolate subtler and contextualised regional and sub-regional change. For example, Parker Pearson's (1995) analysis of south western prehistoric pottery evidences a series of fluctuations between centralised and local production extending from the early Neolithic through to the Roman period.

Pottery Distributions

Artefact distributions, and pottery distributions in particular, have long been used to provide regional frameworks for British prehistory (Brailsford 1957; Cunliffe 1991; Clarke 1970; Ellison 1981b; Hawkes 1959; Hodson 1964, 1980; Kenyon 1952; Smith 1974; Whittle 1977). The dilemma is that pottery traits and their distributions potentially express a range of social identities, cultural mechanisms, and production and exchange contexts (Hodder 1982; Blackmore *et al.* 1979; Miller 1985). To better illuminate these complexities the extant broad regional frameworks of pottery distributions need extensive investigation at a micro-spatial level. Key to this process are i) *the precise typological definition of the content of pottery 'style zones'*, and ii) *the isolation of the detailed structures of pottery trait distributions* (the

associations of fabric types, technologies, forms, and decoration), (Avery 1973; Collis 1977a). Fabric traditions, potting raw materials, and potting technologies might be seen as the best starting point for investigating the basis of style zones.

Broad temporal shifts in the size and mutual exclusivity of the regional distributions of British prehistoric pottery style groupings are well-recognised and summarised in Figure 5.5 (Bradley 1984, 163; Ellison 1981a). Such variation has been attributed to different types of social organization, and specific scales and types of production. Small-scale, regional distributions, for instance, have been seen as reflecting phases of stress or competition with communities expressing their group identity through coherent styles of artefacts (Hodder 1979, e.g. Early Neolithic pottery: Bradley 1984; Late Bronze Age pottery: Barrett 1980; Early Iron Age pottery: Cunliffe 1980). Conversely, one interpretation of larger-scale distributions is that they result from hierarchical societies impeding the development of small, localised prestige groups (Late Neolithic/Early Bronze Age pottery: Ellison 1981b). In the case of Late Iron Age pottery from southern Britain, the appearance of new discrete pottery distributions, of larger-scale output, have been identified with the emergence of 'commercial' production centres and their markets (Cunliffe 1991; Hill 1995b).

Micro-scale Study

I have written at a very general level, but the issues raised remain relevant if we narrow our focus. My intention, finally, is to provide a brief indication of the mechanics of producing a bottom-up analysis of pottery production and distribution, working from a small-scale regional database. This should highlight the potential richness of information which is available in the micro-analysis of a relatively small geographic area. My example is the first millennium BC pottery assemblages of East and West Sussex.

Isolating Viable Assemblages for Analysis

East and West Sussex collectively have more than fifty first millennium BC pottery assemblages of substantial size (*c.* >200–40,000 sherds). Since the mid 1970s, excavations at more than twenty Sussex sites (e.g. Bedwin 1979; Cunliffe 1976) have produced first millennium BC assemblages with detailed stratigraphic information. This adds to the considerable number of assemblages recovered during thirty years (1920s–1950s) of sustained archaeological excavation on Iron Age sites in Sussex by the Curwens, and A.E. Wilson (e.g. E.C. Curwen 1929; E. and E.C. Curwen 1927; Wilson 1940).

Period	Distributions		Pottery traditions (examples)
	Area	Discrete/Overlapping	
Early Neolithic	S	Overlapping	Abingdon Ware Whitehawk Ware Hembury Ware
Late Neolithic/Early Bronze Age	M and L	Overlapping	Grooved Ware Peterborough Ware Beakers
Late Early Bronze Age	S	Overlapping	Wessex Biconical Urns Barrel Urns Food Vessels
Middle Bronze Age	S	Discrete	Deverel-Rimbury fine wares and everyday wares
Late Bronze Age	S	Overlapping	Late Bronze Age post Deverel-Rimbury traditions
Early and Middle Iron Ages	S	Discrete	Cunliffe's (1991) Early and Middle Iron Age pottery style zones (e.g. saucepan pottery)
Late Iron Age	S	Discrete	Durotrigian pottery Aylesford-Swarling pottery East Sussex Ware Southern Atrebatic pottery

Key (after Ellison 1981)
S = small-scale distribution: < 18,000 sq. km.; M = medium-scale distribution: 18,000 to < 250,000 sq. km.; L = large-scale
distribution: 250,000 to >800,000 sq. km.

Fig. 5.5. The geographic scale of British prehistoric pottery style and ware distributions by period (after Ellison 1981b).

With the exception of the later first millennium BC cemetery assemblage from Westhampnett (Fitzpatrick 1997a), the Sussex database wholly comprises domestic assemblages. These assemblages come from a range of site types (hillforts, open settlements, enclosed settlements, and colluvial accumulations). As a whole, British first millennium BC domestic assemblages generally lack 'closed stratigraphic groups' in the strict sense of the term (Collis 1977). The complex stratigraphic implications resulting from cycles of pottery usage, deposition/ discard, and post-depositional disturbance in settlement contexts have been highlighted (Hill 1995a; Lambrick 1984). In order to 're-associate' the original pottery assemblages from Sussex first millennium domestic sites, modes of site and artefact deposition and abandonment were established by isolating intra-context and inter-context sherd joins, and assessing the degrees of sherd fragmentation and erosion (Hamilton 1985; 1987; 1988; 1993). Clearly, this requires sites with good stratigraphic documentation (Figure 5.6).

Sourcing Potting Raw Materials

East and West Sussex have a sedimentary geology which is exposed as a series of distinct west-east bands of limited north-south extent (Hamilton and Manley 1997). These bands provide a range of potting clays and tempers. Definitions of Sussex first millennium BC fabrics and detailed consideration of

the suggested clay and tempered sources are provided in several texts (Hamilton 1977; 1980; 1984; 1993). Most of the inclusions present cannot be sourced to precise geological sources by mineral identification alone, and textural analysis was used to facilitate more precise source attribution.

Isolating the Locales of Production

Evidence for Sussex first millennium BC pottery production comes from seven Late Bronze Age/ Early Iron Age sites, five Middle Iron Age sites and two Late Iron Age sites. This evidence comprises areas/caches of prepared temper, clay, and tempered clay (e.g. Balcombe quarry, Glynde: Hamilton 1993; Bishopstone: Bell 1977; Park Brow: Wolseley *et al.* 1927), potting tools, notably burnishing pebbles (e.g. Bishopstone: Bell 1977; Horsted Keynes: Hardy and Curwen 1937; Figure 5.2); pit kiln fittings (e.g. Bishopstone: Bell 1977; Castlehill Newhaven: Hamilton 1993; Green Street, Eastbourne: Hamilton 1993; Figure 5.3); firing debris (e.g. Bishopstone: Bell 1977; Horsted Keynes: Hardy and Curwen 1937; Figure 5.3). Although this evidence is comparatively sparse, it suggests that there is a separation of raw material source areas from production locations prior to the first century BC. One example is the use of Wealden iron oxide clays during the Late Bronze Age and Early Iron Age. Here, evidence for production occurs on East Sussex downland sites some 20km south of the identified clay sources (Hamilton

Site	Source	Date(s) of pottery assemblages	Type of site
America Farm	Hamilton 1994	LBA	O
Bishopstone	Hamilton 1977	LBA, EIA, MIA, LIA	♣ X
Chantonbury Ring	Hamilton 1980	LBA	♣ X
Caburn	Drewett and Hamilton 1998	EIA, MIA	X
Harting Beacon	Hamilton 1979; Morris 1978	LBA	O
Heathy Brow	Hamilton 1982	LBA	X
Hollinbury	Hamilton 1984	EIA	O
Knapp Farm	Gardiner and Hamilton 1997	LBA	O
Testers	Hamilton 1988	LBA, LIA	♣
Thundersbarrow Hill	Hamilton 1993	LBA	X
North Bersted	Morris 1978	MIA, LIA	♣
Oving	Hamilton 1985	MIA, LIA	♣
Yapton	Hamilton 1987	LBA	O

Key: E = Early; M = Middle; L = Late; O = open settlement; X = hillfort; ♣ = enclosed settlement.

Fig. 5.6. Sussex first millennium BC domestic assemblages with good stratigraphic data.

1993, figs 13.3 and 13.4). Evidence for first millennium BC pottery production (and indeed other craft production) on Sussex hillforts is notably lacking and these hillforts certainly cannot be considered to be central sites in terms of being at the apex of a production hierarchy. Instead, production is located on modest settlements, irrespective of whether production is based on local or non-local resources. In Sussex, it is only during the later first century BC that larger-scale, centralised pottery workshops come into existence and, demonstrably for East Sussex, production now took place at the clay sources (Hamilton 1993, fig. 13.11).

Isolating Scales of Production

In East and West Sussex workshop production, as identified by the use of specific clays or tempers combined with a restricted form and decorative repertoire, is minimal prior to the latest pre-Roman Iron Age. Where such products can be identified their distribution takes up areas of *c.*12km across. One example is the Early Iron Age raised-cordon bowls (made of Wealden iron oxide clays) with incised herringbone decoration found in the adjacent downland hillfort sites of Hollingbury (Hamilton 1984, fig. 2: 19 and 20), and the Caburn (Hawkes 1939, fig. E:74). Another example is the Middle Iron Age saucepan pots (with quartz-sand tempering of Wealden origin) decorated with free-flowing tooled scrolls present in the assemblages from the Caburn (Hawkes 1939, fig. J:70) and, nearby at the settlement of Bishopstone (Hamilton 1977, fig. 54:95; Figure 5.7)).

For the greater part of the first millennium BC the Sussex evidence indicates the acquisition of raw materials at distances of up to 20km from recognised production sites. Both of the 'workshop' examples mentioned in the paragraph above comprise non-local clays/tempers which were *also* used in other contemporary pottery. It would appear that the scale of common resource acquisition was greater than the distribution of products of single communities or workshops. The East Sussex Early Iron Age fabrics made from High Wealden iron oxide rich clays, for example, have been recognised from at least 13 sites distributed across an area approximately 70km across (Hamilton 1980, 1993). The existence of a trade in raw materials, and/or the use of a specific geological resource for clays of tempers by potters from several communities, are all possibilities.

Sussex first millennium BC pottery 'style zones' are at a significantly smaller scale than the regional frameworks of current study. Sussex Middle Iron Age saucepan pot style zones, for example comprise distributions *c.*20–30km across (Fig. 5.7). During the Late Iron Age centralised production can be suggested on the basis of the emergence of standardised forms and fabric recipes. These are a wheel-thrown, quartz-tempered, style tradition in West Sussex, and a handmade, grog-tempered, style tradition in East Sussex (Hamilton 1977; 1985). The products of these putative centralised workshops, have relatively small distribution areas of *c.*50km across and *c.*30km across respectively (Hamilton 1993). By, contrast, Cunliffe's Early Iron Age pottery 'style zones' of the hillfort zone of central southern Britain are, for example, typically *c.*75km across, and his Middle Iron Age saucepan style zones similarly, *c.*70km across (Cunliffe 1991, figs. 4.4 and 4.6).

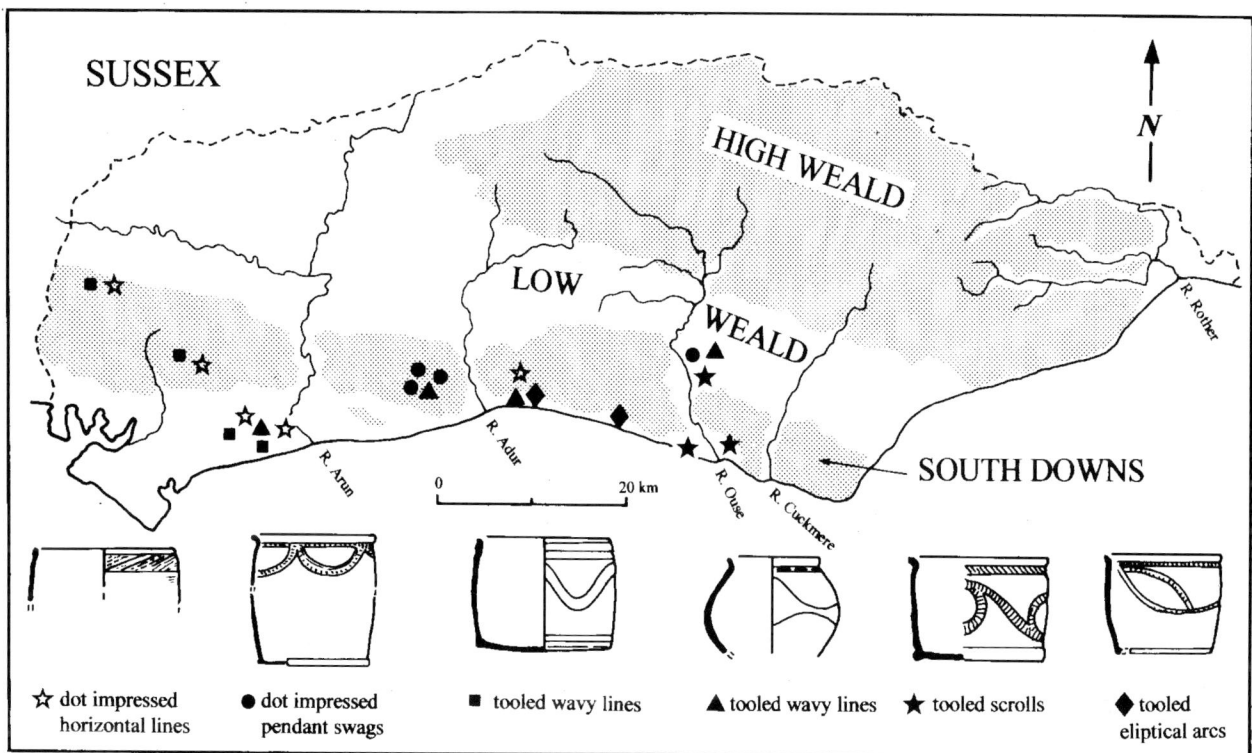

Fig. 5.7. Distribution of major decorative motifs on Sussex Middle Iron Age pottery.

Implications of the Sussex Micro-Scale Study

Sussex first millennium BC pottery style and fabric distributions serve to emphasise that currently established units of synthesis and regional analysis are too large to plot the organisation of specific communities (Champion 1994). While Sussex may be atypical, the results raise important questions about the spatial scale at which we should isolate and interpret socio-economic patterning for the first millennium BC southern Britain, and the presumptions that we make in doing so.

Conclusion

I have opted to provide a general outline of the nature of the evidence for British prehistoric pottery production and distribution, and to consider some of the possibilities relating to its interpretation. The sheer complexity and variability of the evidence challenges many of the traditional generalisations concerning regional variability and socio-economic organisation of British later prehistoric communities.

Without an understanding of the *local* ideological, social, and economic templates within which artefact production took place any starting presumptions relating to artefact distributions as a basis for interpreting period and regional activity will be ill-founded. The British prehistoric pottery database perhaps offers the best opportunity of achieving such an understanding, given that its production covers some four millennia, and that it is abundantly present in much of Britain on a wide range of sites for at least the latter two millennia BC.

Acknowledgements
I would like to thank the editors and anonymous readers for their comments on this paper. Figures 5.1, 5.2, 5.3 and 5.7 where drawn by Jane Russell. The finds and structures illustrated in Figures 5.1, 5.2 and 5.3 were all redrawn from published drawings (Bell 1977, Bradley *et al.* 1980, Gray and Cotton 1966, Harding 1972, Heslop 1987, Needham and Spense 1996, Parrington 1978) and are sourced in more detail in the main text.

6 Staying Alive:
The Function and Use of Prehistoric Ceramics

Elaine L. Morris

"Greater research is needed on the function of pottery as revealed by studies of technology, analysis of residues, the study of physical and mechanical properties and identification of use wear patterns. Such analyses should be integrated into wider considerations of food storage, processing and consumption" (PCRG 1991, 4).

One of the greatest weaknesses of prehistoric archaeologists over the past century has been their manipulation of pottery primarily as a marker of chronology. The pot makers and the pot users never intended to have their vessels tell time. This focus has dominated the majority of our efforts at the expense of so much which could have been done. It has been our collective fault for not demanding more; often this has stemmed from not asking the right questions and occasionally from not asking more questions.

As prehistorians we should have been using pottery to investigate ancient human societies; time is part of that investigation and it provides a framework for exploring change but it is only the beginning. We need to know why pottery was made the way it was in order to inform us about past human behaviour; the making of shapes, application of surface finish and creation of decorative patterns were deliberate activities. We need to know how pottery was used in order to determine which activities occurred at sites and where they took place within sites, the structure of the social groups who used the pots, and the processing and consumption of food in these vessels for both subsistence and social reproduction.

Prehistoric potters made their wares for specific purposes within a social web, and prehistoric people used them in a variety of ways to solve social problems. Thomas emphasizes this in his discussion of the relationships between space and architecture versus portable artefacts brought to that space; while architecture provides a setting for action, 'artefacts can be orchestrated within these settings to provide more detailed and explicit contexts for social dis-

course' (1991a, 83). This is what we should be examining – what prehistoric people did, how they did it and why they did it. Archaeologists need to find the necessary methods for 'reading' or interpreting the many messages encased in pots and their settings.

Food Production, Storage, Processing and Consumption

The focus on chronology has been exacerbated by the compartmentalisation of subsistence studies as the role of environmental archaeologists. Food is the source of life; without it prehistoric societies did not survive. The study of the environment, field systems, and animal and crop husbandry regimes from the Neolithic through the Iron Age (Jones and Dimbleby 1981; Jones 1986, 1992; van der Veen 1992; Ferrell 1995; Huntley and Stallibrass 1995; Bell 1996; Maltby 1994, 1996; Allen 1997) should be integrated with the use of ceramics as food storage, processing and serving utensils, as Jones has mentioned in passing (1996, 33, 36). A society needs food; in the past, pottery was part of the subsistence strategy for obtaining and distributing food and a primary contribution to the process of staying alive in later prehistory. How prehistoric people used pottery in that strategy tells us about their lives and their social organisation. Because pottery can be manipulated in myriad ways and because pottery survives in the archaeological record, it is a major source of information about how people used food and food containers to maintain and reproduce their way of life.

Food is a form of material culture. Whether gathered or hunted, sown, grown and reaped in a field, raised in byres and slaughtered in a courtyard, made from milk and preserved as butter and cheese, boiled in a pot, or roasted in a pit or over a hearth, food was (and still is) a facilitator of social relations. It was manipulated and transformed in a variety of ways for consumption and used as a commodity for displaying wealth and sharing to reinforce or re-negotiate relationships. Strong evidence for feasting or sacrifice at both domestic settlements (Maltby 1985) and, as might be expected, at locations of special social gathering such as causewayed enclosures and henges is based primarily upon faunal studies. These, however, should be reinforced through the integration of ceramic use and deposition since it has been clearly shown that these commonly recovered materials are frequently associated in special ways (Hill 1995a). At South Lodge (Cranborne Chase, Dorset), these relations are presented in opposition as part of the abandonment rituals of the settlement, while the deliberate back-filling of ditches there and at Down Farm contain unweathered and unknawed cattle bone, dog skulls and selected groups of pottery (Barrett *et al.* 1991).

Evidence for the changing inter-relationships amongst the labour of agricultural production or subsistence activities, the places and processes of its transformation, storage efforts, the nature of consumption, and the people who conducted these activities is available in the archaeological record but ceramics must be used to contribute to the investigation of this if we are to fully explore social reproduction (Barrett 1989). In particular we need to concentrate on how pottery was manufactured for use (the ideas and practicalities behind its creation), the many roles it has played in the transformation of produce (cooking, storing, preparation and presentation), how it was employed in the spheres of life and of death (for food and for human remains), and how it was removed from the living world (deposition).

Pottery Practicalities: Intended Use

For the past 50 years or more prehistorians have been describing pottery fabrics and vessel forms to develop sound relative chronologies. Some of those descriptions have been as crude as the wares they describe with the meaningless term 'grit' getting them nowhere in understanding the societies they were investigating. Potters chose raw materials to solve problems. They investigated what was available and found out what worked for them. They were, however, constrained by the social world into making what would be accepted or expected for use

by the people amongst whom they lived and for whom they made their vessels (Barrett 1991a, 201–2). A bead rim, high-shouldered jar would not have been made in the earlier Neolithic, and a Deverel-Rimbury urn would have been an offensive object to someone burying their dead in Kent during the Late Iron Age.

The selection and processing of raw materials according to what is available to a potter tells us about the tasks the vessel may have been required to perform, and how the potter chose to make those tasks possible. A pot is a container required to store, cook, serve or transport food. The food may be a liquid, a solid in a liquid medium or a solid in its own right; it may be animal, vegetable or mineral. This contribution will not discuss the norms of social behaviour which guided potters in choosing forms and tempers for vessels (Walleart 1997) but will examine the nature of vessel shapes and tempering additives which may have restricted their choices, as well as how vessels were eventually used in daily life.

Shapes and Sizes, Tempers and Tantrums, Surfaces and Shine: The Technology of Making for Using

Specific physical and mechanical properties are required to make pots. The clays and tempers, along with fuel and water, are selected and transformed by potters to achieve some of these properties while vessel morphology and surface treatments are responses to the expected use(s) of the vessel (Fig. 6.1). Vessel shapes and sizes present archaeologists with the most obvious clues to finding out what pots were made for. Temper and wall thickness can expand the variation in vessel uses. It is important to emphasize here that this is just the first stage in pottery studies – what the vessels were actually used for is a whole different part of our work.

During the 1980's, a series of articles and books appeared which used ethnographic studies as the potential basis for interpreting the function of archaeological ceramics (Hally 1986; Henrickson and McDonald 1983; Howard 1981; Miller 1985; Smith 1988). By comparing details in the vessel shape or morphology, size and fabric with the known uses of vessels, predictive models of function were presented.

Overall volume, rim diameter, orifice passage, height and openness of vessel profile can be used to predict whether vessels were made as cookpots and general utility wares, preparation vessels, dry storage jars, liquid containers, or serving vessels (Fig. 6.2). The type, size range and density of temper coupled with the vessel wall thickness and curvature of profile create an interplay of assistance in the functioning of these vessels. The goal of pottery

Fig. 6.1. Potting in a perfect world (drawn by Sophia Jundi).

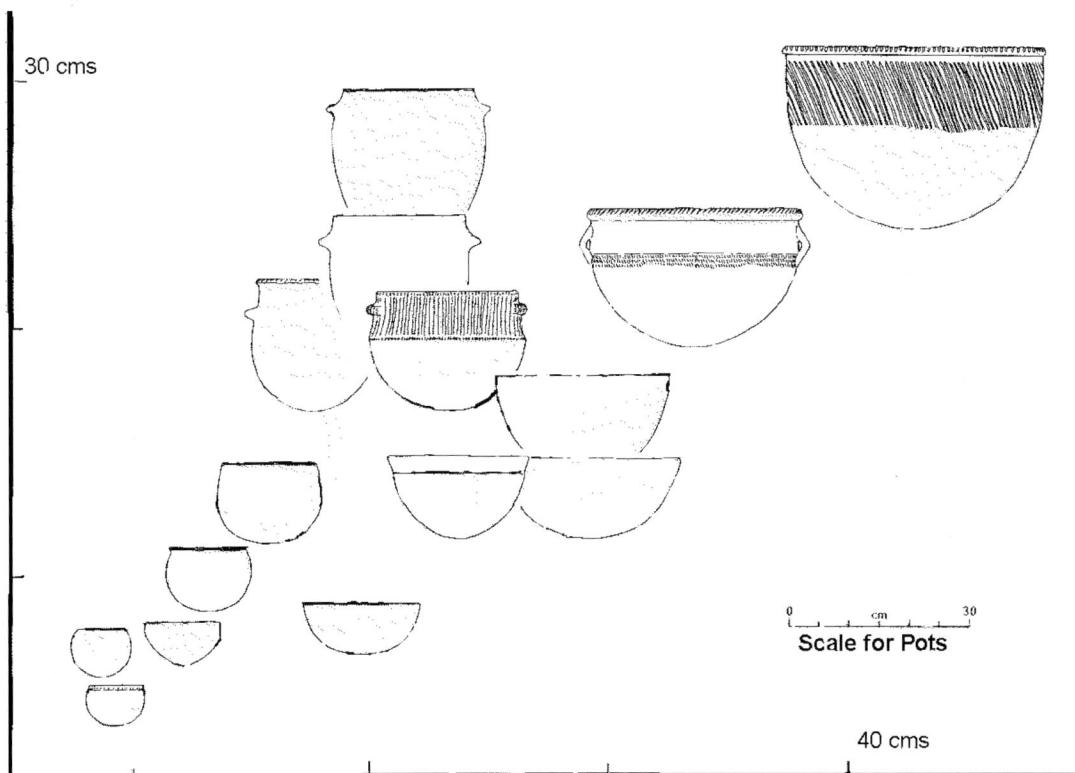

Fig. 6.2. Vessel sizes of the Early Neolithic assemblage from Windmill Hill, Wiltshire presented by plotting vessel height to rim diameter of measurable examples (from Howard 1981, fig. 1.3).

manufacture is to provide the right balance of requirements which prevent breakage during use based on the materials available and within the expectations of the potential users.

These models, however, were infrequently adopted or assessed by prehistoric archaeologists after their first introduction. This pattern of research, innovation but lack of adoption, is an all too strong characteristic of ceramic research. Not until the 1990's do we see these concepts and approaches beginning to be developed and utilised for the Neolithic period in particular (Cleal 1991a, 1992), but still they are not embraced by the general archaeological community. One of the reasons for this may stem from the original models being based on complete vessels from ethnographic contexts and applied to quite special assemblages of archaeological examples. The opportunity to recover whole pots or at least total profiles, and the intensive support to reconstruct fragmented assemblages (Nelson 1985, 316), occur all too infrequently for most prehistorians. Sherds are what most of us deal with, rims are how we classify our vessels and we get excited with the discovery of a partial profile or special deposit containing a complete vessel.

However, changes are at hand. Reimer (1998) has provided a series of ratios based on measuring orifice diameter (the actual opening of a vessel through which all must pass and which is unaffected by variation in rim style) to maximum body diameter, body diameter to height, and vessel capacity which can be plotted and compared to the positions of vessel types with known functions. The next phase must be to find a way of translating this method so that it is applicable at an acceptable level of reliability for sherd assemblages. A start has been made already by Woodward (1997), who has developed a formula for comparing the sizes of selected, very specific Iron Age vessel forms using simply the rim diameters. This model was developed by testing the consistency in rim diameters amongst total profile examples which revealed that the diameters were strongly correlated to capacity for these regional types. It may prove that this formula is suitable for similar rim/vessel types in other regions because of the repetition of forms and consistency of output during this period of prehistory. Similar methods need to be developed for other periods of prehistoric pottery use.

The role of pottery fabric tempers in the use and lifespans of vessels has been an importance concern of ceramicists for sometime (Bronitsky and Hamer 1986; Rye 1976, 1981; Shepard 1956; Steponaitis 1984; Woods 1986). These studies are particularly successful when integrated with the attributes of vessel morphology and wall thickness (Braun 1983) which create a more holistic approach to ceramic functional studies. Recent experimental work on the nature of surface treatments has shown that several have distinct effects on the performance of cooking vessels and abrasion resistance during use (Schiffer 1990; Schiffer *et al.* 1994; Skibo *et al.* 1997). Archaeological analysis has indicated that usewear evidence can correlate to surface treatment and fabric temper (Lambrick 1984), while the visual effects of vessel polish and contrasting colours may hold further information as yet untested on prehistoric material in Britain (cf. Miller 1985).

All of these studies contribute to understanding how, from a technological perspective, the selection of attributes influenced changes we see in prehistory (Schiffer and Skibo 1987). They provide the methods with which we can investigate assemblages and, in particular, what we choose to record and how to measure archaeological assemblages for the purpose of inter-assemblage comparisons. These approaches strongly influenced the creation of the advice manual for the analysis and publication of later prehistoric pottery by the *Prehistoric Ceramics Research Group* (1992, 1995, 1997). What this set of guidelines did not present, however, were the approaches for determining why changes might occur when there are no obvious technological reasons for them to be altered. For example, when tempers could be seen as equivalent in the sphere of engineering performance (cf. Morris 1991), why did one set replace another?

Such developments have been explored more recently from a social perspective which recognises that the users' expectations were having a strong influence on potting technologies, and that we can see these in the archaeological record once we start looking for them (Brown 1995; Morris 1994, 1997a; Raymond 1994). These approaches were inspired by ethnographic study of pottery production and use (Arnold 1985; Sterner 1989), as well as the recognition that pottery can be made easily in a variety of ways to respond to changes in social needs and practice (cf. Barrett 1991a). The realisation that successful local pottery production ceased during certain periods of the ceramic record and was replaced by long distance trade (Morris 1993), that amongst congruent regions one may be aceramic (cf. Royle and Woodward 1993, 74), and that both decorated and undecorated vessels were traded into regions already producing similar wares (Morris 1997a) are beyond simple technological explanations.

Dots and Details: Decoration for Use

It is amongst the variety of decoration, both techniques of application and designs, that the functional uses of pottery take on a whole new range of meaning. It is obvious that decoration is unrelated to direct subsistence activities. Instead the use of this visual effect applied to the surfaces of vessels, as well as the variety of possible vessel shapes and the selection of temper recipes discussed above, create a world of possible responses to the necessities of food preparation, eating, socialising and social order.

Thomas (1991a, 84–7) has reminded us that the reasons for decoration and the selection of specific decorations and traditions of manufacture are both infinite and specific. Decoration can be culturally specific for reasons of ethnic identification, used as a mechanism or expression of social stress, and may indicate locations to be respected or avoided. Decoration of pots has been used as an analogue for the decoration of the human body, or not used as such. The centralised manufacture of vessels along with the use of decoration suggestive of cosmological constructs can be seen to reflect the control of political power and the mediation between commoners and the cosmos by elites (Pauketat and Emerson 1991). While the decentralised production and distribution of pottery with visually distinct representational decoration may have had special meanings for families, clans and lineages rather than for demonstrating the power of elites (Gilman *et al.* 1994). The adoption of alien vessel types with decoration, and the incorporation of these into a group's material culture when pottery is not produced locally, is telling us about how pottery is used in society and how it can articulate and mediate social behaviour and culture change (Dietler 1990; Marshall and Maas 1997). Acculturation may occur when a dominant intrusive society merges with a conquered one, and pottery is a means for exploring and measuring the degree of this change. New foods and activities may be introduced and some adopted, while new vessel forms and styles of ceramics provide a mechanism for coping with these changes (Okun 1989).

Prehistoric archaeologists are necessarily still immersed in the characterisation of regional styles (Cleal 1992; Gibson 1995; MacSween 1995; Sheridan 1995). Yet once the usefulness of these classification schemes is resolved and adopted for description, and the dating clarified (Elsdon 1992; Kinnes *et al.* 1991; Thomas 1991a, 85–7; Gibson and Kinnes 1997), the function of decorated vessels, along with vessel size and distribution, can be explored (Brown, N 1995; Woodward 1995). The recognition that similarly decorated vessels have been found to be used in both domestic and funerary contexts, or that different but contemporary styles are used exclusively to one or the other (Healy 1995), still needs considerable research. The extraordinary variation in decorative techniques and styles between coarsewares and finewares in the later prehistoric period

Fig. 6.3. Things aren't always what they seem (drawn by Sophia Jundi).

cries out for interpretation. Why at some periods is decoration most commonly applied all over vessels, while during other periods it is focused on the upper half of vessels only? And equally important must be the study of why some vessels are decorated and others are not. The application of new methodologies, such as those derived from psychology (Tomalin 1995; Wallaert 1997), which have already been shown to be impressively effective in the examination of material culture transference and adoption, need to be explored.

'Wear-and-Tear': Actual Use

Great progress has been made during the past 15 years in the recognition of usewear evidence from ethnographic observations and the application of that knowledge to archaeological assemblages (Bronitsky and Hamer 1986; Hally 1983, 1986; Skibo 1992). The realisation that we can determine how at least some of the vessels we recover were actually used and the correlation of that usewear evidence to vessel forms and fabric recipes is a major step forward in prehistoric ceramic research (Fig. 6.3). However, all too few analysts detail this information in reports or articles, with notable exceptions (Lambrick 1984; Allen 1990, 39–42; Swain 1987, 64).

The presence of soot on the exterior surface and burnt residues on the interior surface of vessels are the most readily observed and universally expected forms of usewear evidence. In certain areas, additional markers such as limescale from the boiling of hard water and internal pitting-out of calcareous inclusions due to the presence of acidic contents can be common. Other forms of pitting and abrasion (surface attrition) on the interior can be found due to the scraping of vessel surfaces during stirring, grinding or cleaning, while exterior abrasion zones such as around the rim or base can indicate repeated food processing activities. In contrast to this 'wear-and-tear' is the absence of any evidence for use which, when coupled with vessel size, morphology, wall thickness and fabric, can suggest that a vessel was used for long-term or short-term storage. All of these indicators can only be identified if due care is taken in the recovery of pottery from archaeological deposits and during the cleaning and processing stages of analysis. This evidence is easily lost but provides the most cost effective way to interpret pottery assemblage function and use.

A new development in the study of function and use is the application of absorbed lipid residue analysis using gas chromotography and gas chromotography/mass spectrometry to ceramics (Charters *et al.* 1997; Dudd and Evershed 1999; Evershed *et al.* 1991, 1992; Heron *et al.* 1991a; Morris 1997b; Skibo 1992, 79–102). Lipids are organic solvent – soluble components of living organisms such as animal fats (cholesterols), plant leaf oils, and waxes. When porous ceramic material is used to cook and prepare foods, the chemicals in the food are absorbed into the walls of the vessels where they remain in a protected condition for centuries (Heron *et al.* 1991b). The application of resins to the walls of vessels for long-term storage of perishable foods also can be detected. The various chemical compounds of these foods or organic matter have diagnostic 'finger-prints' that have been characterised and can be identified. If a food type has a long chain of compounds, it is likely to be well-preserved in the potsherds, while short-chain compounds such as milk and milk products are suspected to degrade more rapidly. In addition, water-soluble liquids such as wine and beer or volatiles such as perfumes will not be resistent to post-deposition processes.

The application of this new technique to archaeological ceramics must be conducted within an holistic research strategy which examines specific vessel forms and capacities within an assemblage, between assemblages of similar period and site type, and amongst assemblages of different site types or different timespans. Results from such studies are likely to make major contributions to the integration of research into ceramics, agriculture, and paleo-diets, as well as influence our interpretations and understanding of cultural biases, ritual behaviour and lifestyles of prehistoric people.

Food, Families and Friends: Archaeological Examples

Before it is possible to tackle the desirable holistic approach to ceramics, subsistence and society (Plog 1980), much can be achieved by researching specific avenues of enquiry as presented above. This has already been achieved in many studies of prehistoric pottery, such as that by Blitz (1993) to investigate the nature of small-scale societies, food storage and feasting using ceramic, contextual and faunal data, and much more work needs to be focused in this manner.

Cleal (1991b), Parker Pearson (1995), Pierpoint (1980) and Woodward (1995; 1997) have presented several examples for England. In each of these cases, the approach of enquiry has been the same: what can vessel form, size and capacity tell us about society. Early Neolithic vessels appear to be consistently gradual in vessel capacity variation, as do Peterborough-style bowls. This contrasts with Late Neolithic and Early Bronze Age pottery that appears to have restricted sizes for some classes of pottery, especially when larger assemblages of pottery can be investigated. The interpretation of these differences reflecting different types of sites, ritual and domestic, needs to be tested. Variation in vessel sizes, particularly limited size ranges and/or bi-modal variation in assemblages can be shown to be regionally specific for the Early Bronze Age of both southern and northern England. During the Middle Bronze Age, the type of ware (fine, everyday and heavy duty coarsewares), variations within styles (Fig. 6.4) and the regional location appear to have influenced vessel size and frequency. This expansion of vessel size range and the introduction of new types of identifiable forms had previously been recognised as a hallmark of the Late Bronze Age (Barrett 1980; Woodward 1990) but could be the ceramic response to long-term social change beginning in the Bronze Age and continuing into the Iron Age (Barrett 1980; Barrett and Bradley 1980; Hill 1995a, 117–123).

Much more work needs to be conducted along this avenue of research and coupled with the identification of actual vessel use in order to investigate the regional responses to social requirements (Sharples 1991, 261–263). Are these responses influenced simply by social identity rather than environmental conditions, as has been indicated for intra-regional variation in agricultural practices in northern England (van der Veen 1992) or is it simply functional differences between sites? It has been demonstrated that within individual Iron Age pottery assemblages from the same region, there is considerable variation amongst the types of vessels present and their frequency as well as strong

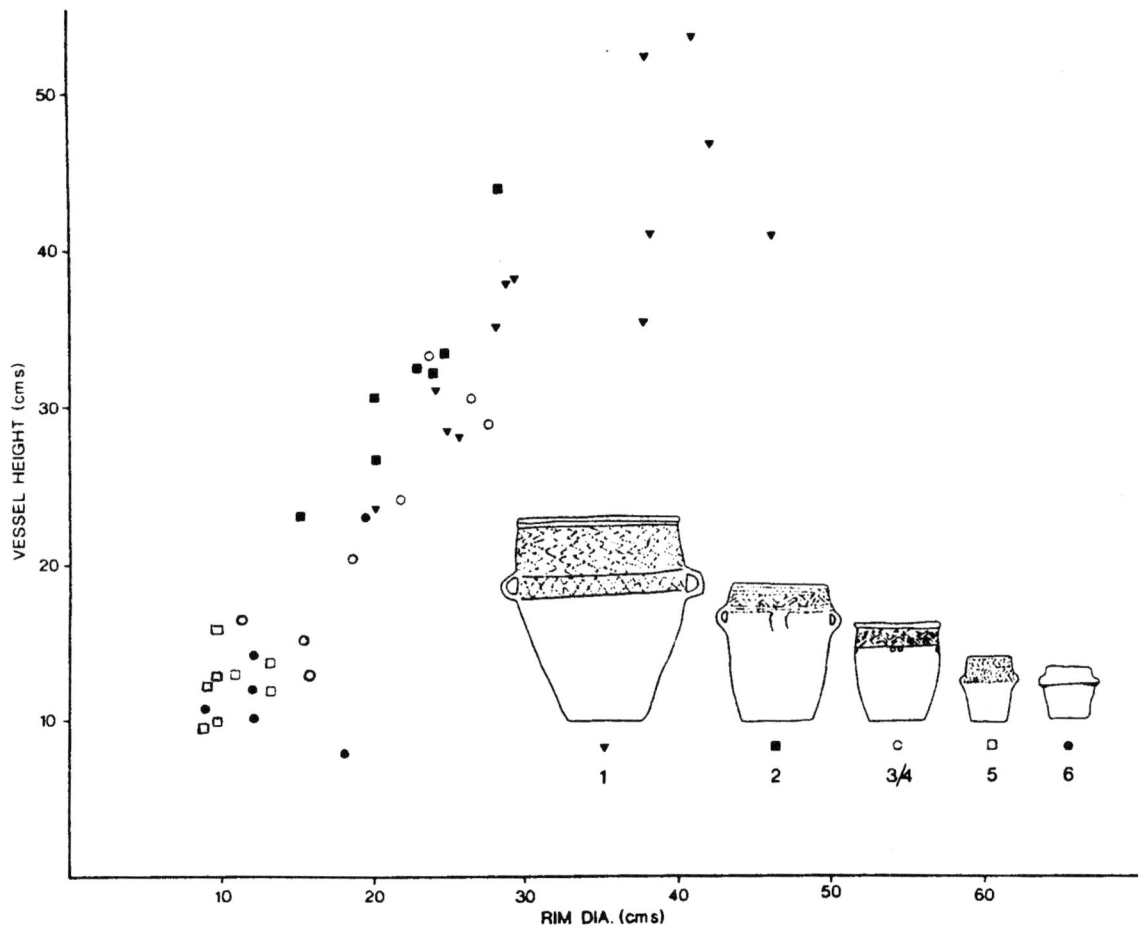

Fig. 6.4. A plot of the relationship between vessel height and rim diameter for Middle Bronze Age Trevisker-style pottery from southwestern England (from Parker Pearson 1995, fig. 9.1).

contrasts in variation of the size ranges within specific vessel types found on the same sites (Woodward 1997) (Fig. 6.5). Is this discovery particular to one part of the country only? Is it dependent upon the type of site? What size of assemblage is required for this form of analysis to be considered statistically sound? Comparison of data from similar-sized and similarly dated assemblages should be conducted between eastern and western England settlements such as the many sites in Northamptonshire and Hampshire, and also within more tightly defined regions such as the Upper Thames and east Gloucestershire.

Tackling the inter-relationships between ceramics and subsistence strategies are already being explored for the Neolithic. Work has begun on the absorbed lipid residue analysis of Peterborough and Grooved Wares from Welsh sites with excited results (Dudd and Evershed 1999). One simple study of Neolithic pottery residues has already been published (Needham and Evans 1987), and another which utilised the presence of marine food deposits

on Late Bronze Age pottery has questioned the lack or paucity of fish remains in faunal assemblages in later prehistory generally (Sergeantson *et al.* 1994).

If vessel sizes and capacities can be shown to vary regionally and intra-regionally by site type, this needs to be tested using residue analysis to assist in determining how the vessels were used. Comparison of Late Bronze Age pottery, for example from Cheshire, the Upper Thames valley and Essex would be an exciting prospect, as would the examination of residues from later Iron Age settlements found in eastern and southern England. A major project that selected a concentrated area containing Neolithic, Bronze Age and Iron Age sites with sizable assemblages could investigate four thousand years of agricultural, ceramic and social prehistory. In contrast, a project which compared the vessel types, capacities, decoration and actual use between sites with small, posthole roundhouses of Late Bronze Age date, large post-ring roundhouses of Early Iron Age date, and those of curvilinear gully construction from the Middle to Late Iron Age could indicate the

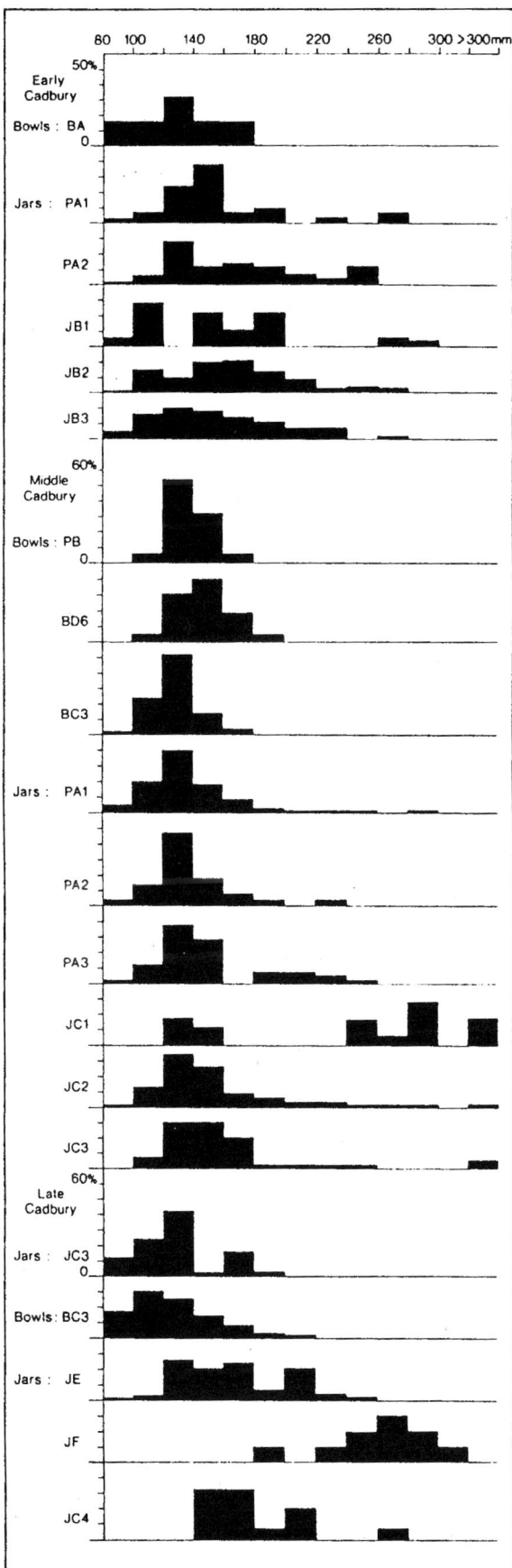

Fig. 6.6. Food and drink – pots, people and parties (drawn by Sophia Jundi).

changing pattern in food consumption and family life in later prehistory.

In addition to using pottery form and function to explore subsistence and social strategies, it is remarkable how few publications there are which manipulate vessel function and use-life, or breakage rates, to explore settlement longevity (Mills 1989), activity areas (Halstead *et al.* 1978), and discard practices (Hill 1995a, 129–131) (Fig 6.6). If these approaches are rigorously applied, a whole new perspective on chronology and pottery usage can be explored.

Ceramics Beyond Subsistence

Integration of approach has been the focus of this contribution, using a variety of questions and investigative methods to examine how food processing links to subsistence production and how social practices beyond subsistence can be elucidated through ceramic variation. A great deal has already been achieved in our investigations of prehistoric life through ceramic analysis but much more needs to be focused on comparative research, which explores the great wealth of data which is available in publications (cf. Woodward 1995) and boxed in museums. In relative terms we have examined the equivalent of a single sherd and still have the whole pot yet to explore.

Fig. 6.5. The frequency of rim diameters by vessel form type and period from the Iron Age hillfort at Cadbury Castle, Somerset (from Woodward 1997, fig. 4.1).

7 Sherds in Space:
Pottery and the Analysis of Site Organisation

Ann Woodward

"Where relatively complete, or reliably representative settlement assemblages are available, consideration should be given to how far ceramic and other artefacts reflect internal settlement organisation...." (PCRG: General Policies 1991, 5).

A Forgotten Initiative

One of the sites that has most influenced our conception of settlement space in British prehistory is Little Woodbury. Bersu's revolutionary excavation strategy of the late 1930s was decades ahead of its time, and led to the total investigation of a wide transect across an Iron Age enclosure. The structures defined served as a basis for a fundamental discussion of rural life and economy in the Iron Age (Bersu 1940) and subsequently Little Woodbury became the type site naming the earlier Iron Age culture province in southern England (Hodson 1964; also see Evans 1989a). Many archaeologists are familiar with the plan of the Little Woodbury house and occupation features, but how many are familiar with the pottery report (Brailsford 1948)? The approach encountered here is just as revolutionary as that enacted in the field, and includes a very early example of the application of the spatial analysis of pottery within a site.

The pottery was divided into four groups: fine heamatite ware, coarse ware, smooth dark ware and miscellaneous. The relative distribution of these ceramic groups was calculated for different context types: the house, different ditch segments and working hollow, and was indicated by shaded pie charts superimposed upon a site plan (Brailsford 1948, Pl.1). Furthermore, the pits were perceived to lie in distinct groups and the composition of the pottery assemblages from each group were represented in a series of similar pie charts (Brailsford 1948, fig 1, p4, reproduced here as Fig 7.1). The conclusions presented were mainly of a chronological nature but functional observations also were

made. For instance, 'From House I there is an outstandingly high proportion of heamatite ware. This ware as a class, of course, is of superior grade: one would expect such 'best' pottery, devoted to family use, to be kept (and then occasionally broken) in the house' (Brailsford 1948, 4–5). Such comments, and the use of pie-charts are reminiscent of many state-of-the-art spatial ceramic studies of the 1990s. Although many eminent prehistorians were privileged to work with Bersu, his general approaches and techniques were not accepted into archaeological practice in Britain for another thirty years, and Brailsford's novel approach to the inter-site spatial analysis of pottery was not matched until the early 1970s. During the intervening decades most pottery research concentrated on unravelling details of relative chronologies and the development and discussion of regional typologies. It was the development of the New Archaeology in the United States, linked to the greater availability of funds for large-scale rescue excavation of prehistoric settlement sites in Britain, that finally stimulated a renewed interest in the investigation of patterning of pottery distributions within structures and across sites.

A Brief History of Spatial Archaeology in British Prehistory

The most substantial and influential summary of the set of approaches grouped under the term New Archaeology produced in Britain was David Clarke's *Analytical Archaeology* of 1968. The analytical processes which were presented and developed in this

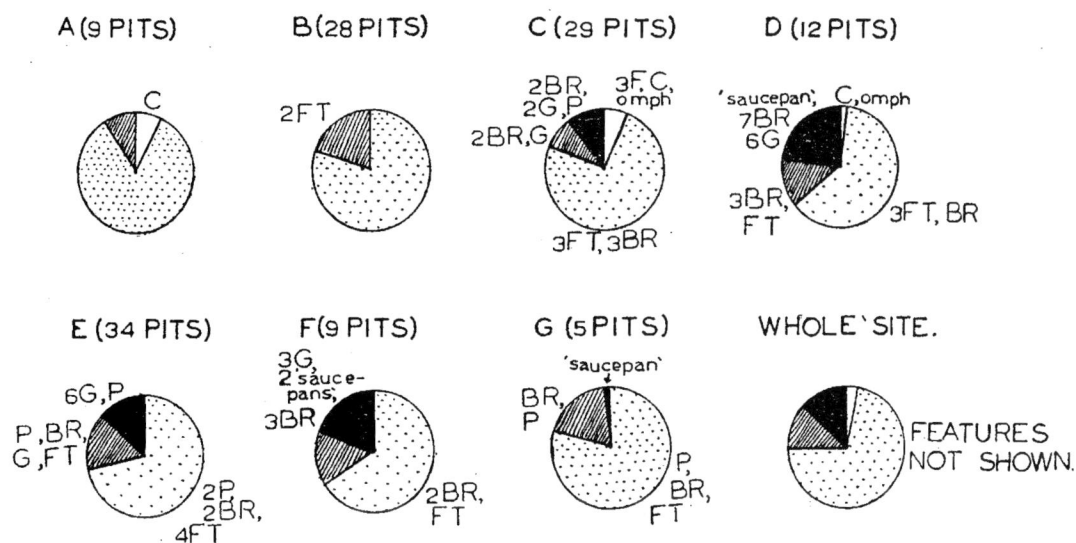

Fig. 7.1. Little Woodbury: spectra showing proportions of different wares from each group of pits. White segments indicate haematite ware; stippled, coarse ware; black, 'smooth dark ware', and hatched, miscellaneous. The letters refer to features. (Brailsford 1948, fig.1).

strikingly innovative volume included one termed 'Spatial Trends', discussed in the section on 'Methods of Analysis'. This discussion focused mainly on the analysis of large-scale settlement patterns derived from the work of scholars who had been following new avenues in the study of geography eg. Chorley and Haggett; and geology eg. Krumbein and Graybill, during the 1960s, and comprised only 4% of the book. However, in the chapter on computer methods, readers were introduced to some novel American research concerning the spatial analysis of pottery within a settlement and adjacent cemetery site (Clarke 1968, 601–5). The site was the Carter Ranch Pueblo in Eastern Arizona, occupied cAD 1100–1250 and Clarke described the various studies conducted by Freeman, Brown and Longacre which had involved the analysis of vessel types and of decorative motifs represented in different locations across the site. The questions posed were three-fold: 1) were there any clusters of pottery types exhibiting 'behaviour' on floors? 2) were there any associations between pottery types within the settlement? 3) were there spatial differences in the distribution of pottery types across the settlement? Thus the three main areas of spatial pottery analysis within settlements were established: intra-structure patterning, the definition of structure function, and the definition of activity areas across a settlement (intra-settlement patterning). The results of the computer analyses at Carter Ranch indicated the existence of four distinct groups of vessel forms which could be tied to four structurally different room types. Furthermore, the distribution of a

sample of decorative motifs and of the different ceramic activity zones indicated the probable existence of two social groups within the settlement, probably two localised lineages or lineage segments.

By the time *Analytical Archaeology* was published in 1968, David Clarke was well advanced in his programme of detailed research into the potential patterning of occupation debris from the Glastonbury lake village. The results of this work, which will be discussed in the next section, had a far-reaching effect. The Glastonbury research, influenced directly by that of American scholars such as Freeman and Longacre, seems to have stood alone in the development of spatial archaeology in Britain for a period of at least five years. For instance, Hodder and Orton's synthesis *Spatial Analysis in Archaeology*, published in 1976, concentrated entirely on methods designed for analysis at the regional scale. The next major step in the elaboration of settlement analysis is illustrated in *Spatial Archaeology* (Clarke 1977), where David Clarke introduced the term 'Semi-Micro Level' for within-site analyses and 'Micro' for spatial studies at the level of the individual structure. The contemporary processual stance was clearly reflected in his definition of spatial archaeology as:

'the retrieval of information from archaeological spatial relationships and the study of the spatial consequences of former hominid activity patterns within and between features and structures and their articulation within sites, site systems and their environments'

(Clarke 1977, 9)

Although Clarke devoted less than a page of text to the discussion of the Micro and Semi-Micro levels of analysis, he did point out the overriding relevance of social and architectural models rather than economic ones, and Fletcher's (1977) contribution illustrated the analysis of such topics as kinship patterns in relation to residence units, the occurrence of preferred spacing and modal measurements, door widths, and room dimensions.

The subsequent development of spatial archaeology in Britain can be divided into two main phases. Firstly, and building on the basis of the functionalist agenda outlined above, there was a flurry of studies which attempted to define activity areas and zones within structures and settlements. Many of these were inspired directly by David Clarke's work on Glastonbury. Such work continued until the mid-1980s when a significant theoretical realignment became evident. This involved the important concept of structured deposition which itself was connected intimately with the more general development of structuralism and other post-processual approaches. Interestingly, these major changes coincided with major differences in the chronological periods of the sites subjected to analysis. These changes are illustrated in Fig. 7.2. Following Clarke's analysis of the Iron Age settlement at Glastonbury (published in 1972) there was a cluster of studies using data from sites of Middle Bronze Age, Late Bronze Age and, to a lesser extent, Iron Age date. The development of studies investigating structured deposition began in 1984 and initially concerned Neolithic and Early Bronze Age sites only. By the late 1980s this approach had spread to Iron Age studies and analyses of Iron Age sites (and re-analysis of earlier functionalist Iron Age studies) dominate the graphs for the 1990s. One final point of general interest is that a great deal of the research carried out in Britain has utilised the finds and archives from sites excavated previously and by other archaeologists. In only 31% of the cases consulted in the preparation of this essay were the spatial analyses undertaken by the excavator of the site concerned. This lies in direct contrast to parallel work in the United States where developments in spatial analysis have occurred mainly within on-going multidisciplinary field projects.

The Glastonbury Model

The site of the Glastonbury lake village, totally excavated by Bulleid and Gray between 1892 and 1907 produced a massive array of archival and artefactual data, selections of which were published in two substantial and detailed volumes (Bulleid and Gray 1911 and 1917). The assemblage is one of the

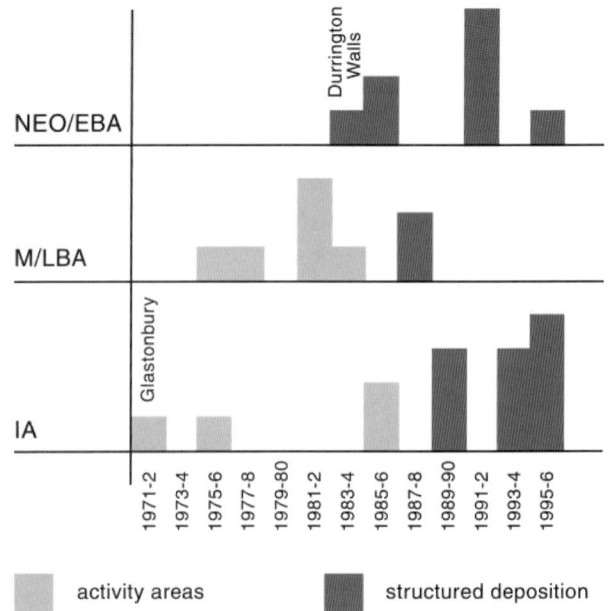

Fig. 7.2. Major prehistoric pottery reports which include spatial analysis, arranged by year of publication.

most varied ever recovered by excavation in Britain and many of the finds were recorded according to context. David Clarke's 'Provisional Model of an Iron Age Society and its Settlement System' (Clarke 1972, 801–869) outlined the preliminary results of a programme of research designed to analyse the spatial aspects of the Glastonbury site at the structure, intra-settlement, territorial and regional levels. It was intended that the data would be investigated further and tested by computer methods, although it appears that this stage had not been reached before Clarke's untimely death. Four groups of analyses were attempted; studies of vertical spatial relationships, horizontal spatial relationships, structural relationships and artefact relationships. The first and third were designed to facilitate a phasing of the site whilst the last three were employed to investigate the distribution of different types of structure and activity areas. In addition, by utilising descriptions of the Celtic social system embodied in the classical texts and the Irish vernacular tradition, he attempted to define some of the kinship patterns and other social customs which may have pertained at Iron Age Glastonbury. The main thrust of the argument rested upon the definition of a modular settlement unit - 'the social and architectural building block of which the settlement is a multiple' (Clarke, fig. 21.1 caption and here Fig. 7.3). The various analyses led to the isolation of a distinct range of structures which clustered into repetitive groups across the site. Each modular unit contained some or all of the structure categories: major and minor houses; huts used as

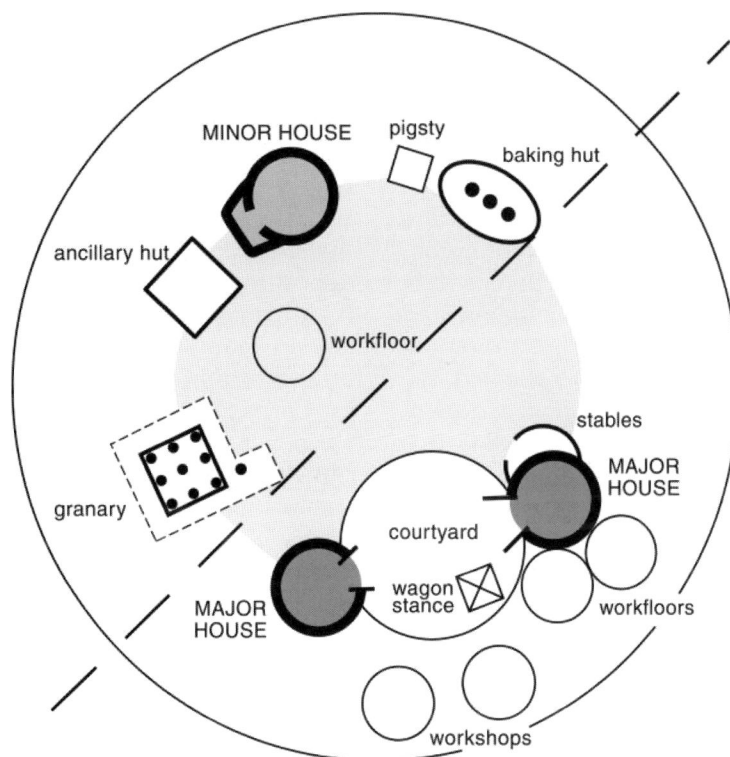

Fig. 7.3. The Glastonbury settlement module (after Clarke 1972, fig. 21.1).

workshops, bakeries, guard rooms, annexes or for other ancillary purposes; courtyards, workfloors and clay patches; storehouses, stables, sties or kennels; and wagon stances. 'The basic division between the pair of major houses (IA) and their satellites, and the minor house (IB) and its ancillaries, may be tentatively identified with a division between a major familial, multi-role and activity area on the one hand and a minor largely female and domestic area' (Clarke 1972, Fig. 21.1 caption). Structural categories were defined in terms of size, shape, method of construction and the array of artefacts found within and outside them. As far as pottery is concerned this included, for example, 'the highest ratio of decorated fine wares to undecorated pottery' (Clarke 1972, 816) in the major house pairs and, for the minor houses 'a comparative abundance of pottery.....but the proportion of undecorated domestic ware is greater than in the major houses' (Clarke 1972, 817).

Even at the time of publication of the Glastonbury paper, those working on sites within the Somerset Levels, and with a detailed knowledge of archaeological deposits similar to those encountered by Bulleid at Glastonbury, were sceptical of Clarke's results, and considered critiques of the approach were published in due course (Coles and Coles 1986; Barrett 1987; Coles and Minnitt 1995). Detailed reappraisals of the excavation records and finds,

both published and unpublished, by Coles and Minnitt have demonstrated that Clarke had underestimated the complexity of deposition on the site, the implications of the available environmental data, the nature of the floors and clay spreads, the severe stratigraphical problems presented and of the undoubted movement of artefacts during the postdeposition periods. Coles and Minnitt (1995) present a reassessment of the data relating to each of Clarke's structure categories and a new phasing which is based on an exhaustive reworking of all the available data. The new phasing is quite different and there can be no doubt that Clarke's conclusions were almost entirely erroneous. However, as Coles points out 'our criticism of Clarke's stimulating and provocative paper should not be taken as outright dismissal of his ideas. It was right, in 1972, to propose new approaches to old evidence .... Clarke's model approach was in itself the achievement; that the evidence did not , could not, fit the model should not matter if it was taken only as a demonstration of the possibilities' (Coles and Minnitt 1995, 181–2). In fact, the achievement was so great that it spawned a school of spatial studies in British prehistory which has spanned two and a half decades, and has influenced research developments across Europe and beyond. The results were wrong, but the idea was devastatingly important.

The Definition of Activity Zones: 1972–1984

Directly stimulated by the Glastonbury model, and using mainly the very clearly defined structural data from Middle Bronze Age settlement sites in southern England, four themes of spatial analysis were developed. These related to the definition of modular units, the patterning of features and finds within structures, the elucidation of kinship systems, and the general distribution of activity areas across entire sites. All the conclusions reached reflected the theoretical framework of their day, and were dominated by economic concerns and functionalism.

The idea of the existence of a simple settlement module comprising two huts, one large and one small and with differing functions, was developed rapidly. Bradley described such a hut pair at Rams Hill (Bradley and Ellison 1975, 212): it included a larger hut containing two cooking holes and most of the domestic rubbish, and a smaller structure which displayed no internal features except for four postholes which may have supported the framework around a hearth. Other Bronze Age timber hut pairs from Chalton, Thorny Down and Trevisker and pairs in stone from Dean Moor, Stannon Down and Zennor were cited as comparanda. Meanwhile, a detailed analysis of the archive and finds relating to the Middle Bronze Age settlement on Itford Hill led to the definition of four probably successive settlement units each consisting of two to four structures (Ellison 1978). Other Bronze Age sites containing similar modules included Cock Hill, Plumpton Plain, New Barn Down, Shearplace Hill and Weston Wood. Detailed plotting of all finds categories from the various structures allowed the definition of major residential houses, defined ceramically by high concentrations of potsherds including a relatively high proportion of fine wares probably used for eating and drinking; ancillary structures with evidence of food storage and preparation, and smaller assemblages of pottery including a higher proportion of coarse wares; animal shelters and weaving huts (Ellison 1981a, 419–20). Using the finds from the extensive excavation of house platforms on Black Patch, a more detailed spatial analysis, using sherd thickness as a definitive parameter, was developed (Ellison in Drewett 1982a, fig. 33). In addition, analysis of all the finds categories from the largest hut had enabled Drewett to plot the likely location of everyday activities within the confines of a single structure (Drewett 1979, fig. 4).

The data from Black Patch was used also to reconstruct the social organisation of the compound, thus developing another of the themes initially introduced by Clarke. The Black Patch compound was deemed to have housed an extended family: a headman's house with an associated animal hut, a hut for the headman's wife in a separate enclosure, and a further pair of huts used by the headman's parents or a sibling (ibid fig.1). Russell (1996) has suggested that, as at Itford Hill, the Black Patch huts may represent modules of more than one phase, so the way is now open for a new analysis in this instance. However, a detailed consideration of deposition factors, as highlighted by Barrett and Needham (1988), would need to be incorporated. A second example of the definition of kinship attributions within a Bronze Age settlement is provided by Gerrish's study of pottery fabrics amongst the various hut platforms excavated at Mam Tor. Each hut seemed to be characterised by a particular combination of fabric types, all of them local, and it was suggested that these differences were due to familial preferences (Gerrish 1983, but also Guilbert and Vince 1996).

On Iron Age sites, a greater variety of context types are found, and it proved possible to investigate the spatial patterning of finds categories, including pottery, across ditches, structures, yard areas and pits. At Wenden's Ambo animal bone debris from prime joints was associated with fine ware ceramics which could have been used at table, whilst the waste bones were found with coarse wares more appropriate to the preparation of food. Pit fillings contained one grouping or the other, but no specific spatial concentrations could be isolated (Halstead, Hodder and Jones 1978). Computerised analysis to test the presence of similar patterning in an Iron Age hillfort environment was however unsuccessful (Fisher 1985). At Winklebury coarse and fine wares did not correlate with different categories of bone waste. However, cluster analysis did demonstrate that the largest and most complex hut produced large sherds in high densities, that fine wares were strongly associated with this and one other hut, and that four different coarse ware types were strongly associated with different huts. There seemed to be two or three major huts and a series of others of varying function. One of the most influential functional analyses of an Iron Age settlement was that presented by Fasham (1985) for Winnall Down. For the Early Iron Age phase, a study of the distribution of metal items, querns, loomweights, worked bone and pottery led to the definition of four specialised activity areas related to weaving, bone-working and crop-processing. Coarse and fine ware ceramics appeared to be fairly evenly distributed except for a concentration of fine cordoned and furrowed bowls in one of the round houses. However, by 1985, a second major development in spatial settlement archaeology was taking place. Such was the size and quality of the Winnall Down archive that it has allowed further analyses to be undertaken which incorporate the new approach. These further analyses will be discussed in a later section; meanwhile the origins of the concept of spatial structured deposition must be explored.

Structured Deposition in the Neolithic and Bronze Age Periods: from 1984

The analysis of the spatial patterning of artefacts within the excavated areas of the great late Neolithic henge enclosure of Durrington Walls (Richards and Thomas 1984) provided a landmark in the development of British prehistory. It combined new techniques of motif analysis on pottery, the developing ideas of contextual archaeology which combined the studies of different artefact categories from varying types of feature, on-site spatial analysis, and new styles of interpretation which attempted to explain patterning in terms of deliberate structured deposition of artefacts and other materials in ritual contexts. The whole analysis depended on the detailed total excavation of two-thirds of the Southern Circle at Durrington Walls, and the meticulous record and publication generated by Wainwright and Longworth (1971).

The new classification of Grooved Ware decoration involved an assessment of design structure, not just the definition of motifs or symbols. Following Hodder's work on Dutch Neolithic pottery (Hodder 1982c), it was explained that the key underlying concepts were the oppositions between decorated and undecorated zones and between bounded or unbounded areas of decoration. Using a new six-stage classification of decoration based on these precepts the decoration on pottery from each context was analysed. The distribution of pottery displaying different decorative stages was shown to be statistically significant, with, for instance, Stages 1 and 3 dominant in the Northern Circle, 1 and 4 in the Southern Circle and Stage 6 – the most complex – on the platform adjacent to the Southern Circle (Richards and Thomas 1984, fig. 12.3). Similar distinctions could also be demonstrated for other categories of artefact such as flint types, bone implements and the faunal remains. At a more detailed level, it could be shown that the density of Grooved Ware varied within the Southern Circle, with the slight concentrations being spatially complementary to the concentrations of flint flakes (Richards and Thomas 1984, figs 12.5–6). It was also observed that the proportion of Grooved Ware displayed a marked fall-off as one moved from the outer post ring towards the centre of the circle. It was concluded that the general patterns which had been discerned: the spatial opposition between flint and pottery, the mutually exclusive deposition of

artefact such as bone pins, bone awls, flint arrowheads and knives (but not scrapers), and the general fall-off in density of material towards the centre of the monument all indicated a clear pattern of spatial arrangement. This arrangement could better be explained in terms of formal deposition than by invoking the former existence of utilitarian activity areas.

One key area of study concerned the development of concepts central to the structuralism school of social anthropology. These included the definitions of deeply embedded structural oppositions such as inside/outside, front/back, east/west and left/right. The concept of enclosure banks and ditches acting as liminal markers, and the ideological symbolism of entrance zones, also became emphasised. Thus, within the Neolithic causeway enclosure at Etton, Pryor was drawing attention to the occurrence of large sherds displaying ancient breaks which could be conjoined. These were interpreted as forming parts of deliberately placed deposits of material and it was shown that such deposits were particularly common in ditch terminals (Pryor *et al.* 1985, fig. 11, left). At the totally excavated small henge monument on Wyke Down, the secondary deposits within the ditch contained Grooved Ware pottery which, as at Durrington Walls, was unevenly distributed. Some sherds were concentrated at the 'back' of the monument but most occurred in the postholes located in the entrance terminals (Barrett *et al.* 1991, fig. 3.22). It was also noted that the more complex decoration occurred on sherds found near to the entrance, and Cleal drew attention to the parallel distribution of vessels bearing internal decoration and complex circular motifs from features on either side of the entrance into the Southern Circle at Durrington Walls (*ibid* fig. 3.26), and also at Woodhenge. The Thickthorn Down long barrow contained no burials, but it has been suggested that human bones may have been replaced symbolically by a series of intentional deposits in the ditches. These deposits included pottery of earlier Neolithic, late Neolithic and Beaker date, in all cases concentrated in the ditch terminals. This pattern formed part of a more general phenomenon, cumulative patterns of '… segregation within association. Certain materials occur together repeatedly but are kept separated from each other within long barrow ditches. In brief, these deposits are commonly concentrated at the butt-end of ditches, and the patterns of 'segregated correspondence' emerge from items either being placed in ditches on opposite sides of the barrow or at opposite ends of the same ditch. One of the most significant of these patterns is that the bones of domestic animals are rarely found in direct association with red deer antler. Potsherds and antler, similarly, seem to be kept apart.' (Thomas 1991a, 68–9 and fig. 4.5).

The theme of deliberate deposition within a Neolithic tomb can be illustrated best by reference to the work of Thomas and Whittle (1986) in the reinterpretation of the results of the excavations of Thurnam and Piggott at the West Kennet long barrow. Piggott (1962) had interpreted the ubiquitous distribution of Peterborough and Beaker sherds as indicating that filling of the stone chambers took place as a single act. However, a modern and detailed reanalysis of the ceramics by Thomas suggested a more gradual process of infilling with a three-fold phasing apparent in each chamber. It was also noticed that some sherds appeared to have been deliberately placed, that sherd quantities varied considerably and that there was a patterned distribution of ceramic styles and decorative motifs. Thus, looking at the Peterborough Ware, the west chamber showed greatest diversity, the north east chamber contained more sherds with fingernail decoration and no curvilinear motifs, the pottery from the north west chamber was characterised by herringbone patterns, jabs, incisions and incised lines, and in the south east chamber sherds with jabs or incisions were most common. It was suggested that these varying assemblages might have reflected the existence of sex or lineage groupings, or at least different groups of potters, using the individual chambers, whilst the variation in condition of the sherds further suggested that there had been deliberate additions of pottery to gradual deposits of secondary blocking. Such activities may have served to aid ritual communication with the distant ancestors. Overall, four sorts of ceramic deposit could be defined: deliberate pot smashing and the spreading of debris amongst the chambers; the deliberate placing of groups of sherds, for instance in corners or behind wallstones; the deliberate additions of relatively clean fresh chalk rubble, containing very little pottery and, finally, the inclusion of dirty black layers with sherds already contained in the deposit i.e. from an occupation area or culthouse.

Some recent commentators have displayed some misgivings concerning these detailed and exciting conclusions. Barrett has criticised Thomas and Whittle's analysis of the earlier Neolithic human remains, emphasising that the actual form the spatial categorisation of the dead may have taken (left:right, back:front etc.) may have been regularly reworked, but he also suggests that it seems unlikely that we should ever understand the processes of infilling in any detail (Barrett 1994, 60). A slightly more positive stance is taken by Case (1995b) who is unhappy with the sequences outlined by Thomas and Whittle. Case avers that burial continued until c.2000 BC when the capstones were pulled aside, and the chambers were filled with material selected from two middens. Case links this act to significant intakes of land and the

presumed destruction of some former settlements during the Beaker period, but many other hypotheses could be advanced. Even if the deposits in the chambers do derive entirely from middens they most certainly reflect a considered selection of material from those heaps. Thus we my be dealing with a two-fold process of structured deposition: the careful spatial segregation of materials within a midden, whether it be domestic or ritual in nature, and the subsequent reworking or reinforcement of these spatial references during their deliberate placement within the tomb. When the results of current analyses of suspected midden material from the ditches of enclosures such as Windmill Hill and Hambledon Hill become available, new avenues of enquiry may unfold.

Meanwhile it is interesting to explore some recent analyses of henge monuments where the study of spatial patterning amongst artefacts has been related to the possible former patterns of bodily movement around and within the monument itself. At The Sanctuary, Pollard (1992) has argued that Piggott's original four phases may be reduced to two, one in timber and one in stone, although it could further be argued that the stone and timber settings were themselves contemporary. Finds were plentiful, although the sherds were small and weathered, possibly the remnants of a substantial surface accumulation. These may have resulted from activities such as feasting, rites of passage or celebrations of seasonal observance. Deposition occurred especially in the north and east sectors and in relation to specific post rings, with the central area and entrance being kept clear. This pattern indicated more than a simple backspace/frontspace division and the eastern focus can be matched at Woodhenge. It appears that movements between the rings of posts and stones and the central zone may have been controlled in a specific manner.

At Woodhenge, Grooved Ware sherds were concentrated in the ditch terminals, thus replicating the pattern already established for sites such as Wyke Down, but there was a subsidiary concentration on the eastern side (Pollard 1995). In the interior, pottery was concentrated in the postholes of particular post rings (especially ring C) and near the location of the two stone holes at the 'back' of the monument. A distinct eastern bias was also discernible. These distributions have been contrasted with those of other artefact categories to build up a model of probable movement within the monument (Fig. 7.4). The faunal remains pattern in various ways and, whilst worked bone items were restricted to the ditch, carved chalk was limited exclusively to the interior. The entrance was emphasised by deposition of elaborate artefacts in the ditch terminals and by the placing of a human skull and deposit of cremated

WOODHENGE

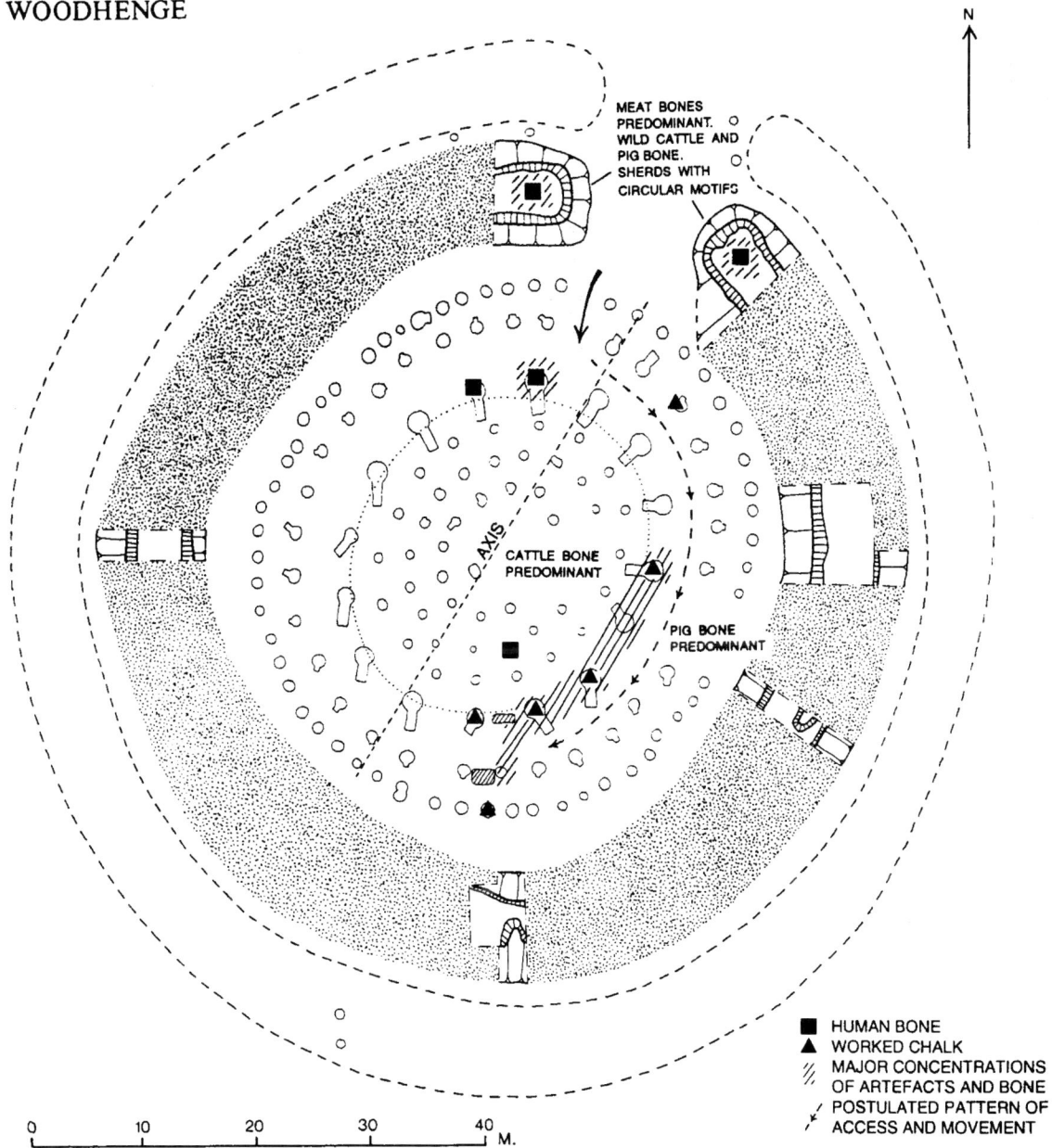

MEAT BONES
PREDOMINANT.
WILD CATTLE AND
PIG BONE.
SHERDS WITH
CIRCULAR MOTIFS

CATTLE BONE
PREDOMINANT

PIG BONE
PREDOMINANT

■ HUMAN BONE
▲ WORKED CHALK
⧄ MAJOR CONCENTRATIONS
OF ARTEFACTS AND BONE
⟋ POSTULATED PATTERN OF
⟋ ACCESS AND MOVEMENT

Fig. 7.4. Woodhenge: spatial organisation of deposition (Pollard 1995, fig. 12).

bone near to it in ring C. The massive ring C posts were ascribed importance by the placing of pottery, lithics, animal bone, carved chalk and human bone around their bases. Within the area enclosed by ring C pig bone was almost excluded. Many categories were deposited mainly on the east and it seems that people were allowed to enter the monument, turn left at a point just before the major post ring, and advance as far as the stone settings, but not beyond. A similar process of clockwise procession between the post rings was adduced for the Southern Circle of Durrington Walls by Thomas (1991a, fig. 3.7).

Structured Deposition in the Later Bronze Age and Iron Age Periods: from 1987

By the late 1980s a subtle change in the interpretation of later Bronze Age and Iron Age settlement spaces was becoming apparent. The attribution of age, gender or kinship groups was more cautious, and more effort was concentrated on defining scales of patterning than on overarching social interpretation. Thus at the Middle Bronze Age settlement of Thorny Down a sequence of settlement modules were adduced 'but no direct evidence of division of labour by sex is apparent', and details such as the concentration of artefacts in and around doorways, or specific deposits in the back of individual huts were described (Ellison 1987, 289–391). Such observations were not dissimilar to those that were being made in relation to long barrow ditches and henge ditch terminals, and very soon the exciting issue of symbolic and structured deposition within Iron Age settlements began to emerge.

Much of this new approach was introduced and summarised in a masterly paper by Parker Pearson (1996). This paper, although not published at the time, was in wide circulation from 1990 onwards and influenced much of the research undertaken in the early 1990s. Influenced directly by anthropological writing rather than by the analyses of Neolithic and Early Bronze Age sites summarised above, the essay discussed the symbolic ordering of household space. Many studies from around the world demonstrate that the symbolic referents of human activities are embedded in architecture and settlement layout. Parker Pearson argued that it should be possible, by interrogating settlement records in an appropriate manner, to recover 'those symbolic principles which constituted the cosmologies of past societies' (Parker Pearson 1996, 119). The anthropological studies repeatedly revealed principles governed by basic binary oppositions such as:

MEN	WOMEN
front	back
right	left
east	west
outside	inside
light	dark
high	low
north	south
cold	hot
red	black
MEN	WOMEN

In relation to the round house, type fossil of the British Iron Age , Parker Pearson's argument ran as follows: 'Perhaps, as in so many other places, the house acted as a microcosm of the universe, with the passing of time measured around the walls of the house. The entrance to the east might be related to the sunrise and the daily rebirth of the cycle of light and darkness which revolved around the house' (Parker Pearson 1996, 119). He also noted that the porch and doorway seemed more important architecturally than the hearth and that many huts were organised around an east-west axis which divided the enclosed space into north and south areas. The same principle applies to entire settlements, as at Aldermaston Wharf where two Late Bronze Age housed occupied north and south zones, with fine ware occurring only in the northern house (Bradley et al. 1980). The ideological importance of middens

was noted, and a tendency for them to be located near front doors and to be associated symbolically with the concept of fertility (Parker Pearson 1996, 126). He also drew attention to the importance of symbolic reversals. For instance, houses with western doorways which thus face 'the wrong way' may be seen to be associated with the inauspicious: profanity, darkness and death. Such huts usually occur as singletons on Iron Age settlement sites and, where evidence is available, are associated with coarse wares only.

The elaboration of ceramic form types in the Late Bronze Age, and in particular the development of fine ware jars and cups associated with the consumption of food and drink (Barrett 1980), has allowed the development of spatial studies on several Late Bronze Age sites excavated mainly in the Thames Basin. As an example we may consider the analysis by Parker Pearson (1996, 121 and fig. 9.1) of the results of excavation at the Mucking North Ring (Bond 1988). The large circular enclosure was entered from the east to face a monumental timber screen running north-south. This served to hide from view three houses. Disposition of fine and coarse pottery indicates that the northern one was associated with food preparation while the southern house was used for eating. Each of these houses also contained a north-south screen and appeared to replicate the form of the enclosure on a smaller scale. No metalworking debris was found in the enclosure's interior but much was found outside and in the ditch, in layers deposited from the outside. 'The North Ring exhibits a number of oppositions: metalworking outside but not inside; the clean front of the enclosure and the hidden occupation zone ('dirty') at the back; cooking debris to the north and serving debris to the south' (Parker Pearson 1996, 121). The Mucking North Ring and other similar sites such as Springfield Lyons appear to have held strong religious or ceremonial connotations and indeed have been compared to henges of the late Neolithic by Collis (1977b). Feasting was important and the spatial segregation of everyday food preparation and food consumption was highly developed. This may have been associated with strong social segregation according to gender, wealth through the procuration of metal, and the existence of strong age sets or powerful kinship groupings.

Thus the clue to many new interpretations of symbolic patterning in the Late Bronze Age and Iron Age is the detailed spatial analysis of pottery. This applies equally in the Midlands and in Wessex as well as in the metal-rich zones of the lower Thames Basin. At Mingies Ditch (Allen and Robinson 1993, figs 42 and 43) and Wasperton (Woodward and Candy forthcoming), phasing is complex and artefactual debris relatively sparse. However, consistent patterns such as the concentration of potsherds in entrance areas of both enclosures and houses are apparent. Deposits were often made in right-hand (southern) terminals of house gullies and pit fillings in near-doorway locations may reflect the former presence of middens.

The cosmological house model conceived by Parker Pearson has been well illustrated at Dunston Park (Fitzpatrick 1994). Within a large Early Iron Age round house there was a concentration of material near the south east-facing doorway and its porch, and especially on the right-hand side as one would have left the building. The finds distributions indicated a clean living area on the left side and a storage area with pits and furniture on the right. Daytime activities may have taken place in the right half of the house, with the left half reserved for sleeping. Thus the use of the built space varied through the hours of daylight, with activities following the sunlight around the house, just as the sun moved across the firmament above (Fig. 7.5). A similar large round house excavated at Longbridge Deverill Cow Down also displayed an uneven distribution of pottery, with concentrations in the porch area and the right half of the hut (Hawkes 1994). Furthermore a pair of large post pits may have supported the superstructure of a substantial and imposing wooden dresser. Upon this the prime material possessions of the family of group could have been displayed. In this case the house had been destroyed by fire, possibly deliberately at the time of abandonment, and the remains of the ceramic assemblage which may have stood on the dresser were preserved in situ. The assemblage includes mainly small bowls and cups – not decorated, but embellished with bright scarlet haematite coating – an Iron Age version of the family silver.

The programme of research into the depositional practises of Iron Age Wessex carried out by Hill has encompassed a thorough analysis of all finds categories from different context types such as enclosure ditches, pits, gullies and structural features. Culminating in a volume entitled *Ritual and Rubbish in the Iron Age of Wessex* (Hill 1995a), Hill has demonstrated that most of the deposits of Iron Age material, much of it pottery, which have been interpreted previously as rubbish dumped and scattered in a random fashion, are in fact the result of deliberate acts. These acts involved ritual behaviour carried out on a daily basis within domestic environments which comprised a network of symbolic spaces. Thus the ideas promoted by Parker Pearson have been extended to a much wider range of archaeological contexts and the detailed analyses of large sets of artefactual data have allowed statistical testing to take place. The nature of the approach can be considered with reference to the results of Hill's re-analysis of the Early Iron Age enclosure on Winnall Down.

As described in an earlier section, the finds distributions within the enclosure were analysed by the excavator (Fasham 1985), and four activity areas associated with a single settlement unit were defined. Subsequently Parker Pearson (1996) suggested that there were two household units represented, arranged north and south of an east-west axis. In-depth study of the finds from all contexts, including consideration of sherd size and abrasion, has provided a much more detailed hypothesis to be built up. The deposits in the filling of the enclosure ditch appear to have been placed along its course, as part of prescribed acts which served to confirm the identity of the inhabitants in relation to outsiders (Hill 1995a, 79 ff). The deposits were related to various structural principles such as distinctions between inside-outside, front-back and an emphasis on the threshold at the west of the enclosure. Certain categories of animal debris, especially the bones of birds and dogs, were confined to areas outside the enclosure. Debris was concentrated in the entrance terminals, where fine wares were very well represented. Pottery was more common in the north terminal as opposed to animal bone and other small finds in the southern terminal. The front of the enclosure in general was characterised by greater proportions of animal bone, fine ceramics, small finds and fragments of adult human bones, whilst the slighter ditch at the back of the enclosure contained more coarse pottery and complete human infant burials.

Within the enclosures the pits can be divided into four spatial groups (not the same as Fasham's four activity areas), which can be linked to imply that the enclosure was divided unequally into north and south sectors along a line from the west entrance to the back corner (Fig. 7.6). Group 1 pits associated with the porched houses in the north contained most of the well-preserved animal bone deposits and two 'hoards' of loomweights. Fine wares were not concentrated near the most elaborate huts but in a central zone of pits, Group 3, along with other key items such as a saddle quern. The other major concentration of fine ware was within the ditch terminals. Pit groups 2 and 4, located alongside buildings in the south and east zones of the enclosures both produced low finds densities, but significant quantities of minority pottery fabrics – sandy and organic types in Group 2, and shell, coarse flint and flint/organic types in Group 4. The Group 4 deposits also echoed the 'back ditch' deposits in the occurrence of low bone densities and an infant burial. As Hill explains: 'The architectural and semi-permanent fixtures provided the setting

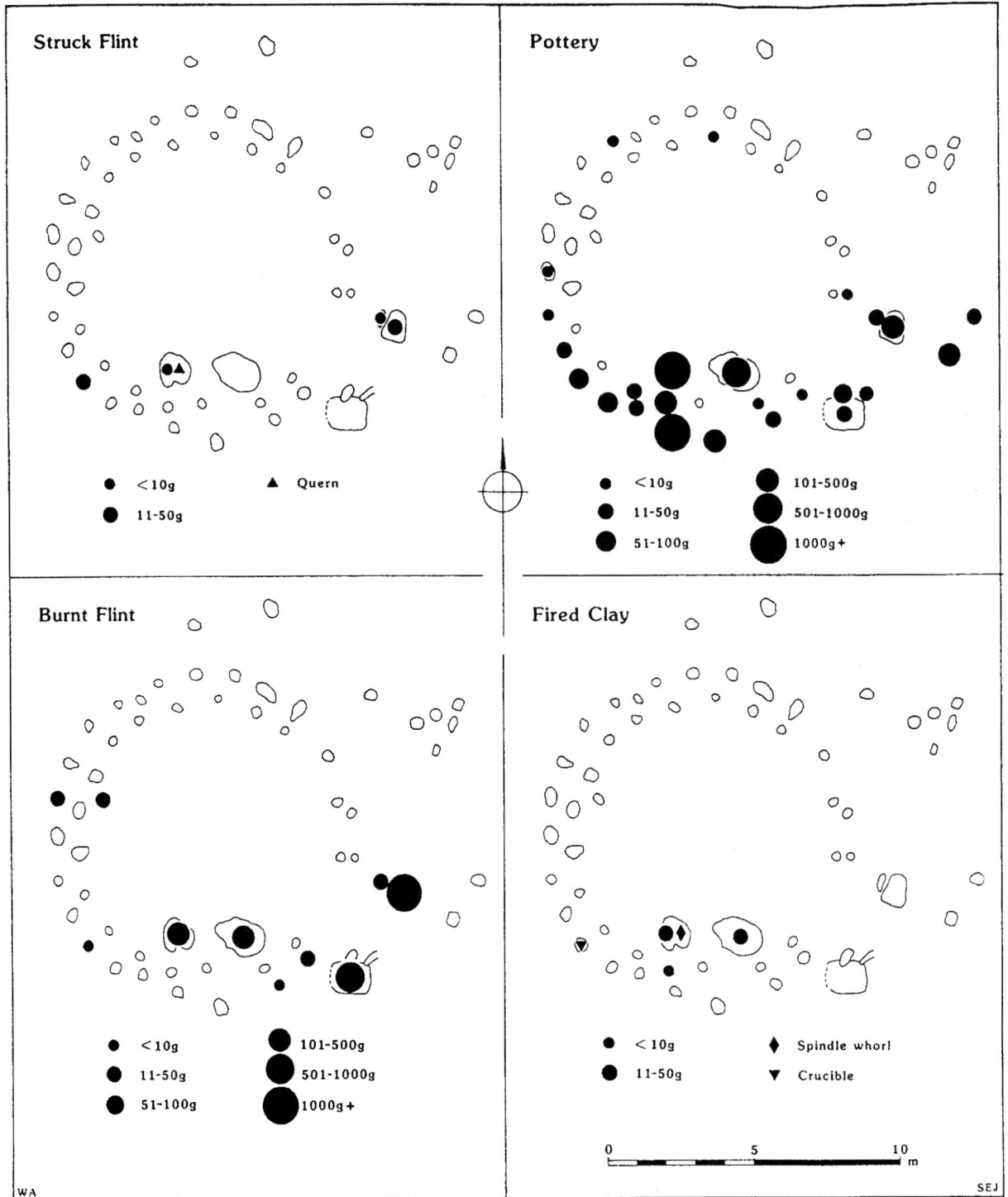

Fig. 7.5. Dunston Park: distribution of material within the round house and possible cosmological referents (Fitzpatrick 1994, fig. 20.3).

for the choreography of daily, routine activities. However, the depositional patterns are not a direct indication of the locations of some of these routine activities, as previously assumed, but were created through brief events spaced over years/decades/centuries..........The interior depositional patterns

represent a coherent entity, and are not divided into clear elements as might be expected if the enclosure contained two spatially distinct household units' (Hill 1995a, 85). Thus, Fasham's hypothesis of a single unit comprising primary houses in the north and ancillary structures around the rest of the

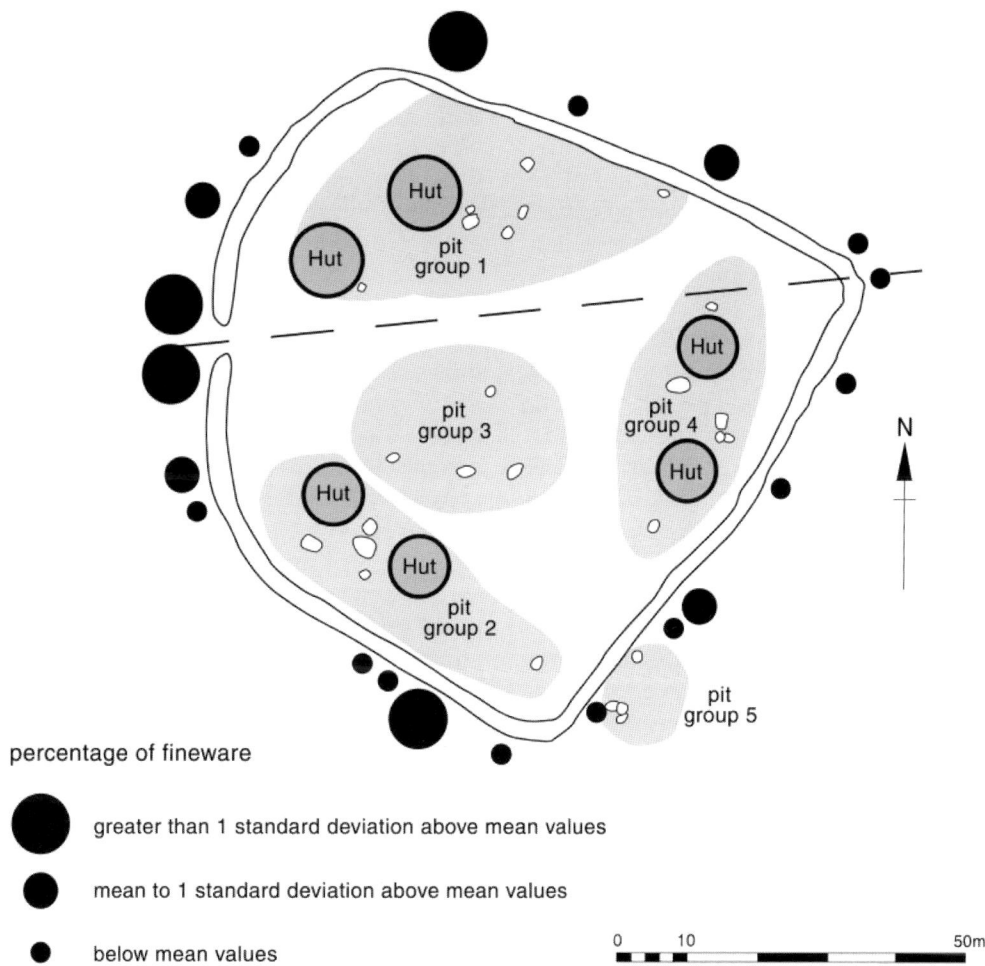

percentage of fineware

● greater than 1 standard deviation above mean values

● mean to 1 standard deviation above mean values

● below mean values

0   10   50m

Fig. 7.6. Winnall Down: Early Iron Age pit groups and the distribution of fineware (after Hill 1995a, figs. 8.5 and 9.4).

enclosure is confirmed. If two porched houses existed at any one time they may have been associated with different sets of ancillary buildings, each household utilising different minority pottery fabrics. Alternatively, the types of minority fabrics in use may have varied through time, with pit fillings in area 2 later than those of area 4.

In recent years this kind of analysis has also been attempted in areas outside Wessex and the Thames valley. By studying the Middle and Late Iron Age pottery from the site at Wakerley, Northamptonshire in terms of its detailed contexts, Gwilt (1997) was able to define a distinct pattern of deposition for the Late Iron Age 'Aylesford-Swarling Affined' fine wares which appeared to repeat a similar pattern displayed by the Middle Iron Age burnished globular bowls and jars. Both sets of fineware material were deposited particularly within the ditch deposits, with a bias towards the righthand sides (looking outwards) of the enclosures. Also various interesting associations between pottery and other types of material such as objects of worked bone or

antler, slag or infant burials could be interpreted in terms of significant liminal boundary locations and the possible location of an excarnation platform, later replaced by a timber shrine.

The Way Forward

The development of spatial studies and the analysis of structured deposition over the last two decades has been fast-moving, wide-ranging and highly stimulating. Further progress can be made through two main avenues of enquiry. The first avenue involves the new excavation of prehistoric sites in areas producing large quantities of pottery. Inevitably, such excavations will mainly result from decisions reached during the planning process and thus will be hedged in by constraints of time and finance. In such circumstances it is essential that statements of minimum requirements in terms of levels of recovery and record should be formulated. In order to further the kinds of spatial research that we have been discussing several requirements are necessary. Firstly, spatial research can best be tackled across large areas, preferably using data from excavations of entire enclosures, units, or, even better, sets of adjacent settlement or burial units within their natural or agricultural setting. The excavation of individual features and contexts must be as complete as possible – 2% samples of ditch fillings are not likely to reveal the levels of patterning that we are seeking. In addition, the pottery and other finds should be recorded according to context or a one metre grid, and three-dimensionally in the case of surviving floors or special deposits. Also the pottery should be recorded in such a way that analyses of sherd size, form and fabric distribution, conjoins and abrasion can readily be undertaken. Through the general wide adoption of the *PCRG Guidelines* the post-excavation recording of pottery in Britain is widely perceived to have reached very high standards. However, the adoption of more detailed recording systems in the field, and of excavation specifications designed to encompass the current requirements for analysis, needs to be encouraged at all levels. Experimental work aimed at devising suitable minimum sampling levels required to answer the questions relating to specific research themes might be one way forward.

Secondly, there is a need to re-interrogate archives relating to sites already excavated. Work in this sphere has concentrated mainly on monuments, especially long barrows and henges of Neolithic date, and Early and Middle Iron Age settlements. New areas to be tackled could include research into the disposition of ceramics within burial and other deposits beneath Early Bronze Age round barrows. A start has been made on the spatial analysis of ceramic types within cemeteries for the later Bronze Age period (Ellison 1980a) and parallel studies should be devised to test patterning in cemeteries of the Late Iron Age. However, the over-riding need is to commence a detailed consideration of any spatial trends displayed within some of the larger pottery assemblages excavated and recorded to high standards in recent decades. Such assemblages include those from Iron Age hillforts such as Cadbury Castle, Crickley Hill and Danebury, and very long-lived settlement complexes such as Beckford, Mucking and Little Waltham. We are poised on the brink of some major steps forward.

Acknowledgements
I am very grateful to Philip Rahtz, Niall Sharples and J.D. Hill, all of whom commented on earlier drafts of this paper. I am grateful to Robert Read for preparing Figures 7.2, 7.3 and 7.6.

8   Pottery and the Expression of Society, Economy and Culture

J. D. Hill

"The role of pottery in overtly or indirectly reflecting social and economic status, social hierarchies or social identity needs further study at both inter-site and regional level" (PCRG 1991, 5).

Introduction

The central place of the study of pottery in writing British prehistory has diminished considerably, and its role changed, over the last thirty years. In the decades before and after the Second World War pottery, its identification and affinities, was literally the 'stuff of history'. Pots were the basis upon which the narratives of prehistory were constructed, debated and challenged. Since, however, the demise of the cultural historical approach in British prehistoric archaeology, it could be argued that the role of pottery has been demoted and routinised.

Within the cultural history paradigm of the 1920s to 1960s pottery, and the people that used the pots, became blurred so that they became indistinguishable and it might often seem that Britain was inhabited by different types of pots who fought and interbred with each other (see picture on page 10 of Catherine Hills' 1984 book, *The Blood of the British*). Different styles of pottery such as Windmill Hill, Beakers or 'Iron Age C' were the key to identify different cultural groups, peoples, and their succession as waves of migrants entered the British Isles to replace or interact with the pots/peoples already here. In this way prehistoric pottery lay at the heart of reconstructing, in however limited a way, the social and cultural lives of people in the past. It also meant that the study and identification of pottery were central to the education of all prehistoric archaeologists. While, with the passing of the culture history approach in the 1960s and 1970s, the potential sources of information which ceramics could provide about the past considerably expanded (particularly with the application of scientific tech-

niques), pottery has nevertheless lost its central position. Few students of prehistoric archaeology now consider they need to learn their pottery.

With the replacement of the cultural history approach in British archaeology, pottery shifted from being the primary indicator of culture to being a chronological marker (although in earlier prehistory this primary role has been lost to radiocarbon dating). It has become an area of specialist study and one whose full possible contribution is unrealised. Since the 1960s, where pottery has been considered in British prehistory other than to refine – or demolish – chronologies and sequences, studies have tended to concentrate on distribution, with less attention to issues of formation processes, function and production (see Chapters 3 to 6). There has been comparatively little attention to social, cultural or symbolic issues in British prehistoric pottery studies. This is despite the recognition of the potential for research in these areas provided by ethno-archaeology and archaeological studies from other parts of the world (e.g. Arnold 1985; Barnett and Hoppes 1995; Bey and Pool 1992; Howard and Morris 1981; Kingery 1986; Kramer 1985; Longacre 1991; Nelson 1985b; Peacock 1982; Rice 1987; Sinopoli 1991; Van der Leeuw 1984 etc.). This mirrors both the limited functionalist framework that has structured much archaeological work in Britain, especially on 'finds', but also the structural role which the pottery specialist is given in this country (see below). This lack of attention to social, economic and cultural aspects of prehistoric ceramics is reflected in the content and position of this chapter. This is the last academic issue defined by the *PCRG* (1991), and the one covering the most broad and least clearly defined range of topics: 'The role of pottery in overtly or indirectly reflecting social and economic status, social hierarchies or social identity needs further study at both inter-site and regional level' (PCRG 1991, 5).

This situation may be changing. Recent publications and meetings have been marked by a wide range of new studies that address social and cultural issues through pottery from all periods (e.g. papers in Sheridan and Sharples 1993; Kinnes and Varndell 1995; Blinkhorn and Cumperpatch 1997; Gwilt and Haselgrove 1997, papers presented at recent PCRG meetings and at TAG '95 and '96 etc.). What might be described as a new cultural historical approach typifies a number of recent studies of prehistoric pottery, although a culture history with very different aims and understanding. These are changes that are in varying ways linked to broader shifts in archaeological philosophy initiated in the 1980s. Different types of earlier prehistoric pottery, with their often markedly different distributions, treatments and contexts of deposition, have increasingly played a role in defining social discourse. This is perhaps superficially similar to the preceding tradition of the 1930s to 60s, but in a refined and enriched manner using notions such as ideology and discourse. Alongside, a growing number of newly published and ongoing studies of the British Neolithic, Bronze and Iron Age are exploring a diverse range of social and symbolic aspects of ceramic production, use and, especially, deposition. While all of these recent approaches can be labelled as examples of post-processual archaeologies, it might be wrong to explain them away as just a reflection of intellectual fashion. The increasing quantity and quality of fieldwork in this country has certainly been an important factor, as has the patterning that ever closer and more detailed study of that data have revealed. Equally, a simple equation of stylistic, ritual and social interpretations of prehistoric pottery with the emergence of post-processual archaeology ignores the important work of David Clarke and his students such as Ian Hodder, Steven Shennan and Ann Ellison (Woodward) in the 1970s (e.g. Blackmore *et al.* 1979; Clarke 1970, 1972; Ellison 1980a, 1980b, 1981; Halstead *et al.* 1978; Hodder 1982a, 1982b; Shennan 1982 etc.). Although studies of style, ritual and the social implications of pottery have concentrated on Neolithic and Earlier Bronze Age material, the 1990s has so far witnessed an expansion of such approaches into later periods. While there is a danger of glossing over the important differences between the uses and contexts of pottery in earlier and later British prehistory, many common themes and problems in the study of ceramics from both eras are emerging. In particular, work on structured/ritual deposition of pottery in

Neolithic, Bronze and Iron Age contexts has been seen as an important key to unlocking the social and symbolic aspects of pottery use, linking the first and last academic themes discussed in this volume (see Chapter 3).

This chapter aims to provide an overview of work that has considered British prehistoric pottery in explicitly social, cultural and symbolic ways. As such it covers those areas of ceramic analysis beyond the six main academic issues the *Prehistoric Ceramics Research Group* identified for the study of pottery (1991), all of which were seen as essentially technical, economic and functional issues. A key point made, however, in many recent archaeological studies, is the impossibility of separating these issues from concerns of social organisation, gender, and cultural meaning. These arguments imply that treating social and cultural aspects of pottery as the residue left over after considering site formation processes, production, distribution and function are flawed, as meanings and social relations are enmeshed in every aspect of a pot's life history.

The chapter will briefly discuss work that has examined issues such as the uses of pottery, social and stylistic aspects of both production and distribution, the decoration of pottery and their possible meanings, the role of pottery in ritual and the use of ceramic evidence for inferring the organisation of society. The absence of explicit discussions of gender issues and prehistoric pottery will be touched upon. Inevitably in a chapter of this size coverage of any one issue must be brief, but the aim is to provide an introduction to the relevant literature and to show the potential that exists for further work of these kinds.

Production

The making of a pot is often seen as a purely technological concern. This can be seen in the way in which ethnography and ethnoarchaeology is often used to illuminate pottery production; studies usually concentrate purely on the technical aspects of clay acquisition, forming or firing and with little discussion of the social and cultural context in which this activity was taking place. The actual technology of British prehistoric pottery has generally received little attention (see Chapters 4 and 5), perhaps because it is perceived as simple and unchanging until the Later Iron Age. With this, there has been almost no consideration of the symbolic and social aspects of the production process itself. Ethnographic studies of technology have often shown how a process such as pottery, stone tool or metal production, or any other technical processes, are inevitably caught up in the processes by which societies' social and cultural orders are continuously brought into being (e.g. Dobres 1995, Thomas 1996, Sillar 1996). Many of these studies emphasise the role of ritual and symbolism, explicitly recognised or just tacit, in the choice of raw materials and their sources, or the processes of production themselves. Recent work on fabric recipes in British pottery has considered some of these issues, stressing that the choice of inclusion/temper type and the complexity of the recipe were not just determined by technical properties or local availability. Rather, fabric recipes were enmeshed in the nature of settlement, the desire to achieve particular surface colours, the possible symbolic importance of certain material and the changing social roles of pottery and other activities (e.g. Woods 1986; Gibson 1995a, *especially* Cleal 1995). Interestingly, while the possible magic associations and technological importance of the use of fire to melt the first human use of metals is often discussed, the first use of high temperature pyro-technology – potting – has not received anything like as much attention (Barnett and Hoppes 1995). The sociology of technology has also been particu-larly influential in studies of stone tool production, and, to a lesser extent, pottery, especially through exploring the concept of *Chaine Opératoire* (Lemonier 1986; Pfaffenburger 1988). This work often considers the sequence of decisions and unconscious motor actions involved in a process such as knapping, weaving or potting (Balfet 1965, Edmonds 1990, Gosselain 1992; Waellert 1997; Van der Leeuw 1977). These non-discursive processes and sequences are seen to be thoroughly cultural products (Arnold 1981). How such motor skills are learnt from copying another potter, usually mother to daughter, has formed the basis for several studies on matrilocality in archaeology (Deetz 1965, Hill, J.N. 1970, but see Herbich 1987), and this has also been tied to lan-guage in one British example (Tomalin 1995). These tacit knowledges of how to make a pot are largely inexpressible through spoken language and as such may be very deep rooted. They may represent a possible major barrier to technological innovation, the techniques of coiling, use of the paddle and use of the wheel all involving very different motor skills (Arnold 1985; Roux and Corbetta 1989). Possibly more importantly, these perspectives from the sociology/anthropology of technology stress how techniques, such as making pots, are not a separate sub-system of society, but rather an integral part of a group's *habitus* and closely tied to how that society operates on a household and larger level. This type of approach has been emphasised in studies of stone tools by Edmonds (1995; Bradley and Edmonds 1993) for the period covered by this chapter, and clearly has great potential for the study of pottery.

Distribution

Studies of the distribution of ceramics have been an important feature of prehistoric pottery studies since David Peacock's pioneering work of the late 1960s (see Chapter 5). The growing body of work on pottery distributions has largely concentrated on the sourcing of different types of pottery, although some work has considered the nature and mechanisms through which pottery and other ceramics such as crucibles and briquetage passed (Morris 1985, 1993). These studies are directly tied to the reconstruction of social organisation, as the mechanisms of ex-change and distribution are a crucial aspect of how social systems are held to operate (e.g. Renfrew 1977; Bradley and Edmonds 1993). It is in this context that the debate about whether the distribution of south western Iron Age pottery ('Glastonbury Ware') represented the operation of market exchange or a socially embedded exchange network (Peacock 1968, 1969; Blackmore *et al.* 1979) is central to the under-standing of later prehistoric social organisation. As are studies such as whether pottery and salt were distributed across Iron Age Wessex through a hillfort based chiefly re-distribution system (Cunliffe 1984a, 1984c; Gosden 1989; Morris 1994, 1997), or how Late Iron Age wine amphorae and Gallic pottery reached south east England (Cunliffe 1987; Haselgrove 1982, 1989; Fitzpatrick 1989 etc). Can it now be proposed that where British prehistoric pottery (or the clay and temper) are found long distances from their source they did not arrive at a site through the medium of *market* exchange systems? However, alternative explanations, and their social conse-quences, have perhaps not been elaborated in great detail beyond either general notions of gift exchange or long distance seasonal movement of peoples. This is possibly because with the widespread availability of suitable local clay sources and ample evidence in many periods for predominantly local production, it is hard to understand why fragile pots or bulky clays were moved long distances by land and water in prehistory except for social, political and cultural reasons. Like recent work on long term changes in fabric recipes with different styles of vessels (Cleal 1995; Chapter 11), so too changes in the sources of pottery may relate to important social and cultural associations with particular types of pottery (e.g. Parker Pearson 1990, 1995).

Briquetage containers could be regarded as ex-ceptional as they were containers for a basic necessity: salt (Morris 1985, 1994a; Lane and Morris 2001). As such it is understandable why this essential commodity was exchanged long distance in later prehistory. Yet Morris (Lane and Morris 2001) has shown that the decision to transport salt in a ceramic container as opposed to a perishable bag or barrel is a regional phenomenon that is not explainable by other than cultural factors.

Studies of distribution and sourcing have been one area where British prehistoric ceramicists have drawn on North American approaches. Morris (1985, 1994a, 1996), in particular, has championed the cross-cultural studies of Arnold (1981, 1985) on the distances potters travel to acquire clays and tempers. However, noticeably absent from British ceramic archaeology are studies which integrate production, distribution, environment and society in the 'Ceramic Ecology' approach (Matson 1965; Arnold 1985; Kolb 1987, 1988), as are other similar approaches considering the whole life cycle of vessels (Van der Leeuw 1977 – exceptions include Howard 1981 and Lambrick 1984).

Pottery Use and Aceramicness

The importance of considering the use of pots has been discussed earlier in the volume (Chapter 6). But the 'need' for vessels to meet particular functions are culturally and socially embedded. Possibly one of the key aspects of the ceramic record for British prehistory is that large parts of the British Isles for long periods needed few or no pots at all. For obvious reasons, these aceramic phases have not received much attention from ceramicists, although they have important implications for how ceramically richer phases are understood. How aceramic some of these phases really were can be questioned. Lack of settlement excavation, poor post-depositional preservation or partial excavation ignoring pottery rich contexts are all factors to be considered. The available evidence does, however, support the notion that the quantities, functions and circumstances in which pottery was used changed through time and varied from region to region.

Aceramicness need not be a reflection of economic backwardness, nor a lack of social complexity as cases such as later La Tène Ireland shows (Raftery 1994, 1995b). Ethnographic cases provide evidence of societies with complex subsistence bases, exchanges networks and elaborate social hierarchies which successfully did not rely on ceramic containers (e.g. Polynesia and New Zealand, north west coast of USA and Canada). Some of these societies may have had a pottery using heritage (e.g. Polynesia – Marshall 1985, Andrew Crosby *pers comm*) or bordered on pottery-using groups (e.g. north west Coast – Arnold 1985). Alternatives to pottery such as wood, bark, basketry or leather etc. do not normally survive in the British archaeological record except on some waterlogged settlements, or where deliberately deposited in bogs (Earwood 1993; Coles and Coles 1986; Evans 1989b; Fitzpatrick

1997b). Another alternative, metal, may rarely have entered the archaeological record because of its value and ease of recycling, unless deliberately deposited in graves or wet places (Bradley 1990a). It may be highly probable, for example, that every household in the ceramically poor regions of northern and western Iron Age Britain had an iron cauldron and also used wooden and other organic serving and storage vessels. The fact that in different times and places in prehistory communities successfully fed and watered themselves without using pottery does not in itself explain why aceramic communities chose to make no or few pots. This is particularly so when communities they were in contact with were ceramic to different degrees, or when these communities may have made pots in the past.

There need be no single explanation for the aceramicness in British prehistory. Ethnographic examples provide a variety of options for understanding the total absence or limited use of pottery in parts of prehistoric Britain. Arnold (1985) stresses the importance of climatic factors in limiting production, although pottery can be made in the most extreme conditions if there is an economic or social need, such as the Arctic. In Britain, climate alone cannot explain aceramic phases as pottery could be and was made in all parts of Britain in different periods of the past. Pots may not have been valued highly enough to justify the time invested in their manufacture, especially if alternatives were available. Pots could have been made at any time through the year in Britain (Woods 1986). Yet studies suggest that the time required to collect and prepare raw materials, make and fire the vessels represents a significant investment of time on the behalf of (usually) women and children and this needs to be scheduled in the agriculture year. Difficulties in scheduling such activities within the annual cycle of women's subsistence and other activities have been argued to be a major factor in the failure to adopt pottery in some parts of the world (Crown and Wills 1985).

Clearly the degree of sedentism is an important factor in the degree and frequency with which pottery was used. A possibly relatively mobile population in Pre-Roman Iron Age Ireland may explain the extreme rarity of pottery in this period (Raftery 1995b). However, some sedentary societies do not make pots, while some relatively mobile pastoral or gatherer-hunter communities, such as Late Mesolithic/Early Neolithic groups across northern Europe, have made and used pottery (see papers in Barnett and Hoppes 1995).

More important factors may have been what pottery was used for. Certain types of food storage, preparation such as soaking or fermenting, methods of cooking and the organisation of the meal may all require, or not require, pots of particulars types and shapes (papers in Barnett and Hoppes 1995). Cooking methods appear to be an important factor in the absence of pottery in Polynesia, despite their earlier use (Crosby pers comm, Marshall 1985). Certainly, the absence of cooking jars in aceramic parts of first millennium BC Britain and Ireland point to significant differences in how daily meals were prepared compared to those areas which did use pottery.

How foodstuffs were consumed, and the broader social settings in which important meals, feasts and sacrifices took place were probably also different between aceramic and ceramic areas. The ways in which pottery forms reflect styles of eating and drinking, or the size of the group participating in the meal, have required some attention in the wider ceramic literature (Deitzler 1990; papers in Barnett and Hoppes 1995; Blitz 1993). The roles of pottery in enhancing the social occasion of eating and feasting has been suggested as a reason for its original adoption in many societies. This includes its initial adoption across Britain where pottery appears as part of the new cultural, rather than purely subsistence orientated, package that marks the Neolithic, and probably provided a new medium in which to serve foodstuffs in probably ceremonial situations (Thomas 1991a). In other periods of prehistory the roles pottery played as containers for serving and consuming food and drink on both daily and special occasions were important in defining the forms, sizes, colours and surface treatments of different styles of pottery. Much earlier prehistoric pottery was possibly used for serving rather than storing or preparing foods and beverages. Differences in the capacities of Grooved Ware bowls between henges and other sites may relate to the needs of large scale feasting at sites such as Durrington Walls (Wainwright and Longworth 1971; cf. Blitz 1993; see also Howard 1981; Thomas 1991a). While the Beaker's function is so obvious, its innovation as a container distinctively designed for drinking alcoholic liquids is taken for granted. In later prehistory, the importance of pottery as a medium for embodying different styles of eating and drinking was probably just as important (Barrett 1989, 1991a; Willis 1994, 1996; Hill – Chapter 13 this volume). Closer attention to the roles of pots as tools in prehistoric foodways offers considerable potential for unlocking the social and cultural information pottery assemblages contain (see Chapter 6).

The varied roles of pottery for consuming foods, and the fact that food can be consumed without using pots, has an important bearing on the question of aceramicness. The possibly restricted use of Early Neolithic pottery for ceremonial eating, feasting, and not daily activities serves to remind us that throughout British prehistory the distinction was not simply one of between the use and non-use of pottery. Rather, it was a blurred scale in which the quantities and specific uses to which pottery were put varied considerably. In some places and times, relatively little pottery was made and probably used in quite restricted social situations, be it feasting or burial. In such situations the making and use of pots was possibly of much greater significance than those where pottery was plentiful and in common daily use. The latter situation, 'normal' to our modern eyes, was generally only a feature of southern Britain from the Later Bronze Age onwards. Even in these ceramically rich situations just how abundant and widespread the use of pottery was should possibly not be taken for granted – certainly when compared to the sheer quantity and broad range of 'Belgicized/ Romanized' Late Iron Age and Early Roman pottery (Willis 1997).

Shape and Colour

Important aspects of the appearance of a vessel are both shape and colour. Perhaps because it is so obvious, what a pot looks like often seems to be relegated in importance compared to the fine detail of rim form and, particularly, fabric. As such the distinction between Post Deverel-Rimbury/Early Iron Age fine and coarse wares is really a distinction between two basic types with very visually different shapes and colours, and even textures on touch. Similar basic visual and tactile differences, before getting down to the details of specific forms or surface treatments, must have been very apparent between different types of Later Neolithic and Early Bronze Age pottery (Grooved Ware cf. Peterborough cf. Beaker etc.). Several ethnographic studies suggest there might have been implicit or explicit conceptual links made between the shape of a pot and the human body (e.g. the use of terms such as 'neck', 'shoulder' or 'body') (Barley 1994; David *et al.* 1988) (see Chapter 1). Establishing such links, however, with British prehistoric material is difficult.

Colour symbolism, however, is an easier aspect of prehistoric pottery to consider. The colours of vessels may be of great significance, as is shown by several ethnographic and archaeological studies of pottery. Although only a limited range of colours were available to a British prehistoric potter, she could clearly control the firing to produce unoxidised blacks/dark browns and oxidised reds/ light brown surfaces, or use red slips etc. While Cleal (1995) has argued that the controlled production of the red surfaces of Beakers was a deliberate choice, not an accident of techonology. Thomas (1991a) and

Gibson (1995) have also discussed the importance of colour in the choice of inclusions or surfaces in Neolithic pottery. Colour also may have played an important role in the adoption of 'Romanized' imported fines in the Latest Iron Age and Early Roman era. There was a preference for black against red imported pots in one large cemetery and the red colour of samian may have been important in its rapid take up after the conquest (Millett *pers. comm.*). Although there has been little work in this area, the colour of pottery may have great potential for future research.

Decoration and Design

Decoration and surface treatment attract considerably greater attention than surface colour. Only a comparatively limited range of treatments were applied to British prehistoric pots and overt symbols and recognisable motifs are rare. Atlantic Scottish Iron Age pottery is unique in British prehistory for its small number of inscribed figurative motifs. Much Neolithic and Early Bronze Age pottery had surface treatments such as cording or pinching or incised decoration all over the complete vessel bodies. In contrast later prehistoric pottery is plain or with only a small area of the total surface decorated/treated. This may suggest a changing importance of pottery as a signalling medium, as the roles pottery played changed over the last three millennia BC.

Almost all reports consider the different types of surface treatment/decoration found in a collection, although detailed investigations of design grammars, geographic distributions or detailed studies are not common. These have been restricted to a few particular styles of pottery; La Tène decorated Iron Age pottery (e.g. Cunliffe 1974; Elsdon 1976; Stanford 1974), Grooved Ware (Wainwright and Longworth 1971) and, particularly, Beakers (Clarke 1970) and Collared Urns (Longworth 1984). This is because these styles have complex patterns of surface treatment that often contain distinct motifs. This appears to be of a different order of treatment and meaning than generalised surface treatments such as the scoring of East Midlands Scored ware, the cordoning of a Cornish Late Iron Age vessels, or, the impressions all over a Peterborough ware vessel. Some of the latter can be explained in functional terms such as making it easier to pick up a pot (e.g. for later Iron Age 'Scored wares' or combed/rilled 'cooking pots' – Elsdon 1992 – such treatments may also help reduce fracture from thermal shock – Schiffer *et al.* 1994). They, however, also make an obvious visual distinction between categories of vessel (see above).

Studies of Beakers and Grooved Ware have often placed considerable attention on their surface treatments. The distinct motifs found on Grooved Ware have been studied in a number of ways including the distribution of different types of motif regionally, between classes of site and within sites, and also considering the complexity and combination of motifs (e.g. MacSween 1995; Richards 1993; Wainwright and Longworth 1971). Similar approaches have been applied to other types of pottery with distinct motifs (e.g. Tomalin 1995). This Grooved Ware 'art' is closely linked to contemporary 'megalithic art' found on small portable stone objects and within passage graves (Cleal 1991). That this ceramic art shares a mutually exclusive distribution with the 'megalithic art', except on Orkney, has generated much discussion (e.g. Bradley 1984, 60ff, Clarke, D.V. 1995, Thomas 1991). Links between decorative styles on pottery and other mediums provide important links to help interpret the role and meanings of certain styles of pottery. Late Bronze Age/Early Iron Age fine wares share similar types of incised motif with types of metalwork (Barrett 1980) and more general links exist between La Tène decorated pottery and metalwork (Elsdon 1976). Beakers share similar decorative styles with Irish gold lunulae although, like Grooved Ware and megalithic art they have largely exclusive distributions (Clarke, D.V. 1985). These vessels also have complex patterns of decoration that have lent themselves to detailed studies of their design grammars (e.g. Clarke 1970; Case 1977; Boast 1995).

Interestingly, except in relation to Beakers, there have been few/no studies of the design grammars of the types conducted by Hodder (1982c), Shanks and Tilley (1987b) and common in the States (e.g. Plog 1980; Arnold 1994; Braun 1991) on British prehistoric material, although such approaches may be applicable to a range of pottery styles. Nor has the broader issue of why decorate British pots received great attention. Why artefacts may be decorated has received considerable attention in the general debates on style and symbolic archaeology over the last 30 years. This has lead to many recent enthnographic studies, some directly inspired by initial questions about British pottery (Braithwaite 1982; David *et al.* 1988; Hodder 1982a, 1991; Welbourne 1984). Although not necessarily directly applicable, these studies may provide many fruitful possibilities for considering British material in the future.

Identity

Pottery's great flexibility of form, surface treatment and decoration offers considerable potential as a medium for displaying 'messages' of all kinds. Indeed it has been argued that it is this quality of fired clay that explains the initial adoption of pottery in many cultures (Barnett and Hoppes 1995, but see Armit and Finlayson 1995). Although given clay's potential for creating diverse forms, more attention is needed to explain why in most British prehistoric contexts only a limited range of long lasted styles was made (Barrett 1991a).

Decoration and other aspects of ceramic style, including technology, appear to have played important, and possibly active, roles in defining and reaffirming different forms of identities throughout British prehistory. Ellison (1981a; Woodward 1995) and others (e.g. Bradley 1984; Hill 1995b) have argued that material culture becomes increasing a medium (consciously or unconsciously) marking differences between local areas, or regions in later prehistory. This is not to argue that pottery could not be used in this way earlier. For example, Armit and Finlayson (1995) suggest that the distinctive styles of the first pottery in Scotland, and the distinct lack of pottery in one region (see above) indicate the existence of distinct ethnic(?) groupings of pre-dominantly gatherer-hunter communities. Equally, throughout the Neolithic and Early Bronze Age pottery from different parts of Britain often shows local characteristics. The question that needs to be asked, however, is to what extent such differences are the result of local unconscious variations, or highly recognisable differences which appears to have been the case increasingly throughout the first millennium BC (Ellison 1981a; Hill 1995b).

Regional differences in Later Bronze Age and Iron Age pottery have long been recognised, even if their implications have not been fully discussed. Cunliffe's work in Wessex developed the notion of 'style zones' (1974, 1991) to describe differences in the distribution of different forms of pot, or styles of decoration. These were explicitly linked to the emergence, ethnogenesis, of Late Iron Age 'tribal' entities known from historical sources. Ellison (1980, 1981a) has shown how this pattern has its origins in the Middle Bronze Age. During the course of the Iron Age local distinctive pottery become part of a multi-dimensional kaleidoscope whereby parts of northern Europe are distinguished from each other by different social practices – presence/absence of burial, different settlement patterns and types, non use/use of decorated metalwork or coins of particular types, use of different types of pottery. This 'regionality' (Bradley 1990, Hill 1995b) can be seen clearly in later Iron Age eastern England. Here areas were marked by differences in take up of new technologies, in the rate of take up of Romanization before and after the conquest, in the range of styles and forms, and in manners of deposition. All of which point to marked and noticeable differences in all aspects of a pot's life history which would be

hard for people living in the area to ignore (Elsdon 1992; Green 1980; Gwilt 1997; Hill 1995b; Rigby and Freestone 1997; Willis 1996, forthcoming).

Pottery was involved in marking and possibly making identities other than those of the regional or tribal. Beakers in particular appear to have been actively used in displaying personal identities. Thomas (1991b) has argued that Beakers and other goods placed in the graves were messages to be read by mourners at the funeral. This and other studies have shown that different shapes and surface treatments of Beakers were placed in the graves of different aged and biologically sexed individuals (Mizoguchi 1995). Other explicit links between different types of pottery and genders are harder to demonstrate. However, a range of highly versatile tools such as pots, probably made by women and linked to activities of food preparation and serving, are likely to have been consciously and unconsciously thoroughly involved in the working out of gender relations throughout the period covered by this book.

Ritual

The key to most of the studies which consider the meanings, roles and social roles of pottery have been the ways different types of pottery were deliberately deposited with or without other categories of objects, plant, animal and human remains, in particular parts of a site or landscape. Such structured or ritual deposition has been the subject of much attention in recent years (e.g. Bradley 1990; Brown A. 1991; Hill 1995a; Pollard 1995; Richards and Thomas 1984; Thomas 1993) (see Chapter 3). Much Neolithic and Early Bronze Age pottery comes from burials or monuments such as henges or causewayed enclosures. Pottery is also found in the less common burials of later prehistory, while ritual deposits on settlements are increasingly recognised. The specific types of cult or ritual pottery or figurines found in many European and other cultures do not typify the British sequence, although there are a few exceptions. However, some vessels were made specifically to accompany human burials, (e.g. this is true for some Beakers, Food Vessels and Late Iron Age wheel turned vessels) and it has been argued that much Neolithic pottery was restricted to use in feasting and ceremonial (see above). But as Pollard (Chapter 3) and others suggest (Thomas 1991a; Hill 1995a) a substantial proportion, even a majority, of all British prehistoric pottery was deposited as the end product or intimate parts of ritual, feasting, and ceremonial at settlements, communal monuments and burial sites. Indeed, if it had not been deliberately deposited in pits, ditches, graves or tomb chambers, the ceramic record for British prehistory would be significantly poorer and reliant on very fragmented material.

Different aspects of the role of pottery in rituals throughout prehistory have been a significant focus of attention in the last 15 years. The placing of pottery in particular places within tombs, communal monuments or domestic sites have received attention in all periods (e.g. Nowakowski 1993; Gwilt 1997; Hill 1995a; Pollard 1995; Richards and Thomas 1984; Thomas 1991a; Thomas and Whittle 1986 etc.) (see Chapters 3 and 7). Other areas that have been investigated include differences in the styles of pottery ritually deposited in different circumstances, the exact manner in which pottery was treated in such deposits and how this changed through time – an area which includes the deliberate breaking or 'killing' of pots and the quite common situation of only depositing a portion of a vessel (Hill 1995a; Gwilt 1997; Woodward 2000b). In these situations where pots were an intimate parts of ritual deposits and essentially for preparing or serving food and drink at feasts and sacrifices, these group rituals may have been the motivation for bringing, or procuring, pots to a site.

A question that has received considerable attention is if the bulk of British prehistoric pottery entered the record as the result of ritual activity, how can we talk about pottery's roles in daily life? (e.g. Allen and Robinson 1993; Hill 1995a; Needham and Spence 1996). This is a particular problem for earlier prehistory where 'domestic' sites are not common except as field walking scatters. However, the problem is also present in later periods where well preserved sites surviving as more than sub-soil features are rare. A common answer is to explore the connections drawn between common actions and categories in daily life and the actions of ritual. Many writers have emphasised how the sacred and secular worlds in British prehistoric societies were not radically separated, and how rituals drew upon a repertoire of activities, categories and meanings from daily life. It is through these processes, such authors argue, that the categories and activities of daily life which used pottery were ritually sanctioned (e.g. Barrett 1994; Boast 1995; Edmonds 1995; Hill 1995a; Thomas 1991a).

Social Organisation

In comparison with North American archaeology, there has been almost no explicit use of pottery to investigate issues of social organisation in British prehistory. What work there has been on this question has tended to concentrate on pottery distribution and exchange (see above). As such, in later prehistory, the distributions of particular types of pottery and the inferred mechanics of their distribution have been used to consider issues of social hierarchy and organisation (e.g. imported pots and amphorae – Haselgrove 1982; Cunliffe 1987). Although even here it is perhaps surprising that so little use has been made of pottery in considering these issues.

The lack of work of this nature might partly be due to the simplicity and limited range of pottery in use through out the period. Unlike other cultures in other parts of the world or time, British prehistoric pottery is characterised by basic cylinders, open vessels that at any one time exist in a restricted range of forms and sizes. It is only with the Late Pre-Roman and Roman Iron Age that a diverse repertoire of pots – ceramic tools – was used. This partially explains the lack of work on craft specialisation and standardisation in pottery production. There does not appear to have been an equation of fine or exotic wares and high social status until the Late Iron Age/Early Roman period in this country. Nor are there the range of specialist forms or styles of decoration that might be limited to particular social groups and particular activities before this time. As such, pottery does not appear to have been used to reflect social status and hierarchy in the bulk of British prehistory, although this may be a product of the lack of research in this area.

Until the very end of the Iron Age, British prehistoric pottery lacked the wide repertoires of pottery forms that typify many cultures world wide. Instead, the defining characteristic of British prehistoric pottery from the Early Neolithic onwards is a very limited range of vessel forms, usually just one or two. Throughout British prehistory it is possibly the differences between different 'styles' of pottery, rather than between different types of vessel within a style that are more important. Different styles of pottery throughout British prehistory were often visually very different to styles of pottery used before, after or at the same time. These different styles of pottery often were deposited in different contexts; burial, henge, settlement or pit complex etc. A clear example of this pattern is the visual and contextual differences between Peterborough Ware, Grooved Ware and Beaker traditions in the Middle/ Late Neolithic (Bradley 1984; Braithwaite 1984; Thomas 1991a). But similar patterns can be seen between Deverel Rimbury and Post-Deverel Rimbury traditions in the Later Bronze Age, or between 'Middle Iron Age' and 'Belgicized/Romanized' Late Iron Age traditions (Bradley 1984, 48) (see Chapter 13). What must be stressed is that the differences between these traditions were not simply ones of different shapes, but often of repertoires, fabric recipes, decorative grammars, and contexts of deposition and contexts of use. A particular type of pot seems to have been made of a particular fabric, used in a particular set of ways, and entered the archaeological record through a particular route. This also appears to be the case with prehistoric metalwork and stonework (Barrett 1991b; Barrett and Needham 1988; Bradley 1990; Bradley and Edmonds 1993; Edmonds 1995).

It is the recognition of these differences between traditions that has led in Neolithic and Early Bronze Age archaeology, to a different, if generalised, use of pottery to address social organisation through the notion of, first, ideology and, subsequently, social discourse (e.g. Shennan 1982; Braithwaite 1984; Thorpe and Richards 1984; Clarke D.V. 1985; Thomas 1991a; Barrett 1994). The differences between the manufacture, use and deposition of particular types of pottery, and the social meanings and categories they reproduced have been seen as an integral part of the social discourses through which people lived their lives. Such discourses, value systems, ways of life, are inseparable from peoples' actions and material culture. They offer a bottom-up perspective on how society was organised as the product of daily activities and encounters. This influential perspective has interpreted the different, but chronologically, overlapping styles of Neolithic and Early Bronze Age pottery in terms of alternative social discourses available to individuals and groups in this period. The choice to use a particular type of pottery in a particular way was an active decision by people in the past. Such a perspective also imbues prehistoric pottery with much wider social implications than might have been hitherto thought, suggesting that all aspects of pottery are thoroughly cultural and social phenomena. Pots are social facts as well artefacts.

Gender

If there has been little work explicitly considering issues of social organisation using British prehistoric pottery, there has been very little discussion of gender issues except for a few suggestions and comments (e.g. Barrett 1989; Rigby and Freestone 1997; Tomalin 1995). This reflects the lack of attention to gender issues in British prehistory in general, possibly because it is difficult to 'see' women in prehistoric Britain. Pottery may provide a fruitful area for future work on gender issues. Direct associations between specific genders (male, female or other) and particular types of pottery are rare in mortuary and other data from the period (exceptions include Beaker pottery – Mizoguchi 1995). However, Gero and Conkey (1991) argue that an engendered archaeology is not about finding women (or men) in

the past, rather it is an archaeology which always tried to work within the realisation that gender is and was a central aspect structuring all areas of life and society. These issues are particularly relevant to pottery (e.g. Marshall 1985; Rice 1994; Sassaman 1992; Skibo and Schiffer 1995; Wright 1991; papers in Barnett and Hoppes 1995). Pots were a class of tools it *might* be assumed were predominantly made by women and children throughout British prehistory. Although individual cases must always be considered on their own merits, ethnographic studies suggest where pottery is organised at a household activity, its is often done and organised by women (Arnold 1995; Skibo and Schiffer 1995; Peacock 1982; Rice 1997). This is an assumption, and one that needs to be considered critically. If relatively few pots were made and used in many parts of prehistoric Britain at different times, traditional conceptions of domestic modes of production may be inappropriate. However, if we make this assumption, how might the perspective that most British prehistoric pottery were tools probably made by women, and tools commonly used by women in the storage, preparation and serving of food and drink shed new light on all aspects of the study of pottery?

Conclusions

This chapter has provided an overview of the current state of and future potential of using pottery to address a range of social, economic and cultural issues in British prehistory. It has briefly touched on how examination of production, distribution, decoration has been used to consider such issues as style, symbolism, gender relations and the organisation of society. The overall tone of the chapter has possibly been a little negative, stressing the comparatively little work that has been attempted directly on these issues, despite the lengthy history of studies on prehistoric ceramics in this country. This is not to dismiss the exciting and important work that has been accomplished in these areas so far. These have made an important contribution to the study of British prehistory.

Compared to North American archaeology, there appears to have been far less attention to questions of style, the organisation of production and distribution, ritual and social organisation in British approaches to pottery of all periods over the last 30 years. While this is partly a case of the grass appearing greener on the other side of the fence, the number of North American studies on these issues speaks for itself (e.g. Arnold 1985; Barnett and Hoppes 1995; Bey and Pool 1992; Kingery 1986, 1993; Kolb 1987, 1988; Kramer 1985; Nelson 1985; Longacre 1991; Plog 1980; Rice 1984; Sinopoli 1991 etc.). It is important to ask why these differences exist, and not simply to import wholesale North American theoretic approaches, with their heavy reliance on statistics and systemic models of society. We need to think more about the nature of British prehistoric pottery studies. One possible factor is the small scale of British prehistoric pottery research and the lack of formal training in the study of pottery for many workers. The latter point relates to an important structural difference between the position and expectations of people working on British prehistoric pottery and those North Americans producing the sorts of studies mentioned above. In Britain there have been relatively few full time academics, specialists or full time research students researching prehistoric British ceramics. The bulk of workers are producing site reports which are often seen as no more than that; a report on the pottery. Pottery specialists may not feel themselves, or are seen/ expected by others, as having either the appropriate material or qualifications to address broader social, economic and cultural concerns. While a similar position applies to ceramic specialists working in

North American salvage archaeology, perhaps a key difference lies in the larger number of graduate students working on pottery as part of their advisor's/mentor's field projects in North America. In such a situation students have the time to address these questions, and are working within a framework where such broader issues are expected to be addressed. Perhaps the expectation and realisation that pottery is a product of, and involved in, a key range activities that can address the broader questions discussed in this chapter is a key difference. This optimistic expectation of the North American processual archaeology perhaps never took root in British archaeology outside a few exceptional teachers, such as David Clarke, and their students. It has perhaps been rediscovered by the post-processualists in the last ten to fifteen years who from a different perspective, have also stressed how all aspects of material culture inevitably provide evidence for a very broad range of social questions. Such optimism offers considerable potential to address the issues touched on in this chapter, and more, in the near future.

9 Ceramic Lives

Alistair Barclay

"He had grown a passion for ceramics. I entered his collection (as a bull vase) when it was already fully developed with dozens of flasks, bowls, double vases, juglets and ewers, ... and some misshapen accidents of firing that he thought were works of genius" Tibor Fischer, The Collector Collector.

Introduction

There is a tradition in British archaeology of cataloguing and publishing collections of objects by material with little regard for their context of recovery. Yet it is often argued that it is only the context and the material associations that provides the necessary meaning for our understanding and interpretation of the past and this is no less true of research into prehistoric ceramics. This paper attempts to take the view that by looking at ceramics from a contextual perspective something can be said about why they were created, how they were used and why they were disposed of. Similar approaches have been made to other categories of material culture (e.g. metalwork and lithics) and have proved most rewarding (Bradley 1990a; Needham 1988; Schofield 1995).

These ideas are presented in three studies based on pottery of Neolithic and Early Bronze Age date from the Thames Valley. The first study looks at the distribution of decorated Early Neolithic pottery and its possible social context. The second study is concerned with votive deposits and how these relate to contemporary burial practice, while the third study looks at the use of Early Bronze Age pottery as containers and pyre offerings. Collectively these studies present three very different contexts for the disposal of vessels: monument ditches, rivers and cremation pyres. A common theme to all three studies is that various choices determined how a vessel was used in everyday life and that these choices eventually influenced the method and context for disposal.

Abingdon Ware: Why Decorate Early Neolithic Pots?

This section looks at the context and use of decorated Early Neolithic pottery, in particular what is generally referred to as Abingdon Ware, from the Upper Thames region and its relationship to other categories of Early Neolithic pottery (e.g. Plain and Carinated Bowl). The approach is deliberately contextual. Despite the potential of such analysis few such studies have been undertaken with reference to pottery. One of the few important studies of this type was the structuralist based analysis undertaken by Thorpe and Richards in their study of the introduction of Beaker pottery (1984). Thomas has also discussed the distribution of earlier Neolithic pottery around Avebury (1991a) and the relevance of this work is discussed below.

Decorated Early Neolithic pottery has a very restricted distribution in the Thames Valley and by far the bulk of this material is found at enclosure sites. Very little decorated pottery is known from the wider landscape, an observation that has certain implications for its everyday use and discard. From its limited spatial distribution several points can be made. First, the absence, presence and degree of decoration may have held some form of meaning in terms of social categories (see Miller 1985). Sterner also makes the point in her ethnographic study of Sirak Bulahay pottery that the original form and function of vessels can sometimes influence their eventual discard (1989, 458).

Abingdon Ware was first defined by Leeds in the 1920s (1927; 1928), redefined by Piggott (1954) and by Case (1956), and this definition has changed as ideas have developed. Piggott defined Abingdon Ware as:

> "... a pottery style which is an evolved form of Windmill Hill Ware .... rims thickened and rolled over, with abundant stroke ornament or punctuations across them....lugs are frequently developed into strap handles".

At one time all Early Neolithic pottery from the Upper Thames was referred to as belonging to the Abingdon Ware style, but now the use should perhaps be restricted to only those vessels that have more elaborate decoration (Smith 1974, 106; cf. Cleal 1992 for a similar argument).

The use of such terms as Abingdon Ware to describe assemblages generally mask their complex character. Cleal has argued that the use of such type-site terminology should be abandoned or at least not given such primary importance (1992, 303). Whilst there may never have been an Abingdon Ware, it is certainly possible to recognise an Abingdon Style. A better and more sympathetic approach to Early Neolithic pottery would be to classify and to quantify vessel types in a standardised way as advocated by Cleal (1992). At present the finer detail such as the similarities between different assemblages is perhaps lost by attempts to classify the entire assemblage to a particular style. Smith was able to identify several Abingdon Ware style vessels at Windmill Hill (1965, 223–7 vessels 194, 198–9, 201), while at Abingdon it is possible to recognise vessels more typical of the decorated assemblage from Windmill Hill. At Staines some of the decorated pottery appears more like the Mildenhall style vessels that occur at Orsett (Robertson-MacKay 1987, fig. 48: p1. 36; Kinnes 1978), while other vessels are more like Abingdon Ware and others more like those from the open site at Runnymede (Avery 1982; Kinnes 1991). A similar argument came be made for the pottery from the probable enclosure at Maiden Bower (Piggott 1931, 90 and fig. 6).

Whittle's renaming of the Early Neolithic pottery styles as South-Western, Decorated and Eastern was primarily designed as a way of looking at coarse cultural patterns in southern Britain in relation to Europe (1977). Again this type of broad-brush approach tends to ignore the finer detail in favour of constructing a form of cultural entity. One point made by Bradley is that the distribution of the decorated styles approximates to the regional groupings of causewayed enclosure (1984, 34). There is of course the question of what do such style groups mean in terms of socio-political geography or social territories. However, the regional groupings of enclosures as originally defined by Palmer (1976) can be questioned and perhaps broken down into groups

that are much smaller than the distribution of the decorated ceramic styles. Interestingly some of the enclosure groups are then located at the boundaries of style distributions (e.g. Staines), while others are located well within the style zones (e.g. Abingdon and Orsett). It is perhaps more apparent that Whittle's style zones have overlapping distributions. Thus the discovery of a large assemblage that could be described as belonging to either the Eastern or Grimston style at Dorney, Bucks is well outside the usual geographical zone (Barclay in prep.). As Herne suggests it is possible to identify Carinated Bowl assemblages across all of Britain and the same is true of Plain Bowl (1988). Whilst it is also possible to detect a change in dominant forms (e.g. the number of Carinated Bowl forms seems to decrease over time, while ledge-shouldered and uncarinated bowls become more common).

Part of the problem is that the assemblages could belong to different chronological phases or horizons. Whilst the decorated styles might have had geographically restricted distributions this appears not to be the case with the so-called Grimston or Eastern style. Herne's review of Grimston Ware reinforces this point (1988). His approach was to identify a common characteristic of Early Neolithic assemblages, in this case the so-called Carinated Bowl, and use this as an indicator of a primary date. If we return to Piggott's seminal work on Early Neolithic pottery we can see that he identified a number of vessel shapes (1931). Herne's work is based on just one of these basic forms. Cleal in her more recent article went on to identify a number of basic pot shapes that could then be used to classify Early Neolithic assemblages (1992). Cleal's scheme does suggest a way forward for the classification of Early Neolithic ceramics, and as she points out, instead of assigning assemblages to styles more work should be undertaken to characterise different vessel types (1992). Many forms are common to both plain and decorated assemblages with the notable exception of Carinated Bowls.

Abingdon Enclosure: Assemblage Characterisation

The assemblage from the Abingdon causewayed enclosure includes a large number of plain vessels (approximately 75%) and of the remainder only a small proportion have elaborate decoration (i.e. on both the rim and shoulder zones or on the neck zone as well). At the Abingdon site it was noted that a very high proportion (95%) had shell filler in the fabric and a considerable proportion of vessels (20–25%) have handles. The assemblage from Abingdon includes a wide range of vessel types that include cups, bowls and jars (Avery 1982, 29: figs 14.11; 14.8–10, 15.12–6; 16.28, respectively). However, it is the bowls that appear to have been singled out for special treatment. These tend to be heavy rimmed and sometimes weakly and high shouldered.

For the purpose of this analysis the bowl component of the assemblage is divided into three categories: 1) plain bowls, 2) bowls with minimal decoration (usually on the rim), and 3), elaborately decorated bowls (with decoration occurring on both rim and shoulder and also extending over the upper body surface). Although this analysis singles out decoration other traits such as fabric, colour, shape and burnish, were perhaps of equal importance in signifying vessel categories.

Category 1 bowls are very common at the Abingdon causewayed enclosure. It can also be noted that the majority of cup and jar forms are also plain. Category 2 bowls with minimal decoration are more frequent than elaborately decorated vessels. Obviously where only rim or shoulder fragments are present they could belong to either category 2 or 3, and for this reason it is noted that the number of elaborately decorated vessels is perhaps under-represented. This is perhaps only a problem where large assemblages occur. Category 3 with profuse decoration are characterised on the whole by heavy rimmed shouldered bowls, sometimes with handles, where the decoration covers either the rim and shoulder zones or more extensively the top half of the vessel. In the Upper Thames this type of vessel has so far only been recovered from the Abingdon causewayed enclosure.

The type of decoration found on these bowls can be divided simply into incised and impressed (see Avery 1982, 29). Incised decoration takes the form of simple lines usually on the rim. Impressed decoration is created by a variety of techniques that include finger-nail, stick/point, bone, reed and twisted cord. The occurrence of these on different parts of the vessels is summarised in Table 9.1. Several patterns can be noted. Incised decoration on rims is very common and accounts for 62% of all the decorated examples. In comparison incised decoration is less common on necks or shoulders and is never found on the lower body. Oblique twisted cord is only ever found on rims, while certain types of impressed decoration are more common on shoulders than rims.

The distribution of Early Neolithic Pottery in the Upper Thames Valley

Early Neolithic pottery is found on a variety of sites both on the Upper Thames gravels and on the more upland areas of the chalk downs to the south and the limestone hills of the Cotswolds to the north. The distribution of pottery is given in Figure 9.1a.

If we start by looking at Carinated Bowl assemblages (or what can be considered as Early Plain Bowl) then what is noticeable is that very little of this pottery occurs on the low-lying gravel terraces (Fig. 9.1a). In fact most of this pottery has been found in the more upland areas of the Cotswolds and there is similar albeit slight evidence from the Berkshire Downs (e.g. the Lambourn long barrow) (Herne 1988). It has so far only been found at one site on the upper Thames gravels (Corporation Farm, Abingdon) (Shand *et al.* forthcoming). In many cases it is associated with artefact spreads or middens that in some cases directly pre-date monuments (e.g. Hazleton North and Ascott-under-Wychwood). These assemblages only ever contain plain pottery and it is arguable that decorated pottery is a later development perhaps appearing some 100 or 200 years later alongside the construction and use of causewayed enclosures.

Developed Plain Bowl assemblages have a more widespread distribution and occur in both the upland and lowland areas (Fig. 9.1a). Like assemblages containing Carinated Bowl they are found in association with spreads or middens and more rarely in pits. On the gravels finds of this type of pottery occur often only in small quantities. The spreads of ceramic material are usually found with flint and the suggestion is that they represent domestic debris perhaps from short stay camps or temporary occupation. In the Upper Thames Valley there is little evidence for contemporary pit-digging, so deliberate burial of material for whatever purpose is seldom recorded. Minimally decorated vessels (Category 2) are also recorded from sites on the gravels. Very little of this pottery has been found in the Cotswolds and only isolated examples of minimally decorated sherds or vessels have been found on sites located on the Upper Thames gravel terraces, where the dominant associ-

Table 9.1. The types of decoration found on the assemblage from Abingdon (after Avery 1982).

Body part	Incised lines	Twisted cord	Stamp	Stick	Reed	Bone	Finger-nail	Fluting	Total
Rim	88	23	5	6	4	4	1	10	141
Neck	5		1	3	1	3	1	5	19
Shoulder	8			18	4	4	1		35
Lower body								1	1
Total	101	23	6	27	9	11	3	16	196

ation is with burials or mortuary enclosures (e.g. a flat grave at Pangbourne, the mortuary enclosures at Radley and New Wintles Farm (Piggott 1928; Bradley 1992; Kenward 1982)). Other examples have been found from pit deposits at Yarnton and Steeple Aston (Barclay in prep a; Barclay in prep b). One site of particular interest is the long cairn at Hazleton North (Saville 1990). This monument was built on a midden deposit that was associated with an assemblage of Carinated Bowls, yet none of this pottery was deposited once the long cairn was constructed and in use. In fact very little pottery was found, although two notable deposits occur. One is a plain cup that was placed near the entrance to a chamber, while the other was a rim from a minimally decorated bowl that was found associated with a hearth in one of the long cairn's flanking ditches. While the cup from the chamber was complete, only the rim from the decorated bowl was deposited around the hearth. We can suggest that the cup might have held drink or food that was placed as an offering, while the decorated rim fragments must have been deliberately placed as a token deposit within the hearth. At Ascott-under-Wychwood a similar deposit occurs (detail from unpublished archive). Again a long cairn was built on top of a midden that contained Carinated Bowl, yet once the tomb was built and in use this type of pottery was never deposited. Yet placed against the outer edge of one of the burial cists was approximately half of a Plain Bowl. This vessel had at some stage been repaired. Its life prolonged it had been curated and it was only perhaps when it eventually split in two that half of the vessel was selected for deposition.

It can be suggested then that both plain and minimally decorated vessels could have been in everyday use and that certain parts of these vessels were selected for burial at mortuary sites as token deposits, not as grave goods but perhaps as offerings to the ancestral dead. One further point concerns decoration. Abingdon Ware is decorated in two ways either linear incised or impressed (finger-nail, cord, stick/point, bone or reed). So far the only minimally decorated vessels found outside causewayed enclosures are those that have linear incised rims and it is these vessels that are found at mortuary sites.

Finally the distribution of more elaborately decorated vessels is restricted to the Abingdon causewayed enclosure. To date not a single example of a Category 3 bowl has been found on any other type of site, either on the gravels or the upland areas of the downs and Cotswolds. The suggestion then is that more highly decorated vessels were seldom used away from enclosures or rather their use was strongly bound up with the social activities undertaken at enclosures that were perhaps more to do with the living than the dead. It is interesting to note that all three categories of bowl occur at Abingdon. Vessels of similar form can be either plain, minimally decorated or be elaborately decorated. This would suggest that decoration could have been used to mark out social boundaries such as age or gender. A more complex argument could look in more detail at the ways these vessels are decorated and further analysis could look at association with other types of artefact that might have gender associations, such as leaf-shaped arrowheads, axes or bone combs. If decoration was used to reinforce social categories then it is not surprising that decorated pottery is largely absent from mortuary deposits. Our understanding of contemporary tombs is that while multiple burial tended to mask individuality bones were often re-arranged by age and gender (Edmonds 1993, 114).

The patterns found in one area of the Upper Thames Valley can also be identified elsewhere. Julian Thomas also makes a similar point for the Avebury area (1991a, 165). Again highly decorated pottery is only found at enclosures, while both Plain and Carinated Bowl and minimally decorated vessels are found from a variety of contexts in the surrounding area (Fig. 9.1b). In the middle Thames Valley a similar pattern is found, although some sites such as the open site at Runnymede Bridge do not appear to fit the explanation. There could be two suggestions why. One is chronological development in that part of the site at Runnymede Bridge could be quite late in the Early Neolithic sequence and at a time when enclosures were beginning to go out of use. The second is a question of regionality. Not all societies built monuments and there are areas of southern England were particular types of monument become rare or absent. The meaning of decorated pots in the Upper Thames may well have been tied to a particular set of circumstances that were simply not manifest in other parts of lowland England.

Mortlake Ware Bowls from the River Thames

This section reviews the evidence for Neolithic pots recovered from the River Thames. In this country recent research into river finds has mostly focused on stone axes or metalwork, although many of the ideas concerning these items are equally relevant to other categories of material culture (e.g. Early Bronze Age flint daggers, jet belt sliders and crown antler maceheads). The Thames is perhaps the best known river for finds, although other rivers in Britain and beyond have also produced Neolithic material (Bradley 1990a).

Peterborough Ware is perhaps the least under-

Abingdon area

Yarnton

River Thames

Abingdon

Goring

N

Enclosure
Plain bowl
Decorated bowl
Carinated bowl
Highly decorated bowl

0   5   10 km

a.

Avebury area

Windmill Hill

N

River Kennet

Enclosure
Plain bowl
Decorated bowl
Carinated bowl
Highly decorated bowl

Rybury

Knap Hill

0   1   2 km

b.

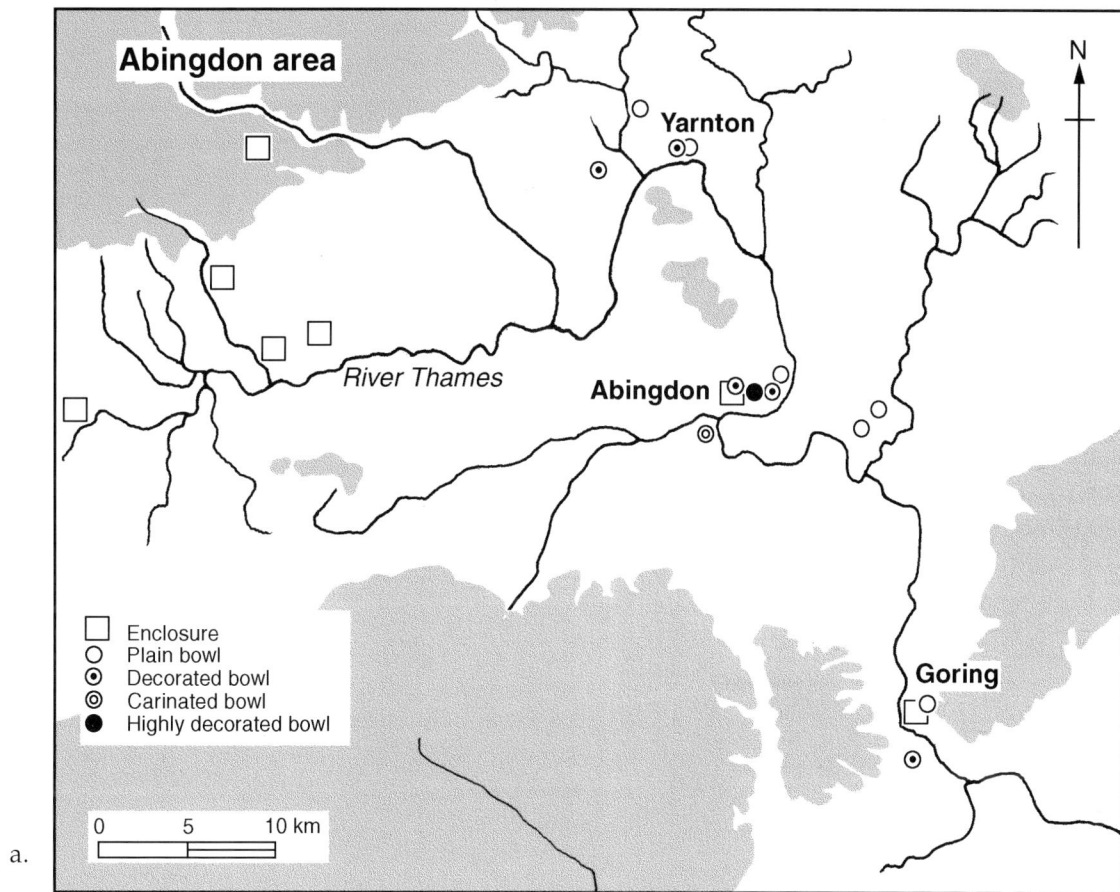

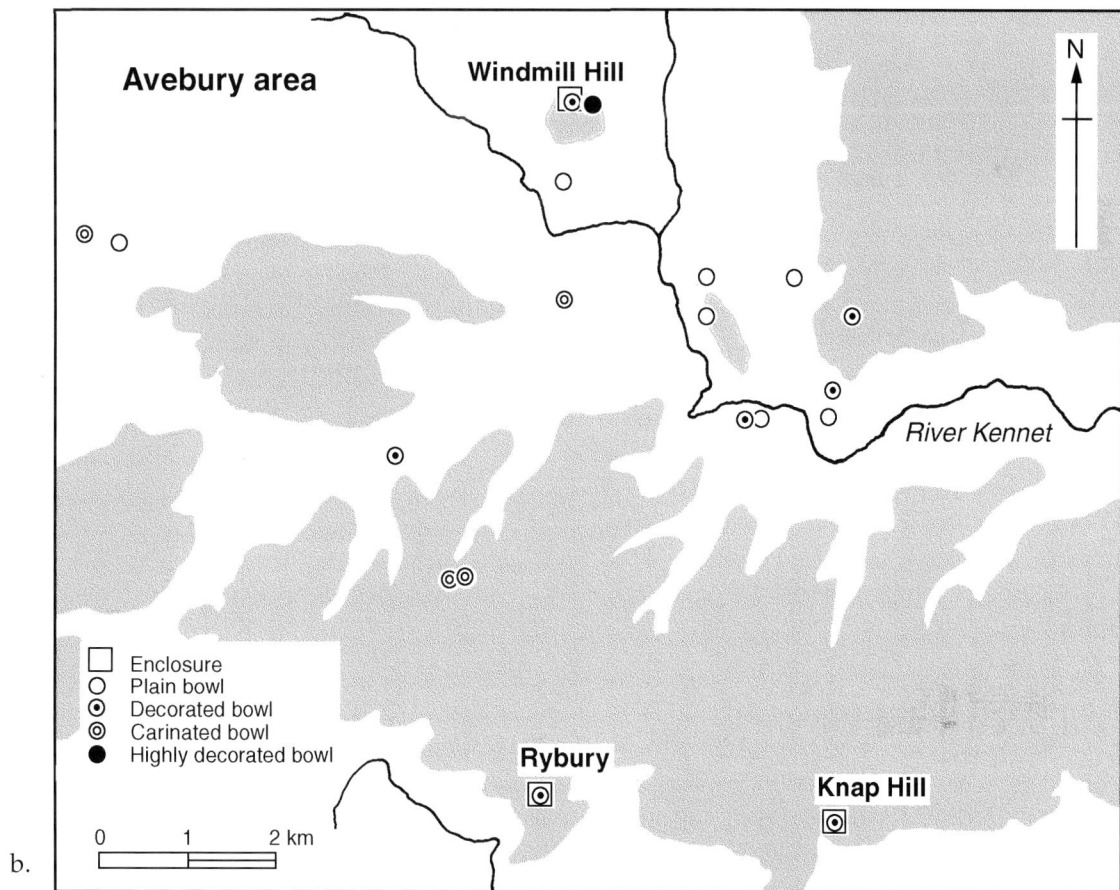

Fig. 9.1. Above, distribution of earlier Neolithic pottery in the eastern part of the Upper Thames Valley and, below, around Avebury (after Thomas 1991a).

stood of the later Neolithic pottery styles and unlike Grooved Ware or Beakers there has been no serious attempt at typological analysis. This is exemplified by the fact that its chronologically development has recently been drastically reviewed (see Gibson and Kinnes 1998). However, this is presently far from resolved and its actual typological development and relationship to other styles remains obscure. What we do know is that the Fengate and Mortlake substyles are much earlier than previously thought, while we are less sure when the Peterborough Ware tradition started and at what point it came to an end. There is clearly a relationship with earlier bowl forms and the suggestion of an overlap with Grooved Ware and less certainly if at all with Beaker (Barclay 1999b). There is increasing evidence that the Peterborough Ware tradition belongs to a middle phase of the Neolithic period. An estimated range for its use would be 3500–2800 cal BC. The typological sequence outlined by Smith can perhaps be condensed into just two phases (1974). An early phase in which so-called 'early Ebbsfleet' appeared, perhaps alongside other forms of Decorated Bowl (*c*.3500–3300 BC) and a second phase (*c*.3300–2800 BC) during which the Mortlake and Fengate styles developed. It is argued elsewhere that in the Thames Valley the use of Grooved Ware but not Beaker overlapped with Peterborough Ware (Barclay 1999b).

Unlike other types of pottery Peterborough Ware has never been defined in terms of vessel forms. Like earlier Neolithic assemblages Peterborough Ware can occur in a variety of forms, although the shouldered bowl is perhaps the dominant form. Such assemblages include a variety of vessel forms and although bowls are most numerous other types such as jars, dishes and cups also occur (Barclay in prep c). The size range is similar to that of earlier Neolithic pottery with rim diameters ranging from 50–400 mm. Of the three defined substyles (Ebbsfleet, Mortlake and Fengate) more variation is perhaps found within Mortlake Ware assemblages. Variety of forms also occurs with Fengate but rarely with Ebbsfleet.

In the Thames Valley Peterborough Ware is found in a variety of contexts which includes pits, surface spreads or middens, monument ditches (cursus, mortuary enclosures, ring ditches and causewayed enclosures), burial chambers and watery deposits. Ebbsfleet Ware can be found in very similar contexts to Early Neolithic Bowl, while it is very rarely found in pits. Like some Early Neolithic pottery it can be found at open sites as surface material or in middens. In contrast both Fengate and Mortlake Wares are more commonly found in pits. Vessels of all three substyles have been found in the River Thames while smaller numbers of Early Neolithic,

Beaker and other Bronze Age vessels have also been recorded.

Peterborough Ware from the River Thames

Holgate lists 25 Neolithic pots from the Thames, to which at least 11 Beakers can be added (1988, 283; Clarke 1970; Cotton and Wood 1996, 12 & fig.8). Up to 21 Peterborough Ware vessels are recorded as coming from the River Thames and whilst at least some of these may derive from the erosion of bankside settlements most appear to be votive deposits. A number of Peterborough Ware sites have been located near to present day river courses and some occur in or near silted up palaeochannels (e.g. Drayton, Oxon and Ebbsfleet, Kent). Analysis of the Peterborough Ware from the River Thames indicates that while all three substyles are represented, Mortlake Ware vessels are more prevalent (Fig. 9.2, upper). The distribution of these vessels is again concentrated in the middle Thames Valley, with notable outliers at Crowmarsh (Wallingford), Oxon, Hedsor, Bucks and Weybridge, Surrey. The remaining vessels are all from Greater London. Some like Crowmarsh represent multiple find spots. Interestingly the site at Crowmarsh has also produced stone axes and finds of Neolithic material have been recorded on the adjacent east side of the river. While the concentration of pots from Greater London corresponds with concentrations of other artefacts such as axes and maceheads.

Many of the vessels recovered from the Thames can be described as large bowls or jars. Some of these bowls are very large and fall towards the top end of the size range for Peterborough Ware vessels. As such their production would have required a greater expenditure of both labour and materials. Successful firing could have been more hazardous and the risk of breakage through movement and use could have been greater. Because of their size some of these pots may have had a more prestigious role as either communal cooking or storage pots. Their movement when empty either within or between settlements may have required the careful effort of one or more people. It is interesting to note that few vessels of this size come from pit deposits and their possible heightened importance could have demanded special treatment upon deposition. Outside the Thames Valley it can be noted that very large vessels have sometimes been deposited in the ditches of funerary monuments, such as the flanking ditches of some long barrows (e.g. Badshot, Surrey – Keiller and Piggott 1939) and from the blocking of a number of Cotswold-Severn tombs.

Peterborough Ware assemblages include a variety of vessel shapes although these are dominated by bowl forms (Barclay in prep. c) (e.g. assemblages

Vessels from the river Thames

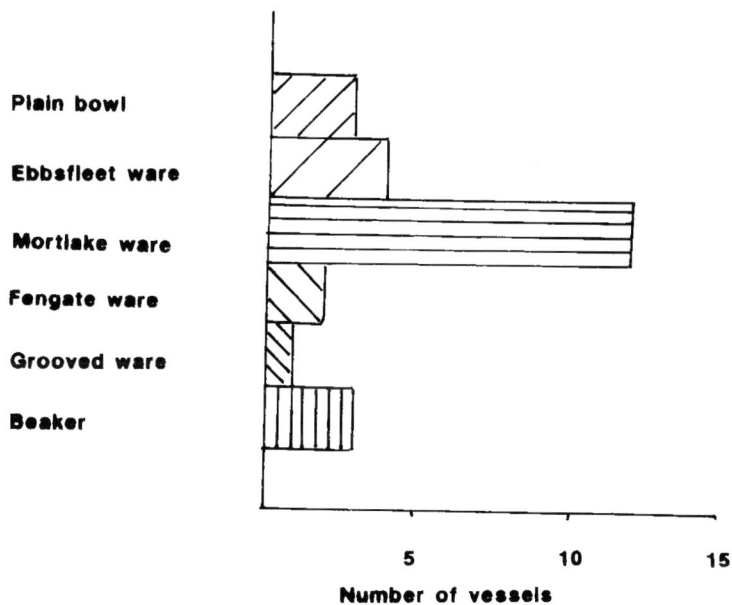

Peterborough ware from the Thames valley

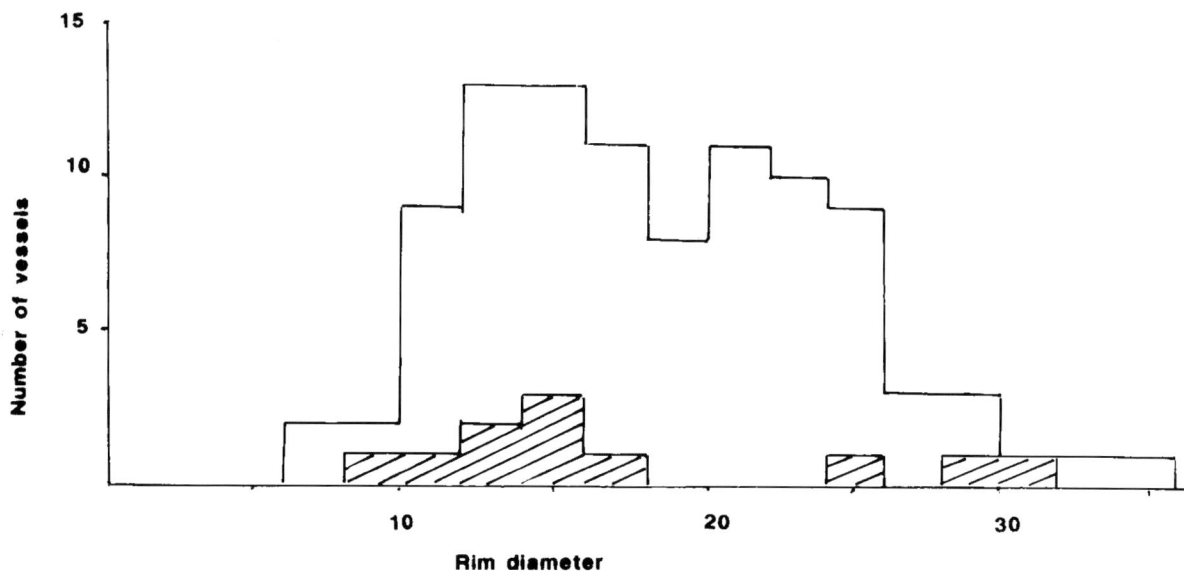

Fig. 9.2. Above, vessels from the river Thames and below, Peterborough Ware: rim diameters of vessels (shaded = vessels from the river).

from West Kennet, Wilts, Ecton, Northants and Heathrow, Middlesex: Piggott 1962; Williams and Moore 1975; Grimes 1960). Thomas has noted the types of context where Peterborough Ware is fre-

quently found (1991a, fig 5.9). Paradoxically one of the largest known Peterborough Ware assemblage is from the infilled chambers of the West Kennet long barrow (Piggott 1962). However, on the whole most assemblages are recovered as surface material (remnants of middens) or from pit deposits. Peterborough Ware from burials is very rare and the few known vessel forms are quite heterogeneous (e.g. the Liff's Low flask – Bateman 1948; Clarke *et al.* 1985, pl. 3.34). With the Liff's Low flask was found a crown antler macehead decorated with a cut lozenge pattern that recalls other portable objects with passage grave art affinities. Incised lattice patterns are common on Peterborough Ware vessels often applied around the rim zone of vessels. The association between these two objects at Liff's Low is important. There is also a connection between the antler crown maceheads and a series of stone maceheads, termed Maesmore, that also carry similar lattice motifs (Roe 1968, 161). Examples of both have been recovered from the river Thames. In fact of the 58 known crown antler maceheads some 41 come from the River Thames (Simpson 1996, 295), while three other examples come from rivers in Norfolk and Nottinghamshire. The most famous of these is the Garboldisham macehead with its incised double spiral (Clarke *et al.* 1985, 255).

The incised lattice and facetted lattice decoration found on a few maceheads can be found on some types of later Neolithic pottery. Incised lattice is found on all three styles of Peterborough Ware, where it is often used to elaborate the rim margin. At Yarnton a pit placed near to the entrance to a long enclosure contained part of a macehead, Fengate Ware sherds with lattice decoration and cremated human bone (Gill Hey *pers comm.*). This deposit recalls the Dorchester-type cremation deposits. A second pit also contained lattice decorated sherds together with a flint macehead fragment. One thing we can look at is vessel selection for deliberate deposition and my example concerns vessels recovered from the River Thames. There are various Neolithic pots from the river, some of which may derive from the erosion of riverside settlements although most can be considered to be votive deposits, and although Mortlake Ware vessels are more frequent the other Peterborough Ware substyles are also represented. A comparison of rim diameters between these vessels and all Peterborough Ware bowls from the Thames Valley reveals a preference for the deposition of both large and small vessels (Fig. 9.2, lower; shaded vessels from Thames). This distinction is more apparent if we consider the actual vessels and it can be argued that their deposition involved some degree of deliberate selection. It could be suggested that the size range represents individual and communal pots and it is interesting to note that the few pots from secure burial deposits are also quite small.

From Mongewell, just south of Wallingford, a substantial Mortlake Ware bowl and two small cup-

sized bowls were dredged from the riverbed (Smith 1924, 127–8 & pl. 26 no 1). Two small cups were recovered from the river from Greater London (Curle 1924, 150 & pl. 28 no 1–2). One is said to have been found in the Thames at Mortlake, while the second is suppose to have been found at the site of a 'pile-dwelling' in the Thames at Putney. There is the suggestion that some of these vessels were perhaps placed at the river edge. If the wooden piles were indeed contemporary then maybe 'offerings' were placed against such structures. Some of these finds could of course simply represent casual loss. But some rivers, especially the Thames, might have held ritual significance as natural features of the landscape. Mortlake Ware bowls are just one type of river find, while they argue that certain monuments and monument complexes were deliberately sited near to rivers.

Most of the vessels belong to the Mortlake style. The small cups are rare finds and it is unusual that two similar cups should be recovered from two places along the Thames. A Fengate Ware bowl from the Thames at Wandsworth, from near Hammersmith Bridge, in form is very like other vessels of this style, however, the body decoration of concentric lines is very unusual and this feature could have set it apart from other vessels. This vessel like the cups described above and other Ebbsfleet and Mortlake bowls are all relatively rather small in size (with internal diameters up to 150 mm). From their size it is possible to suggest that many functioned as the vessels of individuals. Of the remaining vessels that are illustrated in the literature all fall towards the top of the size range for Peterborough Ware bowls. Two massive Mortlake Ware bowls have internal diameters of 270 mm and 300 mm, while the large vessel from Mongewell has a diameter of almost 300 mm. Unlike the small bowls their usage could have been communal. What is so far missing from the Thames is the range of medium sized bowls with diameters between 150–270 mm. It can be noted that vessels with diameters within this range are quite common and have been found on occupation sites from spreads, middens and pits.

Most of the Peterborough Ware vessels recovered from the river are from the middle Thames, an area which has produced other votive deposits including antler and stone maceheads and possibly some contemporary human bone (Bradley and Gordon 1988; Simpson 1996). In parts of northern England contextual association (i.e. as grave goods accompanying burials) links some of these artefacts.

Along the Thames Valley there is a contrast between an area of Neolithic knife burials in the Oxford area of the Upper Thames and an area of votive deposits in the middle Thames. The burials have quite restricted grave assemblages in which

Peterborough Ware vessels are excluded unlike some of their more northern counterparts (Kinnes 1979). In the middle Thames Valley many of the artefact types found in burials elsewhere in the country are recovered as votive deposits from the river. These two areas stand to represent quite different practices both of which can be linked by the Mortlake Ware associated grave group from Liff's Low, Newbiggin, Derbyshire.

Cremains of the Clay: Refired Pottery and Ritual

The refiring of pottery in prehistory is one particular process that seldom attracts comment in the archaeological literature. Some Food Vessels, Collared Urns and accessory vessels along with a range of other artefacts, for example flint and bronzework, appear to have been burnt on cremation pyres in the earlier Bronze Age. Some vessels were no doubt completely destroyed during this process, whilst others either whole or fragmentary were retrieved and buried with or without cremated bone. Considerable work on cremated bone or what are today called cremains (Barley 1995, 39) and the understanding of the cremation process has been undertaken in recent years (McKinley 1994a-b; Boyle 1999). However, in contrast very little work has been undertaken on the associated artefacts. This practice of placing objects on the pyre has its beginning in the Neolithic as potential pyre goods have also been recognised at Dorchester-on-Thames (Atkinson *et al.* 1951).

It is a matter of fact that pots are frequently seen as classifiable types rather than functional tools or containers. To date perhaps too little attention has been given to food residue and use-wear studies. Needless to say there is more to pottery studies than typo-chronology. Pots like other objects were created, used, damaged and discarded. Some were repaired and curated, whilst others may have been deliberately broken. During its life a pottery vessel could have had a variety of functions and use may have varied according to social context. This study looks at Early Bronze Age vessels from the Upper Thames region, which were largely recovered from ritual funerary contexts. At present we know very little about contemporary domestic sites, which remain archaeologically elusive. In the absence of tangible domestic evidence we make the assumption that vessels used in funerary rituals were selected from a wider domestic assemblage. This section of the paper will attempt to identify some patterns of selectivity, such as the choice of vessel, and in so doing will try to demonstrate greater variability in the funerary record.

In undertaking this study I have so far found two clear examples of distorted pots. The first example is a late style Food Vessel (Fig. 9.3a:A) from a secondary cremation deposit within a Bronze Age barrow at Merton (Barclay 1997, 70). This vessel was found in a pit with charcoal and only a token deposit (approximately 5gms) of cremated bone (Bradley *et al.* 1997, 56). Another example is from a pit at Overton Down (Ashmolean Museum Collection). It is a Biconical type urn and again it is grey and distorted and was found in a pit with charcoal.

These vessels are grey in colour, are relatively hard fired and their surfaces have a rough and broken texture. They have the same appearance as warped vessels that have melted due to being fired at a temperature sufficiently high to cause vitrification (Rye 1981, 108). Vitrification can begin at 700°C and becomes extensive at over 900°C. Owen Rye has illustrated the damage caused to modern pots by accidentally overfiring (1981, fig. 94, 96–7). I would like to suggest that some Bronze Age pottery was in fact refired and overfired during the cremation process, most probably on the funerary pyre. Some pots might have been intentionally fired on a pyre, while others could have been refired. McKinley notes that to cremate a person you only need a minimum temperature of 400°C, although it is possible that temperatures as high as 1200°C were reached (1994a, 84). In comparison flint will begin to crack or calcine at 400°C and bronze will melt at between 800–1000°C. The temperature needed to fire Bronze Age pottery would be in the range of 650–900°C, which would be more than adequate to cremate a corpse. If serious distortion only occurs at around 900°C then this could explain why most pots only undergo a superficial change of surface colour. The distorted vessels are obvious examples of pyre goods, although others may have gone unnoticed in the literature. Ian Longworth's corpus on Collared Urns illustrates at least one clear example from Melbourn (1984, pl. 178h. 92) (Fig. 9.3a:B). This vessel contained only charcoal and is believed to have come from a secondary deposit within a barrow. Longworth provides no further comment on the transformed state of this or any other vessel in the corpus.

Other vessels such as an accessory vessel from a Wessex Culture grave at Stanton Harcourt show signs of spalling (Case *et al.* 1964/5, 25 and fig. 9:1). It is reported that the spall was found inside the pot where it had broken away from the surface and the fabric of this vessel is hard and grey in colour. Examination of this vessel by the author indicated that it had indeed been refired to a very high temperature. This vessel was recovered from within a deposit of cremated bone, along with a bone pin and a flint tool that had also been burnt. The cremation deposits found beneath this barrow are of great interest as they reveal

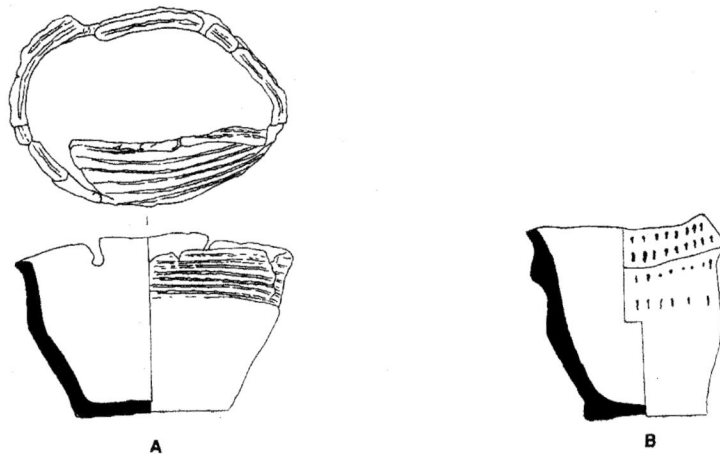

Fig. 9.3a. Distorted vessels from Merton, Oxon and Melbourn, Cambs (after Bradley et al. 1997; Longworth 1984).

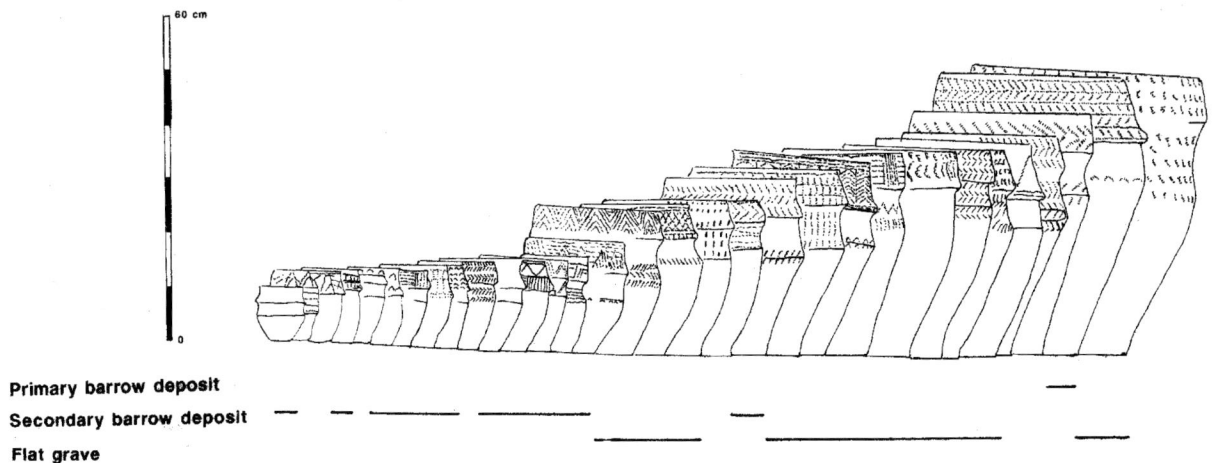

Fig 9.3b. The size range and contexts for Collared Urns and related vessels from the Upper Thames region.

much of the funerary process that has been described by Barrett (1988). Abercromby described a distorted Aldbourne Cup from Durrington Down, Wilts as a 'vessel of pale bad colour, burnt and cracked by fire' (1912, 26). Other vessels that appear as plates in his catalogue also look distorted, damaged and/or overfired (e.g. 249, 288, 291 and 299).

Other vessels such as a Collared Urn from Northampton had suffered only superficial damage to its surface, whilst another vessel from this county had been refired to the same white colour as oxidised cremated bone (Ashmolean Museum Collection). Here it is relevant to note Longworth's observation that most urns are oxidised to either a reddish or yellowish brown (1984, 4). Although surface colour may have been a difficult property to control in open firings, we know from the highly oxidised finished appearance of certain pots that this

could be achieved. There is of course also the methodological problem that most pots are depicted in the contemporary literature as line drawings rather than as photographic images. Further, profiles are reconstructed and pots are often shown as complete, while texture is not always evident. A photographic record perhaps provides a better opportunity to assess differences in firing, distortion and texture. A book like *Symbols of Power* provides over 30 colour images of Early Bronze Age pots (Clarke *et al.*1985). Many of these pots have reddish-brown or yellowish-brown surfaces but others are blackened or greyish-white. Perhaps the more extreme examples are the Food Vessel from Kinneff, Kincardineshire and two accessory cups from near Dunbar, East Lothian and North or South Ronaldsay, Orkney (Clarke *et al.* 1985, pl. 4.89, 5.38).

The examination of typologically similar forms of

pot from the Upper Thames can be used to demonstrate the transformation of colour during the cremation process. The best example is a pair of pots, one from Yarnton and the other from Merton which are typologically very similar (Barclay 1997, fig. 11.1; Case 1956b, fig. 4). The outer surface of the Yarnton pot is a reddish-brown, while the Merton pot is grey. At Radley, the excavation of Barrow 16 produced two refired pots, a miniature Food Vessel and a small Collared Urn (Barclay 1999a, 318). Neither pot was directly associated with cremated bone, but the Food Vessel came from a pit that contained charcoal. It is likely that both were pyre goods that were separated out from the rest of the cremation deposit and buried. I would like to suggest that where pots appear grey or whitish grey there is the possibility that they have been refired in cremation pyres.

The smallest of these pots would have been too small to contain a complete cremation and like other objects may have served as pyre goods. The work of Jacqui McKinley indicates that there is a need to differentiate pyre goods from grave goods as grave assemblages can contain a combination of the two (1994b, 133). Like a deposit from Llanddyfnan, Anglesey that contained burnt and unburnt metalwork (Clarke *et al.* 1985, 291-2 and pl. 4.85). Here it is assumed that the axe was burnt on the body, while the dagger and chisel were pressed into the cremated remains and capped by an unburnt Food Vessel. Another deposit from Bedd Emlyn, Denbigh involved an inverted urn placed over cremated bone that contained 11 calcined flint tools (arrowheads and a flint knife) (pl. 4.86). With the latter example we can question whether the pot which is greyish black and was found in an incomplete state was also a pyre good.

Collared Urns were manufactured in a range of sizes from 10 cm to over 50 cm in height. However, there is a correlation between vessel size and contexts (Fig. 9.3b). Most but not all of the vessels below 20 cm in height occur as secondary deposits within barrows. Vessels in excess of 20 cm predominantly occur in flat graves or pits either away from or adjacent to barrow cemeteries. Exceptionally Collared Urns occur with primary barrow deposits.

At Radley, City Farm, Hanborough and Stanton Harcourt large vessels occur outside barrows, while small vessels occur as secondary deposits at Radley, Merton and City Farm (Barclay 1999; Bradley *et al.* 1997; Case *et al.* 1964/5). These pots and their associated deposits represent different stages in the cremation process. The larger vessels seem to have been used as containers to transport the residues of the cremation to the place of burial. Smaller vessels,

where they are refired, form part of the cremation residue itself having been placed with the corpse on the pyre.

What I have tried to demonstrate is that there existed an element of choice in the selection of Early Bronze Age vessels and that this can be detected by examining the funerary record. Not all vessels were urns or containers as some were pyre goods, whilst others were grave goods. The differences, both apparent in these deposits and in the appearance of these refired vessels enable us to further understand the cremation process. Refired or overfired sherds have also been found in assemblages of Neolithic and Iron Age date. Occasionally they have been found on sites of Late Bronze Age and Early Iron Age date. At the late Bronze Age site at Whitecross Farm, Wallingford refired sherds came from a deposit that also contained burnt timbers that might have come from a demolished structure (Cromarty *et al.* forthcoming). At Kirtlington, Oxon part of a fine bowl which had signs of warping and sooting and is of transitional Late Bronze Age/Early Iron Age date was recovered as the only find from a pit (Harding 1966, 157 & fig 14.A). There are other deposits of this date recorded from Standlake and from New Wintles Farm, Eynsham (Harding 1972, 81–2). In both cases inverted bowls capped deposits that included refired or overfired sherds.

Finally, I would like to suggest that in the Late Bronze Age and Early Iron Age pottery vessels may have undergone similar transformations that is deliberately damaged by fire. Although this need not be taken to suggest a cremation pyre, the pots as objects could have been killed off along with other objects or possessions. Thus pots were both given life and killed by fire.

In future we should try and not be too dogmatic in our approach to ceramic analysis as use and context, rather than typology, is often the key to understanding the social life of pots and people. Just as much attention needs to be paid to signs of use, traces of residues and to damage, alteration and completeness.

Acknowledgements
I would like to thank Angela Boyle, Pippa Bradley, Richard Bradley, J.D. Hill and Ann Woodward for their advice and comments on various sections of this text. I am also grateful for the comments of the two readers of this paper and to the staff at the Ashmolean Museum for access to the collection. Separate sections of this paper have been presented to the Neolithic Studies Group and at the 1995 TAG conference.

10   Pots as Categories: British Beakers

Robin Boast

British Beakers have been intensely studied for over 120 years in an attempt to classify their enormous variety. So far, all attempts have failed in one way or another. This paper argues that the problem is not so much with the Beakers themselves, nor with, as is the usual alibi, the 'lack of data', but with the classifications that Beakers are meant to embody and what we expect pots to 'mean'.

Within archaeology, pottery is still largely seen as a cultural-historical marker. Rarely, if ever, do we use pottery as a point of discussion for understanding social praxis, other objects are seen as far more appropriate. Monuments and metals are far more acceptable records of the social than mere pots. Pots are certainly seen as objects embedded in social practice – especially in their role in burial, but, ultimately, pots are for dating. But why are pots just for dating? There is no doubt that we recognise the importance of certain pots as signifiers of social position and status, and though we clearly recognise the status of the object in many social roles, we remain enamoured with the various details of the pot only to the degree that it can aid in its classification. Form, decoration and fabric are means to an end – the end being the dating of the pot, or better the pot's depositional context.

As the anthropologist Nigel Barley notes:

'... while we have a primordial Stone Age, and revolutionary Iron and Bronze Ages, there is no glamorous Pottery Age. Instead, we have whole ethnicities named after the shape of their pots and Beaker People still confidently stalk the pages of European prehistory. From the almost infinite possibilities offered by clay, each culture has opted to develop only a few and so pottery becomes the embodiment of style and the key to studies of diffusion. The presumption of the inward-looking domesticity of pots is written – in advance – into the archaeological maps so that metals are cast in a techno-innovative role while pots are conservative and passive bearers of culture.'

(Barley 1995, 9,17)

Nigel Barley's comments are a perceptive summary of the vast amount of archaeological work that has been generated about classification and style in regard to this apparently 'conservative and passive bearer of culture'. The endless studies attempting to resolve the way in which pottery bears this obligation have become less stages in an analytic process than statements of common knowledge. This 'common sensical' view of pottery is summed up in one of the first paragraphs of David Clarke's *The Beaker Pottery of Great Britain and Ireland*:

'Beaker decoration is surprisingly conservative in its execution, disposition and content, showing a traditional approach of the kind one might expect from a non-specialist, peasant craft, probably passed from mother to daughter from generation to generation. In this way, a continuity is achieved not only within families but also within social groups linked by inter-marriage and the common communications which define those networked groups; a continuity further accentuated by external isolation, by topography, ecology and poor transport. Pottery making, especially amongst primitive peoples, is usually a periodic group activity of the womenfolk. . . . In this sort of production, conscious experiment is rare, the unconscious model is usually the vessel made for the purpose on the last occasion, varied only slightly by stochastic accident or whim, rather than by deliberate experiment. However, since no artisan produces exactly identical results from a given set of repeated actions, inevitable variation in pot and decoration will occur, within traditional limits. By exercising human choice and repeating the most pleasing satisfactory and fashionable results, the tradition does not become static but develops distinct trends amongst interlinked societies.'

(Clarke 1970, 9)

This image of pottery as a normative media reflecting continuity, tradition, group identity and fashion, and always associated with women, is contrasted with specialist, innovative, dynamic and individualistic media, such as metals or stone, which is always associated with men. This has lead to the emphasis in pottery analysis, if there was ever any other focus, on the defining of ceramic stylistic traditions. Whether these 'traditions' are called types, variants, styles or schools, they all point to the desire to categorise the pot as the passive reflection of cultural norms, as a coherent cultural statement. The outcome of a set of conventionalised, usually domestic, practices – conventionalised in their ultimate goal of standing for social groups.

There is no doubt that pots, as well as all other forms of material culture, are actively used in the construction of social identity, in one form or another. However, pottery analysis tends to assume that this demarcation is simply reflected in the pot itself, as though the object constituted a simple signifier, complete and self contained within its relationship to the social group that it signified, a fashion accessory that signifies tradition through its reference to the pots of the foremothers.

The various attributes of pots are treated as simply a conventionalised sign system that are used to represent specific social relationships or groups. It has been seen to be our role, that of the archaeologists, to simply identify the similarities and differences, to identify the culture that is being borne by the pot. However, much recent research has shown that we cannot assume that pots communicate identity quite so simply (Sterner 1989; Wiessner 1984, 1990). The decorative elements, the aspects of shape, the turn of the corners, the colour, the paste all constitute a grab bag of signifiers that seem to represent an identity through the recognition of similar choices. However, it is not clear that all features represent cultural choices. Many are features of functional necessity, or simply ways of making a pot (Hodder 1990). Certainly these attributes contribute to the look of a pot and, hence, to its identity, but there is a great deal of disagreement about what roles these different attributes fulfil (Hodder 1990; Shanks and Tilley 1987a, 92–96; Sackett 1985; Wiessner 1985). Whatever roles the various attributes fulfil, this argument simply attempts to refine the role of a pot as a passive bearer of culture. It is simply a refinement, a particularisation, of the earlier gross cultural attributions. The

pot remains a simplified system of signs that represent the pot's culture and the role of its owner.

This simplified system of signification is clearly expressed in what I call the hierarchy of ceramic classification. First, the ceramic world is divided by fabric – the coarsewares and finewares are distinguished, the burnished from the smooth, the shell gritted from the grog. Second, we look to the form – the large are distinguished from the small, the tall from the short, and the bowls from the jars. Last of all, we look to the decoration – we distinguish the incised from the applied, the panelled from the frieze, and, of course, there is the endless catalogue of motifs. Although we classify through this hierarchy, the outcome is always the same – a single representative, classified, named and labelled; an appropriate object that can stand for a style, tradition or even a people.

In the endless search for the key to what these objects represent, the pot as representative is taken for granted. We see the pot as a predefined thing in the world, as a thing out there that we can see is a pot first and then a 17cm tall buff red long-necked Beaker with opposing triangles on the neck, of Clarke's S2 style, from grave 4 at Ganton 21 round barrow, Yorkshire. The first is a pure it, a thing that exists conceptually in the world to do something without reference to any particular way of doing it. The second distinguishes the bits of the it that make it 'something made by us'. The functional pot, or should I say 'mundane' pot, is a passive domestic appliance onto which cultural identity is applied. This is essential if the object is to 'speak' to us down through the ages. It must have an essential representation of something cultural that can be distinguished through comparing similarities and differences. Therefore, the object of our study is in a state of constant flux as we continue to find exceptions and contradictions as we attempt to identify more and more attributes in the material world.

This normative response to the variation of material form runs deep within the disciplinary consciousness. It comes from our desire to distinguish boundaries and our long-standing assumption that the social role of objects are to distinguish an owner's place in society. Objects are seen as the billboards that advertise our gender, wealth, status and obligations. Further, for the archaeologist, they advertise a people's and a time's place in the scheme of things. Objects, through their conventionalised difference from other groups, are seen as representing the social boundaries which define convention, define similarity.

But the pot does not arise complete as a conventionalised object, with all its bits perfectly suited to a single social identity. Each aspect of the pot serves to express a variety of social, vocational and practical constraints and choices that vary not only from society to society, but from context to context and from pot to pot (Barley 1994, 159). It is not just a matter of who is making the pot and for what purpose, but also, for each stage of the productive process, what is the social and practical intent of that production and then how are these intentions, expressed materially, employed by users with their separate intentionalities (Baxandall 1985; Latour and Woolgar 1986).

Ceramic analysis often ignores this intentional variety in its goal to classify the object. We assume that public pots must be those that are better made and most highly decorated, even though much work has demonstrated that the opposite may very well be true (Sterner 1989). We still firmly adhere to the compilation of named motifs, fragmenting the pot's design into definable components, even though it has been shown that most indigenous potters do not view their designs as a collection of separate motifs (Torday and Joyce 1910, 216; Price 1989). Most of all, however, we still insist that the pot should be viewed as self-evident; a single signifier that embodies the characteristics of a social group and an age, rather than the specific responses of makers and users to a complex set of social conditions. We look at the pot as a member of a class, as a single pot defined only by its relation to other pots – as part of a field of similarities and differences expressed through a collective of pots whose only relationships may be their material, and perhaps the millennial time and regional place where they were made. The pot simply becomes a combination of functional and techno-logical necessity with the signifying convention of applied decoration.

These assumptions may be clearly seen in Euro-pean Beaker studies. Beakers have been one of the most studied forms of prehistoric ceramic in Western Europe for the last 120 years. As analytical traditions have grown, developed and died, so have the multitudinous interpretations of the Beaker pot and its associated peoples (Thurnham 1871; Abercromby 1912; Mitchell 1934; Piggott 1963; Clarke 1970, 1976; Case 1977; Boast 1990; Barrett 1994). But what has all this pottery analysis taught us? It is clear from the reading of these various studies that they each borrow little from their predecessors, each ap-proaching the pots from a different point of view and reanalysing and remeasuring the collections. Each study brings us not new insights, but a new set of pots with a new and unique set of properties and social positions, a new definition of the cultures that they represent. How does this work in practice? It works through the finding of patterns in form, fabric and decoration and imposing such patterns onto a predefined social reality. I have dealt with the pattern of Beaker fabric elsewhere (Boast 1995), so here I would like to explore the nature of British Beaker shape and decoration.

The key feature of the production of a pot form is that it is a succession of decisions made literally from the base up. Whether producing a pot on a wheel or by coil, basic decisions about curvature, at which point the pot will begin to be narrower rather than wider, and the character of that point, must be made. This does not mean that the shape of a pot is open to extreme variation. On the contrary, as Olivier Gosselain remarks in regard to potting among the Bafia of Cameroon 'the shaping process deserves the most attention because it is completely independent of external constraint. Among the Bafia, it is almost the only stage for which there is perfect uniformity among all potters.' (Gosselain 1992, 581). This is because, among the Bafia, instruction in potting starts at a very young age. Gestures cannot be challenged during learning because they are im-mediately corrected, so the motor habits of youth impose a kind of stability in time and space. But conventionalised motor habits do not apply every-where and there tends to be greater innovation where there is little need to apply new habits or change old ones, such as with the form of decoration (Gosselain 1992, 582).

It is shape that clearly distinguishes British Beakers from other contemporary pottery, their S shaped profile. However, this is an oversimplifi-cation of the actual shape of most British Beakers. British Beakers vary in shape from 'classical' S shaped profile, to biconical, to a W shaped profile, to straight sided handled mugs and even the occa-sional bowl. These basic forms are further varied through the use of cordons, carinations and even collars to enhance certain features of the pot shape (Fig. 10.1). For most of its period of use, the way that Beakers were formed, the decisions and habits of manufacture were extremely conventionalised. The patterns of affinity and difference in Beakers relate to the decisions being made in the production of the forms which literally took hundreds of years to develop. What is clear is that, unlike the preceding Neolithic, conformity, probably imposed throughout the learning process, was being imposed on Beaker shape through a strongly prescribed craft tradition. So what constitutes the shape of a Beaker, and how does this shape reflect what the pot represents?

The study of Beaker form has been dominated by the search for the major patterns of these traditions. These have been conventionally seen as being primarily the height to width ratio, the distinction of tall-thin pots from short-fat ones, and the length of the neck, the distinction of pots with short almost Neolithic necks from those with long necks relative to the proportion of the pots. Figures 10.2 and 10.3 show the range of such Beaker forms as a matrix. In these figures the pot forms change in two dimen-sions. In Figure 10.2, the pots shorten down the

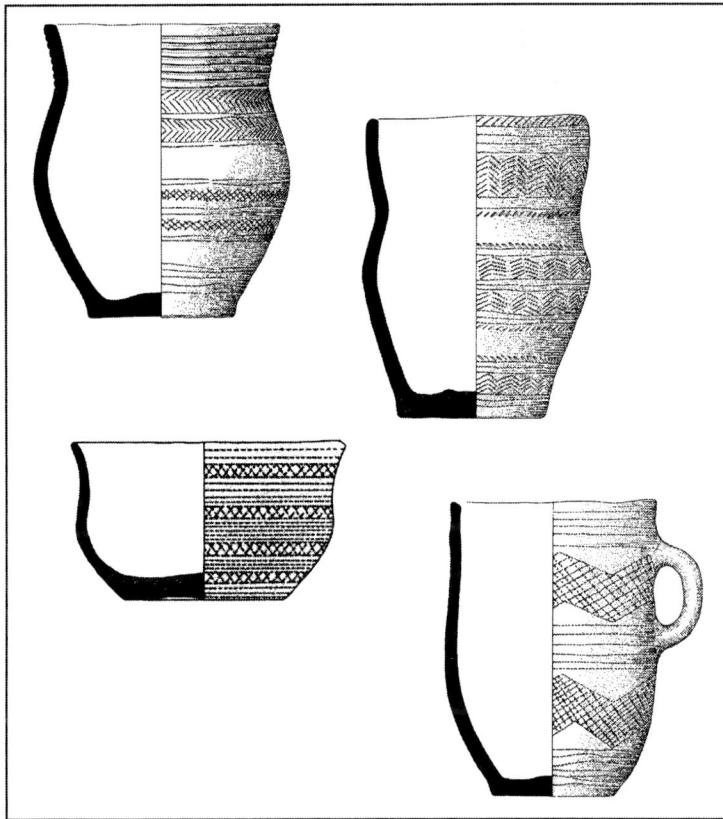

Fig. 10.1. An extremely simplified range of Beaker forms from (left to right, top to bottom) S shaped profile (Stonebridge, Durham, after Kinnes and Longworth 1985), W shaped profile (Northumberland, after Kinnes and Longworth 1985), Beaker bowl (Eynsham, Oxford, after Clarke 1970:305), and handled mug (Goodmanham 113, burial 1, after Kinnes and Longworth 1985).

vertical while they become narrower along the horizontal. In Figure 10.3, the pots also shorten down the vertical but the length of the neck increases relative to the proportions of the pot along the horizontal. This provides a very graphic form of comparing changes in pot shape (Kempton 1981).

In these two Figures, the shaded forms represent the shape of Beakers found in Britain, while the unshaded forms we could say could have been made, but were not. The shading also represents regional distinctions with lightly shaded forms being primarily found in the south of Britain, and the medium shaded forms found primarily in the north (including Scotland), while the dark shaded forms are found in all areas of Britain. This does not represent an absolute distinction, though, in that the lightly shaded forms are represented in the north, and *visa versa*, though in very small numbers.

Though these two matrices represent tendencies, tendencies of a form being significantly more likely to be found in one area than another, rather than absolute dissimilarity, there is a clear distinction seen in both matrices between forms found primarily in the north and those found in the south. There is a tendency for Beakers made in the south of Britain to be short and of medium width, while those of the north tend to be taller and narrower (Figure 10.2). Further, the south seems to have a high proportion of short necked forms or short-wide forms with long necks. The north, on the other hand, has Beakers with a very narrow range of forms of predominantly medium proportion with medium length necks (Fig. 10.3). The forms found in all areas are clearly 'in-between' showing an overlap between the choices made by potters in the north from those in the south.

So, can we say that potters north of the Humber had a different sense of what the proper shape of a Beaker constituted than potters south of the Humber? Though the two traditions of Beaker form created Beakers whose shape was often the same in both areas, the general pattern of shape shows that forms that would have been considered 'extreme' in one area, and probably not accepted by potters or users, was acceptable and even common in the other. I could argue that we are looking at two distinct

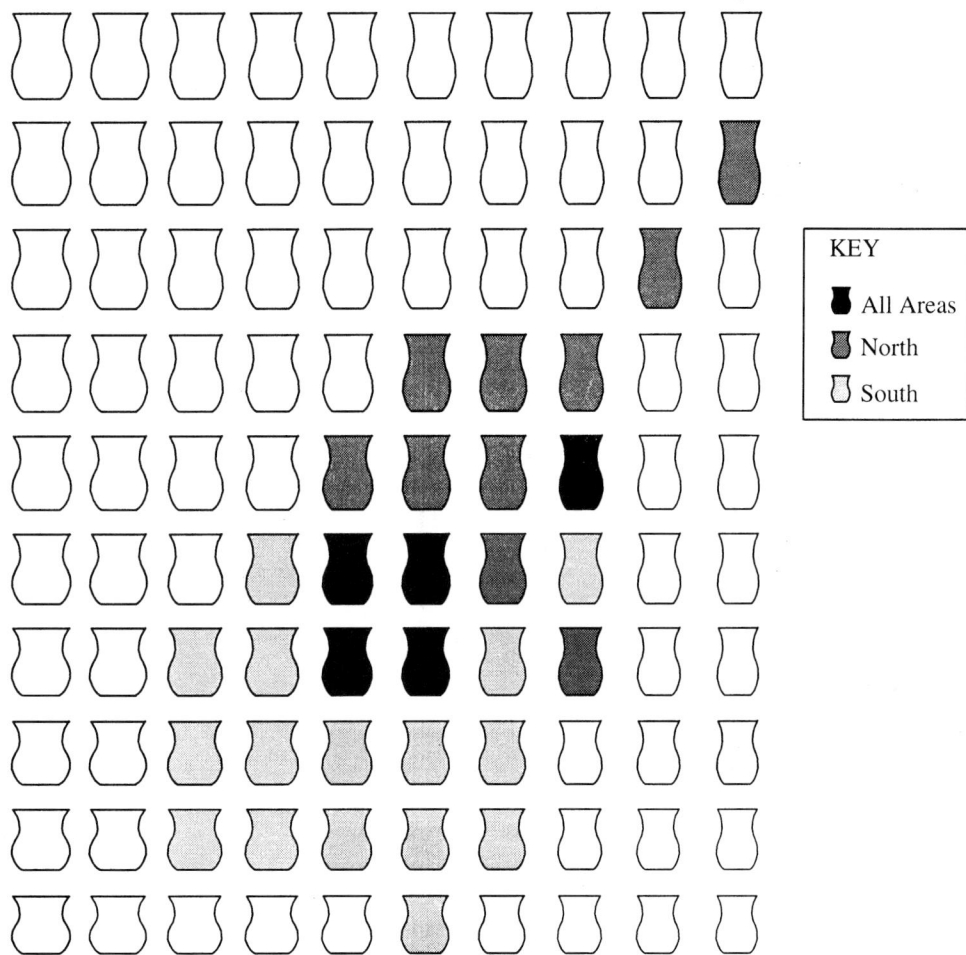

Fig. 10.2. Variation in Beaker shape. In the horizontal dimension the Beakers narrow, while in the vertical dimension they get taller.

traditions of pottery making that necessarily vary due to competence and communication, but I will not.

Even in general terms, the shape of a Beaker obviously is not a single form, or a few forms, that some potters managed to get 'right' and others got 'wrong'. Beakers, like all forms of material culture, are objects made in response to a set of intentions, both immediate and traditional. What matters is the intentions of the potter about what it is that they are making. This will necessarily involve a number of decisions of which some, most or only a few are under the control of the potter. As in Gosselain's example, the pot is not made in response to some abstract image of 'Beakerness' (*contra* Boast 1990), but is made in response to a set of taught skills and negotiations with others before, during and after the making.

However, we do not study pottery in the light of such programme of making or the process by which

such identities are created and delegated. We study pottery as though each pot was an equal member of a large and uniform productive process necessarily always relating to itself. We look at large collections of pottery over large areas and long periods of time. We consider pots as normative responses to the social process of not only needing pots, but needing pots that signal their social roles. We treat these pots as products of an industrial process with the archaeologists as the futuristic sorters, sorting the different objects into their respective cultural bins. But what of decoration, the key categorical feature of Clarke's typology (Clarke 1970)? Certainly it is a means of cultural communication and nothing more. It has no other 'use' than signifying, and signification, as we all know, is culturally determined. Does it too reflect the gross regional distinction found in shape and, if so, what does this distinction distinguish?

Beaker decoration has been less accommodating to pottery studies, both in its definition and descrip-

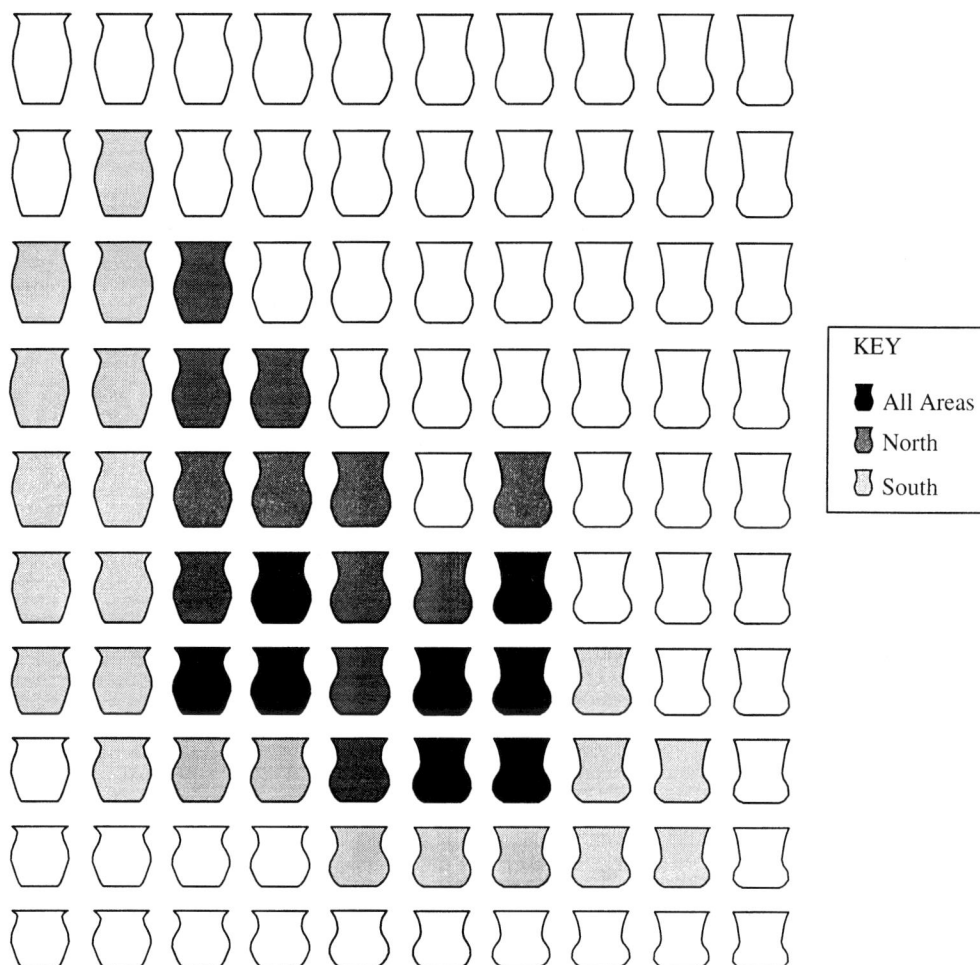

Fig. 10.3. Variation in Beaker shape. In the horizontal dimension, the belly of the Beaker drops lengthening the neck while, in the vertical dimension, the Beaker gets taller.

tion. Many systems for description or measurement of decoration have been devised with very limited success. Traditionally, decoration has been divided into simple and distinguishable motifs or units of design, but we must admit that the design schema must also be significant, and there has been some success in measuring the underlying schema of a number of contemporary design systems (Knight 1983; Washburn 1983; Wiessner 1984). However, in the case of Beakers, such an underlying schema is difficult to identify against a background of remarkable diversity (Boast 1995).

Many have tried to decode the underlying 'rules' of design that guided Beaker decoration (Mitchell 1934; Clarke 1970; Boast 1990). Despite this effort, only the most banal patterns have been forthcoming. We are presented with simple zonal systems (Clarke 1970, 12) or a system of increasing symmetric organisations which are distinguished more by their diversity than their similarity (Boast 1990, 116–117).

Is this because we are assuming that all design systems are just that, systematic – that design, like form, is the outcome of a conventionalised set of representations which denote group or individual identity?

Regardless of such attempts, Beaker design remains enigmatic, perhaps because of its complexity and diversity. Not only is there a vast range of design elements used (Clarke 1970, 16–18), but the organisation of these elements varies greatly over time and space. Figure 10.4 shows the pattern when we compare a very schematised range of Beaker design elements with the organisation of these elements on the pots. Comparing four regions in Britain, we see only subtle differences from Wessex to Scotland. All these elements are widely used with only minor changes over time (Boast 1990, 221–222), but there does seem to be a distinction, again, as we move from the south to the north.

In East Anglia and Wessex, though all elements

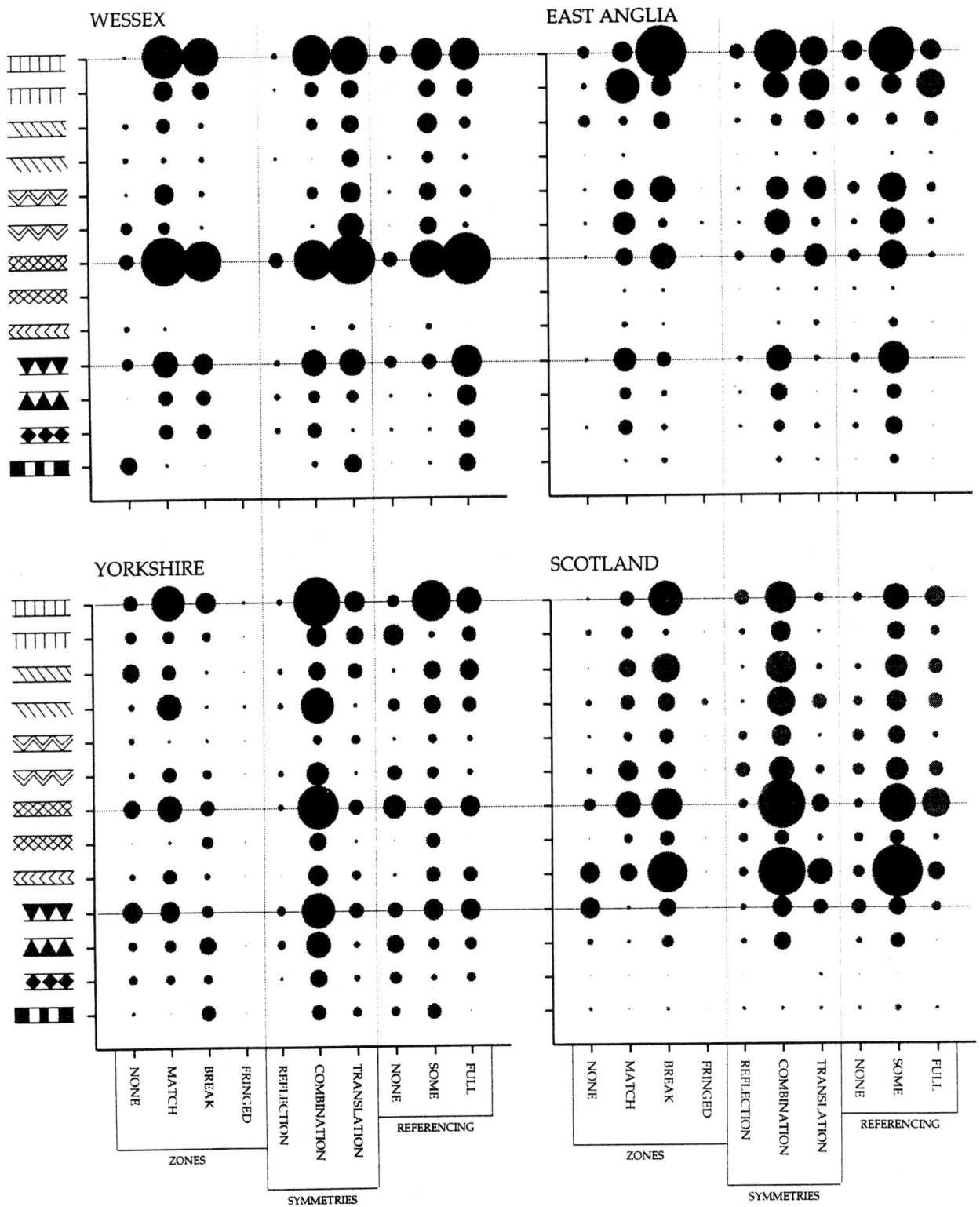

Fig. 10.4. Design element choice. The proportion of association between design element choice and design organisation from a sample of over 800 Beakers from all parts of Britain.

are used, there is a definite preference for the simple ladder and cross-hatch designs, and these are represented in all forms of design organisation. In

Scotland, and Yorkshire in particular, there is a much greater use of all the design elements in all forms of design organisation. Though all elements

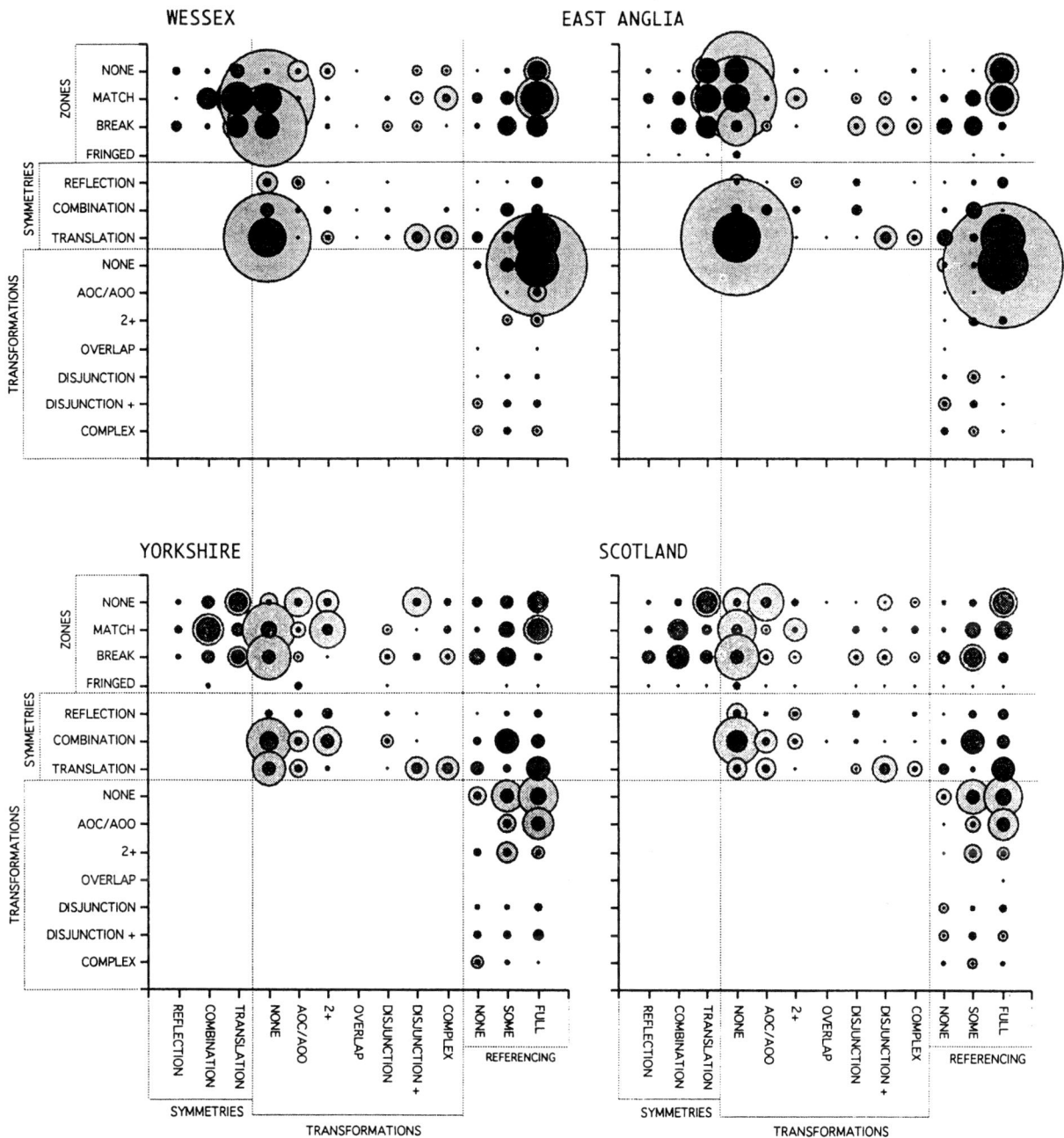

Fig. 10.5. Design organisation. This figure represents the number of pots which share different pairs of design organisational features from a sample of over 800 Beakers from all parts of Britain. The grey circles represent the proportion of pots which share the two characteristics within each category or pair of features. The dark circles represent the proportion of pots weighted by the size of the category, a slightly more representative measure.

are seen as acceptable, in the south Beaker potters were much more cautious about their use of the full range of elements.

This pattern becomes more pronounced when we look at the relationships between different aspects of the design organisation (Figure 10.5). Here we see a clear distinction, as we did with form, between the way that design was organised on Beakers between the north and the south. As with the choice of

elements, Beakers in Wessex and East Anglia represent the full range of design patterns found around Britain, but only a very narrow range is represented in any numbers. The vast majority of Beaker potters in the south use a very narrow range of often quite simple design patterns, while the north used the full range of design patterns in largely equal numbers. This graph shows what most Beaker scholars have known intuitively for some time, that the Beaker decoration found north of the Humber is far more varied and complex than that of the south.

So, the pattern for Beaker decoration follows that of Beaker form. Beaker pots were made and decorated differently north of the Humber than they were south of it. But does this really tell us very much? That there is a distinction, not in kind but in minor aspects of practice, is not new nor particularly informative. Is it that surprising that there is a distinction between the potting traditions of communities that are more than 300 km apart? After all, Wessex is closer to France than to Yorkshire, little alone Scotland. And the pots that we look at, all together and co-present, were made over hundreds of years and across vast areas. They were made and used in communities that probably rarely if ever saw each other and only very few of these pots ever were compared side by side as we do now. In this way we see a broad similarity in Beakers from across Europe, and at this level all British Beakers are alike. But we want something deeper, more indicative of the social distinctions and identities that these pots were suppose to be marking, but can we find it by looking this way?

Because a distinction in the decoration and form of Beakers is demonstrated, this does not mean that a distinction in identity has been discovered. We assume that because the design has a certain intuitive similarity to it, that there must be some underlying identity that guides the construction, and if there are differences then the cultural referent must also have changed. Though this certainly may be the case in some instances (Knight 1983), this is not always the case and I do not think that it is the case with Beakers. Beaker form and decoration does not seem to be determined by a set of explicit codes or grammars, but represents a *bricolage* – a set of designs sharing a common set of elements but formed from a variety of vernacular or even individual traditions. The similarities and differences in an object is not due to its representation of similar and different cultural identities, along with those objects to which its comparison generated the similarities and differences in the first place, but in its participation in specific programmes of action and not in others.

In this way, by saying that Beakers do not have a set of design rules, I do not mean that there is no pattern to Beaker design. Simply that we cannot say that Beaker design represented any one systematic set of identities. It is unlikely that Beaker design constituted anything more than the use of a set of conventionalised forms and design elements with conventionalised horizontal orientation, and, at times, even these conventions were abandoned. However, we cannot say from our analysis what constituted this conventionalisation. What is more

important is to ask what programmes of action required Beakers.

Clearly we see different choices being made at different stages during the production of Beakers, choices that refer to quite different identifications, but they are very small differences. During the initial stages of production, the processes by which the paste is made and the form built seem to be highly standardised, while the process of decoration, though drawing on a set of conventionalised elements and a rough set of rules about design organisation, are allowed to vary quite widely. In fact, what distinguishes Beaker decoration is its almost unique character from pot to pot. The first can be understood through a highly constrained learning process, the second less so (Gosselain 1992, 581).

Through the techniques used in the analysis here, we contextualise the pots as simple type fossils – as representatives of a genealogical progression over time and space. Our generalising analysis gives us little option but to analyse the pots in this light. We do not have the option of asking how the pots constrained and embodied programmes of action, because we have already embodied the pots as genealogical types. The regional differences presented here only show distinctions in making, they are only making Beakers in different ways. This does not tell us about the role of Beakers, whether it was different from one area to another, or not, and what social encounters required something like a Beaker.

Even in the year this paper was written, Humphrey Case was again telling us that 'Beaker pottery thus forms a single tradition, from which burial offerings appear to have been a selection' (Case 1995, 56). I am not sure whether this is true or not. It tells us nothing about Beakers, why and how they formed a 'single tradition', why they were selected as burial offerings, or why a locally made pot should have such uniformity on one level and such diversity on another (Parker Pearson 1995, 93). Certainly, the data presented here shows that as craft tradition, it certainly did not form a single tradition. However, as a means for containing offerings in a grave, a socially appropriate means with the socially appropriate objects, it may form a single tradition.

All interpretations of Beakers over the last 120 years have insisted that the pot functions as a single representative unit – as a unified tradition of cultural representation. It has been held to be an embodiment of certain identities, rather than one of many objects that allows for identity to be negotiated. The pot is not produced as a single stable object, nor is it used as one. Many different decisions are incorporated at different levels of its production, use and deposition. The pot does not mean anything, but allows for social action, and hence social meaning, to take place. Even during the course of the pot's life it can change its identity, or rather shift its identities between programmes of action. After construction, different aspects of its form are delegated different roles and purposes. More often than not, however, these features are used in conjunction to dynamically reference different subjectivities as the need arises.

The identities that pots make possible are not something that is held by someone, or something, but is something that is attributed. Material culture may be used to enforce such attributions through the control of co-presence – through walls and doors and the restriction of access to places and access to goods, and we may signal our intent to hold an identity through the holding and use of objects. But these things do not give us identity, they merely act as material relationships that provide the settings for identities into which we may be allowed to insert ourselves. In our own society, a man who dresses as a woman is not necessarily a woman, but is a man who is asking to be given the identity that is woman. The granting of that identity is not given because of the presence of woman's objects or access to women's places. Rather there is a negotiation for or against the man's right to hold that identity. The agreement between participants and material setting does not constitute the identity, but makes it possible for the conversation to begin.

Beakers as pots allowed identities to be negotiated, but were not a representation of those identities. The fact that pots were made somewhat differently in the north of Britain than in the south only tells us that there are different craft traditions existing in places that were quite a distance away from each other. There is other evidence to suggest that there are quite strong social differences between north and south Britain in the Early Bronze Age, expressed through both monuments and burials, but this does not mean that these differences in Beaker form and decoration are anything more than a consequence of different ways of making the thing we call a Beaker. The Beakers did not have to mean different things nor did they have to constitute different identities, though they may have. The problem is that our study does not tell us nor does it give us a way of finding out. What we need is a radical reconsideration of how we examine pots, and other material culture, and what pasts our examinations are forcing us to create.

By treating pots as inscribed cultures, objects that represent social norms and identities, we do not see pots as the response to a situated set of prescriptions of the makers, the users and the material world, but as the inevitable outcome of social custom. We impose a conventionalisation of form as the determinant of material categories. Through the examination of pots as reflections of social identity, we still demand that pots equal people. Only when we stop treating our pots as type fossils, whose only role is to identify their deposit through an imposed genealogical relation, from identifying the fossilised culture passively represented, will we get away from associating pots with peoples. We should realise that pots, as with all material culture, are diverse signifiers and that these various significations are built into the productive process as an anticipation of programmes of action. Pots do not reflect social identities, but are made to prescribe a certain set of intentions on how we should behave so that we may get on with the process of being defined.

11   Inclusions, Impressions and Interpretation

Ann Woodward

Introduction

The aim of this paper is an ambitious one. It is to strike out from the usual ranges of ceramic analysis in order to investigate the wider social context of pottery use throughout the prehistoric period. The study will consider pottery of all periods between the Neolithic and the Middle Iron Age, mainly in southern Britain, and will discuss the nature of long-term changes in production, form and style in relation to other categories of finds and varying site contexts. Such approaches have been hampered previously by the fact that most specialists have concentrated on the study of a single ceramic tradition, such as Grooved Ware, Biconical Urns or Middle Iron Age fine wares. Thus the study, and methods of analysis used, for pottery of the Neolithic and earlier Bronze Age on the one hand and later Bronze Age/Iron Age pottery on the other are not only different, but often have been developed to answer different sorts of questions. This dual difference is mainly due to the fact that the earlier pottery often survives as whole vessels in funerary or special pit deposits while the later material usually occurs as substantial sherd assemblages in a variety of context types on domestic sites. Furthermore, modern research has concentrated on certain aspects of ceramics at the expense of others. The key works on major ceramic traditions have depended primarily on detailed study of vessel shape, form and decoration and surface treatment only. This applies equally to the analysis of Iron Age pottery, such as the classification of the very substantial assemblages from Danebury (Cunliffe 1984a & b), as it does to the seminal studies of Beakers (Clarke 1970) or Collared Urns (Longworth 1984).

Other aspects of ceramic study, notably the analysis of fabric and consideration of methods of decoration have been less well served. A few studies, such as those of Biconical Urns (Tomalin 1983) and Deverel-Rimbury pottery (Ellison 1975), have attempted to give equal weight to fabric type during analysis of regional variations and possible origins, but on the whole and in spite of the advance in petrological studies, it remains a minor sector of study, often marginalised in reports by relegation to an appendix. And where more extensive fabric analyses have been undertaken, the questions posed seldom relate to a wider ranging investigation of site processes. The description and discussion of techniques of decoration is remarkably unfashionable, to the extent that aspects of technique are seldom described in detail: one is expected to adduce the exact technique by perusal of illustrations which are often inadequate for the purpose. Even worse, these 'poor-relation' fields of study have become compartmentalised. Decorative techniques are only discussed in relation to the technology of vessel production, and analysis of fabrics has become linked to the realms of source characterisation and the analysis of systems of production and exchange. Such compartmentalisation of the subject can now be seen to be damaging to any furtherance of general interpretation of ceramic evidence through time. Recent studies have shown how a study of the basic size ranges of vessel categories, as well as their shape, can lead to novel interpretations in terms of changing function and foodways through time (e.g. Woodward 1995; Hill this volume Chapter 13). A next step is to combine studies of form, size, style, fabric and descriptive techniques in order that the entire aspect of vessels may be perceived period by period and in relation to their changing contexts through time. However, before this can be attempted, the two topics of fabric and techniques of decoration, and their variations by period, need to be reviewed in detail.

Fabrics Through Time

In an important and wide-ranging study, Cleal (1995) has considered major changes in fabric type between the Early Neolithic and the Middle Bronze

Age. Her aim was to identify large-scale changes in the occurrence of key inclusion types, in a single geographical area. The area observed was Wessex. It was the overall pattern which was of interest, not the mechanism which produced it, which she viewed as a fuller stage of research. Cleal's summary diagram is reproduced here (Fig. 11.1) and her main conclusions will be summarised. It will then be necessary to extend her method into the later Bronze Age and Iron Age periods.

Early and Middle Neolithic bowls of the 'Hembury' and 'Windmill Hill' styles were tempered predominantly with flint (see Fig. 11.1). The inclusions are angular and unburnt and appear to have been prepared by crushing the waste from flint knapping. The flint occurs sometimes in association with sand, while some small vessels display sand inclusions only. Shell temper, some of it derived from distant sources, is another category used in these periods. In the Middle Neolithic, Peterborough Ware continues this tradition, although shell is more common in Ebbsfleet Ware and Fengate Ware than in Mortlake Ware. Angular sandstone and quartzite are notable additions to the Mortlake Ware fabric repertoire. By comparison, fabrics recorded for Grooved Ware are predominantly shelly; sometimes the shell is associated with sand, and grogged fabrics occur for the first time in any quantity. A combination of grog and shell forms a particularly characteristic Grooved Ware recipe, especially at the site of Durrington Walls. Little detailed analysis of the source of the shelly inclusions have been undertaken, but some in the Stonehenge region is definitely of marine origin (Cleal *et al.* 1994). Beakers display a wider overall range of fabric types. Amongst these grog or grog plus sand are the most common, followed by flint, sand and then flint. Combination recipes such as flint and grog and flint, grog and sand occur now for the first time. On the other hand, shell or other calcareous inclusions are notable by their absence. The fabrics of Food Vessels and Collared Urns, too few of which have been described in enough detail for them to be included in Fig. 11.1, are in Cleal's Wessex study area dominated by grog. However, it can be noted that in other areas rock inclusions are common. Their petrology, where investigated, invariably reflects the local geology. Within the Deverel-Rimbury tradition of the Middle Bronze Age the dominant filler type in Wessex is burnt flint, although grog continues in use to a significant extent in Dorset. The flint is not usually accompanied by sand and is highly distinctive in nature. The flint fillers usually comprise an even and dense distribution of small to medium inclusions (up to 1mm in diameter). The selective fragment size distribution strongly suggests that the temper was crushed and then sieved to produce

particular size gradings. The flint fragments are blocky and well-calcined and result from the burning, rolling and crushing of large amounts of flint nodules. On the whole however, such material would have been easier to prepare than the crushed knapping waste employed in the earlier Neolithic.

In conclusion, Cleal noted that there were two main periods of striking change in the use of tempering materials. One coincided with the introduction of Grooved Ware and involved the new predominance of shelly inclusions, the first major use of grog and the development of complex recipes, while the second occurred in the Middle Bronze Age with the development of the controlled and selective use of a single filler type: calcined flint.

It is difficult to trace a pattern of changing fabric use through to the Late Bronze Age in Wessex because very few relevant assemblages have been analysed. At Easton Lane, Late Bronze Age sherds were characterised by less well distributed and more angular flint inclusions, often associated with quartz sand (fabrics A7, A9, C5), and similar fabrics were noted amongst the Late Bronze Age urn deposits recently recovered from Twyford Down (Seager-Smith and Woodward 2000: fabrics F11 and F12). In the Salisbury Plain study area of the Wessex Linear Ditches Project, the detailed fabric studies by Raymond provide useful statistics. She notes a significant increase in the use of sand as a filler during the Late Bronze Age. In comparison with the Deverel-Rimbury fabrics described, of which only 2 out of 10 contain 25% quartz sand or more, nearly all the 21 Late Bronze Age fabrics contain sand, 11 at the 25% level or above (Bradley, Entwhistle and Raymond 1994, 154, Tables 29 and 30). A similar pattern may be found for Late Bronze Age sites in the Thames Valley. At Aldermaston Wharf flint inclusions were common, but 29% of the material (in fabrics D, H S and J) also contained sand, while at Knight's Farm Site 3 sandy fabrics (types e, f, g, h, i, j, k, l, m, n – i.e. e to n inclusive) accounted for 27.5% of the pottery (Bradley *et al.* 1980, 232 and 265).

It is even more difficult to follow patterns through into the Iron Age period, because in spite of the many detailed analyses of assemblages of this date in Wessex, summations and analyses of fabric trends through time have seldom been prepared. At Danebury the early period is characterised by coarse flint-tempered and shelly fabrics, whilst finer flint-tempered wares are dominant by the Middle Iron Age. Sandy wares occur throughout (Cunliffe 1984b, 232). A similar pattern is present at Winnall Down, although again detailed results present in the archive are not presented in print (Hawkes 1985). At Cadbury Castle, the fairly uniform shelly and calcite tempered Late Bronze Age wares were replaced by a much more extended repertoire in the Early Iron

TRADITION : / SAMPLE :	NEOLITHIC BOWL (1694)	EBBSFLEET WARE (52)	MORTLAKE WARE (69)	FENGATE WARE (24)	TOTAL GROOVED WARE (163)	DURRINGTON WALLS GROOVED WARE (49)	BEAKER (114)	DEVEREL-RIMBURY (140)
FLINT	46%	60%	38%	25%			12%	73%
FLINT & SAND	9%		22%	21%			8%	13%
SHELL	29%	31%	10%	30%	19%	6%		
SHELL & SAND					14%	12%		
GROG					10%	10%	18%	
GROG & SHELL						8%		
GROG, SAND, SHELL						8%		
GROG & SAND						8%	15%	
FLINT, GROG, SAND							8%	
FLINT & GROG							7%	
NONE VISIBLE					6%	8%	7%	
ANGULAR QUARTZ & SANDSTONE			6%					
SAND	8%				8%	6%	16%	
OTHER FABRICS	8%	9%	24%	24%	43%	34%	9%	14%

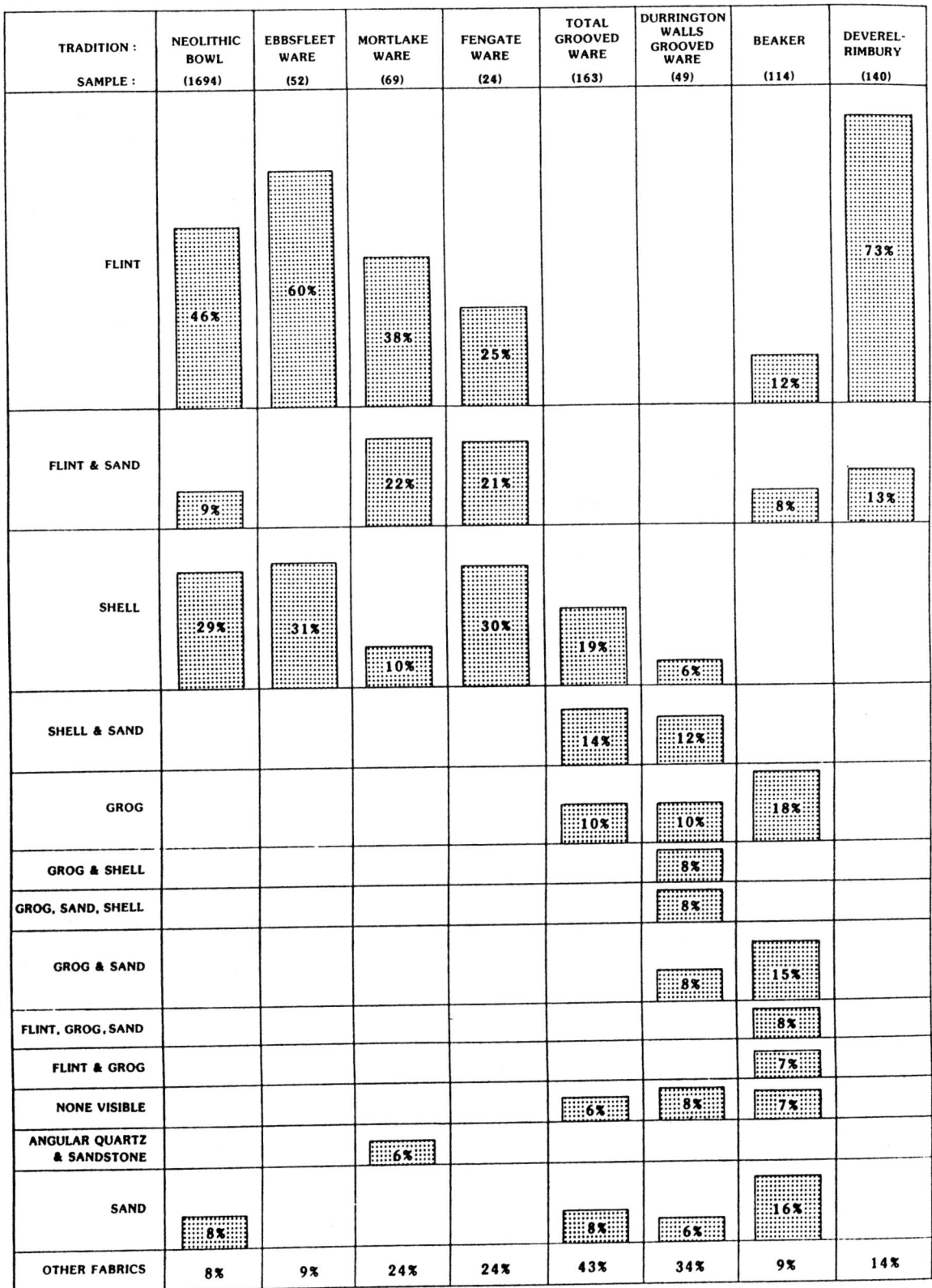

Fig. 11.1. Bar chart showing percentage of vessels within traditions of individual inclusion combinations, for every combination constituting more than 5% of the total for that tradition. (Total percentage of tradition represented by fabrics of less than 5% each also shown) (Cleal 1995, Fig. 16.2).

Age. To the platy shell and calcite fabrics, wares with oolitic limestone and micaceous sand were added. Also, mixed recipes such as shell and sand, shell and grog, flint and shell became common. By the Middle Iron Age the pattern presented became more standardised with fine evenly distributed shell-tempering providing the norm. These wares gave way to sandy 'Poole Harbour' fabrics only just before or at the time of the Roman conquest (Woodward 2000a). At Maiden Castle a similar pattern of a wide variety of fabrics giving way to more standardised types has been clearly presented, but the 'Poole Harbour' fabrics occur very much earlier than at Cadbury (Brown, L 1991a, fig. 149).

To summarise, the Late Bronze Age and Iron Age periods appear to have displayed some significant general trends. Firstly, there was a loosening of the tightly defined sieved flint temper recipes of the Middle Bronze Age and significant inclusion of sand during the Late Bronze Age. The Early Iron Age was characterised by a wide variety of fabrics ranging from fine sandy wares to very coarse platy shell or coarse flint fabrics and combination recipes were very common. Fabrics tend to vary according to vessel size and style. During the Middle Iron Age, fabrics tended to become much more standardised and specific categories such as saucepan pots were made using controlled fine flint-tempered fabrics, in Hampshire, or well-mixed fine shelly recipes as in Somerset. Coarse ware categories were manufactured using much the same recipes.

The Meaning of Fabrics

Fabric types have mostly been discussed in relation to ceramic technology and in relation to the availability of raw materials for use as suitable inclusions. However, a few specialists have begun to recognise that the inclusions themselves may have held symbolic significance in various ways. Three examples will serve to introduce this exciting topic. Gibson (1995a and this volume, Chapter 4) has drawn attention to the white quartz inclusions found commonly in Welsh Peterborough Ware. These inclusions often extrude from the exterior surface of the pot and it seems that they were intended to be seen. Gibson suggests that the fragments may have held important ritual meanings and draws attention to the common recurrence of white quartz boulders on Neolithic and Bronze Age monuments in the highland zone. Other types of filler also may have been intended to be highly visible. The occurrence of white calcareous inclusions, especially shell fragments, within vessels which are black or dark in colour has been emphasised by Cleal (1995). Although there is a technological link in that pots with

calcite inclusions cannot be fired to high temperatures and therefore are less likely to display a red, oxidised coloration, Cleal believes that the white-in-black effect may have been intentional and of symbolic significance. Even when inclusions are less visible they might be of equal symbolic significance. For instance, in his study of Bronze Age pottery from the south west, Parker Pearson has suggested that one explanation for the extreme variation in the fabrics of Beakers may be due to the fact that the inclusions derive from the vicinity of the owner's home or the Beaker was 'perhaps even formed out of the soil from whence that person originated' (Parker Pearson 1995, 93). One very clear example of largely invisible inclusions which may be imbued with considerable symbolic and social value is the usage of grog. Several authors have drawn attention to the fact that the grog employed may have included the ground-up fragments of known individual vessels and that the inclusion of such fragments in new pots may reflect and reinforce familial and ancestral links in various ways (e.g. Bewley *et al.* 1992; Brown, N 1995, 127).

Such social contexts for the use of grog are well evidenced in the ethnographic literature, a particularly clear example having been discussed by Sterner (1989) who described the custom of breaking off a rim fragment from a cracked 'soul pot' belonging to a deceased father to be incorporated as grog in a new one made for his son. Grog is particularly common in the Early Bronze Age period in Britain, a period when pots may have been owned and used by particular individuals rather than by communities (Woodward 1995). It seems highly possible that the grog in such vessels may have derived from particular pots belonging to ancestors or other revered members of society. In order to test such a hypothesis, several avenues of enquiry may be followed. Firstly, there is accumulating evidence that visible fragments of specific vessels are occasionally present. Thus, at Pasture Lodge Farm (Lincs), Allen noted a decorative rim fragment, probably from an Early Bronze Age vessel, as grog in a Middle Bronze Age urn (Allen *et al.* 1987, 214) and at West Kennet, a piece of Fengate Ware (P14) contains a large curved fragment for another vessel (Cleal 1995). Secondly, there are frequent occurrences of incomplete vessels known from Early Bronze Age burial deposits. These are pots which were damaged before entering the grave. They are difficult to identify, owing to the problems afforded by post-depositional disturbance, but can occasionally be confirmed in some instances. Once such situation is where a portion or rim is missing from a vessel which was deposited in an inverted position. It has been suggested that the partially surviving grog-tempered Beaker vessels found over the Early

Bronze Age gold hoard at Lockington, Leicestershire were fragments of such vessels, ancestral pots from which areas had been removed for recycling in new vessels, and a literature search of reports on modern burial excavations revealed eleven examples of vessels from which significant pieces had been removed prior to deposition (Woodward 2000b). It is difficult to identify these instances from published descriptions and illustrations but the impression gained is that such occurrences were not uncommon.

From this standpoint it is not difficult to move on to discussion of rock inclusions in pottery, for which a similar hypothesis of reincorporation may be advanced. Whilst there have been suggestions that broken stone axes could have been used as a source of high quality temper (Wardle 1992, 72), and that the range of rock types utilised for pottery temper at Ewanrigg is broadly similar to those utilised in stone implements (Freestone in Bewley *et al.* 1992, 340), the idea that the source of rock temper may have been specific prized implements in the possession of the potting family or group has not been explored. Some igneous and metamorphic inclusions can be demonstrated to have been present in the glacial drift deposits selected for potting, but in many cases petrological study had demonstrated that the rock fragments were specially crushed for tempering use. It is usually assumed that suitable small erratics were collected for this purpose, but the use of stone artefacts existing within a settlement would have been both more economic of time and effort and allowed a powerful opportunity to imbue a vessel with cultural and social importance. The incorporation of dust or fragments from an heirloom axe could have emulated or even surpassed the incorporation of fragments from the family's drinking or eating vessels. The extended life cycles of stone tools, especially axes, and their changing social roles through time have been the subject of some stimulating research (Bradley 1990b and Skeates 1995). Perhaps the ultimate incorporation of their dust and fragments within pottery vessels marks the beginning of a new life for them in a slightly different social milieu. As with pottery, it is difficult to extract any statistics concerning degrees of completeness of stone artefacts from the published literature. However, it is interesting to note that of the 488 examples of battle axes originally listed by Roe, 15% were found in a partial state, her 'Broken Halves' (Roe 1966, 214). Of course, it may be that the rock fragments incorporated in pots were not derived from stone artefacts but were taken from pieces of rock from a known source which had been revered in its own right since the Neolithic or earlier; such an interpretation would be equally interesting.

Moving forward in time to the Middle and Late Bronze Age, the most common non-flint stone artefacts are querns. These items were of crucial significance within the sedentary domestic environment that became established alongside stable field systems and territorial arrangements from the Middle Bronze Age onwards. Their use in grinding primary foodstuffs gave them an important transformational role (Hill 1995a, 108) and, very interestingly, by the Iron Age it seems that parts of most of the querns ever in existence may have entered the archaeological record through a process of deliberate deposition (*op cit* 131). Querns were so important that they were buried, either whole or in pieces, within pit fillings on Iron Age settlement sites. Similar deposits of quernstones in pits are common on Middle Bronze Age settlements. Notable examples have been excavated at Itford Hill, Thorny Down and Winnall Down (Hawkes 1969), and the intentional nature of these deposits was discussed in her paper: 'A good quern , after all, was an absolutely essential piece of domestic equipment. So the possibility suggests itself that these deposits had some ritual significance, and that the quern-burials, if not also the domestic pots, were some form of religious offering made under circumstances actually unknown to us but nevertheless perfectly imaginable' (*ibid*, 8).

Middle Bronze Age pottery is tempered usually with calcined flint. This substance would have occurred commonly on settlements where it was used in cooking and other heating processes. Indeed, in terms of surface scatters, later Bronze Age settlements are often defined by the occurrence of burnt flint. If, as we might wish to suggest, pieces of quern were ground up also for incorporation within pottery, it is unlikely that the dust and fine sand derived from the sarsen and sandstone employed in quern production could be detected petrologically within the pottery fabrics. A programme of analysis could be designed to test such an hypothesis, although results in the south-western region might prove more promising. At Trethellan Farm in Cornwall, querns and rubbing stones again were deliberately hidden within pits and structured sealing deposits (Nowakowski 1991, 141–56). The stone artefacts were made from a variety of granites and sandstone. The pottery occurs in two main fabric types, one the typical Cornish gabbroic ware and the other of clay including Lizard gabbro together with greenstone (mainly basalt and dolorite). On a few other Trevisker sites, the pottery fabrics also include fragments of sandstone and granite (Williams in Nowakowski 1991, 132). It would be very interesting to see whether these fragments could be matched with any of the sources of raw material for the querns and rubbing stones, for the source of some of the clay tempering may have been fragments of such stone artefacts.

Returning to the East Midlands, a few clues may be provided by the results of the excavations of the Iron Age settlement at Gamston (Knight 1992). Here there were large numbers of querns, some of them possibly imported from the Peak District and Charnwood Forest (*ibid.* 84 and figs. 28–9) and some of the pottery was tempered with granodiorite. The granodiorite probably came from Mountsorrel on the eastern side of Charwood Forest (*ibid.* 42 and Knight, this volume Chapter 13): it was fresh in character and had been deliberately introduced as temper. Although Knight prefers to view the pottery vessels as imports from Charnwood, *c.* 35km away, he does state that the raw material 'could have arrived on the site in the form of querns'. The later Bronze Age vessels from Lockington contain igneous inclusions which also may derive from Charnwood Forest, which of course was the main local source for stone axes of Group XX in the Late Neolithic and Early Bronze Age periods. One might wonder whether significant items made from other raw materials could also have been broken or ground up and incorporated into ceramic vessels. Such a raw material is bone or antler and it is interesting to note that, with the more extensive employment of petrological analysis, occasional identifications of bone inclusions are now being made (e.g. for the Iron Age settlement at Covert Farm, Crick, Northants: Woodward, Hancocks and Ixer in prep.).

If the fabrics of Bronze Age and Iron Age pots may have included the ground-up fragments of stone tools of varying kinds, then it should come as no surprise that Cleal could identify the flint tempering in Early-Middle Neolithic pottery as crushed detritus from flint-knapping activities. It is known that the knapping of flint on the sites of monuments may represent ritual acts (e.g. Thomas 1991a), so the knapping waste used for pottery temper may have resulted from such activities, or the temper may even have been prepared by the crushing of selected implements.

However, the calcined flint temper recipes of the Middle Bronze Age require a slightly different level of explanation. Cleal points out that the Neolithic lifestyle was much more mobile than in the Middle Bronze Age and that it would have been difficult to stockpile quantities of flint. The more settled existence of the Middle Bronze Age, associated with the establishment of more permanent structures, defined social space and eventually, fields, would have allowed the early accumulation of burnt flint which would have been associated intimately with the processes of the drying of crops and other commodities, cooking food, heating liquids and providing warmth. Indeed the importance of flints in such everyday essential processes may have led to them being imbued with a further significance. Burnt flint

may have come to symbolise the very essence of domestic life centred around the hearth, the 'domus' as defined by Hodder (1990a), and as such was the ideal substance to be incorporated within the ceramic containers which were used for the storage, preparation and consumption of foodstuffs. Thus, in all periods for the Neolithic to Iron Age it has been possible to suggest that pottery fabric may have been of extreme symbolic importance. We shall return to these aspects later in a more wide-ranging discussion of systems of meaning through time, but meanwhile the topic of how vessels were decorated needs to be addressed.

Techniques of Decoration Through Time

The incidence of decoration on pottery is not uniform through British prehistory. Some periods and areas are characterised by plain wares alone and many assemblages contain both decorated and plain wares. Furthermore some vessel types carry all over decoration while other types have decorated zones limited to the upper parts of the pot, the shoulder or the rim only. Although the potential symbolic meanings of degrees of zonation of decoration have been subjected to preliminary analysis (e.g. Richards and Thomas 1984), the reasons for these more general patterns are not at all apparent. In order to initiate relevant lines of enquiry a consideration of the different techniques of decoration employed will be attempted. The decoration of prehistoric pottery results from the applications of various designs through acts of impression, or, occasionally, the addition of mouldings. The techniques may be divided into seven categories.

1. incised or grooved linear impressions. These are formed using sharp or blunt instruments, probably of wood or bone. Incision is used to signify sharp narrow lines, whilst grooves are defined as being wider, usually >0.5mm.

2. cord impressions. There are three main types of cord: whipped cord, in which a light thread has been whipped more or less are right angles round a flexible core; twisted cord, in which two strands are twisted together to form a single cord and plaited cord, in which strands are plaited together to form a single cord. Whipped cord was usually bent into a loop in order to make a short impression of the 'maggot' type. Twisted and plaited cord both are usually employed to form straight lines within geometric motifs, but the use of plaited cord is relatively rare.

3. individual impressions. Single impressions may be circular, geometric or irregular in shape and were formed using the ends of a flint flake, a

bone or wooden point, twigs, or hollow reeds. They may occur singly, in rows or as infill within motifs defined by linear impressions. Stab-and-drag is a specific variant of this technique.

4. bird-bone impressions. A specific variation of type 3, these complex impressions are made using the articular ends of the bones from birds and small mammals.

5. comb and stamp impressions. Linear and infilled designs may be executed using a bone comb with short or long rectangular teeth, or one with circular teeth giving a point-line effect. If is often possible to deduce the number of teeth and width of the comb used. Stamped impressions, again usually of bone, may be circular or of complex geometric form. Rows of regular stamped impressions were sometimes formed by the rouletting technique.

6. applied decoration. The main category of applied decoration is clay cordons which may be horizontal, vertical or curved. Lugs, vestigial handles, etc. may be decorative in part, but have not been considered in this particular study.

7. finger and thumb impressions. The most common forms are oval finger-tip or thumb-tip impressions and curved finger-nail impressions. Both often occur in horizontal rows, sometimes on cordons, and finger-nail impressions also occur in pinched pairs or as overall random rustication.

Tools for the fabrication of many of these forms of decoration will have mainly been of natural occurrence and perishable. Cord also falls into the perishable category, and, although bird-bones may survive on sites, their use in pottery decoration is difficult to prove. However, it was the survival of such bones in the West Kennet long barrow that led Dorothy Liddell to first interpret this style of decoration in the 1920s. Tools which do survive include pebbles used for burnishing, and bone combs such as those from Bronze Age contexts at Northton (Harris), Bishops Cannings Down, Dean Bottom and Gwithian (Gibson and Woods 1997, fig. 19). The forms of Iron Age pottery stamps have been deduced and illustrated by Elsdon (1975).

Liddell experimented with various modern bird and animal bones and produced many pattern variations on plasticine (Liddell 1929). She found that bird bones produced sharper impressions than bones from small mammals such as rat, stoat, weasel, squirrel or hedgehog, and that the species of bird from which the bones derived could be determined for impressions on some Neolithic pottery. At Hurst Fen, Longworth produced impressions similar to those on a Middle Neolithic bowl by using the end of a tibia from a bird the size of a fowl (Clark

et al. 1960, Pl.XXV). Another sherd showed the impressions of quills. The nature of the cords used to form impressed decoration on pottery is of crucial interest. Experiments showed that wool would have been too elastic and hair-moss fibres unsatisfactory. One possible source of suitable material is lime bast. Cords and twine made from lime bast are known in deposits from the Neolithic onwards in the Baltic area (Clark 1952, 207). However Sherratt has made the interesting suggestion that the fibres used were those from the hemp plant, *Cannabis sativa* (Sherratt 1987, 97–8).

To demonstrate the changes in the employment of different techniques of decoration through time a chart similar to that compiled by Cleal for the fabric data has been prepared (Fig. 11.2). Owing to the variable incidence of suitable statistics relating to decorative techniques in published pottery reports the geographical spread of information is inevitably wider than that employed in Cleal's study for fabric. This of course means that we may be viewing in part the results of regional variations. However, for the Neolithic period at least, several different regions are represented in the tabulation, and for the later periods most of the figures relate to Wessex. Starting in the Middle Neolithic, using data from the sites of Abingdon (Case and Whittle 1982) and Hurst Fen (Clark *et al.* 1960, fig. 27), we find that incised decoration was the most common, mainly forming simple linear motifs on the neck. Individual impressions formed by bones, reeds, flints or twigs were also significant. However contemporary regional styles of pottery in the south west were mainly plain, as in the earliest Neolithic phases. Moving on to the Late Neolithic, the pattern changes substantially. Peterborough Ware decoration is dominated by two techniques, cord impressions and bird-bone designs. In Wales, bird-bone impressions are extremely common (Gibson 1995, fig. 3.4), while at Windmill Hill and on sites in Cranborne Chase, twisted cord is the most common technique (Smith 1965; Cleal 1991b, data from catalogue). However, one should also note that, although the material from the West Kennet long barrow was not fully quantified, Piggott stated that bird-bone impressions were extremely common in that assemblage (Piggott 1962). Grooved Ware, on the other hand, displays no bird-bone decoration at all. The assemblages from Durrington Walls (Wainwright and Longworth 1971) and Lawford (Shennan *et al.* 1985) contain low proportions of cord decoration, but the main decoration techniques are grooving associated at Durrington Walls with applied cordons and at Lawford with individual circular impressions.

For the Early Bronze Age period, few large assemblages exist, so it was decided to quantify the decorative techniques used on vessels occurring

Period	Site/Area	Technique of decoration										(number of vessels)
		incised	whipped cord	twisted cord	plaited cord	grooves	flint/reed/twig/jab	bird-bone	comb	applied cordons	finger tip/finger nail	
Middle Neolithic:bowl	Abingdon	▓		▒			▒		░		░	(190)
	Hurst Fen	▓					▓	░			░	(187)
Middle Neo: Peterborough	Wales	░	▒	░			▒		░			----
	Windmill Hill/ Cranbourne Chase	░	▒	▓			▒	░			▒	(134)
	West Kennet							▓				----
Late Neo: Grooved Ware	Durrington Walls	░		░		▓			░	▓	░	(3573)
	Lawford	▒	░			▒	▓		░	░	░	(403)
Beaker	Dorset	▒		▒			░		▓		░	(111)
Collared Urn	Dorset	░	░	▓	░		▒			░	░	(147)
Food Vessels	North-east England	▓	▒	▒		░	░		░			(113)
MBA	Kimpton					▒					▓	(46)
	Simons Ground	▒				▒	░			▓	▒	(128)
LBA	Aldermaston/ Knights Farm	▓					░		░	░	▓	(90)
EIA	Danebury	▒				░				▓	▓	(37)
MIA	Danebury	░									▒	(52)

Number of instances

░ 1 - 10%   ▒ 11 - 30%   ▓ > 30%

Fig. 11.2. The percentage occurrence of decorative techniques in selected prehistoric pottery traditions.

within discrete regions. For Beakers and Collared Urns the area chosen was Dorset, with data derived from the works of Clarke (1970) and Longworth (1984); for Food Vessels the corpus of material from north-east England was employed (Gibson 1978). Analysis showed more changes in patterning. Beakers are dominated by comb-impressed designs, while incised and twisted cord designs take second place. Twisted cord, however, is by far the most common technique used to adorn Collared Urns. In distinct contrast, Food Vessels are ornamented mainly with incised decoration and cord impressions, especially of the whipped variety. Deverel-Rimbury pottery of the Middle Bronze Age is exemplified by the Wessex assemblage from Kimpton (Dacre and Ellison 1981) and the Stour Valley group from Simons Ground (White 1982). Although the globular urns are decorated using incised linear and grooving techniques, by far the most common forms of decoration are the use of applied cordons and of finger-tip or finger-nail impressions.

In the Late Bronze Age, following the plain ware Post-Deverel-Rimbury stage, pottery of the Decorated Style is dominated again by finger and thumb treatments, although some incised geometric designs occur. In this case, the assemblages analysed were those from Aldermaston and Knights Farm in the Thames valley (Bradley *et al.* 1980). In the Iron Age period, decoration varies greatly between regions, but the techniques seem to change through time in a fairly standard fashion. Taking the published Danebury assemblage as a guide, we see that a high occurrence of finger-tip decoration and cordons in the Early Iron Age gives way to the use of grooving by the Middle Iron Age. A similar broad pattern occurs in other regions, although various other techniques are evidence by the Middle Iron Age. For instance, Glastonbury Ware carried sharply incised patterns and some stamping, 'duck' stamping is common in the Severn Valley, and in the East Midlands geometric stamps and scored surface treatments are the norm. Another surface treatment which is found commonly during the Iron Age is burnishing. This occurs mainly on thin-walled bowls and jars, as opposed to scoring which tends to be found on larger jar forms. However, few useful statistics of occurrence are yet available. Burnishing has often been interpreted as a means of conveying the shiny surface of metal containers, but it does also occur in pre-metal contexts such as the earliest Neolithic.

The Meaning of Decorative Techniques

Just as the choice of inclusions used in the potting clay may have been determined by symbolic and social, as well as practical, factors, it seems possible that the use of different techniques of decoration employed through time may not have been selected at random. This seems all the more likely in the light of the chronological analysis presented above which has demonstrated that particular types of decoration were strongly associated with particular ceramic traditions, even when several such traditions were broadly contemporary. It is instructive therefore to consider what sorts of symbolic meaning might have been involved.

Hodder's review of the European Neolithic (1990a) emphasised the contrast between the domestic and the wild or natural spheres of perception and how these seemed to have structured economic and social developments through time. Similar oppositions between the wild and the domestic or tame may also have been important in later periods, and this idea has been investigated by Hill (1995a) in relation to Iron Age Wessex. Thus it may be interesting to analyse the tools used for pottery decoration in terms of their domestic or wild origin. The tools used to produce individual impressions appear to have included bones, twigs, reeds, straws, quills or flints. Most of these items would have been gathered in the wild, although the flint and bone implements may have been man-made within a domestic context. Incised linear decoration and grooving seems to have been more systematic, and executed using sharp flint implements or bone and wooden points of standardised widths. The raw material for the cords used to make cord impressions may have derived from the lime tree or the hemp plant. Lime bast fibres had been used extensively since the Mesolithic. They were used particularly in the production of netting, especially fish nets (Clark 1952, 44 and 227). Knotted and fringed network carrying slings would have been used to transport various unwieldy containers, including large pots. As Clark points out, 'the decoration of the earliest cord-ornamented ware, ... clearly reproduces the carrier or sling: in this case, indeed, it is not merely the arrangement, but also the very character of the decoration impressed on the clay, which reveals its origin' (*ibid*, 207). Such decoration is therefore skeuomorphic, but there may be more to it than that. It may be that the cord decoration provides a reference to other spheres of life within which cordage was important, possibly in this case the netting of fish, and boat-building. Pots from the earliest Neolithic periods were usually plain, but the lugs often found on them could have formed both functional and decorative purposes. Sherratt has argued that the possible use of hemp fibres, from the *Cannabis sativa* plant, for the execution of cord decoration on Corded Ware and Beakers may have been a symbolic reference to the stimulating contents of the vessels themselves (Sherratt 1987).

In a similar way, consideration of bird-bone impressions invites allusion to the birds themselves. Most of the species involved were medium to small in size. Such wild creatures may have been caught for food purposes, but Liddell's analysis has shown that certain species may have been preferred

(Liddell 1929). Her firm identifications included goose (4 occurrences), blackbird and magpie (2 occurrences each), carrion crow, rook, sparrow, jay and one small mammal example: hedgehog. She also observed that 'bird-life and bird-ways have from earliest times been invested with magical attributes and made the vehicle of omens and portents some of which ... persist to the present day'. She also notes the finding of the legs of small birds in Breton tombs and a goose from a long barrow near Stonehenge. In the Celtic world, birds formed a natural object of religious significance. Their qualities of free flight and the ability to escape from the earth were indicative of spiritual powers (Green 1986, 186–8). Interestingly, the birds venerated in Late Iron Age times included geese and cranes and also ravens and crows, the very birds whose bones had been used to decorate pots so many centuries earlier. From Iron Age pits in southern Britain there are examples of deliberate deposits of ravens, heron, mallards, other waterfowl and also seabirds: the cormarant and, especially, the kittiwake (Hill 1995a, 63–4 for a summary). It also seems interesting that the birds whose bones were employed in the late Neolithic and Early Bronze Age were either black in colour, or displayed plumage of striking contrasts: the black and white magpie and the jay with its unusual flashes of pink and blue. A similar pattern applies in the Iron Age, with the examples of ravens and the colourful mallard wings, but birdbone decoration on pots is not known from this period. The only probable ceramic connection with birds in the Iron Age is the occurrence of rows of stamped waterfowl: 'ducks' on Malvernian pottery from the Severn valley (Peacock 1968b).

The combs and stamps used to decorate pottery were probably made from bone, certainly the surviving combs were, although we do not know from which animal species the raw material was derived. Many of the 'weaving combs' found on Iron Age sites were made from antler, so that material may also have been employed. Other uses for combs, firmly within a domestic sphere, would have been in personal care of the human body and in the production of textiles. Reference to the human body brings us on to the final category of decorative techniques, the use of the human finger and thumb. This technique not only places the process within the domestic sphere but also introduces an element of individual identification: the vessel is marked by a part of the body who made it.

The Meaning Context

In an important study of the decoration on calabash containers amongst the Ilchamus of Baringo, Hodder (1991) explained how ceramics need to be situated into their own context of meanings. It implies looking for similarities and contrasts along varied dimensions of meaning and breaking down the notion that 'ceramics' form one category with specific intrinsic meaning. For instance, 'if the pots being discussed are painted red, one can ask, "where else in their culture does one find red?' (*ibid.* 72). Hodder goes on to explain the links of meaning between the decorated calabashes which were made and used by women to store milk and also used to feed milk to children and in the exchange of milk with kin. Milk was used in fertility and reproduction ceremonies and is symbolised by other materials, such as hearth ash, which are white in colour. White milk is contrasted with the colour red, associated with danger, blood, men, the wild, and red ochre. However, the complex of meanings is not simple-many reversals and contrasts also occur. One of these involves a double 'V' design painted in red ochre on the chests of young male warriors, a design which also occurs in some calabashes. Throughout Ilchamus life milk and blood, white and red are contrasted, yet they are the same, both involved with life and renewal. 'The calabashes are decorated, and they are decorated in a particular way, because the Ilchamus have a particular set of perspectives that separates and brings together milk and blood, white and red, female and male. Decorating calabashes is one way in which this meaning "game" is played out' (*ibid.* 79).

In an archaeological context, Thomas and Tilley (1993) have attempted to apply such an approach to certain classes of pottery in late Neolithic Brittany. They suggest that, just as the buckler motifs of the tomb art may represent decaying human rib-cages, pottery may represent particular aspects of the female body. The knobs or dots on Chasséen Ware may denote breasts and the pendant swags on Conguel pottery resemble necklaces. Thus the pot may represent a female torso and the breasts may refer to liquid content such as milk or cattle blood. In the passage graves of the Morbihan, Kerogou Ware displays sets of vertical lines below the rim. These may denote ribs or hafted axes and lie in contrast to the earlier tomb art of that area. In contrast, the *allées couvertes* further north mainly contain plain pottery, but the tomb art includes 'breasts' and 'necklaces', motifs which were earlier found only on the Conguel pottery.

Using similar approaches, and employing the data on fabric and decorative techniques that has been assembled above, the possible wider meanings of pottery during British prehistory may be examined. In the Early Neolithic, pottery was not decorated. However, the finely-formed carinated bowls were often burnished and are thought to have been associated with the consumption of large amounts of special food, i.e. feasting (Thomas 1991a). Feasting episodes may have been associated with flint knapping activities of a ritual nature, and it is debris from such activities which was crushed to provide temper for the potting clay. Most vessels were dark in colour and the temper was highly visible. When decoration first appears it is mainly executed by incision. Implements used may have included bones, twigs or reeds, but a particularly likely candidate, especially for fine incised designs, is the edge of a flint tool. Thus a relatively simple linkage of meaning between tools, containers and food may have been maintained.

In the Middle and Late Neolithic, the situation became infinitely more complex. Thomas has discussed in detail the process whereby social identity came to be tied up with the recognition and exploitation of a vast array of different raw materials which were combined and deposited in myriad contexts and combinations (Thomas 1996, figs 6.12–13). Aspects of the contemporary ceramics firmly reinforce these patterns. Firstly, we see a widening of the types of inclusion used, and emphasis on exotic and highly visible tempering materials such as luminous white quartz and the various types of fresh and fossil shell, which reflects the wide range of colourful rocks used for implements and stone balls. Also, there is a greater variety of decorative techniques and these vary according to a series of distinct pottery traditions. We have seen that cord decoration may have involved a raw material, lime bast, gleaned from the forest and that cordage was used also in the catching of fish in the wild and the building of boats. At the same time, it provided carriers for containers, whether of bark, leather, wood or baked clay which would have been used primarily in the storage and preparation of foods and liquids. A little later the fibres of *Cannabis sativa* may have been used to decorate drinking vessels which contained liquids and substances of very special kinds. Also common on Peterborough Ware were impressions made by bird-bones. Birds also derive from trees and the wild forest and it has been established already that the species selected may have been those that were seen to possess supernatural powers. Thus we glimpse a world which valued connections between, the wild, the forest, birds and fish, the supernatural and food. By the end of the Neolithic the consumables may have included commodities which were both alcoholic and hallucinogenic (Sherratt 1987 and 1991).

The late Neolithic Grooved Ware tradition lay in strict contrast to such a complex of meanings. The grooved decoration is executed most probably by man-made tools of bone or wood and the motifs employed are both more extensive and more complex. The tempering agents most commonly employed are novel: shell, grog and mixture recipes involving both. The use of grog may imply that individual vessels were important and became to be used as raw material in newly constructed examples. They occur mainly on 'ritual' sites where feasting, exchange and various ceremonies were acted out. The distinctive shell temper is known, in some cases, to have derived from marine shells (Cleal *et al.* 1994). Such shells are known also from certain pits of Grooved Ware date. Links with the sea and shellfish seem to be implied. The shapes of the vessels, many of them large tubs, evoke themes of storage and consumption on a grand scale. Whether this involved milk or other beverages, grains or dried meat cannot yet be discerned. The meanings of the complex abstract designs found on Grooved Ware are usually viewed as ambiguous, and writers such as Thomas (1996) have argued that this ambiguity was intentional. Other writers have suggested that some of the designs are entoptic in character, depictions of the abstract patterns experienced by the human mind when under the influence of certain hallucinogens. Such designs are well known from the rock art found in megalithic tombs, but in the ceramic context they may relate more directly to the alcoholic and hallucinogenic substances mentioned above.

In the Early Bronze Age, a series of ceramic traditions coexisted and most of them are known largely from funerary contexts. As far as fabrics are concerned there is an overwhelming preponderance of grog, although Beakers also used a variety of combination inclusion recipes. The grog, we have argued, is a highly symbolic substance, which related to individual pots, particular human beings and their descent through time. The main decorative techniques employed are cord impressions, incised lines and, in Beakers, comb impressions. Sherratt (1987) suggests that comb decoration was developed to imitate the impressions made by hemp cord. However, the use of combs may indicate something rather different. Combs and cords were both employed in the production of textiles. Complex weaves known from actual textile finds, and representations such as that on the menhir from Sion, Switzerland (Clarke 1970, 299), give an impression of clothing adorned with rich geometric patterns, similar to the patterns found on Beakers – chevrons, lozenges, fringes, checks and panels, and the more limited motif repertoires of the Collared Urn and Food Vessel traditions. Exactly the same range of designs and motifs is found on certain decorated metalwork of the period – either in gold, the lunulae and 'Wessex' sheet gold ornaments or in bronze, on axes and a few spearheads and daggers. Thus there might have been a complex of overlapping meanings which encompassed decorative outfits and costumes, metal regalia and ceramic vessels used for ceremonial and funereal purposes. In this context, it is also interesting to note the parallel, noted by Tomalin (1995), between the unusual pointillé ornament found on some large bronze daggers and pommels which recurs on the accessory cups of the Aldbourne type.

Throughout the Neolithic period and on into the Early Bronze Age, it has been argued that pottery served highly specific purposes within largely mobile societies. Pottery may have been a generally rare commodity, and was associated particularly with occasional acts of social aggregation connected with feasting and various ceremonies (Thomas 1991a, Ch.5). Pots were associated often with individuals and, in southern England, it was only from the beginning of the Middle Bronze Age period that pottery survives regularly in domestic contexts (Woodward 1995). By contrast, in East Anglia there are many instances of Beaker and Early Bronze Age 'domestic' pottery scatters from the Fen edge (Healy 1995), but these are not associated with settlement structures, and their interpretation is still a matter of debate. In Middle Bronze Age Wessex, for the first time ceramic assemblages are found on settlement sites, and a range of vessel sizes and forms appropriate for storage, food preparation, serving and consumption is represented. These changes link up with the establishment of permanent homes and houses, the greater dependence on farming and, eventually, the development of a divided and enclosed landscape of fields, pastures and trackways. Alongside such changes, we now must add a major dislocation in the fabric types used for pottery production and an equally drastic change in techniques of vessel adornment.

The calcined flint fillers derive from burnt flint nodules which would have been ubiquitous on the farming settlement sites and indeed may have symbolised the hearth, the home and the very essence of settled life. The fact that fillers were often sorted into size grades by sieving provided another interesting link. The origin of the sieve is unknown as they were made entirely from organic materials. However it is postulated that they were used for the separation of weed and grain seeds in agricultural communities from the earliest times, and an example survives from a Neolithic deposit in Switzerland (Hillman 1981, 155–6). Although the mesh sizes of wheat sieves would have been too large for the sorting of some of the size grades of calcined flint filler a technological connection seems highly likely. Thus sieves for pottery temper can be related to cereal agriculture and the new settled farming regime of the Middle Bronze Age period. As far as decoration is concerned, most of the complexity of motifs,

techniques and individualism found amongst Early Bronze Age ceramics was swept away. In its place came a strictly standardised range of fabric types, symbolising the new economic and social regime, and a highly restricted range of decorative techniques. A few geometric motifs can be matched, as in the Early Bronze Age on contemporary metalwork, e.g. the bracelets of Bignan type (Rowlands 1971), but the main means of adornment is finger-tip and finger-nail impressions. Such decoration, formed by the extremities of the human body may have served to emphasise the totally domestic and humanised nature of the new social order, and through its apparent uniformity, the importance of the group and community at the expense of the individual. A change of gender context, from male potting in the Neolithic/ Early Bronze Age periods to female potting in the Middle Bronze Age settlements may also be implied, but it is difficult to see how such a contention might be tested. The picture for northern England could not be more different. As in the south, large numbers of domestic settlements appear from the Middle Bronze Age onwards, but this development coincides with an overall decline in the use of ceramics, and by the Iron Age many regions are practically aceramic.

From the Late Bronze Age we have noted significant additions of sand, and sometimes fragments or grindings from other rocks. The sand will have facilitated the production of more thin-walled vessels and a greater range of sharply angled table wares, thus continuing and developing the possibilities of form variety in the domestic sphere of food preparation, serving and consumption. At the same time, we have suggested that some of the inclusions may have been derived from stone implements, and especially querns, parts of which were deliberately incorporated within the pottery. Querns were the mainstay of grain processing in the domestic context of hearth and home and thus a symbolic link to ceramic tablewares does seem logical. Items designed for overt display in the Late Bronze Age mainly comprised the bronzework. Much of this involves weaponry which may have been employed in social contexts which were mainly male. Decoration of both pottery and metalwork is scarce, but it may be of interest to note that finger-tip treatments, following on the domestic possibly female tradition from the Middle Bronze Age are confined largely to vessels used for storage and cooking, whilst the main embellishment of the fine table wares involves burnishing, and, slightly later on, the application of haematite coatings. Such treatments, as well as the angular profiles of some vessel categories, may have been imitating the finish of metal cups and bowls, or the fine male-orientated Late Bronze Age bronzework in a more general sense.

As the full Iron Age develops, the same distinction between finger-tip decorated or plain domestic coarse wares, and fine table wares now adorned with complex incised geometric patterns, prevails. Most other categories of artefact are plain and functional in design, but certain other categories are decorated. This phenomenon may be investigated by considering the substantial total assemblage from Danebury (Cunliffe 1984b; Cunliffe and Poole 1991b). Most of the tools and weapons, bone tools, whorls, weights, whetstones and querns are undecorated. The main categories of metal which carry decoration are occasional bronze items of a personal nature, such as razors, or the possibly imported openwork La Tène style disc which may have adorned a dagger sheath or a wooden trinket box; and items associated with horse harness: terrets, strap-junctions and other fasteners. Amongst the bone and antler items, decoration occurs on antler cheek pieces, cylindrical toggles and combs. The toggles were probably fasteners and may have been associated with clothing or, again, horse harness. Thus many decorated items were associated with horses. At this stage it may be useful to observe that, at least in Hampshire, the techniques of decoration and motifs employed on the metal, bone and antler items, which mainly involve complex plastic curvilinear designs of La Tène type or sets of ring-and-dot motifs (the latter on bone and antler items only), are in direct contrast to the geometric and loose curvilinear incised patterns found on the ceramic table wares. To investigate the significance of such observations as this, much more detailed analysis of known large site assemblages and their detailed on-site patterning in relation to stratigraphy and different categories of context is required.

Conclusion

This wide-ranging and often contentious study has attempted initially to demonstrate the variations in some of the less well studied aspects of prehistoric ceramics through time. More tentatively, many possible explanations for the changes and cross-correlations observed have been discussed. These explanations have aimed to place the changing ceramic characteristics firmly within a wider archae-ological context which involves the production and consumption of food, the development of settled domestic life, gender roles and cosmologies.

In most cases, the arguments have not been developed very far. The wider employment of petrological analysis for pottery assemblages of all periods is leading to the compilation of an important body of comparative data, but this process is still in its infancy, and has yet to be attemped in many regions. Any analysis of techniques of decoration and motif repertoires is hampered by the variable standards of recording and quantification that have been reached in the past. Hopefully, with the general application of the *PCRG Guidelines* future reports and archives will provide better sources of data upon which such enquiries can be based. Published records of specific surface treatments such as scoring and burnishing are extremely variable and those for the very important characteristic of surface colour are, in modern reportage, virtually nonexistent. Perhaps the posing of more exciting questions will stimulate a more systematic and considered approach to pottery recording.

It is hoped that the ideas and connections outlined in this speculative contribution will serve to stimulate an interest in the compilation of ceramic archives, and also to emphasise the need to consider pottery assemblages in relation to the varying contexts within which they are found, and to other categories of information on individual sites. These categories will include finds made from other materials, the remains of food and drink, structures occupied, avoided or visited, ascribed domestic or ritual space, and the natural and social environments experienced beyond. Thus we may strive to situate the production, use and symbolic importance of pots within the total context of human habitation and experience.

Acknowledgements
This paper was written in 1996. I am grateful to Niall Sharples and to J.D. Hill who made many useful suggestions concerning earlier drafts of this paper, and to Andrew Sherratt for helpful advice on hemp and sieves. I am grateful to Robert Read who prepared Figure 11.2.

12   A Regional Ceramic Sequence: Pottery of the First Millennium BC between the Humber and the Nene

David Knight

Introduction

Much discussion of first millennium BC pottery in Britain has focused upon the comparatively well-known sequence of Wessex (e.g. Cunliffe 1984c) but away from this area very different sequences of ceramic development may be suggested (e.g. Barrett 1980; Cunliffe 1991; Elsdon 1989). The issue of regional variability is addressed in this chapter by reference to the growing body of data from the East Midlands: an area which despite major potential for ceramic research has so far received little attention from students of later prehistoric pottery (cf. Willis 1996). A brief review is presented of the history of ceramic research in the region, followed by a synthesis of the evidence for temporal and spatial variability in vessel fabrics, forms and styles of surface treatment. The possible social and economic implications of these changes are then assessed, with particular emphasis upon the growing evidence for changes in pottery production and distribution.

The East Midlands has been selected for study in recognition of the accumulation over the last thirty years of many large pottery collections, analyses of which have highlighted some interesting patterns of change. This has led to some fundamental revisions in our interpretations of the first millennium BC in this region, which until the rapid expansion of archaeological activity from the 1960's could still be viewed as a scantily populated 'heavily wooded Midland plain' (Piggott 1958, 13). This revolution in our understanding of settlement and hence population densities in the first millennium BC has been most pronounced in Northamptonshire. Here a recent survey of the Late Bronze Age and Iron Age pottery from the county has revealed the remarkable total of almost 500 ceramic collections deriving from excavation, fieldwalking and other activities (Morris *et al.* 1998, 34, table 1). This surpasses the known number of collections in most of the Wessex counties, for long the focus of Late Bronze Age and Iron Age research, and emphasises the key role of such areas for future research into these periods.

Much of the first millennium BC pottery from Northamptonshire and neighbouring areas of Midland and eastern England has been recovered from settlements yielding large ceramic collections with significant research potential. Rarely, unfortunately, have sites with well stratified ceramic sequences been recorded, thus thwarting attempts to construct relative chronologies such as those devised for Cadbury Castle, Somerset (Alcock 1980) or Potterne, Wiltshire (Gingell and Lawson 1984). Further difficulties arise from the paucity of absolute dating evidence, in the form either of associated metalwork or radiocarbon dates, combined with the uniformity and longevity of many pottery fabrics, forms and styles of surface treatment. Despite these problems, major progress has been made towards the creation of a regional ceramic sequence. In addition, detailed fabric analyses have demonstrated significant potential for studies of ceramic production and distribution, while further patterns of interest are emerging from analyses of the distributions of Scored ware, La Tène decorated wares and other pottery styles (cf. Elsdon 1992a; Morris 1994b).

Spatial Extent of Study

The boundaries of the study area have been drawn to include the drainage basins of the Rivers Trent, Welland and Nene. It incorporates therefore mainly the historic counties of Derbyshire, Leicestershire, Lincolnshire, Northamptonshire, Nottinghamshire, Rutland and Staffordshire, together with the northern part of Cambridgeshire. The eastern boundary has been extended beyond the Trent basin to the modern Lincolnshire coast, in order that the important later Iron Age ceramic traditions of Lindsey and Kesteven may also be considered. Southwards, the eastern margin correlates with the edge of the broad zone of low islands, salt marshes and creeks which in the Iron Age would have extended over much of the Lincolnshire and Cambridgeshire Fenland (Fig. 12.1; Hall and Coles 1994, especially fig. 59). Extensive areas of wetland, unsuitable for permanent settlement, would have extended northwards from the Fens into the Lincolnshire Marsh and either side of the Humber Estuary, penetrating deeply inland along the lower Trent and Ancholme Valleys and into the Vale of York (Van de Noort and Davies 1993; Van de Noort and Ellis eds 1995, 1997, 1998). The approximate extent of these areas, which has significant implications for interpretations of pottery distributions within the eastern part of the region, is shown in Fig. 12.1.

History of Ceramic Research

This region has only recently attracted the attentions of researchers concerned with developments in Britain during the first millennium BC (e.g. Haselgrove 1984; Knight 1984; Liddle 1982, 16–27; May 1976a, 1976b, 1984, 1996, 619–44; O'Brien 1979; Smith 1978; Willis 1997) and not surprisingly few attempts have been made to synthesise the ceramic evidence of this period. Kenyon (1950, 58–67; 1952), building upon the pioneering work of Hawkes, was the first to publish a general review of East Midlands Iron Age pottery, mainly within the framework of her East Anglia-Wash and Trent Basin regions (*ibid.* 42–50, 67–73). The evidence was presented in terms of Hawkes' ABC model, and in the greater part of the region the ceramic sequence was compressed mainly into the first century BC and first century AD (*ibid.* 73). Later general surveys of the pottery from this region were conducted by Cunliffe (1966; 1968) and the proposed 'style-zones', summarised in his later syntheses of Iron Age Britain (1974, 1978, 1991), have formed the basis of much subsequent work on first millennium BC pottery (cf. Fig. 12.2). Most recently, a valuable corpus of pottery from East Midlands sites spanning the Late Bronze Age to Late Iron Age periods has been published by Elsdon (1996a), together with a summary of some of the main typological developments of the period.

Other reviews have focused upon either the ceramic sequence of particular areas within the East Midlands, notably the Trent basin (Challis and Harding 1975), Nene basin (Knight 1984) and Leicestershire (Hope 1979), or particular ceramic traditions. The most influential study in the latter respect is that carried out by Barrett, who considered the earlier first millennium BC pottery of part of this

region in his general survey of the later Bronze Age ceramic sequence of lowland Britain (Barrett 1980, 312–3). This was tackled mainly from the viewpoint of developments in vessel typology, with consideration also of the social and economic implications of the observed changes. The proposed sequence from plain to decorated Post Deverel-Rimbury (PDR) assemblages has been widely accepted (e.g. Cunliffe 1991, 60–4) although, as Barrett himself noted, this sequence may have varied significantly regionally (Barrett 1980, 298, 314). Other valuable surveys of specific ceramic traditions include Elsdon's studies of Scored ware (Elsdon 1992a) and La Tène stamped and rouletted decoration (Elsdon 1975). Syntheses of the Late Iron Age pottery from the southern parts of the region are contained in Thompson's (1982) survey of grog-tempered 'Belgic' pottery from southern England, and in Friendship-Taylor's study of the Late La Tène pottery from the Nene and Welland Valleys (Friendship-Taylor 1998, 1999).

The emphasis in most of the discussions referred to above has been upon typology and chronology, but more recently attempts have been made to look at the broader social and economic implications of the ceramic evidence. The most notable contributions in this respect have been Morris's survey of ceramic production and distribution in first millennium BC Britain (Morris 1994b; 1996) and Willis's study of the Romanisation of the Late Iron Age pottery industries in the eastern part of the region, from Leicester northwards (Willis 1996). Efforts have also been made to examine intra-site spatial distributions of pottery, with particular reference to the social and symbolic implications of this evidence (Gwilt 1997).

The above work has been made possible by the steady accumulation of published pottery reports containing the basic data for systematic research, many accompanied by detailed archives. Examples include those for Dragonby, Lincs. (May 1996), Enderby, Leics. (Clay 1992), Fengate, Cambs. (Pryor 1984), Gamston, Notts. (Knight 1992), Mam Tor, Derbys. (Coombs and Thompson 1979) and Weekley, Northants. (Jackson and Dix 1986–7): settlements of highly variable character, widely distributed throughout the region (Fig. 12.1).

The Sequence of Ceramic Change

Consideration of the limited stratigraphic and absolute dating evidence from first millennium BC sites in the region, alongside typological parallels with pottery from elsewhere in Britain, suggests a sequence of four main stylistic traditions post-dating pottery of the Deverel-Rimbury complex (the latter as defined by Barrett 1976). Each is characterised by a range of new vessel forms and/or styles of surface

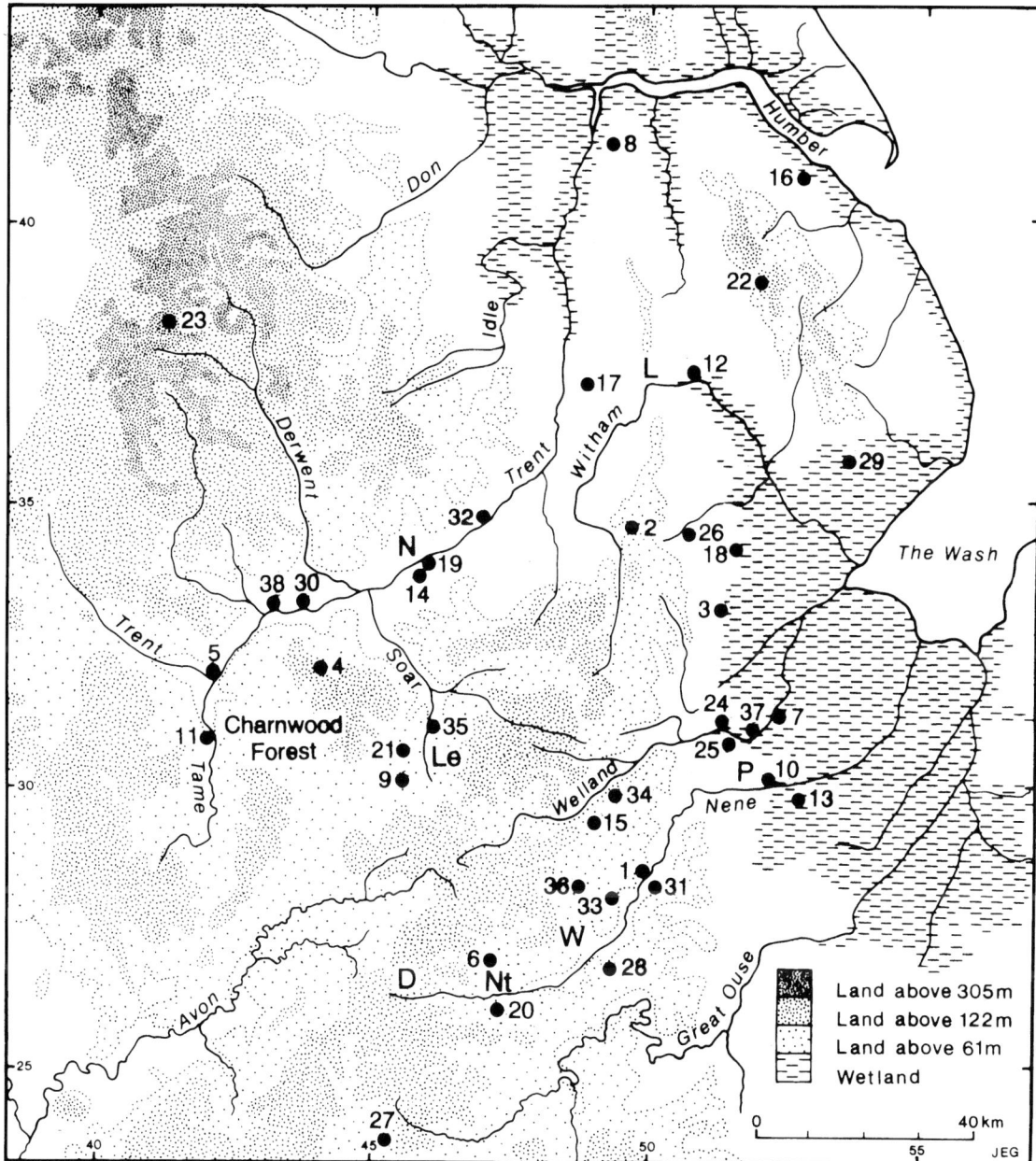

Fig. 12.1. Location map, showing relief, drainage, approximate extent of Iron Age wetlands and main sites referred to in text. 1. Aldwincle; 2. Ancaster; 3. Billingborough; 4. Breedon-on-the-Hill; 5. Catholme; 6. Chapel Brampton; 7. Cowbit; 8. Dragonby; 9. Enderby; 10. Fengate; 11. Fisherwick; 12. Fiskerton; 13. Flag Fen; 14. Gamston; 15. Gretton; 16. Grimsby (Weelsby Avenue); 17. Harby; 18. Helpringham; 19. Holme Pierrepont; 20. Hunsbury; 21. Kirby Muxloe; 22. Kirmond le Mire; 23. Mam Tor; 24. Market Deeping; 25. Northborough; 26. Old Sleaford; 27. Rainsborough; 28. Rushden; 29. Stickford; 30. Swarkestone Lowes; 31. Thrapston; 32. Thurgarton (Coneygre Farm); 33. Twywell; 34. Wakerley; 35. Wanlip; 36. Weekley; 37. Welland Bank; 38. Willington. D: Daventry; L: Lincoln; Le: Leicester; N: Nottingham; Nt: Northampton; P: Peterborough.

treatment, introduced gradually over quite lengthy periods, and by a substratum of inherited ceramic types. The changes occurred at different rates within the East Midlands and did not affect all parts of the region equally. Spatially restricted ceramic traditions may be discerned most clearly in the second half of the first millennium BC, with the development of well defined regional styles of La Tène ornament and Scored ware. Potting traditions in the earlier part of the millennium appear to have been more homogeneous, in contrast to some other areas of southern Britain (cf. Cunliffe 1991, 61–72), although

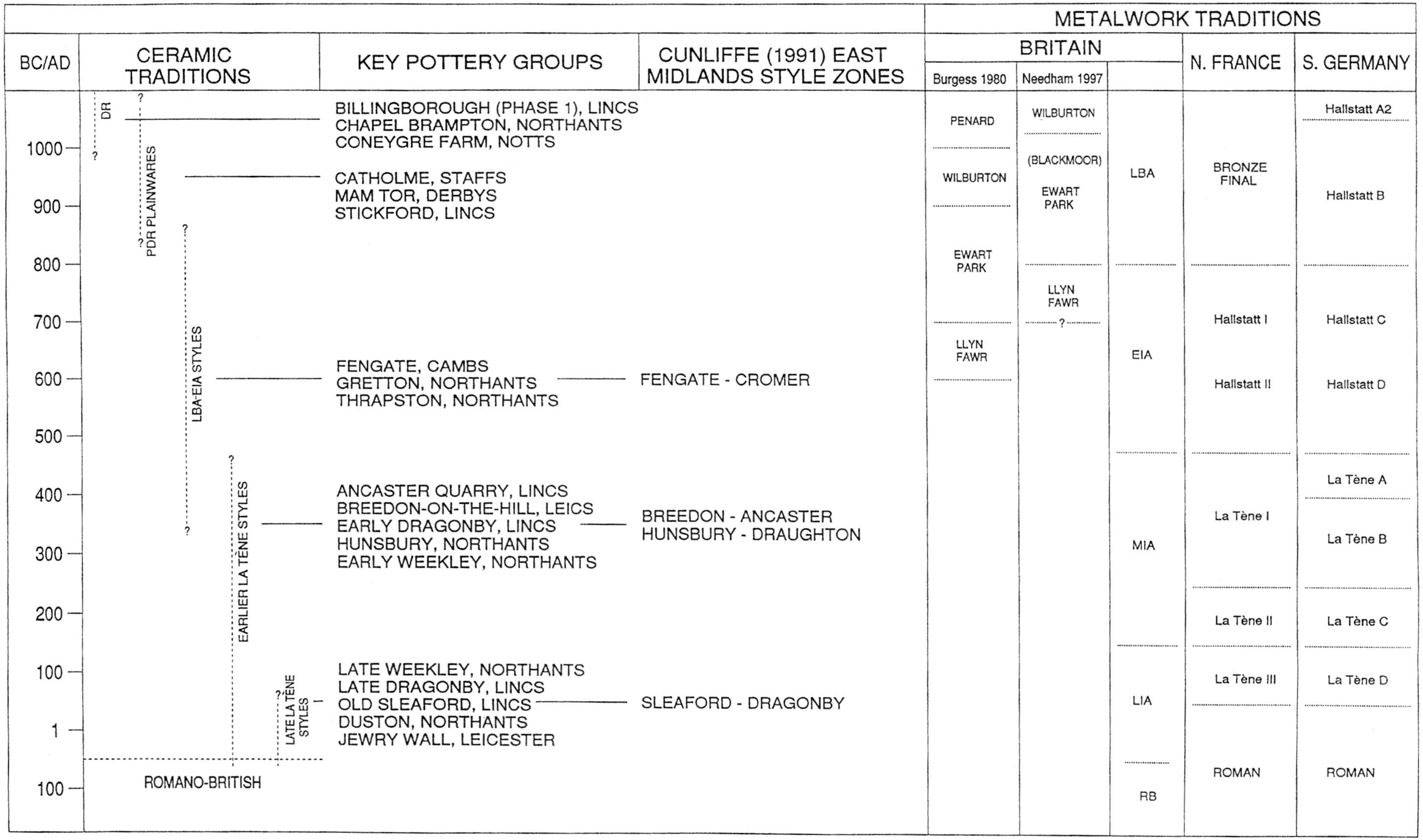

BC/AD	CERAMIC TRADITIONS	KEY POTTERY GROUPS	CUNLIFFE (1991) EAST MIDLANDS STYLE ZONES	BRITAIN			N. FRANCE	S. GERMANY
				Burgess 1980	Needham 1997	METALWORK TRADITIONS		
1000	DR	BILLINGBOROUGH (PHASE 1), LINCS / CHAPEL BRAMPTON, NORTHANTS / CONEYGRE FARM, NOTTS		PENARD	WILBURTON		BRONZE FINAL	Hallstatt A2
900	PDR PLAINWARES	CATHOLME, STAFFS / MAM TOR, DERBYS / STICKFORD, LINCS		WILBURTON	(BLACKMOOR) / EWART PARK	LBA		Hallstatt B
800				EWART PARK				Hallstatt C
700	LBA-EIA STYLES	FENGATE, CAMBS / GRETTON, NORTHANTS / THRAPSTON, NORTHANTS	FENGATE - CROMER	LLYN FAWR	LLYN FAWR / ?	EIA	Hallstatt I	Hallstatt D
600							Hallstatt II	
500								La Tène A
400	EARLIER LA TÈNE STYLES	ANCASTER QUARRY, LINCS / BREEDON-ON-THE-HILL, LEICS / EARLY DRAGONBY, LINCS / HUNSBURY, NORTHANTS / EARLY WEEKLEY, NORTHANTS	BREEDON - ANCASTER / HUNSBURY - DRAUGHTON			MIA	La Tène I	La Tène B
300								La Tène C
200	LATE LA TÈNE STYLES	LATE WEEKLEY, NORTHANTS / LATE DRAGONBY, LINCS / OLD SLEAFORD, LINCS / DUSTON, NORTHANTS / JEWRY WALL, LEICESTER	SLEAFORD - DRAGONBY			LIA	La Tène II	La Tène D
100							La Tène III	
1	ROMANO-BRITISH					RB	ROMAN	ROMAN
100								

Fig. 12.2. A suggested ceramic sequence for the East Midlands during the first millennium BC (cf. Haselgrove 1997, fig. 8.1 and Needham 1997, illus. 15 for metalwork sequence).

this could reflect the smaller sample base and the greater difficulty of identifying spatial variability.

The proposed ceramic sequence is summarised diagrammatically in Fig. 12.2. This shows the broad date ranges of each pottery tradition, examples of key vessel groups, and correlations between the scheme proposed here and the commonly employed 'style zones' of Cunliffe (1974, 1978, 1991). The approximate durations of the contemporary British and Continental metalwork assemblages are also shown (cf. Haselgrove 1997; Needham 1996, 1997; Rieckhoff 1995, especially tab.21).

Deverel-Rimbury Ceramic Styles

This tradition falls beyond the scope of the present work, but some understanding of its character, chronology and spatial extent is essential for an assessment of early first millennium BC ceramic developments within the region. Useful discussions of Deverel-Rimbury pottery and related regional traditions have been published by Barrett (1976, 1980, 298–301) and within an East Midlands context by Allen, Harman and Wheeler (1987; cf. Allen 1988; see also papers in Barrett and Bradley 1980). Pottery related to the classic Deverel-Rimbury style of south-central England is poorly represented in the East Midlands compared to areas farther south (see Fig 12.3,1–6). However, discoveries at settlements such as Barnetby Wold (Didsbury and Steedman 1992, fig.4), Billingborough (Chowne 1988; Chowne, Cleal, Fitzpatrick and Andrews, forthcoming) and Kirmond le Mire (Field and Knight 1992), Lincs., and cremation cemeteries such as Barwell, Leics. (Allen 1988, 330; Liddle 1982, 15), Chapel Brampton, Northants. (Moore 1971; Knight 1984, i, 72), Coneygre Farm, Thurgarton, Notts. and Pasture Lodge Farm, Long Bennington, Lincs. (Allen, Harman and Wheeler 1987) suggest that regional variants may have flourished over much of the area lying south and east of the Peak District (into which region Deverel-Rimbury styles appear not to have penetrated: cf. Beswick 1994). On current evidence a regional tradition of commonly grog-tempered and mainly bucket and barrel shaped vessels is apparent (cf. Allen *et al.* 1987, 211–23). These pots are generally plain, but some were ornamented with finger-nail or finger-tip impressions, forming a row around the upper body or rim or covering much of the outer surface (*ibid.* figs 13–17), a plain or finger-impressed horizontal cordon around the upper body (*ibid.* fig. 13.3; fig. 14.14, 20) or applied bosses (e.g. Chapel Brampton). More rarely, incised chevron or other geometric patterns were applied to the body (e.g. Coneygre Farm: Allen *et al.* 1987, fig. 7.12; Stainsby, Lincs.: May 1976a, fig. 43: urn 8).

Deverel-Rimbury vessels are imprecisely dated. In southern Britain, however, occasional associations with Middle Bronze Age metalwork (mainly Taunton assemblage bronzes of the 14th–13th centuries cal BC) and with organic material dated by radiocarbon, mostly from burials, suggest a predominantly middle to late second millennium cal BC date range overlapping the later period of currency of Collared Urns, Food Vessels and other earlier Bronze Age ceramic types (Barnatt 1994, Appendix 1; Barrett 1976, 290–5; 1980, 306–13; Burgess 1986; Needham 1996, 133–4; 1997, 84–6, illus. 15; Smith 1959). Radiocarbon dates could indicate a continuation of Deverel-Rimbury traditions into the early first millennium BC in some areas, overlapping the Post Deverel-Rimbury styles which in southern Britain eventually assumed dominance (Barrett 1976, 1980, 309–11; Cunliffe 1991, 53–4). The possible late continuation of Deverel-Rimbury styles remains a vexed question, but a recent reassessment of the radiocarbon data failed to find convincing evidence for significant continuation beyond the second millennium BC (Needham 1996, 134–5). In the East Midlands, absolute dating of Deverel-Rimbury wares rests upon rare discoveries on cemetery sites of Middle Bronze Age or less closely datable later Bronze Age metalwork, together with occasional radiocarbon associations. These include a Taunton assemblage bronze bracelet recovered from topsoil at Old Somersby, Lincs., and hence not directly associated with pottery (Chowne and Lane 1987, 40). In addition, a doubled wire bronze bracelet and possibly part of a twisted bronze wire bracelet, both datable to the Middle or Late Bronze Age, were found with a perforated globular bead of blue glass or faience inside a plain bucket urn at Chapel Brampton (Knight 1984, 72). Rare associations have also been recorded with material dated by radiocarbon, including Swarkestone Lowes, Derbys., where a bucket urn had been placed inside a hollow oak tree trunk dated to 3080±60BP (Beta-104495; 1450–1130 cal BC at 2 sigma; Knight and Elliott in prep.), Chapel Brampton, where were recorded fragments of a bucket urn associated with charcoal dated to 3064±120BP (Birm-313; 1600–900 cal BC at 2 sigma; Moore 1971), and Billingborough, where a date of 3140±57BP (BM-1410; 1520–1260 cal BC at 2 sigma) was obtained from charcoal associated with Deverel-Rimbury pottery in an early silting layer of an enclosure ditch (Chowne *et al.* forthcoming; see following section). These dates are consistent with a period of use centred upon the latter half of the second millennium BC, but considerably more dates are required to verify this argument.

Post Deverel-Rimbury (PDR) 'Plainwares'

The changes in ceramic fashion which in this region accompanied the decline of Deverel-Rimbury pottery styles remain poorly understood, largely because of the rarity of stratified sequences incorporating Deverel-Rimbury pottery and the paucity of associated dating evidence. Another problem arises from the comparative rarity of decoration in East Midlands assemblages dating from the earlier part of the first millennium BC. This complicates attempts to examine the transition from 'plain' to 'decorated' PDR styles, proposed originally by Barrett (1980), although there are sufficient grounds to suggest a trend towards the greater use of decoration during the period of currency of Ewart Park metalwork assemblages (c.1020–800 cal BC: Needham 1997, 93–8, illus. 15).

An evolving tradition of mainly plain vessels, some representing developments of established Deverel-Rimbury forms, is suggested by typological comparisons between a growing number of largely unpublished ceramic collections from this region and pottery attributed by Barrett (1980) to his later Bronze Age tradition of 'PDR plainwares' – as exemplified by vessels from the Berkshire sites of Aldermaston Wharf (Bradley et al. 1980) and Knights Farm (Bradley et al. 1980), Ram's Hill, Oxon. (Barrett 1975) and Cadbury Castle, Somerset (Alcock 1980). These have been recovered from sites widely distributed across the region, including Ball Cross, Derbys. (Stanley 1954), Billingborough (Barrett 1980, 313; Chowne 1988; Chowne et al. forthcoming), Catholme, Staffs. (A.G. Kinsley and G. Guilbert pers comm.), Flag Fen (Pryor forthcoming), Mam Tor (Barrett 1979), Northborough Nine Bridges, Cambs. (K. Gdaniec pers comm.), Stickford, Lincs. (Knight forthcoming: a) and Welland Bank, Deeping St. James, Lincs. (Pryor 1998). Important components of this ceramic style include open bowls, bowls and jars of ovoid form or with pronounced rounded or carinated girths, and ellipsoid jars which may have developed from Deverel-Rimbury roots (see Fig. 12.3, 7–12 and cf. Barrett 1980, fig. 5). These indicate a broadening of the ceramic repertoire, including a new emphasis upon bowl forms not represented in local Deverel-Rimbury collections. Several distinctive rim forms may be recognised, including the 'hooked' rims which were first identified by Barrett (1975, 103; e.g. Mam Tor: Barrett 1979, 46, Coombs and Thompson 1979, fig. 22.2), bevelled or tapered rims (ibid., fig. 21.1, 24.2) and distinctive tapered rims differentiated from the vessel wall by a sharp internal angle (e.g. Stickford; cf. Coombs andThompson 1979, fig. 24.1). Bases are generally flat, but rare examples of omphalos bases, possibly derived from metallic prototypes, have also been recognised (e.g. Flag Fen and Northborough

Nine Bridges). The finer wares are sometimes distinguished by thin walls and may preserve burnished surfaces, in both these respects contrasting with the coarse thick-walled urns which characterise the East Midlands variant of the Deverel-Rimbury tradition. Decoration was applied rarely, if at all, and comprises mainly a row of finger-nail or finger-tip impressions along the rim or girth and applied cordons (e.g. Mam Tor: ibid. figs. 18 & 23).

Stratigraphic evidence supporting the case for a progression from Deverel-Rimbury to PDR ceramic traditions has been recovered from several settlements within the East Midlands. The best known of these is Billingborough, where excavations revealed three sides of a subrectangular ditched enclosure yielding within the ditch filling a stratified sequence of later Bronze Age pottery (from earlier to later 'Phase 1' according to the phasing in Chowne et al. forthcoming; published previously as 'Phase 1' and 'Phase 2': Chowne 1978, 18, figs. 5–6). The lower layers of the ditch were dominated by grog-tempered pottery, occasionally combined with rare fossil shell ('earlier Phase 1'); these fabrics gave way in the upper fills to a mixture of grog-tempered vessels and pots with shell and limestone inclusions ('later Phase 1'). The grog-tempered sherds from the lower layers derived from characteristic Deverel-Rimbury forms, either with straight vertical or slightly tapering sides (cf. Allen et al. 1987, 212: type 1) or inturned slightly beneath the rim (ibid. 212: type 2). Some of these have a horizontal cordon or a row of finger-tip impressions on the upper body (Chowne 1978, fig. 5). The upper layers incorporated fragments of comparable vessels associated with several plain sherds deriving from carinated vessels of novel type (ibid. fig. 6). Other new elements include a concave-necked sherd with a row of finger-nail incisions around the neck and fragments of open bowls or cups, embellished in one or possibly two instances by a curious pattern of impressed open circles arranged diagonally or horizontally (ibid. fig. 6.17). Associated sherds, from vessels of uncertain form, occasionally have rows of finger-impressions along the lip. The more diverse pottery from the upper layers invites comparison with typical PDR assemblages, and in view of the comparative rarity of ornament may relate to Barrett's earlier tradition of PDR 'plainwares' rather than later 'decorated' wares. Deverel-Rimbury vessels may have continued in use alongside these new ceramic types for some time, although much of the Deverel-Rimbury material from the upper ditch levels could have been redeposited. Pottery from other contexts at Billingborough may be compared to other PDR ceramic types from southern Britain, suggesting a varied repertoire including bowls with pronounced rounded or carinated girths and ovoid jars with everted necks (cf. Mam Tor: Coombs and Thompson 1979, figs. 16–27).

Another ceramic collection which may incorporate vessels spanning the transition from Deverel-Rimbury to predominantly plain PDR ceramic traditions was obtained from a settlement at Kirmond le Mire – although the small size of the collection must urge caution in interpretation (Field and Knight 1992, 45, figs. 7b, 8: site KM3). A trench through an enclosure ditch revealed four layers incorporating sherds attributable to the Deverel-Rimbury and PDR ceramic traditions. The bottom layer comprised mainly chalk rubble, possibly from a levelled bank, but yielded no finds. Above this was a dark ash-flecked layer which may also have been deliberately deposited and two upper layers which appear to have accumulated more gradually. The lower of the two upper layers yielded an unabraded rim from a grog-tempered Deverel-Rimbury bucket urn, preserving beneath the rim a single finger-tip impression (*ibid.* fig. 8.3), and three abraded shelly body sherds of uncertain affinity, while the dark ash-flecked layer beneath this produced a moderately abraded rim, possibly also from a bucket urn, in a coarse shelly fabric (*ibid.* fig. 8.4). The uppermost layer, by contrast, yielded seven sherds (*pace* Field and Knight 1992, 45), tempered with grog or in a fine sandy fabric, including fragments of two vessels comparing with PDR wares; the latter comprise a rim from a thin-walled vessel with high everted neck and internally bevelled rim (*ibid.* fig. 8.1) and a rounded rim from an ovoid or possibly ellipsoid vessel reminiscent of some of the PDR plainwares from other Lincolnshire sites such as Stickford (*ibid.* fig. 8.2).

A similar sequence may be postulated at several other sites in the region, including Flag Fen (Pryor forthcoming) and probably Welland Bank (F. Pryor *pers.comm.*), but although the sequence seems soundly based, the absolute chronology of the proposed changes remains less certain. A chronological range from the late second millennium BC into the tenth/ninth centuries BC may be suggested for PDR plainwares generally, largely on the basis of radiocarbon and metalwork associations from sites in southern Britain (Barrett 1975; 1980, 306–13; Needham 1996, 134–7). Dating remains problematic, however, and could have varied significantly regionally. Some elements of the tradition can be dated with reasonable confidence to the period from the tenth to ninth centuries BC, on the basis of parallels which have been noted with Ewart Park cast bronze vessels and beaten bronze buckets (e.g. Barrett 1980, 313–4; Cunliffe 1991, 61–4; Needham 1995, 164–5). The chronology of Ewart Park metalwork has been reassessed recently by Needham (1996, 136–7, fig. 1; 1997, 93–8, illus. 15) who, on the basis of associated

radiocarbon and dendrochronological dates, has suggested a *c.*1020–800 cal BC date range, significantly earlier than previous estimates for the duration of such metalwork (e.g. Burgess 1980; O'Connor 1980). Especially persuasive parallels may be drawn between the well-known cast bronze bowl from Welby, Leics. (Powell 1948) and pottery furrowed bowls (Avery 1981; Barrett 1980, 313–4, fig. 5.11), examples of which incorporate several features suggesting that their makers may have been influenced by contemporary metalwork (cf. Harding 1974, 149–51). The composition of the Welby hoard suggests a Ewart Park origin (cf. O'Connor 1980, 387–9), implying that pottery furrowed bowls could date from as early as the tenth century BC (see also Needham 1995, 164–5). Further evidence that Ewart Park metalwork could have influenced pottery styles is provided by the stylistic parallels which have been noted between fine thin-walled carinated bowls, sometimes with omphalos bases and highly burnished finishes, and rare examples of other cast bronze vessels (notably the two beaten bronze cups from Glentanar, Aberdeenshire: Pearce 1970–1; cf. Barrett 1980, 313–4, fig. 6; O'Connor 1980, 193, 285) and between high-girthed carinated jars and beaten bronze buckets (cf. Harding 1974, 138-40; Longley 1980, 68: type 13; O'Connor 1980, 191–2, 285). If these parallels are accepted, we might imagine a ceramic style developing from Deverel-Rimbury roots, towards the end of the second millennium BC, to which new elements, inspired in part by contact with Ewart Park metalworking traditions, had been progressively grafted. Furrowed bowls, therefore, together with other PDR forms that could be related to Ewart Park metal vessels, might represent later elements of this tradition.

Little direct dating evidence has been obtained for East Midlands plainware, the chronology of which hinges at present upon a small number of radiocarbon and dendrochronological dates. The value of radiocarbon dating is limited by the possibility that the later phases of this ceramic tradition overlap the notorious radiocarbon calibration platform of *c.*800–400 cal BC (cf. Needham 1996, 136–7), but with this proviso the evidence supports a very early first millennium BC date range. One of the better known ceramic associations from the region was recorded some years ago at Newark Road, Fengate, where a backfilled pit or post-hole cutting an infilled Bronze Age boundary ditch yielded unabraded joining sherds from a plain tripartite carinated bowl which appear to have been deposited with charcoal dated to 2740±80BP (Har-773; 1120–780 cal BC at 2 sigma; Pryor 1980, 66, 106, 247, fig. 61.39). This pot would fit comfortably within a plainware context, although comparable vessels also characterise assemblages of the succeeding ceramic phase. Another important discovery was made at nearby Flag Fen, where a plain omphalos-based bowl, recalling in shape the decorated globular bowls from Fengate (Hawkes and Fell 1943, fig. 7), was recovered from beneath a timber dated by dendrochronology to *c*.900BC (J. Neve, in Pryor forthcoming). At least two levels beneath this was a Deverel-Rimbury bucket urn ornamented with a row of finger-tip impressions around the upper part of the wall (F. Pryor: *pers comm*.), adding further weight to the case for a progression from Deverel-Rimbury ceramics to PDR plainwares. More recently, excavations of a circular ditched enclosure at Thrapston, Northants., revealed in the ditch fill a possible sequence of plain to decorated PDR wares; from the primary ditch fill was recovered a pig lower mandible dated to 2630±50BP (BM-3113; 920–760 cal BC at 92.5% probability: Hull 1998; calibration by J. Ambers: *ibid*. 10). Six more bone samples from various levels in the ditch have been submitted for radiocarbon dating, and are awaited with interest. Recent discoveries of large plainware assemblages on several other sites within the region, notably Langtoft, Lincs. (Knight 1999), Northborough Nine Bridges (K. Gdaniec: *pers comm*.) and Welland Bank (Pryor 1998 and *pers comm*.), hold out the possibility of further radiocarbon dating of associated organic material, and the next few years may see major developments in our understanding of the earliest ceramic traditions of the first millennium BC.

Late Bronze Age–Earlier Iron Age (LBA–EIA) Ceramic Styles

The changes in metalworking styles which are manifested by Ewart Park assemblages may have coincided in southern Britain not only with the adoption of a range of ceramic forms which could reflect in some cases the influence of contemporary metalwork but also with a gradual renewal of interest in finger-impressed and grooved, incised and impressed geometrical ornament. The apparent resurgence in finger ornament might provide further evidence for links between potting and metalworking, in view of the occasional discovery on carinated jars of vertical and horizontal lines of finger impressions which it has been suggested could mimic the rivets joining the component sheets of Ewart Park beaten bronze buckets (cf. Harding 1974, 139–40). However, the extensive use of finger-impressed decoration in Deverel-Rimbury assemblages should urge caution in relating too boldly the resurgence of finger-tipping and the patterning of metal rivets.

This trend towards more profusely decorated wares was first identified by Barrett (1975, 1980), following detailed analyses of the stratified pottery groups from such sites as Ram's Hill, Oxon. (Bradley and Ellison 1975), Runnymede Bridge, Surrey (Longley 1980), and Cadbury Castle, Somerset (Alcock 1980), and formed the basis of his influential division into 'plain' and 'decorated' PDR wares. The case for a progression during the Late Bronze Age in some parts of southern Britain from 'plain' to 'decorated' ceramic assemblages has been sustained by more recent analyses of stratified pottery groups from sites such as the Potterne midden and settlement, Wilts. (Lawson 1994; E. Morris *pers comm*.), but there is currently insufficient evidence to establish the impact of these changes on the repertoires of potters working in many areas north of the Thames. In the East Midlands, studies of temporal changes in the proportions of plain and decorated wares during the early first millennium BC, together with changes in the variety of ceramic forms and their relative proportions, are complicated by the rarity of well-stratified assemblages dating from this period and by the paucity of reliable dating evidence. At present, the only known site from the region which may preserve a sequence from plain to decorated PDR wares is the partially excavated enclosure at Thrapston, where a collection of plain and decorated PDR wares, associated with animal bone dated by radiocarbon, was found within the ditch fill (see above). The problem is exacerbated by the small numbers of decorated vessels which have been obtained, even from such classic LBA–EIA assemblages as Gretton, Northants. (Jackson and Knight 1985, 81, tables 4–5, fig. 14). The low proportions of decorated sherds stand in sharp contrast to the totals obtained from sites such as the Potterne midden (Lawson 1994: upper levels, stratified above PDR plainwares) or the East Chisenbury midden (Brown, G *et al*. 1994), both in Wiltshire, and underline the spatial diversity of ceramic styles at this time and the pitfalls of underestimating regional variability in the formulation of ceramic sequences.

The wide variety of ceramic ornament which characterises 'decorated' PDR assemblages from southern Britain is aptly illustrated by the pottery from the sites referred to above and by the rich collections recovered from All Cannings Cross, Wilts. (Cunnington 1923), Mucking, Essex (Bond 1988), Orsett, Essex (Hedges and Buckley 1978) and Petters Sports Field, Egham, Surrey (O'Connell 1986; see also Barrett 1980, fig. 1). Typologically related assemblages have been recovered from settlements distributed widely over the East Midlands, including the 'Gravel Pits' and Vicarage Farm settlements at Fengate (Hawkes and Fell 1943; Pryor 1974), Gretton (Jackson and Knight 1985), Harborough Rocks, Derbys. (Challis and Harding 1975, fig. 4; Ward 1890), Rainsborough, Northants. (Avery *et al*. 1967), Red Hill, Ratcliffe-on-Soar, Notts. (Elsdon 1982),

Rectory Farm, West Deeping, Lincs. (Knight, Allen and Appleton forthcoming) and Willington, Derbys. (Elsdon 1979). Parallels with 'decorated' assemblages from other regions of southern Britain, combined with the limited direct dating evidence from sites in the East Midlands, suggest that these pottery groups mainly postdate 'plain PDR' assemblages such as Catholme or Stickford, but with the exception of the above-mentioned site at Thrapston, stratigraphic evidence which might imply a transition from 'plain' to 'decorated' styles has yet to be obtained from the region.

The emphasis in ceramic collections from the East Midlands which may be related typologically to Barrett's 'decorated' rather than 'plain' PDR assemblages lies upon bowls and jars with carinated or pronounced rounded girths, either of bipartite form or with an everted, upright or concave neck, and occasionally with an omphalos base (e.g. Fengate: Hawkes and Fell 1943, figs 1–10). The range of forms also includes ovoid and vertically sided vessels, globular bowls and open bowls (*op.cit.*) but the difficulty of identifying these forms from small fragments may have caused some underestimation of their original frequencies (cf. Knight 1984, i, fig. 3). Footring bases, to the author's knowledge not as yet observed in plain PDR collections from the region, survive occasionally in LBA–EIA contexts (e.g. Vicarage Farm, Fengate: Pryor 1974, fig. 14.19). The distinctive thin-walled ellipsoid jars with tapered or bevelled rims that characterise plain PDR assemblages such as Stickford and Northborough Nine Bridges, together with the hooked rims from sites such as Catholme or Mam Tor, seem not to continue into this phase, implying developments not only in the character and frequency of ornamentation but also in vessel forms. New and distinctive rim forms may occasionally be discerned, notably rims with one or two internal grooves, possibly for lids, or with multiple internal corrugations, as at Gretton (Jackson and Knight 1985, fig. 6.21–22, 8.65, 69–73) and Fiskerton, Lincs. (Fig. 3.9; Field 1985–6). Other distinctive types include the unusual square-headed rims from sites such as Gretton (Jackson and Knight 1985, fig. 8.67–68) and Harringworth, Northants. (Jackson 1981), and a variety of T-shaped and other flanged forms (e.g. Jackson and Knight 1985, fig. 6.23, 8.51). The finer wares commonly have thin walls with distinctive tapered or internally bevelled rims (*ibid.*, fig. 9.89–92), continuing the fashion for delicately moulded rims which is a feature of the preceding 'plainware' tradition.

Some of the coarser wares from the region were embellished with extensive finger ornament or with tooled decoration resembling finger-nail incisions. This comprises most commonly a row of finger-nail or finger-tip impressions along the rim, neck-angle or girth (Hawkes and Fell 1943, figs 3–4). Cordons were sometimes applied to the neck or girth, and were either undecorated or embellished with finger impressions. A varied repertoire of highly distinctive incised and grooved geometric patterns also characterises this ceramic style, including hatched triangles and interlocking multiple pendant and standing arcs (best exemplified at Fengate: *ibid.* figs 6–7; Pryor 1974, fig. 14). These designs can occur in association with geometric impressed patterns, sometimes emphasised by a white calcareous inlay (Barclay 1998), recalling pottery from sites such as Chinnor, Oxon. and All Cannings Cross, Wilts. (e.g. Pryor 1974, fig. 14; cf. Knight 1984 i, 23–4 for range of patterns).

Barrett suggested that a transition from PDR plainwares to pottery assemblages characterised by a more extensive use of decoration may have occurred during the eighth century BC, largely on the evidence of ceramic associations with Ewart Park metalwork and radiocarbon dating (Barrett 1980, 306–13). Subsequent backdating of Ewart Park metalwork to the tenth and ninth centuries cal BC raises the possibility of an earlier date for this transition (cf. Needham 1996, 1997), but the correlation between the observed ceramic changes and the Ewart Park tradition seems to hold firm. Several scholars have also noted the remarkably close parallels which may be drawn between 'plain' and 'decorated' PDR wares in eastern England, notably from Fengate, and Urnfield pottery in the Low Countries (e.g. Barrett 1980, 315; Champion 1975). The parallels are certainly striking, and if genuinely indicative of contact between insular and Continental potters would support the chronological arguments advanced above. The later history of 'decorated' LBA–EIA wares remains unresolved, but in some parts of Britain these may have continued, with modifications, well into the fifth or even fourth centuries BC (cf. Barrett 1978, 276; 1980, 313). Unfortunately, this broad date range coincides closely with the radiocarbon calibration platform of *c.*800–400 cal BC, thus severely limiting the application of this technique (cf. Baillie and Pilcher 1983, 58–60). Absolute dating of LBA–EIA assemblages depends largely, therefore, upon rare associations between typologically diagnostic pottery and closely datable items of metalwork, with the many problems of interpretation which arise from processes such as redeposition or heirloom survival (e.g. Ketton, Rutland: Mackie 1993, 7–9).

Considerable difficulties attend the dating of LBA–EIA ceramic assemblages in the East Midlands, for dating hinges at present upon typological comparisons with more securely dated pottery from elsewhere in southern Britain and rare associations with metalwork dating from towards the proposed

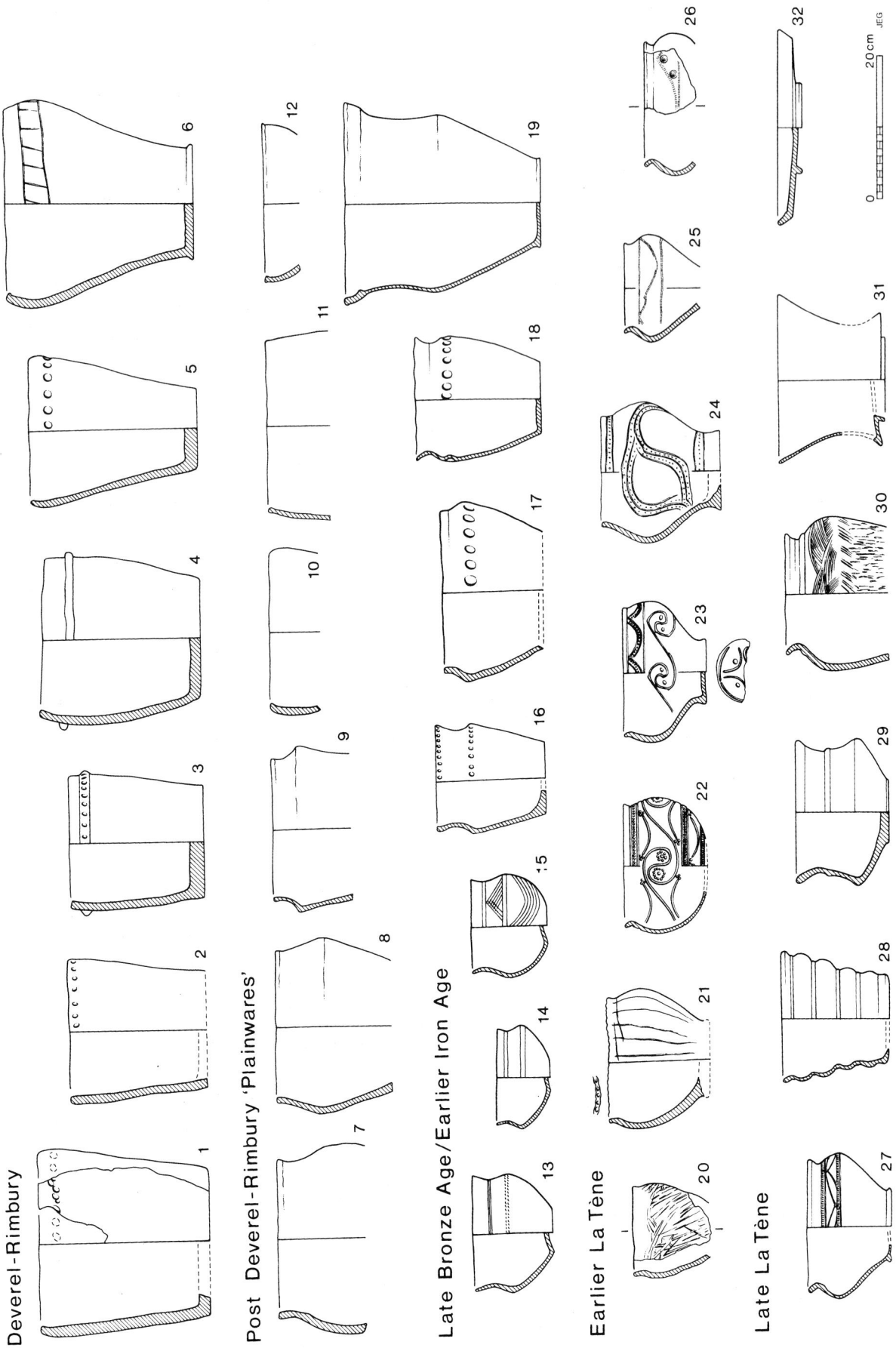

Deverel-Rimbury

Post Deverel-Rimbury 'Plainwares'

Late Bronze Age/Earlier Iron Age

Earlier La Tène

Late La Tène

Fig.12.3. Examples of Later Bronze Age and Iron Age ceramic types from the East Midlands; (see facing page for provenance of pottery).

Catalogue of Pottery Illustrated in Fig. 12.3.

Brief details are recorded of bibliographic source, form and surface treatment. All except vessels 29, 31 and 32 are handmade.

1. Billingborough, Lincs. (Chowne *et al* forthcoming, fig. 23.40). Straight-sided jar, inturned slightly beneath rim, tapering slightly towards flat base. Irregular row of finger-tip impressions beneath rim.
2. Pasture Lodge Farm, Long Bennington, Lincs. (Allen *et al*. 1987, fig. 14.22). Straight-sided jar, tapering slightly towards base. Row of finger-tip impressions beneath rim.
3. Pasture Lodge Farm (Allen *et al*. 1987, fig. 15.23). Straight-sided jar with internally bevelled rim and flat base. Applied cordon beneath rim, decorated with finger-tip impressions.
4. Coneygre Farm, Thurgarton, Notts. (Allen *et al*. 1987, fig. 7.10). Ellipsoid ('barrel') jar with flat base. Plain applied cordon beneath rim.
5. Coneygre Farm (Allen *et al*. 1987, fig. 7.11). Shouldered jar, with straight sides, inturned at girth, tapering towards flat base. Row of finger-tip impressions around girth.
6. Coneygre Farm (Allen *et al*. 1987, fig. 7.12). Approximately ovoid jar with slightly concave lower body above a flat base pinched out around the circumference; rim slightly bevelled internally. Panel of incised rectilinear decoration around girth.
7. Mam Tor, Derbys. (Coombs and Thompson 1979, fig. 27.1). Plain jar, probably of ovoid profile, with slightly everted neck.
8. Mam Tor (Coombs and Thompson 1979, fig. 22.1). Plain bipartite round-shouldered jar (pronounced but not angular change of profile at girth).
9. Mam Tor (Coombs and Thompson 1979, fig. 19.4). Plain carinated jar with high upright neck.
10. Billingborough, Lincs. (Chowne *et al*. forthcoming, fig. 23.35). Plain neckless ovoid ?bowl.
11. Stickford, Lincs. (Knight forthcoming: a). Plain ellipsoid jar.
12. Stickford (Knight forthcoming: a). Plain open bowl.
13. Fengate, Cambs. (Hawkes and Fell 1943, fig. 5.L1). Tripartite carinated bowl with omphalos base and everted neck. Three closely spaced parallel incised lines around base of neck; two rows of semicircular stamp impressions along girth.
14. Fengate (Hawkes and Fell 1943, fig. 5.K1). Burnished tripartite carinated bowl with everted neck and omphalos base. Pair of parallel incised lines around girth and base of neck.
15. Fengate (Hawkes and Fell 1943, fig. 7. R6). Burnished globular bowl with concave neck, tapering towards rim, and omphalos base. Incised multiple pendant arcs on lower body and incised multiple interlocking chevrons around shoulder; upper decorative panel demarcated above and below by pair of closely spaced parallel incised lines.
16. Fengate (Hawkes and Fell 1943, fig. 3. F2). Carinated jar with high concave neck and flat base. Row of finger-tip impressions around girth and exterior of rim.
17. Gretton, Northants. (Jackson and Knight 1985, fig. 7.34). Carinated bowl with very short upright neck. Row of finger-tip impressions around girth.
18. Gretton, Northants. (Jackson 1974, fig. 17.1). Ovoid jar with high everted neck and flat base. Row of finger-tip impressions around girth.
19. Fiskerton, Lincs. (Elsdon 1996a, fig. C.5). Round-shouldered jar with high concave neck and flat base, pinched out around circumference; the interior preserves a pronounced concavity beneath the lip, possibly for a lid.
20. Aslockton, Notts. (Palmer-Brown and Knight in prep). Ovoid jar with short everted neck. A dense pattern of randomly intersecting scored lines covers the body.
21. Breedon-on-the-Hill, Leics. (Challis and Harding 1975, ii, fig. 13.9). Neckless ovoid bowl, preserving on the outer face a series of vertical scored lines. Lip decorated with a row of finger-tip impressions.
22. Hunsbury, Northants. (Fell 1936, fig. 6.D4). Burnished ellipsoid bowl with very short everted neck. Elaborate pattern of grooved running scrolls and single standing or pendant arcs, combined with triple dimple and 'berried rosette' stamps.
23. Weekley, Northants. (Jackson and Dix 1986–7, fig. 33.54). Ellipsoid bowl with everted rim and pedestal base. Tooled running scroll design on lower body, separated by linear girth groove from a shoulder panel of double pendant arcs. Single dimples occur as space-filling devices within the running scroll, while the spaces between the tooled pendant arcs are filled with rows of smaller and closely spaced circular stamp impressions. The base preserves a tooled cruciform pattern, combined with single dimple stamps.
24. Breedon-on-the-Hill, Leics. (Challis and Harding 1975, ii, fig. 13.10). Jar of unusual form, preserving a pronounced rounded girth and a pedestal base. Body decorated with unusual curvilinear pattern of triple parallel tooled lines infilled with rows of dots (influenced probably by contact with the Northamptonshire style of La Tène decoration). Double parallel tooled lines with dotted infill demarcate this design. Burnished externally.
25. Dragonby, Lincs. (May 1996, fig. 19.57:679). Burnished round-shouldered bowl with short slightly everted neck, decorated with a double-notched square-toothed roulette wheel. Rouletted lines demarcate a decorative panel containing a poorly executed rouletted wavy line.
26. Dragonby (May 1996, fig. 19.48:510). Ellipsoid bowl with short everted neck. Shoulder decorated with single pendant arcs, executed with a double-notched square-toothed roulette wheel, combined with triple concentric circle stamps.
27. Old Sleaford, Lincs. (Elsdon 1997, fig. 59.95). Burnished round-shouldered bowl with short everted neck and footring base. The decorative shoulder panel incorporates incised 'leaf' motifs and, at the tip of each 'leaf', triple dimple stamps. The edges of the decorative panel are demarcated by a row of double

square-toothed rouletting confined within parallel
tooled lines.

28. Old Sleaford (Elsdon 1997, fig. 55.47). Burnished
corrugated jar, with narrow cordons either side of
the three upper corrugations.

29. Moulton Park, Northampton. (Williams 1974, fig.
18.113). Wheelmade carinated bowl with central neck
cordon.

30. Dragonby, Lincs. (May 1996, fig. 19.26:117). Ovoid
jar with everted neck and cordon at base of neck.
Body preserves an upper zone of combed arcs and,
beneath this, a dense pattern of short mainly vertical
incised lines.

31. Dragonby (Rigby and Elsdon 1996, 588–9: fig. 21.1:
1502). Wheelmade Central Gaulish tazza (micaceous
terra nigra), Cam 51c; internally burnished lines. A
rare form in Britain, interpreted as almost certainly
pre-Conquest (*ibid*. 589).

32. St. Nicholas Street, Leicester (Clay and Pollard 1994,
69, 80, fig. 50.2; graffito: *ibid*. 72, fig. 49.G1). Wheelmade Central Gaulish platter (micaceous *terra nigra*),
Cam 1, with concentric grooves on base interior and
graffito incised on base exterior after firing. A c.10
BC–AD 25 date range was suggested by Clay and
Pollard.

end of this phase. At Rainsborough, for example,
just outside the boundary of our area, fragments of a
plain iron ring-headed pin and of a bronze ring with
double-spiral terminals compared to Continental
Hallstatt D (HaD) rings (O'Connor 1980, 89; *pace*
Avery *et al*. 1967, 286–8) were recovered in the north
guard room from below deposits interpreted as roof-
collapse layers (*ibid*. 235–8, 284–8, fig. 31.154–171).
Ring-headed pins cannot be closely dated, but the
earliest examples could have developed in HaC/D
from swan's neck pins (cf. O'Connor 1980, 257). A
HaD *terminus post quem* may thus be suggested for
this deposit (i.e. from no earlier than the late seventh
century BC: cf. Fig. 12.2). Another important association was recorded near Gretton, where a plain iron
ring-headed pin was recovered from the bottom
pottery-rich layer of one of two parallel ditches, the
pottery from which is discussed in detail in the
following section. The pin was recovered from layer
3 of ditch A, together with a large assemblage of
mainly unabraded pottery which seems to have been
dumped after the accumulation of c.0.3m of silt. The
pottery included a rich variety of carinated, round-
shouldered and ovoid forms, some with extensive
finger ornament, and may be ascribed on typological
grounds to the LBA–EIA ceramic tradition (Jackson
and Knight, 1985, 81 2). Further evidence for a late
continuation of this ceramic tradition is provided at
Fiskerton by two virtually complete thin-walled jars
with flat bases, pronounced rounded girths and high
everted necks, one with internal corrugations, which
were retrieved from beneath the horizontal timbers
of a causeway (Fig. 3.19; Elsdon 1996a, fig. C.5: top
two vessels; Field 1985–6; Hillam 1985, 21–3; N. Field
pers comm.). A 20m length of the causeway was
excavated in detail. This was constructed mainly of
oak, with some alder and poplar/willow, and
incorporated many untrimmed oak timbers, often
with bark adhering. It was possible to determine
precisely the dates of felling of such trees, permitting
recognition of a complex sequence of repair phases

from 457 to 339BC. The vessels stratified beneath the
causeway had been placed next to each other, in an
upright position, and although crushed after deposition, comprised joining sherds in remarkably
fresh condition. It seems likely, therefore, that the
vessels had been deliberately deposited, prior to
construction of the causeway or during a later repair
phase, and hence a 339BC *terminus ante quem* may be
suggested for their deposition. Large quantities of
Iron Age metalwork, including several La Tène I
swords, were also recovered from along the line of
the timber causeway, although not in direct association with pottery. One of the pots compares closely
with some of the corrugated-neck vessels from
Gretton, and hence the association provides useful
support for the proposed earlier Iron Age dating of
the pottery from the parallel ditches.

Occasional associations have also been recorded
on sites in or just beyond the region between LBA–
EIA ceramic assemblages and material dated by
radiocarbon, notably from the Gretton parallel
ditches (Jackson and Knight 1985, 81), Vicarage
Farm, Fengate (Pryor 1974, 15–22; Knight 1984, i,
93–4) and Rainsborough (*Radiocarbon* 17, 1975, 228–
9; Avery 1993, ii, 276–90). The value of these associations, unfortunately, is seriously limited by the
close correlation between the main period of production of pottery of this style and the calibration
platform of c.800–400 cal BC, and hence the calibrated date ranges are too broad to permit close
dating (cf. Knight 1984, 89–95). The problem may be
illustrated by four dates obtained from pottery-rich
contexts in the parallel ditches near Gretton. All of
the dates were obtained from charcoal derived from
mature timbers, possibly felled many years before
deposition, and were directly associated with substantial groups of LBA–EIA pottery which appear to
have been deliberately deposited (Jackson and
Knight 1985, figs 8–9). Two sections across ditch A
yielded dates of 2410±80BP (Har-3015) and
2390±60BP (Har-2760) from samples in the bottom

of layer 3, while two sections across ditch B produced dates of 2240±70BP (Har-3014) and 2210±70BP (Har-2761) from charcoal at the base of layer 4. Calibration at two sigma yielded date ranges of 800–250, 770–370, 410–100 and 400–60 cal BC respectively, preventing all but the broadest dating. Similarly, twigs associated with a small collection of mainly unweathered LBA/EIA sherds which appear to have been dumped in the bottom waterlogged layer of a pit at Vicarage Farm yielded a date of 2290±125BP (UB-822), calibrating at 2 sigma to 800 cal BC – cal AD 1 (Pryor 1974, 15–22, fig. 14.1–3; Knight 1984, i, 93–4)!

Earlier La Tène Ceramic Styles

A further phase of ceramic innovation can be identified in the East Midlands between the fifth and third centuries BC (see Fig. 12.3, 20–26), with the gradual incorporation into the potter's repertoire of a range of new decorative motifs recalling in some cases the designs applied to La Tène metalwork (Avery 1973; Elsdon 1975, 1976; Grimes 1953) and the growth of the Midlands 'Scored ware' tradition, the latter corresponding broadly to Cunliffe's (1991, 73) 'Breedon-Ancaster' group (Kenyon 1950; Elsdon 1992a). Other important developments of this period include a restriction of finger ornament to vessel rims and a progressive emphasis upon ovoid, globular and ellipsoid forms (cf. Cunliffe 1991, 85–8; Knight 1984, i, 99).

Vessels from the East Midlands which display ornament of La Tène inspiration may be divided stylistically into two main regional traditions (Fig 12.5), the chronological development of which may have varied significantly. These comprise a Lincolnshire group, extending westwards to Nottinghamshire and southwards to northern Cambridgeshire, characterised by the remarkable collections from Dragonby (May 1996) and Old Sleaford (Elsdon 1997), and a Northamptonshire group, exemplified by the pottery from Hunsbury (Fell 1936) and Weekley (Jackson and Dix 1986–7). More localised stylistic variations recalling the mosaic of decorative motifs recorded in the Upper Thames (Lambrick 1984) may also be discerned, as exemplified by the cluster of sites with 'berried rosette' motifs around Hunsbury (Elsdon 1976), and further research may eventually permit the identification of local production centres. The distinguishing features of the La Tène decorated pottery from Lincolnshire have been discussed most extensively by Elsdon (1975, 1996b, 1997). She has noted the strong emphasis upon arcuate and other geometric designs executed with a combination of double-notched square-toothed rouletting, circular stamps and tooled lines, often further embellished with pattern burnishing

(Elsdon 1975, 26–36, figs 6–8, 16–19; 1996b; 1997, 105–110). Rouletting is alien to the Northamptonshire tradition, which displays a greater concern for flowing curvilinear patterns: most characteristically, patterns incorporating the running scroll motif (e.g. Hunsbury: Fell 1936, fig. 6: D1–D7; Blackthorn and Moulton Park: Williams 1974, figs 14.35,38 and 35.28; Weekley: Jackson and Dix 1986–7, fig. 33.50, 51, 54, 58 and fig. 36.96). These curvilinear patterns suggest a familiarity with south western styles of La Tène ornament, acquired partly from imported Glastonbury-style gabbroic pottery, discussed later in this chapter (cf. Elsdon 1975, 3; Jackson and Dix 1986–7, 77), and also perhaps from imported metalwork. The latter is suggested by a remarkable beaten bronze bowl from Hunsbury embellished with three rows of stamps bearing a striking resemblance to the 'duck' motifs of Iron Age Malvernian or Cornish 'duck-stamped' pottery (Fox 1958, 12, Plate 77b; Challis and Harding 1975, i, 73; cf. Peacock 1968, fig. 3.3,7,9 & 11; Peacock 1969, fig. 3.1). Exactly comparable designs do not appear on Northamptonshire pottery, but such items could have inspired some of the local curvilinear designs. There is insufficient space to consider in detail the rich variety of motifs and patterns employed by potters working within these stylistic traditions. The reader is referred instead to the classifications contained in syntheses of the Lincolnshire material by Elsdon (1975; 1996b; 1997) and, for Northamptonshire, a summary by the writer (Knight 1984, i, 26–8) and a more recent discussion of the decorated pottery from Weekley (Jackson and Dix 1986–7, 77–79, figs 33–36; microfiche: M131–133).

A predominantly late date, centred upon the second and first centuries BC, has been suggested for La Tène decorated pottery in Northamptonshire (e.g. Jackson and Dix 1986–7; Gwilt 1997, 155) and Lincolnshire (Elsdon 1975, 36–7; 1996b, 434–6; 1997, 106), although the roots of this style, certainly in Northamptonshire, could lie in the La Tène I period of the fifth to early third centuries BC (cf. Upper Thames: Elsdon 1975, 6–10, fig. 9). Decorative techniques and patterns may have changed over time, as perhaps at Dragonby where a change towards more rigidly rectilinear rouletted patterns has been argued on stratigraphic grounds (Elsdon 1996b, 434), but the dating evidence is currently insufficiently precise to permit a detailed discussion of stylistic changes. The stratigraphic relationships of La Tène decorated pottery from the region would support a generally late date, for pottery of this style occurs consistently in deposits preceding contexts yielding Late La Tène wheelmade wares or in association with these vessels: notably at Aldwincle and Weekley, Northants. (Jackson 1977; Jackson and Dix 1986–7) and the Lincolnshire sites of Dragonby and Old Sleaford (May 1996; Elsdon 1997). In addition, many of the closest parallels which may be claimed with the decorative devices applied to La Tène metalwork, such as the 'berried rosette', suggest that this style of ceramic ornament may have flourished mainly in the late La Tène period (Elsdon 1976), overlapping the wheelmade pottery of La Tène III. Further evidence for the late continuation of La Tène decoration in Lincolnshire is provided by the complex fusion of earlier La Tène and Late La Tène decorative and formal elements. This is demonstrated most persuasively at Dragonby and Old Sleaford, where a remarkable range of necked bowls and other forms which compare closely with the Aylesford-Swarling pottery of south-eastern England were embellished with elaborate stamped and rouletted patterns whose ancestry may be traced to the earlier La Tène decorative style (Elsdon 1996b, 433; 1997, 107–8).

Although the bulk of the evidence would support a late date, there remain compelling arguments in favour of backdating the earliest manifestations of the La Tène ornamental style, at least in Northamptonshire, to the La Tène I period. Crucial to this argument are several close parallels between the decoration applied to La Tène I metalwork from the region and ceramic ornament attributable to the La Tène style. Harding drew attention long ago to a number of close parallels between curvilinear designs applied to pottery from sites in the Upper Thames and La Tène I metalwork (Harding 1972, 95–6; 1974, 170–2). Particularly persuasive parallels may be drawn between the curious serpentine pattern on the back of a bronze dagger sheath from Minster Ditch, Oxon. or the 'proto-running scroll' pattern on the bow of a La Tène Ia bronze fibula from Woodeaton, Oxon. and the designs applied to round-shouldered and carinated vessels from Blewburton Hill, Oxon. (cf. Harding 1972, 93–6, Plates 58G-J, 74D, 79A). These parallels, if accepted, would suggest a La Tène I origin for ceramic versions of this ornament, at least in the Thames basin, and equally crucially would provide further support for the argument that LBA–EIA carinated vessels had continued in fashion in this region well into the fifth and fourth centuries BC. A similarly ancient origin can be suggested for some of the decorated pottery from Northamptonshire. This can be argued most strongly at Hunsbury, where early progress towards the application of curvilinear designs to pottery is suggested by comparisons between the ornament on certain vessels and the row of hearts with foot scrolls and series of concentric semicircles which embellish the bows of two La Tène Ia bronze fibulae from the site (Fell 1936, fig. 2a–b; cf. Jacobsthal 1944, 66, Plate 274.378; Jope 1961a and b). In Lincolnshire, typological links have been

proposed by Elsdon between certain vessels embellished with stamped rosettes and circles and carinated bowls from the Upper Thames with stiff curvilinear or geometric decoration of the La Tène style, notably from Blewburton Hill (Elsdon 1975, 41; 1996b, 436). The Upper Thames vessels appear to combine characteristic LBA–EIA profiles with La Tène ornament, and on typological grounds a date towards the beginning of the La Tène period, between the fifth and third centuries BC, may be proposed. If accepted, the parallels would suggest a more extended chronology for Lincolnshire decorated pottery, more in keeping with the evidence from the Nene and Thames basins.

Other evidence for the dating of the La Tène decorative style is provided by rare associations with material dated by radiocarbon, but the value of the handful of radiocarbon dates which have been obtained is severely limited by their broad error ranges. Elsdon and May have noted the discovery at Helpringham, Lincs., of stamped and rouletted sherds on a saltern yielding dates of 2180±80 BP (Har-2280; 400–30 cal BC at 2 sigma), for charcoal from a hearth attributed to the latest phase of salt-making, and 2330±90 BP (Har-3102; 800–150 cal BC at two sigma), for charcoal immediately beneath this hearth, but in neither case apparently could a direct association with pottery be demonstrated (May 1996, 436, 624; Elsdon 1996a, 20: C3; J. May and B. Simmons: *pers comm.*). At Harby, Notts., a small collection of stamped and rouletted sherds, some joining to form part of the shoulder of a possibly globular vessel, was recovered from the terminal of an enclosure ditch during excavations by Lindsey Archaeological Services (Knight 1997a). These sherds were directly associated with charcoal dated to 2130±80 BP (Beta-101169; 380 cal BC – cal AD 50 at 2 sigma). Other dates, which figure prominently in discussions of Northamptonshire decorated pottery, were obtained from five charcoal samples collected from a single layer extending along an enclosure ditch at Weekley, from which was also recovered a substantial quantity of La Tène decorated pottery (Jackson and Dix 1986–7, 49, 77: ditch K1). These have frequently been employed as evidence of a predominantly first century BC/AD date range for pottery of this style (e.g. Gwilt 1997, 155), but their value for dating purposes is seriously limited by the wide date ranges, arising in part perhaps from repeated cleaning episodes which could not be discerned in the ditch fill. The dates, when calibrated at two sigma, vary as follows: 200 cal BC – cal AD 120 (Har-1725), cal BC 70 – cal AD 340 (Har-1779), 380 cal BC – cal AD 60 (Har-1844), 380–30 cal BC (Har-2007) and 190 cal BC – cal AD 200 (Har-2008). Thermoluminescence dating has also been attempted for selected decorated vessels from

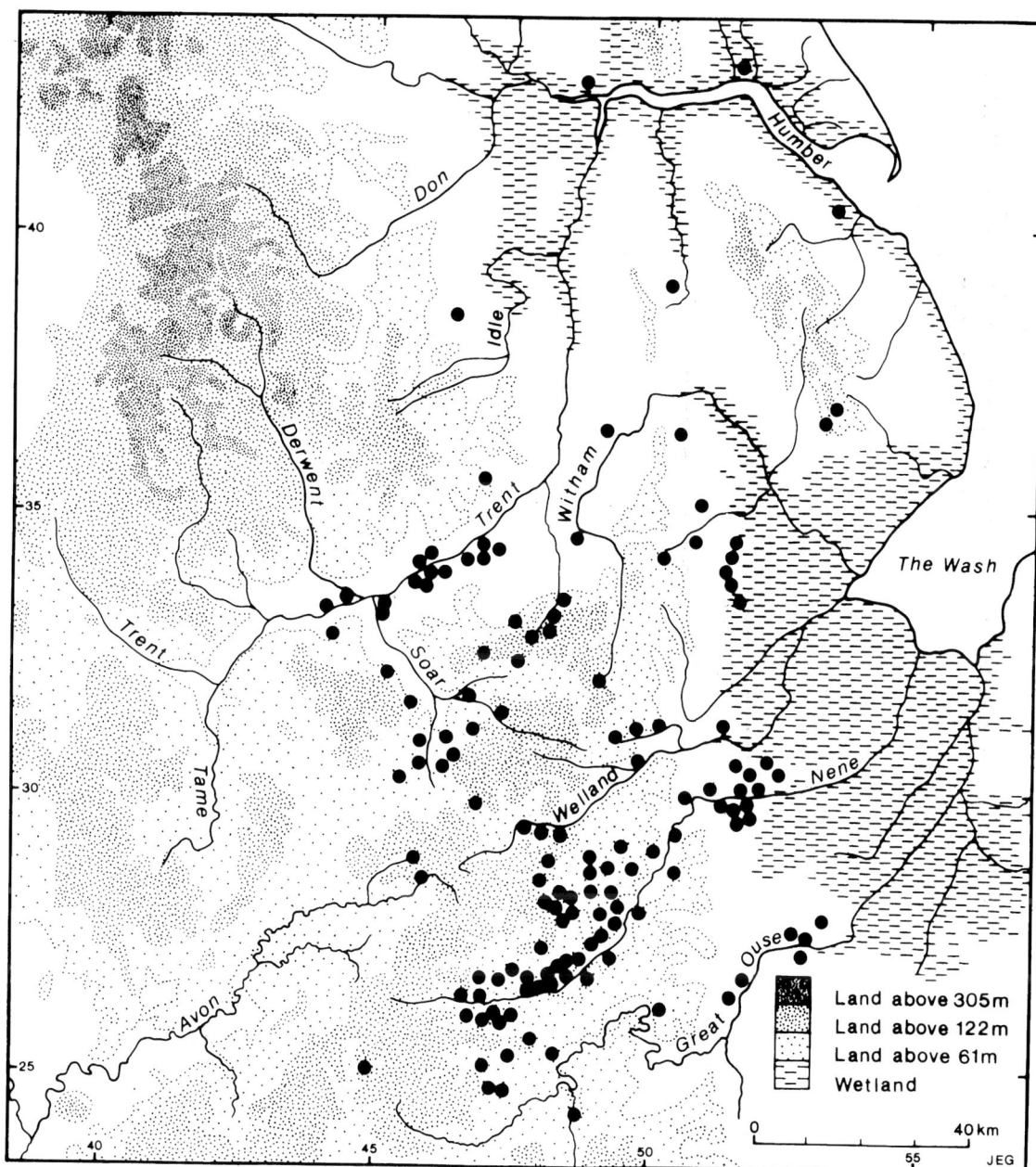

Fig. 12.4. Distribution of Scored pottery (source: S. Elsdon).

Dragonby (May 1996, 438–442; table 19.9), but the date ranges at two sigma are unfortunately too broad to permit close dating (vessel 10, Fig. 19.20: AD 361±366; vessel 649, Fig. 19.54: 169±410 BC).

The dating of the earliest Scored pottery from the region is no less problematic, although there can be no doubt that by at least the second century BC scoring was widespread throughout much of the region, particularly towards the south and east of the Trent Valley (Fig. 12.4). Scored ware was identified many years ago as a distinct style of Iron Age surface treatment in the East Midlands, most notably by Hawkes (Gurney and Hawkes 1940, 235–9) and

Kenyon (1950; 1952), and has been reviewed most recently by Elsdon (1992a). Scored ware is characterised by intersecting deeply incised lines, executed probably with a knife, the end of a bone or other sharp implement (*ibid.* fig.1), and by a variety of lightly to heavily brushed vessels whose outer walls had been roughened probably by a bunch of twigs or fibres (e.g. Gamston: Knight 1992, 45; Enderby: Elsdon 1992b, 43, illus. 25; Willington: Elsdon 1979, 164). Scoring may sometimes have been applied for aesthetic effect, as suggested by rare examples of lattice, horizontal and vertical patterns (e.g. Challis and Harding 1975, i, 80; Elsdon 1992a, fig. 1) and, most persuasively, the unusual hatched triangle patterns observed at Weekley (Jackson and Dix 1986–7, fig. 31.46). In the majority of cases, however, vessel surfaces are characterised by seemingly haphazard arrangements of ragged scored lines (e.g. Jackson and Dix 1986–7, fig. 31.35–43; Kenyon 1950, figs. 4–5, 11–13). It has been suggested, in view of the 'random' nature of most scoring, that this surface treatment may have performed a primarily functional role, serving perhaps to roughen the surface for easier handling (cf. May 1976a, 138). This remains an attractive hypothesis, although it is suggested later in this chapter that cultural factors may also have played a role in the dissemination of this technique.

Recent research has suggested that the roots of Scored ware could lie in the fourth or even fifth centuries BC (Barrett 1978, 287; Challis and Harding 1975, i, 58–62; Cunliffe 1991, 73; Elsdon 1992a, 89), considerably earlier than Kenyon was able to demonstrate (Kenyon 1950; 1952). However, this argument, which rests currently upon a limited number of associations with datable metalwork and with organic material dated by radiocarbon, is at present somewhat tenuous. One of the most frequently quoted metalwork associations was recorded during excavations at Ancaster Quarry, Lincs., where an Early La Tène bronze brooch which May suggested could date from as early as the fifth century BC was found close to a vertically sided scored vessel in the filling of a linear ditch near the main focus of settlement (May 1976a, 138–40, figs 69.1, 69.6; J. May *pers comm.*). More recently, excavations of a gradually infilled palaeochannel near Market Deeping, Lincs., have yielded scored pottery from a layer towards the bottom of the channel from which was also retrieved an iron La Tène II brooch, dated by Fitzpatrick to the third century BC (Fitzpatrick forthcoming). Occasional associations of scored pottery with radiocarbon dated material suggest a wide date range, stretching back at the earliest to the fifth/fourth centuries cal BC. At Padholme Road, Fengate, a date of 2300±46 BP (GaK-4198; 410–200 cal BC at 2 sigma) was obtained from the collapsed wattlework lining of a pit yielding scored pottery (Pryor 1974, 22–9; 1984, 154). While at Cowbit, Lincs, a weighted mean date of 2098±15 BP (UB-4026 & UB-4027; 180–100 cal BC at 2 sigma) was obtained from charcoal in the fills of two shallow flues relating to a saltern hearth or oven yielding scored pottery (calibration by A. Bayliss; Knight forthcoming: b). More recently, valuable series of radiocarbon dates for Scored ware have been obtained from Wanlip, Leics. (Marsden 1998, 48–9), and from material stratified in a palaeochannel at Market Deeping (Knight forthcoming: c; A. Bayliss: *pers comm.*), which together would support the argument for currency from the fifth/

fourth centuries cal BC (see also Fisherwick, Staffs.: Smith 1979, 90–3, 98–9).

Scored ware may have continued in use well into the first century AD in some parts of the region, notably in the Trent basin and lower Nene and Welland Valleys (cf. Challis and Harding 1975, i, 79–80; Elsdon 1992a, 84–6, 89). In the Trent Valley, for example, notable associations with Late La Tène wheelmade pottery have been recorded near Nottingham at Holme Pierrepont (Elsdon 1992a, 84) and Gamston (Knight 1992, 49–50), while in the Soar, lower Nene and Welland Valleys wheelmade Late Iron Age pottery has been recovered with Scored ware at Kirby Muxloe, Leics. (P. Marsden: *pers comm.*), Cat's Water, Fengate (Pryor 1984, 155) and Werrington, Cambs. (Rollo 1988, 116–8). In the middle and upper Nene basin, by contrast, a general absence of associations with late La Tène wheelmade pottery or metalwork suggests that in this area Scored ware may only rarely have outlasted the first century BC (Elsdon 1992a, 88–9; Jackson and Ambrose 1978, 174). Scoring seems to have been replaced progressively by a new range of combed wares in this area and over much of the region of its distribution (Elsdon 1992a, 88–9; Pryor 1984, 156), including Jewry Wall, Leicester (Kenyon 1948), the Northamptonshire sites of Aldwincle (Jackson 1977), Wakerley (Jackson and Ambrose 1978) and Weekley (Jackson and Dix 1986–7), Cat's Water, Fengate (Pryor 1984) and Old Sleaford (Elsdon 1997, 108). Towards the northern fringes of the study area, however, this technique appears not to have been taken up so enthusiastically: as may be demonstrated by its comparative sparsity in the Trent Valley (e.g. rare examples at Willington: Elsdon 1979, 164).

Detailed analyses of Scored and La Tène-decorated vessels provide important evidence for other changes in ceramic fashions during the later Iron Age, most notably from 'extensive' to 'restricted' finger-tipping and from carinated to ovoid and related forms. Many scored vessels have finger-nail or finger-tip impressions along the lip or the outer edge of the rim, but more extensive finger ornamentation of the kind which characterises LBA–EIA pottery is virtually unknown (e.g. Wollaston, Northants.: Hall and Nickerson 1969, fig. 6.84). Scored vessels also indicate a fundamental shift of emphasis during the later Iron Age away from carinated forms towards ovoid and related vessels, notably globular bowls and jars, ellipsoid bowls and ellipsoid ('barrel') jars (e.g. Breedon-on-the-Hill, Leics.: Kenyon 1950; Wacher 1977, figs. 6–7; Cat's Water and Padholme Road, Fengate: Pryor 1974, 1984; Gamston: Knight 1992;). These occur alongside smaller proportions of round-shouldered, cylindrical and open vessels, although the original proportions of cylindrical and open forms remain uncertain in view of the difficulty of identifying such vessels from small sherds. Further evidence in support of this trend towards a greater emphasis upon ovoid and related forms is provided by an assessment of the frequencies of forms embellished with La Tène ornament (e.g. Hunsbury: Fell 1936; Hardingstone, Northampton: Woods 1969; Blackthorn and Moulton Park, Northampton: Williams 1974). These are commonly ellipsoid, ovoid or globular vessels, mainly bowls, with flat, footring or, very occasionally, pedestal bases. More rarely, examples have been recorded in Lincolnshire of globular jars embellished with La Tène ornament and preserving unusual omphalos bases, most notably at Dragonby (e.g. May 1996, fig. 19.54:647, 649). The chronology of these globular vessels remains uncertain, for all were recovered from unstratified contexts. Elsdon (1996b, 434) favoured an early date on the basis of the elaborate interlocking arc decoration, although the distinctive corrugated neck of at least one example raises the possibility of a typological link with Aylesford-Swarling vessels (May 1996, fig. 19.54:647).

The case for significant changes in vessel forms and styles of surface treatment during the mid-first millennium BC is strengthened by occasional discoveries of stratified ceramic assemblages, associated in some cases with typologically diagnostic metalwork or material dated by radiocarbon, which may be argued to span the transition from the LBA–EIA to Earlier La Tène ceramic phases. At Gretton, for example, a stratified sequence of Early Iron Age pottery was obtained from two parallel ditches interpreted as possibly part of a trackway, together with an iron ring-headed pin and charcoal dated by radiocarbon (Jackson and Knight 1985: ditches A and B). Ditch A contained a thick layer of primary silt (4) and above this two layers (3 and 2) incorporating substantial quantities of mainly unabraded pottery which appears to have been deliberately deposited, possibly from an adjacent settlement. This material includes a large proportion of carinated and round-shouldered vessels, plus a number of ovoid vessels and (in layer 2) a small number of sherds deriving from open bowls or lids. Bases are flat or of footring form. Vessels were sometimes provided with strap handles. A small proportion of the pottery displays extensive finger-tip or finger-nail ornament. Ditch B incorporated sherds that were generally smaller and more abraded than those of ditch A. The material appears to have been deliberately deposited, but may have been exposed longer to trampling or weathering prior to deposition than the material from ditch A. The pottery in the bottom artefact-bearing layer (4) was deposited after the accumulation of a considerably greater thickness of silt

(*c*.0.5m) than was recorded in ditch A (layer 4), and, if it is accepted that the ditches had been in contemporary use, may date from later in the sequence. The assemblage compares closely with that from layers 2 and 3 of ditch A, although extensive finger ornament seems to be less well represented. In addition, the upper layers of ditch B (2 and 3) contained noticeably smaller proportions of carinated and round-shouldered vessels, plus comparatively larger numbers of ovoid vessels. Open bowls remain poorly represented. The presence of a small proportion of sherds with extensive finger ornament suggests an affinity with LBA–EIA assemblages, but the changed proportion of carinated and round-shouldered vessels to ovoid forms invites closer comparison with later Iron Age assemblages. The layers might be interpreted on typological grounds, therefore, as transitional between the LBA–EIA and Earlier La Tène ceramic traditions – a conclusion supported by the recovery from layer 3 of ditch A of an iron ring-headed pin, dating from no earlier than HaC/D (cf. O'Connor 1980, 257). Radiocarbon dates were obtained from charcoal in layer 3 of ditch A and layer 4 of ditch B, in both cases in direct association with pottery, but as emphasised above the calibrated date ranges are unfortunately too wide to permit close dating.

Another key stratified assemblage, incorporating material deposited over a protracted time period, was recovered during recent excavations by Lane of a palaeochannel at Market Deeping (Lane forthcoming). This feature yielded a remarkable quantity of deliberately deposited Iron Age pottery and briquetage, together with animal bone, worked wood and other palaeoenvironmental remains. A stratified sequence of pottery, much in fresh condition, was recovered from the lower layers of the channel (Phases 1–4), some directly associated with organic material for which radiocarbon dates are currently being obtained. The pottery comprises mainly handmade Scored wares, but the basal deposits preserved rare sherds with LBA–EIA typological affinities, not obviously redeposited (finger-tip impressions along the girth and plain thin-walled and high-necked vessels). Provisional interpretation of the radiocarbon dates from the lower layers suggests a fifth/fourth century cal BC date for deposition of the earlier material (A. Bayliss *pers comm.*) and hence for the changes in ceramic fashion which distinguish the earlier La Tène ceramic phase. Additional support for an early date is provided by the discovery, noted above, of scored pottery in a layer, attributed to Phase 1 but above the basal layers of the feature, yielding an iron La Tène II fibula dated to the third century BC (Fitzpatrick forthcoming).

Late La Tène Ceramic Styles

Pottery styles were transformed in many parts of the
East Midlands during the first century BC with the
addition to the potter's repertoire of a rich variety of
new ceramic types, commonly wheelmade, many of
which find close parallels in the Aylesford-Swarling
ceramic tradition of south eastern England (Birchall
1965; Thompson 1982). Some of the innovations of
this period represent imports from production
centres outside the region, notably Gallo-Belgic girth
or butt beakers, cups and platters (Fig. 3.31–32; e.g.
Dragonby: Rigby and Elsdon 1996; Duston, Northampton: Friendship-Taylor 1998, 148–70; Leicester:
Clay and Pollard 1994; Kenyon 1948; Jarvis 1986;
Old Sleaford: Rigby 1997). Many, however, represent regional products related to classic Aylesford-
Swarling types (as defined by Birchall 1965, 245–6;
e.g. Old Sleaford: Elsdon 1997, 107–8). Established
ceramic forms and decorative styles also experienced significant modifications, reflecting in part the
impact of wheel technology (e.g. ovoid jars: Knight
1992, 50, fig. 22.45–46; Jackson and Dix 1986–7, 79)
and the combining by potters of Late La Tène with
Earlier La Tène formal and decorative features:
notably at Dragonby and Old Sleaford, where the
potters' imaginative combinations of elements derived from Earlier La Tène and Late La Tène traditions created in first century BC and early to mid-
first century AD Lincolnshire a ceramic industry of
daunting diversity (e.g. May 1996; Elsdon 1997). The
complex ceramic traditions of this period fall beyond
the scope of the present study. However, some
discussion is required of the date of transition from
Earlier La Tène to Late La Tène ceramic styles and
the spatial distribution of pottery comparing with
Aylesford-Swarling vessels, for both have a considerable bearing upon the dating of ceramic assemblages attributable to the Earlier La Tène tradition.
For further discussions of Late La Tène ceramics
from the East Midlands, the reader is referred to the
important published reviews by Thompson (1982)
and Willis (1997). Valuable corpora of ceramic types
are contained in the recent survey of East Midlands
Iron Age pottery by Elsdon (1996a) and of Northamptonshire Late Iron Age pottery by Friendship-
Taylor (1998, 1999), and in reports on excavations at
such key Late Iron Age sites as Dragonby (May
1996), Fengate (Pryor 1984), Jewry Wall, Leicester
(Kenyon 1948), Old Sleaford (Elsdon 1997),
Wakerley (Jackson and Ambrose 1978) and Weekley
(Jackson and Dix 1986–7).

The dating of the earliest Aylesford-Swarling
pottery from south eastern England remains contentious, despite extensive research by Birchall (1965)
and later workers (Rodwell 1976; Stead 1976;
Thompson 1982: Haselgrove 1997). Birchall, on the

basis of associations in graves between pottery and
closely datable metalwork, was unable to date the
earliest pottery of this tradition before Caesar's British
campaigns of 55 and 54 BC, thus confounding
previous attempts to correlate such pottery with
Caesar's Belgae (e.g. Hawkes and Dunning 1931),
although she did identify a possibly pre-Caesarian
group of hand-made coarse wares (Birchall 1965, 248).
Rodwell investigated this early group of vessels in
greater detail, but again was unable to establish
beyond doubt a pre-Caesarian origin (Rodwell 1976,
221–36). A review by the present writer of the Iron
Age pottery from the Nene basin identified a typologically early group of so-called 'earliest Belgic'
pottery recalling the early pottery from Aylesford
(Birchall *op. cit.*) and exemplified by material from
the Northamptonshire sites of Aldwincle (Jackson
1977) and Irchester (Hall and Nickerson 1967) and
the unpublished collections from Rushden (Woods
Group Ci) and Yardley Hastings (Knight 1984, 63–4,
69–71; for parallels see Birchall 1965, 248: 'Earliest'
group, no. 73–79, and 'Early' group, Type Va vessels;
also Rodwell 1976, figs 15–17; Thompson 1979). This
distinction remains valid, although with hindsight it
is suggested that the term 'Belgic', with its unfortunate
connotations of links with the Belgae mentioned by
Caesar, is best avoided. A date for this group from at
least the latter half of the first century BC in some
parts of the region was suggested on the basis of
brooch associations at Rushden (Knight 1984, 82),
but later work on the chronology of insular and
continental La Tène III metalwork necessitates
reappraisal of this conclusion.

A recent reassessment by Haselgrove of the
chronology of La Tène brooches and their ceramic
associations raises the possibility that La Tène III
wheelmade pottery could have been current in some
areas of southern Britain from the late second
century BC, considerably earlier than was previously
contemplated, although the date of its introduction
may have varied significantly regionally (Haselgrove 1997, 58, Hill Chapter 13 this volume). The
implications of this revised ceramic chronology for
the dating of Late Iron Age pottery in the East
Midlands must await a full reassessment of the La
Tène III ceramic tradition and, in particular, the
brooch associations – a task well beyond the scope
of the present study – but we may note here the
possibility of a markedly earlier origin for Late La
Tène pottery than has hitherto been contemplated.
Despite this, the bulk of the Late La Tène pottery
from the region would seem, on the basis largely of
associations with La Tène III metalwork or coins and
stratigraphic relationships with Gallo-Belgic imports
and Romano-British pottery, to date from very late
in the Iron Age, within a time bracket from the end
of the first century BC to the mid-first century AD

(e.g. Jackson and Ambrose 1978; Jackson and Dix 1986–7; May 1996, 405–7). There is also every likelihood of significant intra-regional variation in the chronology of this material.

Attempts to formulate a regional ceramic chronology are complicated further by the observation that in some parts of the East Midlands the ceramic innovations discussed above appear to have made little if any impact upon established potting traditions. The Trent Valley marks in this respect an important zone of transition. Vessels displaying affinities with Aylesford-Swarling types have been recorded on a scatter of sites along the Trent terraces, including Gamston (Knight 1992, 50, fig. 18.22), Holme Pierrepont (Elsdon 1996a, fig. B.2.12), Rampton, Notts. (*ibid.* fig. B.5), Swarkestone Lowes (Elliott and Knight 1999, fig. 17.1) and Willington (Elsdon 1979, 163), although major difficulties are encountered when attempting to disentangle Late Iron Age from early post-Conquest products. Iron Age pottery collections from sites to the north and west of the Trent, by contrast, rarely incorporate such vessels; exceptions to this pattern include the Nottinghamshire sites of Dorket Head (Turner and Turner 1997), Scratta Wood (Challis and Harding 1975, i, 94; R.S. Leary: unpublished pottery archive, Trent and Peak Archaeological Trust) and Dunston's Clump (Leary 1987). Vessels with Aylesford-Swarling affinities are also rare on Iron Age sites in the Cambridgeshire and Lincolnshire Fens (cf. Lane 1992b, 233) where earlier stylistic traditions may in some areas have continued up to and beyond the Roman Conquest – defining perhaps, in Evans's memorable phrase, areas of 'cultural backwaterness' (Evans 1997, 224). The longevity of earlier Iron Age ceramic traditions poses major problems for the identification of Late Iron Age and early Romano-British sites: a problem which is exacerbated in areas such as mid- or south Lincolnshire where Iron Age shelly fabrics continue, with no discernible change, into the early Roman period (cf. Darling 1988). The social or economic mechanisms underlying these stylistic contrasts remain uncertain, but there are hints of differences in status or wealth, reflected by variable access to Gallo-Belgic imports, or possibly of cultural variations which have so far eluded discovery.

Processes of Change

Attention is focused in this final section upon the pottery traditions of the first millennium BC prior to the major changes which accompanied the spread of Late La Tène ceramic styles. The latter is a subject in its own right, best assessed with reference also to the impact of Roman pottery industries (cf. Willis 1996).

Particular emphasis is placed upon the evidence for ceramic production and distribution, the organisation of which may be shown to have changed fundamentally in parts of the region during the later first millennium BC.

Late Bronze Age and Earlier Iron Age

Petrological analyses of the fabrics of vessels attributable to the PDR plainware and LBA–EIA ceramic traditions, from sites such as Billingborough (Allen 1988; Chowne *et al.* forthcoming), Fengate (Williams 1984, 134), Gretton (Jackson and Knight 1985), Mam Tor (Guilbert and Vince 1996) and Willington (Elsdon 1979), support the case, made recently by Morris (1994b), that in this region the emphasis in the early half of the first millennium BC was upon local production – in other words, that the majority of pottery manufacture was probably carried out employing clays and tempering materials located up to about 5km from the focus of production (cf. Arnold 1985, 32–60, fig. 2.5). Similar conclusions may be drawn from analyses of Late Bronze Age and earlier Iron Age ceramic collections in other regions of southern Britain. Examples of specialised production and distribution are known from scattered sites in Wessex, south western England and the west Midlands (Morris 1994b, 374–7), but the emphasis in this early period appears to have rested firmly upon the production of both fine and coarse wares for limited consumption (*ibid.* 384).

Later Iron Age

Petrological analyses of later Iron Age pottery from the region and of the briquetage containers known as 'stony VCP' (Morris 1985) have provided convincing evidence for the development of complex distribution systems, extending ultimately as far as the Cheshire Plain and, most remarkably, the Lizard Peninsula of Cornwall. This contrasts with the apparent emphasis in the earlier part of the millennium upon local pottery manufacture, and suggests a shift during the later Iron Age towards non-local systems of production and distribution. A similar trend has been proposed for some other areas of Britain, most notably the Marches, Wessex and south-western England (Morris 1994b, 377–81, fig. 3), although the closest parallels lie with areas such as Wessex where evidence is preserved for both local and regional pottery distributions.

The most convincing evidence from the East Midlands for non-local pottery production is provided by petrological analyses of sherds incorporating igneous inclusions derived from a source in south Cornwall, some 380km to the south-west. The case for exchange links with Cornwall hinges upon the discovery at Weekley of ten sherds from at least four vessels whose mineralogy closely resembles the gabbroic clays of the Lizard peninsula (Fabric Group D: *ibid*. 77, fig. 36. 91; Williams 1986–7; cf. Peacock 1969a, 44). The elaborate scroll decoration on one of these pots invites close comparison with Glastonbury-style products from Castle Dore (Jackson and Dix 1986–7, fig. 36.91; cf. Radford 1951, fig. 14) and there seems little doubt, in view of the close correlation between petrology and typology, that the vessel had originated at a production site in south western England (cf. Peacock 1969a, 52–3). The discovery supports the typological evidence for contact between these widely separated regional ceramic traditions, discussed in an earlier section of this chapter. The nature of the links between these regions can only be guessed at, but comparisons with other areas raise the possibility of a down-the-line exchange network, perhaps utilising kinship relationships (cf. Morris 1994b, 378). The identification at Weekley of imported gabbroic vessels spurred a programme of thin-section analysis of other vessels with La Tène ornament from Northamptonshire, including sherds from Blackthorn, Northampton (Williams 1974, fig. 35.28 & 32), Hardingstone, Northampton (Woods 1969, fig. 25.161), Hunsbury (Fell 1936, fig. 6:D4), Ringstead (Jackson 1980, fig. 6.1), Twywell (Jackson 1975 fig. 22.38) and Hemmingwell Lodge, Wellingborough (Williams 1986–7). The samples were shown to incorporate inclusions, such as shell, ironstone and quartz, that could have been obtained from numerous local or non-local sources. The wide distribution of these inclusion types frustrates attempts to identify raw material sources, but the restricted distribution of distinctive motifs such as the 'berried rosette' (Elsdon 1976) would support the case for the distribution of some vessels from nearby production centres. We might suggest, therefore, a combination of local and non-local production, in the latter case involving exchange networks stretching as far south as Cornwall.

A similarly complex system of production and distribution may be indicated by the distribution of Lincolnshire stamped and rouletted wares, although the positive identification of regional exchange networks is hindered in this area by the emphasis upon fabrics incorporating fossil shell obtainable from countless locations along the Jurassic escarpment (cf. Elsdon 1997, 124). Several scholars have noted major contrasts between the decorative techniques and patterns applied to pottery from sites in Lindsey and Kesteven, and have raised the possibility of specialised production centres in these areas (Elsdon 1997, 108; May 1996, 436). Petrological analyses have been carried out on pottery from a variety of Lincolnshire sites with the aim of investigating this hypothesis,

notably at Ancaster, Dragonby, Kirmington, Old Sleaford and Sapperton (Elsdon 1997, 124; Middleton 1996), but unfortunately at none of these sites was it possible to distinguish products which had undoubtedly derived from elsewhere. Petrological studies were supplemented at Dragonby and Ancaster by neutron activation analyses of selected decorated sherds (Colston 1996). These indicated different clay sources for most of the pottery from each site, but unfortunately the locations of these clays could not be determined. Two samples from Dragonby could not be separated chemically from the Ancaster group, and the possibility was raised of some movement of pottery between these sites (*ibid*. 427–8). This is possible, but considerably more research would be required before we could rule out the option of the utilisation of other clay sources of similar chemical composition, possibly close to Dragonby.

Other evidence which it has been suggested might indicate movement of Lincolnshire stamped and rouletted wares is provided by rare discoveries of typologically related vessels well away from the focus of this decorative style (Fig. 12.5; e.g. May 1996, 640). One of the more convincing examples is a small sherd from Gamston, preserving a pattern of square-toothed rouletting which is entirely alien to the potting traditions of the middle Trent Valley (Knight 1992, 43, fig. 15.4). The vessel was manufactured from a shelly fabric, derived probably from a non-local source – possibly in Lincolnshire. Further hints of contacts between Gamston and communities farther east are provided by the discovery of a footring-based ovoid vessel with a rather poorly executed interlocking arc pattern around the shoulder (*ibid*. 49, fig. 17.14): unique in Nottinghamshire, but finding many close parallels in Lincolnshire (notably Salmonby: Elsdon 1996c, fig. 3.2). Several scholars have also drawn attention to the occasional discovery in Lincolnshire of vessels preserving decoration which may indicate contact with other regional styles of La Tène ornament (cf. Elsdon 1996a, 22, 26) – for example, at Weelsby Avenue, Grimsby, where excavations unearthed a curious sherd with infilled rouletted decoration which Elsdon has compared to LIA1 stamped and rouletted vessels from Hengistbury Head, Dorset (Elsdon 1996a, 22, fig. C6b: bottom sherd; cf. Brown, L 1987, 309, 317, ill. 147: form JD4.3). The unusual sandy fabric contrasts with other pottery from the site and has been interpreted as non-local (S. Elsdon *pers comm*.), but further analyses are required before the range of possible sources can be assessed.

Additional evidence which may indicate the development of regional distribution systems in the later Iron Age is provided by the discovery in Nottinghamshire, and subsequently on several Iron

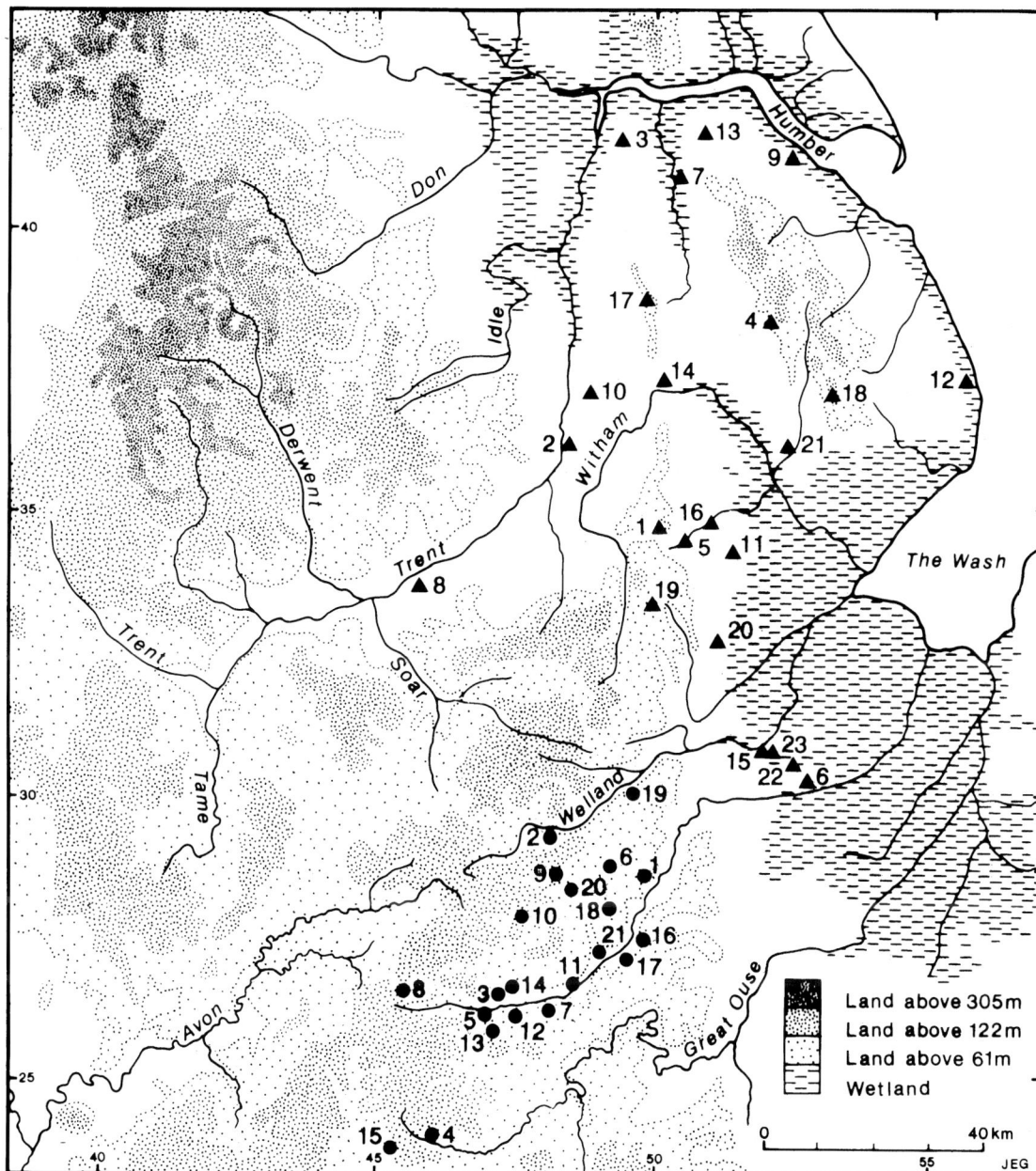

Fig. 12.5. Distribution of La Tène decorated pottery of the Lincolnshire and Northamptonshire traditions (sources: S. Elsdon and author).

Lincolnshire tradition (triangles): 1. Ancaster Gap; 2. Collingham; 3. Dragonby; 4. East Barkwith; 5. Ewerby; 6. Fengate; 7. Fonaby; 8. Gamston; 9. Grimsby (Weelsby Avenue); 10. Harby; 11. Helpringham; 12. Ingoldmells; 13. Kirmington; 14. Lincoln (Holmes Grain Warehouse); 15. Market Deeping; 16. Old Sleaford; 17. Owmby; 18. Salmonby; 19. Sapperton; 20. Stainfield; 21. Tattershall Thorpe; 22. Werrington; 23. West Deeping (Rectory Farm).

Northamptonshire tradition (circles): 1. Aldwincle; 2. Ashley; 3. Blackthorn (Northampton); 4. Brackley; 5. Briar Hill (Northampton); 6. Brigstock; 7. Cogenhoe; 8. Daventry (DIRFT); 9. Desborough; 10. Draughton; 11. Earls Barton (Clay Lane); 12. Hardingstone; 13. Hunsbury; 14. Moulton Park (Northampton); 15. Rainsborough; 16. Ringstead; 17. Stanwick; 18. Twywell; 19. Wakerley; 20. Weekley; 21. Wellingborough (Hemmingwell Lodge).

Age sites in Derbyshire, Leicestershire and Northamptonshire, of pottery tempered with igneous inclusions which may have derived from granodiorite sources in or on the fringes of Charnwood Forest. This recalls the discovery, many years ago, of similar inclusions in 'traded' Saxon pottery from the Midlands and eastern England (Walker 1978; Williams and Vince 1997), and raises the possibility of an exchange network in Iron Age pottery which could provide a Midland equivalent of the widely distributed Malvernian or gabbroic wares of south-western England (Peacock 1968; 1969a). This fabric was first recorded in an Iron Age context at Gamston, where petrological studies by Williams identified coarse angular inclusions deriving from a medium-grained rock of granitic texture with pink to grey feldspar, abundant grey quartz and flakes of biotite in several plain quartz-gritted sherds (Fabric Q1A) and a plain grog-tempered sherd (Fabric G1A; Knight 1992, 42–3; Williams 1992; Carney 1998a and b). The granitic inclusions were identified as grano-diorite, comparable to that outcropping close to Mountsorrel on the eastern edge of Charnwood Forest (Hains and Horton 1969, 27; Sylvester-Bradley and Ford 1968, 51), and in view of their angularity were interpreted as material crushed for use as temper. A drift source for the granodiorite, in local river-terrace deposits, was regarded as unlikely, and it was suggested that pottery vessels or temper had been transported to Gamston from the Mountsorrel area, possibly via the Soar and the Trent over a distance of *c.*35km (Knight 1992, 42). Work on another Trent Valley site at Swarkestone Lowes some 30km upstream, has identified further sherds with coarse angular granitoid inclusions which appear to have been crushed as temper (Elliott and Knight 1999). The inclusions within one thin-section were identified as of granodiorite composition, comparing reasonably well petrographically with the Ordovician granodiorites of Mountsorrel, while those in another sample were interpreted as of dioritic or syenodiorotic affinity, possibly from the Mountsorrel granodiorite (Williams 1997; Carney 1998a).

The possible sources of the granitoid inclusions recorded in the pottery from Gamston and Swarke-stone have been considered by Carney (1998a; 1998b) and Williams (1992; 1997). It was concluded that granitoids similar to those recorded at Gamston and Swarkestone *could* occur as pebbles or larger cobbles in the gravels of the Soar Valley or in the Trent Valley gravels downstream of Swarkestone. They would, however, be extremely rare (most clasts in Trent or Soar Valley drift consisting of vein quartz, flint or Triassic sandstone) and are unlikely to have occurred in a condition readily amenable to crushing. More likely sources would be gravels derived from streams strictly local to granitoid outcrops (such as Mountsorrel) which would in-corporate concentrations of granitoid debris in an easily crushed form. Alternatively, loose weathered-out fragments of granodiorite could have been obtained from the post-glacial scree or 'head' de-posits which mantle the Charnwood/Mountsorrel region. Further evidence supporting a non-local

origin for pottery attributed to this fabric group may be provided by the occurrence in both of the above samples of silt-size quartz grains, suggesting that the clay had been obtained from Triassic mudstones or from glacial till derived from these; an abundance of mica in one of the samples could indicate that the clay had been dug from the highly micaceous Sneinton formation of the Mercia Mudstone. The nearest exposure to Swarkestone is some 5km to the south-east, to the south of the Trent between Castle Donington and Breedon-on-the-Hill, although more distant sources of suitable potting clay closer to readily available supplies of Mountsorrel grano-diorite could have been exploited.

Farther afield, examples of granodiorite which might have derived from the Charnwood area have been reported in Northamptonshire at Weekley, following petrological analyses by D. Williams (A. Gwilt *pers comm.*), and the Daventry International Rail Freight Terminal (DIRFT; A. Woodward *pers comm.*). In Leicestershire, at locations closer to the Mountsorrel outcrop, discoveries of granodiorite have been reported at a number of sites, notably Kirby Muxloe and Wanlip (Marsden 1998, 45–6; P. Marsden *pers comm.*). The presence of such fabrics at the latter sites is not surprising, as both are located on the edge of Charnwood Forest, but the presence of a similar fabric in Northamptonshire suggests that the early discoveries in Nottinghamshire and Derby-shire may form part of a much wider pattern extending north and south of the production source during the later Iron Age.

Few of the other inclusion types which character-ise later Iron Age pottery from the region, such as shell, quartz and flint, can be tied closely to particu-lar raw material sources. There is, however, a growing body of evidence to suggest that the regional distribution systems which have been postulated for pottery incorporating localised gabbroic or granodiorite inclusions may have ex-tended to pottery incorporating more ubiquitous raw materials such as shell. Excavations in the south Lincolnshire Fens at Cowbit, for example, yielded a small collection of 144 potsherds dominated by non-local shelly limestone fabrics (Knight forthcoming: b). Similar fabrics are common on Iron Age sites along the south Lincolnshire Fen margin, and are generally assumed to indicate the use of local Jurassic clays. At Cowbit, however, the nearest available sources of comparable shelly limestone are located a minimum of 14km to the west of the site, near Thurlby, implying the import of either pottery or temper. The evidence for the use of non-local raw material resources is not unexpected perhaps, in view of the need to import a broad range of re-sources into the specialised wetland environment of the Fens, but it raises some difficult questions of interpretation. In particular, were these goods transported from production sites to permanent settlements, or are these seasonal sites, utilised for salt production and summer pasture, with pots brought from permanent home bases? In the case of Cowbit, where the small collection of pottery sherds is overshadowed by briquetage derived from salt production, we may propose a model of seasonal movement by communities who for practical reasons may have relied mainly upon basketwork or other organic containers, supplemented by a small number of imported pottery vessels. Non-local shelly fabrics have been suggested elsewhere, notably at Gamston (Knight 1992, 42–3), where vessels tempered with fossil shell which could have been obtained from sources at least 5–6km from the site were identified – including one rouletted sherd which is related typologically to Lincolnshire stamped and rouletted ware. Similarly, at Hamilton, Leicester, shell-tempered scored pottery for which a non-local source has been suggested was obtained during recent excavations by the Oxford Archaeological Unit (P. Marsden *pers comm.*; pottery report in prep.). However, shell is so common within the region that non-local sources may only be identified in exceptional circumstances.

The petrological and stylistic evidence for the development of non-local pottery production in the region is supported, finally, by the Iron Age briquetage data assembled by Morris (1985; 1994b). Clear evidence has been obtained for the penetration into the upper and middle Trent Valley of salt containers, manufactured in the Cheshire Plain from 'stony VCP', notably at Fisherwick (Smith 1978, 45–57), Fox Covert Farm, Aston-upon-Trent, Derbys. (Hughes 1999), Gamston (Knight 1992, 65), Swarkestone Lowes (Elliott and Knight 1999) and Breedon-on-the-Hill and Enderby (Morris, 1994b, 385). The penetration of Cheshire salt as far east as Nottingham is surprising in view of the comparative proximity of the Lincolnshire salterns (Lane 1992a), although the distribution network associated with the latter has yet to be elucidated. Perhaps Cheshire salt was more prized than the Lincolnshire product, or perhaps Lincolnshire salt was traded in organic containers. As yet, no evidence has been obtained from the Fens for ceramic salt containers, despite the accumulation of a substantial body of excavation data, and it must be assumed that other means of transporting the salt were employed. The easterly distribution of stony VCP suggests movement along the Trent and Soar Valleys, and against this background the postulated 'trade' in pottery between Charnwood Forest and the middle Trent Valley may merge into a wider pattern.

Conclusions

A sequence of four chronologically successive ceramic traditions has been proposed in this chapter, commencing in the late second millennium BC or early first millennium BC with a range of highly distinctive post Deverel-Rimbury 'plainwares', and culminating in the first century BC with the earliest wheelthrown Late La Tène pottery. This scheme is summarised diagrammatically in Fig. 12.2, and is presented as a framework for future research within the region. Further ceramic work must be directed towards closer dating of key ceramic assemblages, although the obvious longevity in this region of many ceramic forms, styles of surface treatment and fabrics, combined with the formidable interpretative problems posed by redeposition and other taphonomic processes, should urge caution when formulating more precise chronologies. Closer dating may only be attained by concentrating resources upon large stratified assemblages, ideally spanning two or more ceramic phases, combined with a greater investment in the radiocarbon and dendrochronological dating of directly associated organic materials. Radiocarbon is unfortunately of limited value for pottery overlapping the calibration platform of *c*.800–400 cal BC, but recent dates for later Iron Age pottery, from sites such as Wanlip, Cowbit and Market Deeping, have raised hopes of refinements in the dating of pottery either side of this platform. Thermoluminescence dating may also play an important role eventually in the refining of Iron Age ceramic chronology, to judge by the initial results of research by Sarah Barnett, including analyses of selected vessels from Cambridgeshire, Leicestershire, Lincolnshire and Northamptonshire (S. Barnett *pers comm.*; cf. Beamish 1998, 24–7). Particular efforts should also be focused upon vessel fabrics as potential chronological indicators: a subject which in this region has yet to be systematically investigated. Thus, although certain very basic contrasts may be discerned, such as a heavy emphasis in the Trent Valley upon grog-tempering in Early to Middle Bronze Age pottery, little systematic change has yet been identified. Attempts to rectify this problem have been made by the formulation of a common fabric terminology for East Midlands later prehistoric pottery, permitting ready comparison of the fabrics from different sites (Allen and Knight 1995; Knight 1997). This system has been adopted by the Prehistoric Ceramics Research Group (PCRG 1997, 25–8) and it is hoped that the steady accumulation of data will permit eventually a systematic investigation into temporal patterning in first millennium BC fabrics from the region.

Recent ceramic studies have also enhanced our knowledge of the production and distribution of pottery, and hence the exchange relationships between settlements in this area and beyond. Petrological analyses of selected vessels, combined with stylistic analyses of La Tène decorated wares, have demonstrated a progression in some parts of the region during the latter half of the first millennium BC towards non-local production – mirroring a development observed in other areas of southern Britain during this period. The case for non-local pottery production rests in part upon the discovery at Weekley of Glastonbury-style gabbroic vessels, produced in Cornwall, and at sites in the Trent and Nene basins of pottery incorporating granodiorite inclusions which suggest a production source in or close to the Mountsorrel area of Charnwood Forest. Other non-local fabrics have occasionally been recorded in later Iron Age contexts, notably the shelly limestone wares from Cowbit, although the wide distribution of most of the inclusions contained within first millennium BC pottery fabrics from the region generally prevents positive identification of non-local products. Evidence for the long-distance movement of decorated finewares may be provided, finally, by rare discoveries of stamped and rouletted vessels well away from the focus of their distribution in Lindsey and Kesteven, notably in the middle Trent Valley. Confirmation of the complex distribution networks which linked later Iron Age sites in the region is provided by scattered discoveries of stony VCP on sites in the Trent and Soar Valleys, indicating the movement of ceramic containers for the distribution of salt manufactured at unidentified locations in the Cheshire Plain.

Additional petrological and chemical analyses are required to investigate further the observed trend from local to regional production during the first millennium BC, although the potential value of petrology is limited in this region by the wide distribution of most of the inclusions which occur within the clay matrix. One of the key research questions for this region, from the viewpoint of ceramic production, is the role of Charnwood as a possible focus of manufacture. Current evidence supports the contention that vessels had been distributed from this area during the later Iron Age, but this hypothesis needs to be tested rigorously by additional petrological work, supplemented by chemical analyses to narrow the range of potential sources of raw material. Other crucial questions for

consideration include the possibility of alternative drift sources for granodiorite and the factors which may have attracted potters to this raw material source. Since examples of granodiorite have been claimed in at least one Neolithic context, in Grimston Ware from a ring-ditch at Great Briggs, Holme Pierrepont (G. Guilbert and D. Williams *pers comm.*), study could usefully be extended to the prehistoric period generally.

Another issue of significance is the growing spatial diversity of ceramic traditions during the first millennium BC, as exemplified by the clustering of La Tène decorated pottery in areas of Northamptonshire and Lincolnshire (Fig. 12.5) and the concentration of scoring in Leicestershire and Northamptonshire (Fig. 12.4). This trend towards greater clustering of ceramic types is not easily explained, but could relate in part to the known changes in the organisation of production and distribution. Alternatively, we might speculate whether these patterns relate in some way to social groupings. Particular styles of pottery could well have been employed as symbols of social identity, but on present evidence we can only guess as to the possible social implications of these distributions.

Acknowledgements
This paper was submitted in March 1999 and has not been revised subsequently. Valuable comments on this text have been provided by Carol Allen, Sheila Elsdon, Colin Haselgrove, J.D. Hill, Jeffrey May, Elaine Morris, Stuart Needham, David Williams and Ann Woodward. Thanks are also extended to Sarah Barnett, Pauline Beswick, John Carney, Ros Cleal, Maggi Darling, Naomi Field, Ron Firman, Kasia Gdaniec, Graeme Guilbert, Adam Gwilt, Graham Hull, Dennis Jackson, Gavin Kinsley, Tom Lane, Ruth Leary, Patrick Marsden, Lorraine Mepham and Francis Pryor for helpful discussions and for the provision of unpublished data on ceramic collections. Calibrations of the radiocarbon dates have been calculated by Steve Malone, employing OxCal v2.17 (after Stuiver, M., Long, A. and Kra, R.S. 1993. *Radiocarbon* 3[1]), unless stated otherwise in the text. The illustrations were prepared by Jane Goddard and Fig. 12.2 with the assistance of Steve Malone. The approximate extent of the Iron Age wetlands, shown in Fig. 12.1, was established with advice from Andy Howard, Tom Lane, Malcolm Lillie and Francis Pryor. Eileen Appleton assisted in the compilation of the list of references.

13 Just About the Potter's Wheel? Using, Making and Depositing Middle and Later Iron Age Pots in East Anglia

J. D. Hill

"The identity and differentiation of the group is brought out in the practice of eating together or separately, as well as in the content of what is eaten by different collectivities; this is the arena of feasts and fasts, of prohibitions and preferences, of communal and domestic meals, of table manners, and modes of serving and service." (Goody 1982, 38)

Introduction

This paper is about the adoption of wheel turned pottery in south east England during the last two hundred years of the Pre-Roman Iron Age (c.150 BC–AD 43) set within the wider changes in the deposition, use and manufacture of pottery that were taking place at this time. The discussion will concentrate on the uses of pottery, arguing that the production of specific types of pots were intimately tied to particular ways in which those pots were used, and the social settings of that use. It is also suggested that the differences between hand made Middle Iron Age pottery and wheel made Late Iron Age pottery are another example of how throughout later British prehistory the manufacture of a particular type of artefact almost seems to go hand in hand with a particular way for that artefact to enter (or not enter) the archaeological record (Barrett 1991b; Bradley 1990).

The adoption of wheel turned pottery has often been seen as one of the key defining features of the Late Pre-Roman Iron Age in southern Britain (e.g. Hawkes, Myers and Stevens 1930). A distinctive style of wheel turned pottery, sometimes labelled 'Belgic' or 'Aylesford-Swarling', appeared in parts of Hertfordshire, Essex, Kent and West Sussex during the first century BC. This innovation is one of the major changes that took place in these areas during this period. These included the adoption of new burial rites, emergence of 'oppida' types of settlement, a system of coinage and the appearance of a stratified, if not class divided, society. Many of these changes involved borrowing or modifying cultural elements from north east Gaul, and close links are very evident with this area before and after it was conquered by Rome in the 50's BC. This borrowing included the wheel made pots themselves that are often identical to vessels made in northern Gaul (Cunliffe 1991,1995; Haselgrove 1982, 1989; Hill 1995a; James and Rigby 1997; Millett 1990a).

The paper considers the initial take up of wheel turned pottery in Hertfordshire and Essex, and how this pottery was adapted to fit within existing ceramic traditions further north. The adoption of wheel made pottery in other regions outside East Anglia is not considered in detail. It will concentrate on the roles and use of pottery suggesting that an examination of pottery forms/repertoires and styles of deposition add extra dimensions of variability to consider alongside the distinction between hand or wheel made. The paper draws on a study of pottery forms and sizes from 22 settlement and 18 cemeteries dated between c.300 BC and AD 60 from East Anglia – defined here in a broad sense as the counties of Norfolk, Suffolk, Essex, Hertfordshire and Cambridgeshire[1]. This region contains one of the most important foci of rapid change and social development in later Iron Age Britain (Hertfordshire and Essex), while the north is often considered peripheral and unchanging (Bryant 1997; Champion 1994; Haselgrove 1982; Hill 1995a). These broader changes will not be discussed in depth in this paper, which concentrates on issues of pottery interpretation that may be of wider interest than just to Late Pre-Roman Iron Age specialists.

From Middle to Late Iron Age Pots: Immigration and New Technology

Despite the importance of the appearance of wheel turned pottery as a chronological marker to define the Late Iron Age, there has been surprisingly little attention paid to the adoption of this new technology. While many authors mention wheel turned pottery, greater discussion is usually given to other features of the Aylesford-Swarling culture such as the cremation burials, or the presence of Dressel 1 wine amphorae. With the identification of this wheel turned pottery with invading Belgic peoples from north east France, the problem of how the potter's wheel arrived in south east England was easily solved. However, despite the rejection of the notion of immigrants causing all change in Late Iron Age south east England, the assumption that foreign potters are necessary to start wheel turned production remains to this day – on those rare occasions people have considered the problem (e.g. Cunliffe 1991, 133). As Freestone and Rigby (1997, 57) argue, in what is notably the *only* serious discussion of this question:

> 'These first wheel-thrown ceramics are very similar to the pottery being produced at this time in the Belgic areas of Gaul. Although the British pots are made in local fabrics, typologically and technically they are identical to assemblages in northern France.... These exceptionally strong parallels seem to imply that the first of these new wheel-thrown wares were produced by immigrant or itinerant potters from Gaul, working in Britain and using local clays.'

As well as the clear links in pottery forms with northern Gaul, the assumption that new people are needed to initiate a new ceramic technology can be tied with the widespread assumption that pottery traditions are resistant to change (e.g. Rice 1984; Kingery 1993). In particular, the customary motor patterns of forming pottery vessels – habitual postures, actions and ways of doing things – are regarded as particularly resistant to change (Arnold 1985; Rice 1987; Raina and Hill 1978). Arnold (1985) and others (Roux and Corbetta 1989) have argued that on average two generations are required to fully integrate new motor habits, and the use of the wheel inevitably means a far longer 'apprenticeship' period to acquire the skill. These arguments do strongly support the notion that the introduction of wheel turned pottery into Late Iron Age south east England represents a marked break in customary habits. But does this necessary imply immigrant wheel using potters, and what was the wider context of pottery use in which this innovation was set?

From Middle to Late Iron Age Pots: Contexts, Categories and Use

In essence the key differences between Middle and Late Iron Age pottery can be seen by comparing Figures 13.1 and 13.2. These graphs show the relationship between the height and the rim diameters of measurable vessels (i.e. those with complete or reconstructable profiles) from a selection of sites in East Anglia.[1] They show two clear differences between Middle and Late Iron Age vessels. Firstly, there is no clear relationship between vessel height and rim diameter for Late Iron Age vessels compared to Middle Iron Age vessels. This is a marked break from the pattern that typifies British prehistoric pottery from the fourth to the end of the first millennium BC (cf. Howard 1981; Woodward 1995, 1997). Secondly, there are considerably more Late Iron Age vessels that can be measured than there are Middle Iron Age vessels. These differences reflect important changes in both the uses of pots and the ways pots entered the archaeological record. Although the use of the potter's wheel is linked to both these changes, on its own it did not cause them.

Later prehistoric pots were tools (Braun 1983) for storing, preparing, cooking and serving food and drink: the 'foodways' of these societies. The term 'foodways'[2] not only refers to Iron Age food preparation technology and the types of foods consumed, it also embraces the social facets of food such as the conventions of the meal; how cooking and eating reflect and reproduce the structure of family life; the use of meals to incorporate or distinguish, express or compete for status etc. As such, this allows us to move away from the largely technological and functional discussion that has surrounded Braun's notion of 'pots as tools'. Instead, the need for specific types of ceramic tools directly relates to how specific cultural foodways require tools to prepare and serve certain foods and drinks in specific ways. From this perspective it might be proposed that any change in the range, form and types of pots, ceramic tools, is direct evidence for a change in the foodways of those groups.

The most obvious change with the adoption of Late Iron Age pottery was the greater range of different shaped pottery tools available, each with different rim diameter to vessel height ratios (Figs 13.1, 13.2). Before, eastern English Middle Iron Age ceramic traditions were characterised by a narrow range of simple open containers (see drawings in Cunliffe 1991: Figs A:17, 22–24). Potters drew on a restricted range of basic vessel categories from which to make vessels of different sizes. Details of vessel proportions, wall form, rim type or surface treatment varied, but in general people made and used a limited range of open cylinders – deep bowls

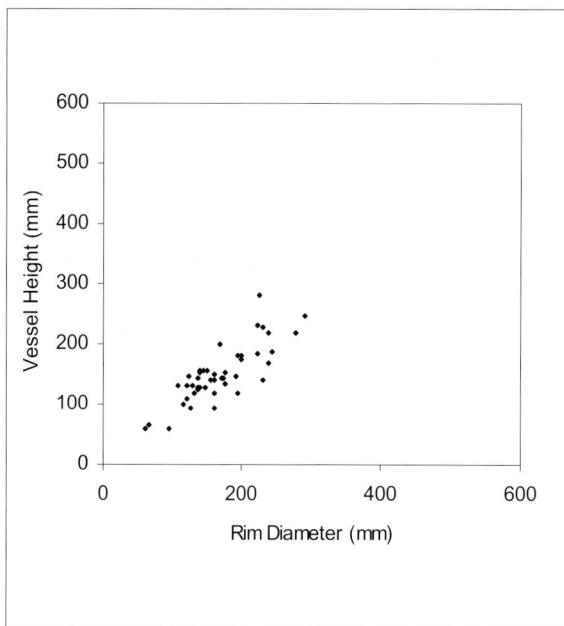

Fig. 13.1. The ratio of rim diameter and vessel height for 48 Middle Iron Age vessels from Anglia.

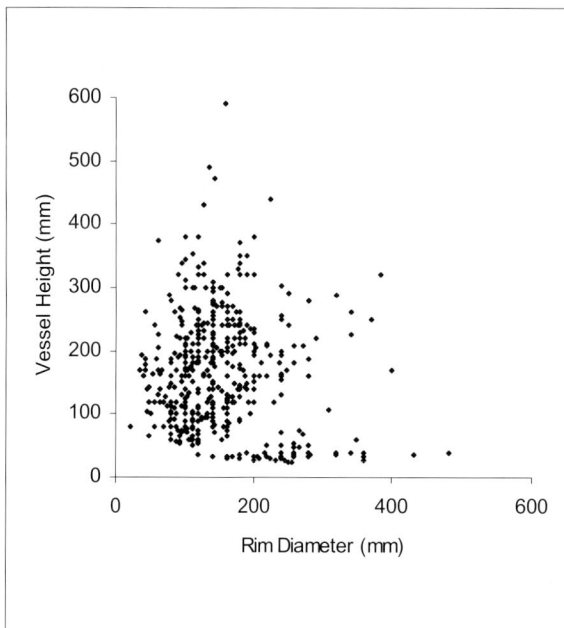

Fig. 13.2. The ratio of rim diameter and vessel height for 500 Late Iron Age vessels from Anglia.

or tubs – of varying sizes (Fig. 13.1). Distinctively constricted or narrow necked jars were very rare. Pots were all hand made, in relatively small numbers, with little apparent exchange (Morris 1994). The ubiquitous open bowl/jars were used in aspects of food storage, preparation and serving. Functional differences did exist, notably between burnished vessels (more often used for serving than cooking) and plain vessels (more often used for cooking than serving), and between larger (storage/cooking) and smaller (serving/cooking) sized vessels (Hill and Braddock forthcoming). However, there was little specialism according to vessel shape. The same shape of vessel could be plain or burnished, large or small. The potential role of organic and large metal containers in the Middle Iron Age foodways is difficult to assess. Metal, leather, cane, bark and wooden containers could, *but need not*, have been used; the majority of which would also have been open cylinders (Earwood 1993; Evans 1989b; Fitzpatrick 1997b). Overall, the impression given is of multi-purpose pottery vessels; the same size, even the same bowl/jar, used for a range of functions.

This is in sharp contrast to the Late Iron Age, when potters produced a larger range of types, each with a tighter range of vessel sizes. A Late Iron Age site will produce a rich assemblage of pottery, in terms of sheer quantities, proportion of non-locally made vessels and range of vessel shapes compared to a Middle Iron Age assemblage.[3] It is due to the presence of these very different forms that there is the diverse range of vessel heights to rim diameter ratios for Late Iron Age pottery (Fig. 13.2). As some of the names of pot types imply, specific forms of Late Iron Age vessels had specific functions which can be identified on the basis of form, physical evidence, and, classical literary and artistic evidence (e.g. beakers, cups, flagons, platters, cooking jars, storage jars etc.). A greater range of ceramic tool types were now used which points to important changes in how a meal would be served and looked 'at table', in the manner and types of foods eaten, and in the basic categorisation of this (and other?) spheres of material culture. This pattern was not restricted to ceramic foodway tools, there is evidence also for a wider range of metal and wooden vessels in this period.

The Rate and Scale of Change

This important change in the ceramic repertoire was not a sudden break. The range of ceramic tools essentially expanded in two well-recognised phases (Birchall 1965; Stead 1976; Thompson 1981). This paper does not intend to discuss the chronology of Late Iron Age pottery in any depth. The dating of earliest Late Iron Age pottery has been tied up inevitably with proving, or disproving, the truth of Caesar's account of the Belgae's migrations (Hawkes and Dunning 1930; Birchall 1965; Rodwell 1976 etc.). Birchall's (1965) untying of the two phenomena

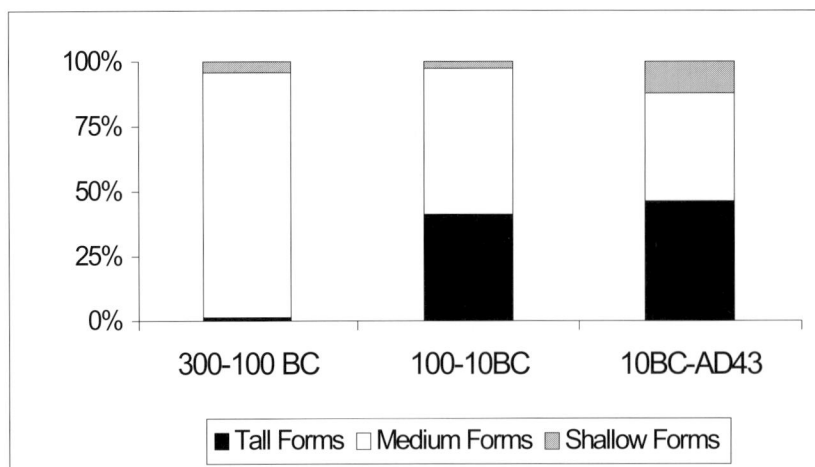

Fig. 13.3a. Change in basic pot forms through time in southern East Anglia (Hertfordshire, Essex).

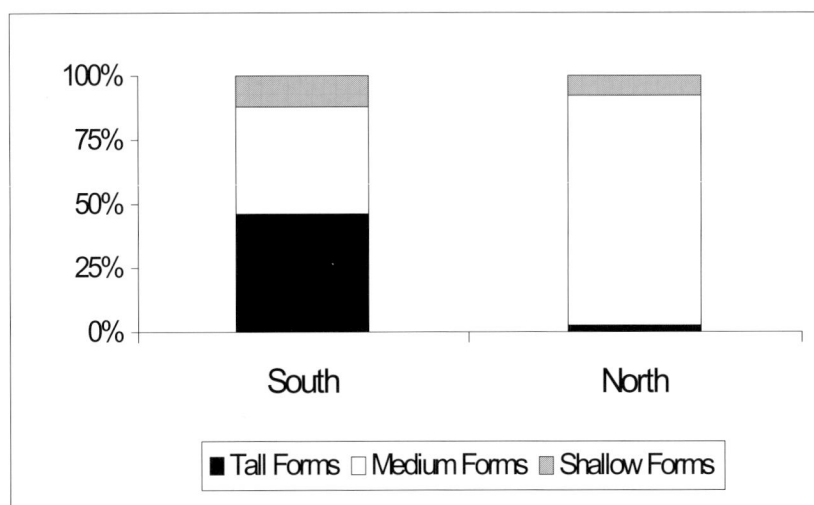

Fig. 13.3b. Comparison between assemblages dated C.1–50 AD from southern and northern East Anglia.

Fig. 13.3. The changing proportions of tall, medium and shallow vessels in assemblages from southern and northern parts of East Anglia from c.300 BC to AD 43.

rested on proposing a short chronology for Late Iron Age pottery, all post dating the Roman conquest of Gaul (c.50 BC+). Grounds for a long chronology, with the inception of Late Iron Age pottery before Caesar was in Gaul, have gained strength over the last twenty years as ideas have changed about cultural change, and continental chronologies have been revised (James and Rigby 1997; Fitzpatrick 1997a; Haselgrove 1997). A long chronology, starting as early as 125 BC, is accepted here although the changes in repertoire and deposition discussed in this paper were the same whenever they happened.

The exact details of the development require more work, but two broad phases can be identified in the development of Late Iron Age pottery convention-ally dating to before and after the Roman Emperor

Augustus' re-organisation of Gaul and actions in Germany c.20/10 BC. These correspond to Stead's (1976) Welwyn and Lexden phases. However, 'Augustan' ceramic forms begin slightly earlier on the Continent (Colin Haselgrove pers comm.). In the first phase a large proportion of new 'tall' forms and constricted forms were added to the open bowls/ jars, which were themselves now made in new shapes (Figs 13.3a, 13.4). These tall forms (vessels with maximum widths considerably smaller than their height) included a range of basic tall 'beakers', necked or cordoned jars and also pedestalled urns. This addition possibly took place before the next trend where assemblages were also distinguished by an increasing division into visually distinct types of vessel with specific forms and surface finishes, each

Fig. 13.4. Changes in the range and shapes of pottery in East Anglia from c.200 BC (top row) through the first century BC (middle row) and to the immediate pre-Conquest period (lower row) (drawn by Sophia Jundi).

with specific functions (Fig. 13.4). These include burnished carinated open bowls/jars such as *tazze* of different sizes, which along with necked or cordoned bowls are special serving forms. At the same time the visually distinct 'cooking pot' with repeated vessel proportions and a combed surface become increasing common, along with very large storage jars, with similar surface treatments. Certainly by the mid-first century BC ceramic assemblages were marked by a range of distinct tools, a visual and tactile distinction between kitchen wares and serving wares, and an emphasis on tall forms (Fig. 13.4).

The new tall forms were probably vessels designed for drinking alcohol. Okun (1989, 47–49) showed that a high proportion of tall drinking forms characterised pre-Romanized assemblages in the upper Rhineland. In south east England these tall forms included a range of essentially tall cylinders (Thompson 1982 types B5, C8–1 etc.). These early tall jars occur in a wide range of different local forms and are often definitely or probably hand made (e.g. Thompson's (1982) – 'smallish jars with slack shoulders and slight everted rims' (form C8–1), many of Rodwell's 1976 group 1, 2 and 3 vessels etc.). They also include the *handmade* tall, neckless or slack shouldered open jars from Gatesbury Track, Braughing (Partridge 1979) and Baldock (Rigby 1986). Single examples also occur in Middle Iron Age assemblages at Wenden's Ambo (Hodder 1982d, fig. 29.5) and Little Waltham (Drury 1978, no 286). These cylindrical tall open forms represent some of the earliest pottery of this tradition in south east England. These forms are included in Birchall's (1965) and Rodwell's (1976) 'Earliest' and 'Early Belgic' pottery which predate the main Welwyn phase cremation burials which contain pedestal urns. Outside this region, a similar pattern occurs at Westhampnett, West Sussex, where the mid-first century BC cemetery contains a high proportion of *handmade* versions of tall north Gallic and other forms (Fitzpatrick 1997a).

These tall cylindrical jars are largely replaced later by wheel made, undecorated, cordoned necked and other tall jars in the later first century BC (Thompson 1982, type B2–2 etc.), and later by beakers. Pedestalled urns, the most distinctive first century BC wheel made vessels, should also be connected to drinking. Their functions are unclear, but if their replacement by beakers as grave goods in the first century AD was a direct replacement with a vessel of a similar function, then these other 'tall' vessel forms may also have been drinking, or liquid serving, vessels (Table 13.1). Pedestal urns are clearly wheel made and copy north east Gallic types. Drinking out of a pedestalled urn or a later beaker is difficult to image, without much of the content missing the mouth and flowing down the chin. This might be intended, although other scenarios could be envisaged; use of straws? Constricted forms, narrow necked jars and flasks etc. were another prominent addition – forms again probably used for holding and serving alcohol. These forms comprised only 1.4% of assemblages dating before c.125–100 BC, but comprise 10% of those dated c.100–10BC and 12.2% of those dated 10BC to AD43. These new Late Iron Age assemblages occur on settlements and also in the cremation burials that become common in the first century BC. The early and late burial assemblages show the new emphasis on drinking and eating forms in a more exaggerated way, with rich and poor graves almost exclusively furnished with table forms (Table 13.1).

This range of distinctive pottery forms widens further in later assemblages (c.10BC onwards), with the addition of platters, cups, beakers, flagons, flasks etc. (Fig. 13.4, lower). Almost all of these additions were either imports from Roman Gaul or copies of Romanized Gallic prototypes (Freestone and Rigby 1997). Almost all were new tableware forms. The typology, dating, origins and distribution of Gallic fineware table forms have received considerable attention (e.g. Rigby and Freestone 1986; Timby 1987). Less attention has been paid to the local versions of these forms (except Rigby 1986; Thompson 1982) and the wider implications of copying (Willis 1994, 1997a). Beakers, another variant on the tall cylindrical vessel form, add to the large drinking forms. The distinctive shaped and small volume of cups, another drinking

form, were possibly for a different alcoholic beverage or context for drinking (cf. modern differences between beer and wine glasses etc.). Flagons for serving alcohol were added to the existing range of constricted pouring vessels, while the platter and other shallow dishes mark a new way to serve food from this time (Fig. 13.4). Kitchen wares continue little changed, the surfaces of cooking pots now usually being rilled rather than combed. This full repertoire continues with changes after the Roman conquest in AD 43. New additions post AD 43 follow the trends of adding new food preparation and serving 'tools' such as purposely made sieves, wide open bowls/dishes and *mortaria* (Going 1987; Swan 1988; Tyers 1996).

This paper argues for a use-lead view for these ceramic changes. Studies of pottery have often concentrated on production and distribution rather than use and deposition. Seeing pots as food storage, preparation and serving tools helps to correct this emphasis as we have to ask why people would want to use new forms of pottery? The increasing repertoire of Late Iron Age pottery included almost exclusively new tablewares which implies that the types, look and ways meals were served were changing. At the same time, the existence of distinctive kitchenwares as opposed to tablewares also suggests a stronger conceptual differentiation was now being drawn between the cooking and eating (and those involved in both activities?). The latter is important as it raises the need to set these changes in terms of changing gender and age relations at this time. A conceptual difference between kitchen and table may imply that a far stricter distinction was drawn between those who cooked and those who consumed at these meals. Certainly the changing tools for cooking suggests, along with other evidence, changes in cooking practices that may have required longer periods of direct attention to food preparation and cooking. The basic Middle Iron Age bowl/jars were probably used primarily for preparing carbohydrate rich stews and porridges etc. These types of food can be easily prepared and left to cook/keep warm (see Hill and Braddock forthcoming for an interpretation of Middle Iron Age vessel use). Do the changes in the Late Iron Age mean a shift away from this pattern? Steamers, firedogs for roasting, new foodstuffs – including fish – and the preparation of meals to be served on the new plates suggest so. Certainly, the widespread use of platters from c.10 AD onwards represents a marked actual and conceptual change in the types of foods (no longer sloppy stews etc. but boiled, roasted or baked more physically intact, recognisable, foods), the food's 'look' and presentation (how the foods are arranged on the platter can be far more easily manipulated than with a stew/porridge),

Table 13.1. The different proportions of broad types of vessel between settlements and cemeteries in Hertfordshire, Essex and south Suffolk in the first centuries BC and AD.

First Century BC (pre-Augustan settlements and cemeteries)

		Settlements		Cemeteries	
		n.	%	n.	%
Tall Forms	Pedestal Urns	20	6.7	33	29.2
	Tall Constricted Jars	13	4.4	1	0.9
	Tall Open Jars	3	1.0	2	1.7
	Storage Jars	79	26.6	18	15.9
Medium Forms	Cooking Pots	10	3.4		
	Open Bowls	20	6.7		
	Tazzae	97	32.7	28	24.8
	Small Bowls/Cups	2	0.7	9	8.0
Shallow Forms	Specialist Cups	26	8.8	21	18.6
	Dishes, Shallow Bowls			4	3.5
	Platters	3	1.0		
Other Forms	Medium height, Constricted Jars	2	0.7	2	1.7
	Flasks	13	4.4	4	3.5
	Lid	8	2.7	2	1.8
	Strainers	1	0.3		
	Total Number of Pots	297		113	
	Percentage of Tall Forms		41.1		46.0
	Percentage of Medium Forms		48.9		54.9
	Percentage of Shallow Forms		8.4		7.1
	Percentage of Constricted Forms		11.5		6.2

First Century AD (Augustan and later settlements and cemeteries)

		Settlements		Cemeteries	
		n.	%	n.	%
Tall Forms	Pedestal Urns	47	2.7	38	5.0
	Flagons	135	7.7	81	10.7
	Beakers	198	11.3	235	30.9
	Tall Open Jars	159	9.1	128	16.8
	Storage Jars	112	6.4		
	Cooking Pots	160	9.2	4	0.5
Medium Forms	Open Bowls	253	14.5	26	3.4
	Small Bowls/Cups	56	3.2	41	5.4
	Gallo-Belgic Cups	75	4.3	45	5.9
Shallow Forms	Dishes, Shallow Bowls	82	4.7	2	0.3
	Platters	204	11.7	106	13.9
	Medium height, Constricted Jars	104	6.0	15	2.0
Other	Flasks	20	1.1	26	3.4
	Lid	68	3.9	7	0.9
	Mortaria	13	0.7		
	Strainers	41	2.3		
	Spouted Vessels	4	0.2		
	Other	16	0.9	6	0.8
	Total Number of Pots	1747		760	
	Percentage of Tall Forms		30.9		63.4
	Percentage of Medium Forms		33.3		9.3
	Percentage of Shallow Forms		20.7		20.1
	Percentage of Constricted Forms		14.8		16.2

along with a possible shift towards individual servings in individual vessels (cf. Deetz 1978, Yentsch 1991 on changing seventeenth and eighteenth century American colonial foodways). Those involved in the preparing of these meals were probably spending more time in their preparation than before, leading to a greater separation of cooks and eaters/drinkers (women and child cooks with male eaters in most households? Servants, slave or dependents as cooks in higher ranked households?). More time was probably also being spent brewing beer. As beer would easily sour, any large quantities would need to be prepared several days in advance of its planned consumption.

Early assemblages have a considerably high proportion of tall forms which have been argued were probably for drinking or holding beer or mead (Figs. 13.3a and 13.4). That specific pottery vessels were now required for drinking suggests changes in the importance and setting for drinking, an activity often attached considerable social and symbolic importance (e.g. Dietler 1990; Sherratt 1987; Vencl 1994; Woolf and Eldridge 1994). Specific vessels separated out drinking alcohol as a distinct activity and provided the props to embellish that activity. (A good malt whiskey may taste the same out of a student's chipped mug, but drinking it out of cut glass glasses poured out of a lead crystal decanter indicates and helps to construct a very different social milieu.). The exact details of these new drinking activities remain vague to us, but who was drinking (gender/social group), the circumstances (payment for work parties, feasts, family gatherings, rites of passage) and whose labour was most involved in producing the alcohol consumed (gender/age group) all have important social implications. Equally, there is no need that this increasing emphasis on drinking is connected with the consumption of Mediterranean wine. There are some amphorae in south east England at this early date (Fitzpatrick 1985), but it is likely that locally brewed beverages were drunk out of the vast majority of these drinking forms. Other new foodway tools that appeared with this early Late Iron Age pottery included firedogs, possibly implying a new emphasis on grills and spit roasting, and wooden 'buckets' (Earwood 1993). The latter are usually seen as wine mixers but are possibly for serving other cold liquids, as opposed to hot liquids cooked in metal cauldrons (Colin Haselgrove *pers comm.*). Wooden tankards, sometimes sheaved in bronze, were also another new drinking form in the Late Iron Age repertoire (Earwood 1993).

Other distinct tablewares also feature in early assemblages, such as large and small *tazze* bowls, pointing to similar changes in how food was presented and consumed as well. This is not to imply

that eating and drinking were unimportant in the Middle Iron Age, rather that the specific forms and social roles of eating and drinking were altering both at the level of the big social event and the daily preparation and serving of meals. The social context and importance of first drinking and then eating as well changed, requiring new forms of material culture to create and sustain the new contexts and meanings associated with these activities.

The importance of the meal was sanctioned by its central role in the cremation burial rite adopted in south east England later in the first century BC. In this rite the deceased was portrayed to mourners and to the afterlife as a participant in a meal: the cremated remains of the deceased accompanied in the grave with serving vessel, foods and beverages (Haselgrove 1984; Fitzpatrick 1997a; Stead and Rigby 1989; Whimster 1981). This meal, through the types and range of serving vessels and foodstuffs provided, came to reflect the status of the deceased or their family.

The funerary meal expressed the importance of the meal in wider society, and its use as a specific 'tournament of value' (Appadurai 1986); a key arena in which households could both express and compete for social status. I would suggest that it was this importance of the meal that led to the accelerating developments seen in Late Iron Age pottery repertoires and all other aspects of foodways (e.g. presence of Mediterranean wine and other imports). Such competition created the need to acquire fineware pottery, metal vessels and glass ware from Gaul and further afield to display and create distinctions. It also lead them to commission local craft people to make fire dogs, cauldrons, stave built wooden buckets or shale vessels. It could be argued that it was this situation also that provided the demand for exotic foods and drinks to consume at these meals. These include Gallic delicacies in mica dusted jars, but particularly the Mediterranean wine, olive oil and fish paste contained in the amphorae which have attracted so much attention (Fitzpatrick 1985; Peacock 1984; Williams and Peacock 1983; Tyers 1996). Local changes in foodstuffs are less well documented, as they could involve changes in the cuts of meat or how foods were prepared, rather than gross differences in bone or seed assemblages (see Trow 1990 for an overview). However, an increasing proportion of pork, fish and chicken bones can be documented from some sites (e.g. King 1984), while the intensification of cereal production (Jones 1996) might possibly be related to increased brewing.

These changes should not just be seen as operating at the level of overt social competition or display at feasts and 'dinner parties'. The transformations of the meal witnessed in the change from

Middle to Late Iron Age pottery have deeper, more insidious, social implications. For many the daily meal, its preparation and consumption are seen as one of the key areas in which the structure of the family (its form, division of labour, gender relations, expectations, forms of authority etc.) are made manifest and reproduced. Preparing and eating daily meals are, as such, one of the ways in which a society's norms are expressed, inculcated, reproduced and challenged. These norms included an acknowledgement of the different forms of authority and obligation through which people led their lives (e.g. Barrett 1989, Beaudry *et al.* 1991; Douglas 1975; Murcott 1982). These ideas have important implications for the study of the tools used in preparing and serving meals (e.g. Blitz 1992; Deetz 1977; Dietler 1990; Yentsch 1991). The transformation of the pottery repertoires in the course of the Late Iron Age would have affected all meals, not just special occasions. As such, they provide evidence that changes in family structure, social norms and the sources of social authority were probably taking place, even if it is felt the details of such changes will remain obscure to us.

John Barrett's (1991a) discussion of the social basis of pottery classification is pertinent here. The change from Middle to Late Iron Age ceramics can be seen as the production of a wider range of basic categories of vessel in use. Categories are a product of peoples' thinking on and practical engagement with their worlds. Pottery and other artefact categories can be seen as physical resources drawn on by people in the daily negotiation of their relations with others. As such the very existence of different categories of artefacts helps maintain the particular systems of social authority and power in that society. The addition of new categories and redefinition of others, and, by inference, the changing social practices that drew on those categories, were an essential part of attempts to renegotiate the basis of authority and power within the family and society at large. New forms of pots, made in new ways, imply conscious attempts to break both with the customs and history that surrounded making 'traditional' pots, but also with the ways meals and drinks were consumed (cf. Reina and Hill 1978, 230–250). The resulting compartmentalisation of ceramic categories (and by extension, other aspects of the meal including foods, their preparation, the organisation of the meal?) may also parallel similar processes in greater separation of functions in other aspects of material culture, settlement space, and the landscape (Hill 1995b, 122; James and Rigby 1997, 81; Jundi and Hill 1998). It also implies a compartmentalisation of how people were seen or saw themselves at all levels of social life; 'The ordered system which is a meal represents all ordered systems' (Douglas 1975, 273).

The Potter's Wheel: Chicken or Egg?

These changes in repertoire and categorisation represented a change in the ways potters thought about making a pot. Rather than work from a single prototypical category or shape whose size, exact details of wall shape, rim form and treatment could be varied, Late Iron Age potters from the outset choose from a wider range of different prototypical categories to reproduce. Such changes accompanied, and might have sprung from, the technological changes involved with producing Late as opposed to Middle Iron Age vessels. These include the use of the potter's wheel, but also include greater investment in clay preparation, changes in firing to produce a more controlled and consistent product, and the use of grog tempering. It has been suggested that the potter's wheel allowed the creation of new forms in the Late Iron Age, facilitating in particular the manufacture of the tall forms the make up much of the pottery of this period. In these arguments, the introduction of a new technology, usually by foreign immigrants, leads to change.

However, does this argument put the egg before the chicken? It certainly pays little attention to either the social contexts in which pottery was manufactured or used in the period. The wheel was used in parts of north west Europe close to southern England from the fifth century BC (Collis 1984; Freestone and Rigby 1997). There has been no discussion about why the wheel was *not* introduced to southern England for another 300 years, although if the wheel was a technologically superior way of making pots simple functionalist explanations would suggest its rapid adoption in Britain as well. Possible arguments could be based around the isolation of British communities from the continent in the Middle Iron Age (Cunliffe 1991, 1995), although this isolation or inward focus is a feature of western Europe as a whole at this time (Champion *et al.* 1984; Collis 1984). It also overlooks the direct and indirect evidence for cross channel contacts throughout this period (Stead 1984; Fitzpatrick 1989). These contacts make visible a level of exchange, movement of people, and marriage between apparently 'isolated' groups across La Tène western Europe. There are some imports of wheel made pottery into south west England in the second and early first century BC (Cunliffe 1987). However, coinage points to strong links between south east England and northern France in the second century BC, if not earlier (Fitzpatrick 1992, Haselgrove 1993): i.e. up to a century or more before the potter's wheel crossed the channel.

Other evidence for contacts in the Middle La Tène period include clear evidence that some wheel turned continental pedestalled vessels had been seen by, or closely described to, British potters as hand made, local, examples of pedestalled vessels apparently imitating continental forms are known. There are a small number of hand made versions of continentally inspired pedestal vessels known from the fifth to second centuries BC. These include the pair of vessels from Swallowcliffe Down, Wiltshire (Clay 1925), a small number of pedestal bases from Danebury, Hampshire (Brown 1984) and that from Eastbourne, Sussex (Hodson 1962). In East Anglia examples include unpublished vessels in pre-first century BC contexts from Broom, south Bedfordshire (Hill 1996b) and an unusually large number of pedestal bases in the very small assemblages from Lakenheath (Gell 1949). Although not confirmed through scientific analysis, these vessels are probably all locally produced and some must have been made by potters who had seen such wheel made vessels. If these few hand made vessels were produced by local (female) potters who had knowledge of Gallic prototypes – including, presumably, how they were made, why need immigrant potters be required to introduce the wheel in the first century BC?

That such forms or the technology did not become widespread was not because such vessels were unknown, but probably because a pot is not just pot. A number of studies of pottery and other material study demonstrate that particular forms of objects, how they were made and used are related to a complex web of religious, social and political factors. A particular type of object may not be simply replaced by an apparently similar object with the same function. As such, the potter's wheel or the north French types of vessel may have been well known to (some) people in southern England throughout the third and second centuries BC. There could even have been wheel using potters from Gaul. However, neither the forms nor the technology were adopted because they did not fit within the categories of vessels, and the webs of social practice and authority they were made and used within. This explanation of the 'failure' to adopt the potter's wheel for so long is to link the technology, organisation of production and the uses of specific forms of pottery to the specific social and cultural orders in which these activities were carried out and helped to sustain. The later Iron Age is marked by the 'regionality' of forms of material culture and social practice (Hill 1995a; Cunliffe 1995). That use of the potter's wheel, the forms of organising pottery production it might imply, and the specific forms of vessels used might be part of these dimensions of differentiation between Iron Age groups is to be expected.

This type of argument also suggests that the notion that the introduced wheel led to new ceramic shapes may not have been the case. Even if the new technology was brought to southern England at the start of the first century BC by immigrants, we need to understand why it was possible for immigrant potters to successfully introduce the technology at this time *and not before*. Again, to assume the adoption of a new technology then led to the appearance of new forms may place the chicken before the egg. By stressing the importance of the roles (specific types of) pots played in the foodways of groups, suggests there would need to be a demand for these new vessels which the wheel made so easily. It could be argued that it was only when the shift in emphasis to drinking and tablewares had taken place, that the wheel could have been effectively exploited in southern England. Evidence from the earliest pottery assemblages, however poorly dated, supports this argument. A number of assemblages contain definitively, or probable, hand made tall jar/beaker forms later produced on the wheel (see above). These are all settlement, not cemetery assemblages, and show considerable local variation in vessel forms. This variability and the absence of the wheel does not, in my opinion, suggest the presence of immigrant potters. Rather, the changes witnessed in the ceramic assemblages were being caused by local potters producing new forms. Later in this process the wheel was adopted. Given the long links between southern England and north east Gaul from before these changes in the pottery, there is probably as strong a case to be made for local adoption of the wheel than for the immigration of (many) wheel using potters.

The subsequent widespread adoption of the wheel did have considerable implication for the organisation of production. Grog (crushed pottery) added to well prepared clays are a characteristic of Late Iron Age pottery over much of south east England (Thompson 1982). Well sieved, levigated (?) clays are required to use the wheel effectively, and grog has excellent physical properties as a temper and to provide a highly burnished surface. But purely technical, as opposed to cultural, factors need not solely determine the fabric recipes used at this time. South Cambridgeshire Late Iron Age wheel turned pottery was made in dense sandy fabrics, despite the familiarity with grog products made in adjacent areas, and occasionally locally (Thompson 1982). That pots should contain other pots at a time when pots' social and ritual roles were clearly changing may not be coincidental (cf. Brown, N 1995; Cleal 1995; Sterner 1989).

The wheel, carefully prepared clays and well controlled firings – complementary changes – all imply fundamental changes in the actual activities of potters, their investment in time, scheduling to fit other, especially agricultural, activities, and the division of labour (Freestone and Rigby 1997). The use of the wheel itself involved different motor skills to hand building, skills which are related to deep seated predispositions often considered as slow and difficult to change (Arnold 1985; Rice 1987; Raina and Hill 1978). Although this is clearly not the case in first century BC southern England. These changes not only imply changes in the organisation and distribution of pottery, but in the perceptions and associations of the pots themselves. Middle Iron Age pots were probably produced in small numbers and infrequently. They may have been produced by family members, immediate or more removed, and moved through links of kinship and alliance. This implies that the small numbers of pots used by Middle Iron Age domestic groups may have had relatively well known histories as it would be easy to remember how and when individual vessels were acquired, and who was involved in their making or acquisition (cf. Willis 1999). This situation would have become more unusual in the course of the first centuries BC and AD as the numbers of vessels in use in a household grew (see below) and with increasingly specialist production, the social distance between producers and consumers probably grew. Who made a Gallic *terra nigra* platter would be unknown to most British users, what probably mattered more was the symbolic capital that these foreign pots provided to the users.

The increasing specialisation of, and between, potters can be assumed from these changes, although there has been little detailed consideration of the organisation of production or distribution. The trend towards increased specialisation (see below) may itself lead to the adoption of the wheel as the output of individual potting households increased. The potter's wheel is usually found in modes of production described as a *household industry* (Van der Leeuw 1977) or *individual or nucleated workshop* by Peacock (1982) (see also Arnold 1985; Rice 1987, 181ff). No production sites have been identified as not even the firings regularly left archaeological traces. Although better controlled firings are evident from the fabrics produced, no permanent kiln structures have been recognised till the middle of the first century AD; most clearly post dating the Roman conquest (Swan 1984; Tyers 1996; Woods 1974). Potters were probably dispersed throughout the region (Thompson 1982), unlike the organisation of the Late Iron Age pottery industry in Dorset (Brown, L 1996), although more concentrated production may have taken place in the Upchurch Marshes of Essex.

The changes that took place in the organisation and scale of production possibly imply a change in who was making pots (Freestone and Rigby 1997). There has been very little discussion of the issue of gender in all aspects of British Iron Age studies (Freestone and Rigby 1997 are almost the only exception). Where the gender of potters is rarely considered, the types of small scale *household production* or *household industry* level production usually envisaged for the Middle Iron Age are commonly associated with women (e.g. Wheeler 1954, 30; Freestone and Rigby 1997). While both the larger scale of production and the use of the potters wheel are ethnographically most commonly associated with men (Balfet 1981; Peacock 1984; Skibo and Schiffer 1995; Van der Leeuw 1977). Most early Romano-British pottery is assumed to have been made by male potters. These types of generalisation are fraught with dangers and difficulties, especially as there is no direct evidence for the gender of Iron Age potters. However, the changes in the uses of pots discussed here and other changes in agricultural practices and everyday life attested in the first centuries BC and AD all imply important changes in the relative workloads of men, women and children. *If* we assume most Middle Iron Age pottery was made by women, and most immediately pre-Roman wheel made pottery was made by men then the changes in pottery discussed in this paper were associated with an important change in the gender of potters. This change raises important questions. Did women originally simply respond to male demand for new drinking forms, or how active were they in creating new categories of pottery, and changes to social practices to subvert and change the patterns of authority they reproduced (cf. Hodder 1991 & previous discussion of Barrett 1991a's ideas)? At what stage did men become potters? If women continued to pot, to what extent did this change their relationships and status within their families and wider society? Should we envisage different scales of production with male (immigrant?) specialists producing more exotic products such as pedestal urns and copies of Gallo-Belgic finewares and women still producing more 'mundane' cooking jars and domestic vessels at a household level of production (Freestone and Rigby 1997)? Or should we envisage different, more complex and fluid situations including a high degree of participation by women in all types of production?

Such issues may seem removed from the original questions of technological innovation, but only serve to show how all aspects of making and using pots were thoroughly implicated in the organisation of society as a whole. From such a perspective, the foil of a technological innovation, the wheel, causing change may be an unlikely explanation. The cultural and social conditions (and not just the technical and 'economic' conditions) needed to be right for the rapid adoption of the technology and of its products by others. If this technological innovation on its own

J. D. Hill

right was the cause of all the changes we see in the pottery use of this period, it needs to be argued why these changes did not happen earlier. It is possible that some wheel using potters, their products or knowledge of the potter's wheel were present in south east England from the fifth century BC onwards. However, it was how using particular types of pots, made in particular ways and by particular people were socially embedded that meant that communities choose not to adopt the potters wheel from groups they had contact with for hundreds of years. It was when such conditions were changed, were possibly deliberately challenged, that new uses for new types of pots, made in new ways, were possible.

From Middle to Late Iron Age Pots: Deposition

The changes outlined here were not just changes in pot forms and use, they were also changes in the ways pottery entered the archaeological record. To return to figures 13.1 and 13.2, it is clear that there are far more Late Iron Age vessels with complete or reconstructable profiles to compare vessel height and rim diameter than there are Middle Iron Age vessels. This is not simply a factor of more excavation of Late Iron Age sites, or simply because there was more pottery in the Late Iron Age. Rather, it points to significant changes in the ways pottery entered the archaeological record.

There almost certainly was more pottery in use in the Late Iron Age, if only because households needed a greater number of more specialist pots to fulfil the roles which previously required fewer vessels. The increasing quantities of pottery in circulation imply important changes in attitudes to pottery (Willis 1997a). But this increase in itself cannot directly explain the increasing quantities of pottery entering the archaeological record, nor that the sherds are often of a larger size. The stronger qualities of Late Iron Age pottery is an important factor. But, again, it need not directly lead to larger sherds entering the archaeological record, as a wide range of factors intervene between the breakage of a pot and its possible entry into the archaeological record (Deboer and Lathrap 1979; Hayden and Cannon 1983; Hill 1995a; Needham and Spence 1996). Recent work on Iron Age settlements has shown that much of material found on such sites was deliberately deposited, often in a ritual context (Gwilt 1997; Hill 1993, 1995b). Similar practices did take place on Middle Iron Age sites in East Anglia, although these have not been studied yet in detail (Ashwin 1996; Fiddler 1995; Hill and Braddock forthcoming, Hill and Horne forthcoming). How-

ever, it is clear that large deposits, containing large proportions of large numbers of Middle Iron Age pots are unusual.

This pattern changes in the Late Iron Age. Pottery was clearly placed as part of the mortuary ritual in graves at this time. In addition, the types of deposits found on settlements change with large quantities of freshly broken pottery deposited in ditches, pits and wells. This may reflect changes in refuse maintenance on sites and the need to dispose of larger quantities of broken pottery. Although not studied in detail, many of these are possibly ritual deposits, a transformation of earlier ritual practices. Some examples appear to be closing deposits marking the abandonment of a settlement and containing all(?) of the site's deliberately broken pottery (e.g. Willis 1997b; Hill and Horne forthcoming). Other deposits have similarities to burial offerings, but were not placed in a grave (e.g. Stead and Rigby 1986). Others have less clear single explanations, but contain freshly broken sherds from considerable numbers of vessels. Examples of these include the deposits from the Ermine Street and Skeleton Green sites at Braughing, where large quantities of early imported and locally produced pottery were deposited in pits on a scale it is hard to imagine as normal wear and tear (Partridge 1981; Potter and Trow 1988). Braughing also provides a clear example of ritual in the large deposits of pottery deposited in a boundary ditch with disarticulated human bone and animal bones, including those of white tailed sea eagles (Partridge 1978).

Large quantities of well preserved pottery are common in the Roman period. So common that it is rarely asked why they occur. This pattern starts in the Late Iron Age and represents another significant break in ceramic culture from the Middle Iron Age. Along with vessel repertoire, differences in the types of deposits can be seen as two dimensions of variability to compare assemblages; dimensions of variability that can be added to, or even replace, the opposition of hand made versus wheel made pottery. Using these dimensions of variability, two extremes can be recognised that represent the major differences between Middle and Late Iron Age assemblages (Fig. 13.5). But thinking about these dimensions also allows us to ask if other combinations can occur, and occur independent of the technology used to produce pots. Are there examples of Middle Iron Age hand made pots deposited in a Late Iron Age manner? Or are there assemblages of Late Iron Age wheel turned pottery dominated by open bowls and deposited in a Middle Iron Age manner?

Range of Vessel Forms

		Limited Reportoire	Wide Reportoire
No. of Pots in Deposits	Few	'Middle Iron Age' Settlements	?
	Many	?	'Late Iron Age' Settlements

Fig. 13.5. Common features of the deposition of 'Middle' and 'Late Iron Age' pottery in Anglia.

Being Different, Different Being: The Initial Adoption of 'Late Iron Age' Pottery in Southern East Anglia

Some of these possibilities can be seen when Middle and Late Iron Age assemblages outside the 'heartlands' of Late Iron Age south east England are considered. Looking at northern East Anglia (Norfolk, Suffolk, Cambridgeshire) also demonstrates that the terms 'Middle' and 'Late Iron Age' used so far as chronological labels in this paper really describe ceramic and broader social traditions that could exist simultaneously in different parts of the region (Bryant 1997; Hill 1997). There was no simultaneous change to Late Iron Age styles of pottery across East Anglia c.125 to 75 BC. Rather, some northern parts of the region still used 'Middle Iron Age tradition' pottery after the Roman conquest (Hill 1995a; Willis 1996). It is important to ask why southern East Anglia developed Late Iron Age tradition pottery so early and why other areas continued with Middle Iron Age tradition pottery for much longer. The answers support the interpretation advanced here: that changes in pottery forms, deposition and production were intimately tied to changes in foodways and wider aspects of social discourse.

The development of Late Iron Age tradition pottery was one of several aspects of social life that marked out southern East Anglia as distinctive and different from neighbouring areas (Fig. 13.6). Others aspects included the early use of coinage, the adoption of north Gallic cremation burial practices and changes in personal appearance (Haselgrove 1982, 1989; Cunliffe 1995). Because of these links with parts of the continent, and the well known later developments and dominance of this core area of southern England, the early developments in

Hertfordshire and Essex have often been treated as part of a unique phenomenon requiring a distinct, individual explanation. However, the development of the new pottery, use of coinage and adoption of cremation can also be seen as another expression of the marked differences seen in material culture and social practices between different regions in the later Iron Age.

Across later Iron Age Britain and Ireland communities often had distinctly different settlement forms, pottery styles and ritual practices from neighbouring groups. These differences were not an accident of isolation between groups, rather the opposite, as they appear to have actively distinguished regions (Hill 1995a; Millett 1990b). Nor should they be regarded as just skin deep but rather pointing to deep seated differences in the organisation of daily life and structure of society. Examples include the major differences between different parts of later Pre-Roman Iron Age Scotland and the 'Arras' culture of East Yorkshire with its continental style of burial. Across later Iron Age eastern England differences in the types of pottery in use reveal this pattern of regionality (Fig. 13.6). As well as the distinctive Late Iron Age tradition pottery in the south, two types of the basic 'Middle Iron Age' open bowl/jar traditions can be distinguished (East Midlands assemblages with Scored wares, north East Anglian assemblages with unscored pottery). Communities in Lincolnshire used the very different 'Dragonby-Sleaford' pottery marked by a distinctive repertoire of decorated and early wheel made forms (Elsdon 1996). These were again in stark contrast to the basic open forms used in the 'Arras culture' of East Yorkshire (Rigby 1991). In this context there is nothing unusual in a region developing distinctive pottery and social practices which used distinctive pottery. What was unusual was the scale of the close links and similarities southern East Anglia and Kent had with other regions across the Channel – themselves characterised by material cultures and social practices different from their neighbours (Fitzpatrick 1989; Haselgrove 1996; Roymans 1996; Willis forthcoming b; Woolf 1993b). Equally unusual may have been those features of the social practices that developed in southern East Anglia in the second and first centuries BC that fostered the developments in social organisation that rapidly took place over the next 100 to 150 years.

The immediate context of the development of the use and production of Late Iron Age tradition pottery probably also played an important role. The new pottery appears in areas into which permanent settlement expanded in the Later Iron Age. Hertfordshire appears to have been relatively empty in the third and second centuries BC as Middle Iron Age handmade pottery (c.300–100 BC) is extremely rare

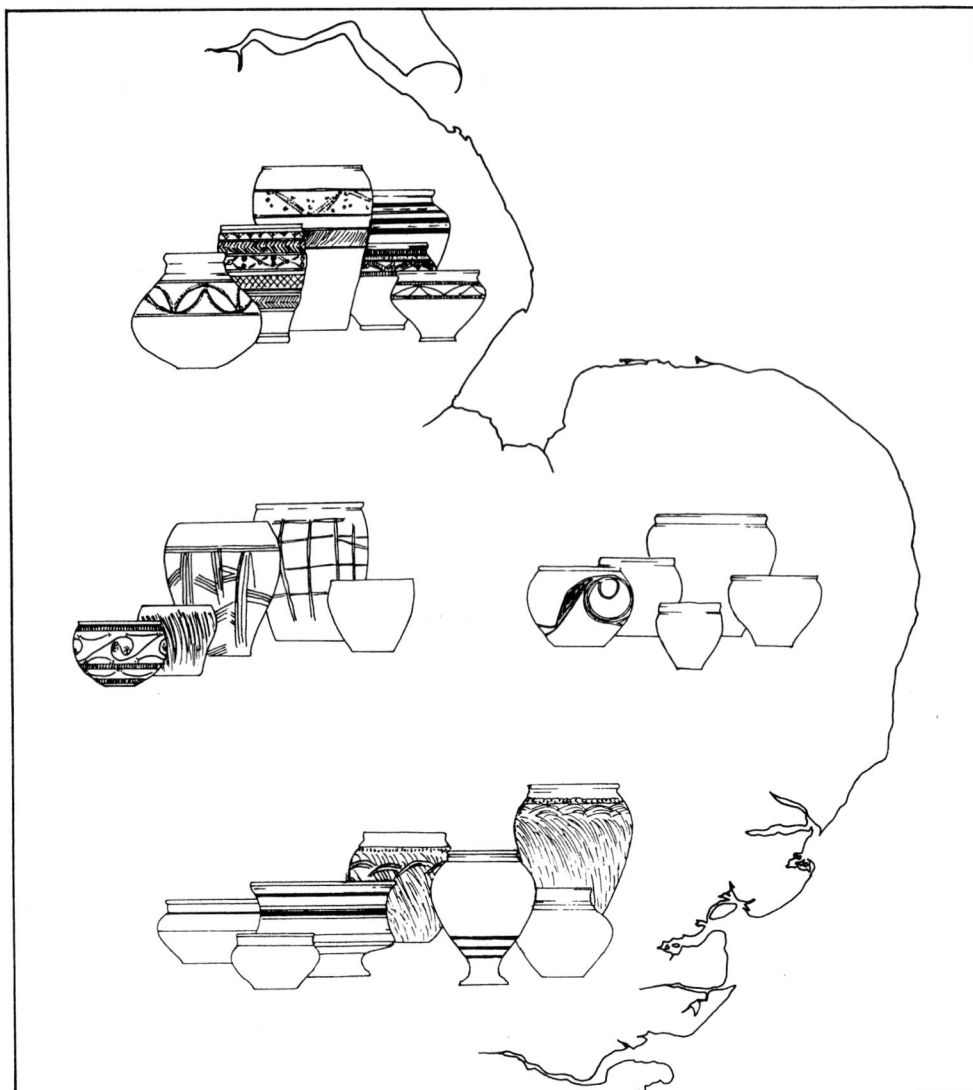

Fig. 13.6. Eastern England c.50 BC. Regionally distinct styles of pottery forms and repertoires across East Anglia and the East Midlands in the middle of the first century BC (drawn by Sophia Jundi).

(Bryant 1995, 1997; Hunn 1992). Reviews of collections and the literature suggest as few as seven find spots of Middle Iron Age pottery in Hertfordshire, compared to ninety plus with Late Iron Age pottery (Hill 1997 unpublished). Settlement expansion into previously under utilised areas is a key feature of the Later Iron Age. Many of these previously 'marginal' areas developed specialist economic activities or allowed novel social forms to emerge (Haselgrove 1989; Hill 1995a; Sharples 1990). The exact mechanics of settlement expansion and the movement of peoples are poorly understood, but probably involved a piecemeal process. Equally, it is unclear where these people came from, although no single origin need be envisaged. Some people may have crossed the channel *in both directions* as part of this process.

The development of new eating and drinking practices needs to be seen in this light, as does the earlier adoption of coinage. This represents a distinct change in both the categorisation of material culture and the social practices such categories sustained. Potters were allowed in these circumstances to experiment and change the types and categories of vessels they or their teachers had previously made. New styles of eating, greater distinction between 'kitchen' and 'table', a new emphasis on social drinking in different ways represent a distinct shift away from the customs and norms from the parent cultures these peoples came from. Given that similar changes did not happen in all areas which witnessed similar expansions of settlement, that such changes may have been a deliberate challenge and shift to established ways of doing things is likely. Movement into areas with previously little permanent occupation may have allowed greater freedom to escape from deeply sedimented practices and their related structures of authority; the creation of new social practices and categories of action and things as an active strategy of challenge (Barrett 1991a – see above). At the same time there may have been a greater openness to adopt and adapt alien practices, along with a need to create new identities to bring together peoples with different backgrounds and stress their separation from the old. A range of other economic and social factors also were probably at work, such as the decreasing size of local kinship groups or greater need for short term strategies to produce agricultural surplus all possibly leading to an emphasis on social drinking and beer production. Craft specialism, such as some households increasingly scheduling larger amounts of their time to pottery production, was possibly also born out of similar economic and social factors (Haselgrove 1989; Sharples 1990). As was the initial adoption of coinage – to facilitate relations between strangers?

Social drinking is often connected with the construction of social solidarities and as a way to pay for the mobilisation of work groups. It is suggested here that drinking helped to construct new relationships, and the emphasis on drink was necessary in a situation where deeper, longer term relations of reciprocity existed. In this sense it may have been a more short term social strategy than those used in traditional core areas where 'special deposits' point to irregular (separated by years) meat feasting with large numbers of people present (Hill 1995a). The size of the social groups involved in most of these drinking and eating parties appears to have been far smaller. Whatever the cause, drinking and slightly later eating in new ways became increasingly important as a way to mobilise people and as an arena for competing for and displaying power and rank.

As such, these changes in the repertoires of pottery, in the foodways they served and in the ways pottery entered the archaeological record in areas such as Hertfordshire and Kent represent another example of the way in which different regions of later Iron Age Ireland and Britain were distinguished from each other. Different styles of pottery, supporting regional differences in cuisine, in first century BC eastern England were probably closely identified with corporate community identities. Other regionally distinct styles of pottery and other aspects of society maintained the identities of long standing groups. However, what is different about the adoption of the potter's wheel, or other aspects of southern East Anglia in the later Iron Age such as coinage or cremation burial, is not their links with northern France, but rather that these communities

can be observed to create for themselves a new distinctive society over the second and first centuries BC. Part of the explanation for this may have been that this was an area relatively little permanently settled at the start of this process. As such it could have been that the impetus to develop new social practices and forge new identities were born out of the novel social conditions created by the movement of peoples into this area.

Being Different, Different Being: The 'Failure' to adopt 'Late Iron Age' Pottery in Northern East Anglia

If regionality helps to explain the adoption of 'Late Iron Age' tradition pottery in the south of the region, it also helps us to understand the 'failure' of many groups in the north to adopt this pottery. It is important not to see northern East Anglia as a backwater, or a periphery that just reacted to a core to the south (*contra* Haselgrove 1982; Cunliffe 1988, 1991). After all, the distinct identity of the southern core was itself a reaction to the established communities to the north and west (Hill 1995a). The later Iron Age across the region was a dynamic period of change. Settlement expansion into eastern Norfolk and parts of the Fens was an important feature, as were the creation and shifting relationships of various identities and polities, including the Iceni (Bryant 1997; Hall and Coles 1994; Davies 1996; Martin 1988).

Pre-Augustan Welwyn phase 'Late Iron Age' tradition pottery had a very limited currency north of Hertfordshire and Essex. In south Cambridgeshire this pottery does appear in cremation burials identical to those further south, although at present no settlement assemblages similar to Brickhill, Grubs Barn, Baldock or Braughing are known (Fox 1923; Thompson 1981; Hill *et al.* 1999). This is possibly a factor of site discovery, but a relatively large number of excavations and evaluations in southern Cambridgeshire have produced 'Middle Iron Age' handmade assemblages and early-middle first century AD wheel made assemblages, but clearly later first century BC wheel made pottery is rare. On those few sites where it has been found it is in very small quantities as a minor component in hand made 'Middle Iron Age' assemblages e.g. Green House Farm and Wardy Hill, Coveney.[4] As such, it appears on current evidence that early wheel turned and grog tempered pottery may have been mainly being used in death in south Cambridgeshire. While in life either only small quantities of grog tempered, wheel made pedestalled urns, *tazze* and other forms were present on settlements, or only a minority of hitherto undiscovered settlements used such pottery. Widespread adoption of the full repertoire of southern forms, often produced in local sandy fabrics, and Gallo-Belgic imports probably took place post 10–1 BC in this area.

In others (and potentially on some sites in the former area) a different pattern is evident (Fig. 13.3b). Around Peterborough, the Fens, Norfolk and northern Suffolk communities appear to have adapted southern wheel turned ceramic traditions to fit within existing patterns of pottery use. The limited range of 'Middle Iron Age' handmade open forms continued to be made in these areas until after the Roman conquest (Mackreth 1988; Pryor 1984; Willis 1996). Dating these assemblages when they lack datable brooches or imported pottery can be difficult. Varying quantities of wheel made 'Late Iron Age' tradition pottery are found on many sites in the middle first century AD (c.25 to 75). Some were originally made further south, others local products. What is noticeable about these wheel turned vessels is the very limited range of forms acquired or locally produced. The bulk are carinated bowls and cups or necked bowls; all basic open bowl forms which clearly fit within the limited range of open forms traditionally used by these communities. Other parts of the developed southern repertoire are markedly absent or rare. There are almost no tall neckless jars, beakers, flagons, cups or platters, be they Gallic or British products, nor amphorae. This is also true on many clearly post-Roman Conquest non-military sites. The large ritual enclosure at Fisons Way, Thetford, is an exception with slightly higher proportions of tall, shallow and constricted forms (including Gallo-Belgic and samian imports) and a large number of specific vessel forms in its later phase. But contemporary sites such as West Stow (West 1989), Fengate (Pryor 1984), Haddenham V (Hill and Braddock forthcoming) and Coveney (Evans forthcoming, Hill and Horne forthcoming) lack almost any tall, shallow or constricted forms (Note 4).

Seen from the perspective of the use of pottery and foodways these differences were not that there were 'just' different forms of pots in both areas. The differences between these groups of communities were differences in kind, indicating significantly different foodways in a different cultural environment. As has been argued in other, very different, contexts (Ferguson 1991), a striking feature of early first century AD ceramics in northern Anglia is the relative lack of differentiation and categorisation. There are few shapes and little decoration. Unlike southern Anglia there is little evidence for social differentiation or hierarchy represented in the pottery or wider aspects of the foodways these ceramic tools were a part of.

However, I would argue that it was not because these groups were peripheral that Gallo-Belgic pottery or amphorae are extremely rare in these area (*contra* Haselgrove 1982; Cunliffe 1995). Rather, there was little demand for these forms – be they made locally, in southern East Anglia or further afield. Nor was there the demand for the exotic foodstuffs and beverages that were eaten and drunk from them. Whatever changes took place in these areas in cooking and serving meals, the setting and social contexts of such meals, and the larger social discourses they sustained or changed, did so within the existing foodway traditions. Acquired or locally made wheel turned pottery replaced or was used alongside small to medium sized hand made bowls/jars. Wheel turned vessels would have been visually distinct in such settings, and where local production is probable, potters were at pains to reproduce distinctive southern carinated and cordoned forms (Hill 1996).

These patterns of pottery use in northern East Anglia should not be seen as a product of backwardness, nor isolation. These were dynamic societies with contacts between each other and with those to the south. Rather, the maintenance of these ways of life – increasingly seen as 'traditional' – was probably a conscious choice (cf. Willis 1999). In this context, as in others throughout Later Iron Age eastern England, 'it is obvious that ceramics were often symbols as much as they were everyday objects' (Beaudry *et al.* 1991,172).

Conclusions: Are Pots a Chronological Marker?

The paper has emphasised the importance of the use of pottery in contrast to many approaches to pottery in archaeology which emphasise production or distribution and trade. It has been suggested that it was changes in ways foods and drink were prepared and consumed, and the social importance of different aspects of eating and drinking that created the demand for new forms or vessel, the desire to acquire non-locally made pottery and the adoption of new technologies. This is not to say that these innovations did not themselves have far reaching and unintentional consequences once taken up. Nor is it to separate off pottery production and its social contexts from the social context of pottery use and deposition.

The interpretation offered here has tried to tie pottery closely to the social discourses and gender relationships through which particular social forms were reproduced. In this respect Iron Age and Roman pottery can be interpreted in similar ways to those applied to British Neolithic and earlier Bronze Age pottery. The differences between Middle and

Late Iron Age pottery in terms of forms, fabric recipes, methods of production, contexts and form of deposition, are similar to such differences that existed between different styles of Late Neolithic and earlier Bronze Age pottery. Equally, it has become recognised that different styles of Late Neolithic and earlier Bronze Age pottery did not simply replace each other through time. In fact their use overlapped and they were in use in different areas simultaneously (Bradley 1984; Braithwaite 1984; Thomas 1991a, 1996). This is also the pattern for Middle and Late Iron Age pottery and probably for other later prehistoric and historic pottery as well. This is to suggest that later, like earlier, prehistoric pottery should be seen not primarily as a chronological marker. Rather, pottery could be seen as evidence for the existence of particular social discourses – ways of life; a term that tries to link the apparently inconsequential aspects of daily life, values and norms which people lived by with the structures of authority, ideology and meaning.

The initial adoption of 'Late Iron Age' pottery signals a break with the dominant social discourses that shaped previous societies in the region. Similar arguments might be used to explain how other new elements in the material culture and social practices in this region were adopted, such as coinage and cremation burial. New forms of pottery are witnesses to changes in the everyday lives of people, with new styles of food preparation and consumption. It has been suggested that these changes were integral to changes in other aspects of relationships within and between families. I have argued that they predate and provided the incentive for the adoption of the potter's wheel. The increasingly social and ritual importance of the meal as an arena for display led to accelerating demands for different and exotic foodstuffs, and the means to serve them. That is that it provided the demand for imported pottery, glass and metal vessels and for the contents of Mediterranean amphorae. Eating and drinking in these ways also expressed a clear difference from neighbours, relatives or people living in different parts of the region. The 'failure' to adopt new styles of ceramics, and so also the failure to create a demand for Gallo-Belgic finewares or amphorae, in many parts of northern East Anglia can be seen as a conscious rejection of this alternative set of foodways and the broader social baggage they carried with them. Groups in northern East Anglia accommodated and transformed selected elements of the new ceramic traditions, but may have never necessarily adopted the whole package had it not been for the Roman conquest. This is because what and how you ate and drank in the eastern England of the later Iron Age were not incidental activities, as their labelling as mundane or everyday often implies.

They were essential to defining who you were, or aspired to be.

Acknowledgements
This article is based on a paper presented at TAG '96. The original data was gathered together and the first draft written in 1996. This study owes a great debt to Isobel Thompson, without whose massive corpus of Late Iron Age pottery from south east England this study would have been impossible. I would also like to thank the comments and help with my English from Colin Haselgrove, Sam Lucy, Sander Van Der Leeuw, Elaine Morris, Steve Willis and Ann Woodward. Sophia Jundi drew Figures 13.4 and 13.6.

Notes
1. The basis for this study: The pottery dimensions and proportions of different pot forms on sites used in this paper are based on a study of pottery form and size carried out by the author in 1995–96. With the exception of four sites, the study relied on published illustrations and other information contained in site reports and Isobel Thompson's (1982) corpus of Late Iron Age pottery. Information from a total of 40 sites was collected for the counties of Norfolk, Suffolk, Essex, Hertfordshire, Cambridgeshire and Bedfordshire.

    For the graphs of Middle Iron Age pottery dimensions (Fig. 13.1) information was collected from the few published Middle Iron Age sites with illustrations of complete vessel profiles and from the author's measurements of reconstructed pots. In East Anglia complete or reconstructable vessel profiles of pottery of this period are unusual for the reasons discussed in this paper. This is not a problem for Late Iron Age tradition pottery from both cemeteries and settlements (Fig. 13.2). Only a sample of 500 of the available drawings of complete or reconstructable Late Iron Age profiles were measured. The illustrated vessels were selected from Thompson's (1982) corpus and other sites to provide a large and representative sample of different forms.

    The data on pottery forms and repertoires was harder to extract. Very few published reports offer any quantification of different pottery forms, even for imported material. The graphs and tables of pottery repertoires were drawn up by counting the numbers of different types of vessel illustrated, unless reliable quantitative information was provided in the reports or it was clear from the way vessels were individually discussed in the text. This is a far from satisfactory situation. The figures presented here must be treated with caution. However, in the absence of quantitative data, and without consulting archives or studying the collections themselves, this is the only approach feasible. The approach used here is certainly biased towards those vessels chosen for illustration, or listed individually in the text. Unless only a selective sample of vessels is illustrated, most Late Iron Age reports do illustrate large key groups of vessels or complete grave groups. Lists of individual sherds/vessels on Late Iron Age sites tend to be of imported vessels, and this fact and, the greater likelihood that imported vessels will be illustrated in reports, is a strong bias in the data. Also given that coarse ware cooking, serving and storage vessels may be given less attention in reports than other forms, the figures presented here are probably skewed in favour of table wares on Late Iron Age tradition settlements. This bias would be even greater had not Isobel Thompson illustrated the large proportion of the available complete or partial vessels included in her corpus.

The difference between settlement and cemetery assemblages has already been mentioned, with cemeteries providing accurate vessel counts for the different types of pots placed in each grave. Unlike cemetery assemblages, using simple raw counts of pottery from settlement sites cannot securely reconstruct the actual proportions of pottery in use by the inhabitants. The complications of the choice of vessels for ritual deposition on sites, differences in normal breakage rates between vessels with different functions and the selective reuse and curation of broken vessels (Deal and Hagstrum 1995; Hill 1995b; Moorhouse 1986) all indicate that archaeological assemblages need not reflect the original proportions of vessels in use.

Despite these biases in the data, the broad patterns outlined in this paper about the changes and differences in the pottery repertoires are felt to be useful. Only detailed studies of the quantification of different pottery forms can establish how distorted the figures used here are. Even if the proportions of the different vessels are not exact, this does not change the existence of the different forms, the emphasis on categorisation and the changes in the appearance of new table wares in the Late Iron Age tradition over time.

Copies of the basic data collected for this study are available from the author.

2. Foodways: Jack Goody (1982, 38) credits the invention of this term to Simoon: 'the modes of feeling, thinking, and behaving about food that are common to a cultural group' (1967, 3). The term now has wide currency in North American archaeology. These social and cultural aspects of eating and drinking are areas of life that have received considerably attention in recent sociological, anthropological and archaeological studies (e.g. Blitz 1993; Beadsworth & Keil 1997; Counihan and van Esterik 1997; Fiddes 1991; Goody 1982; Yentsch 1991).

3. For this study 38 different types of pot form were established to analyse assemblages. The types were chosen to reflect broad shapes of vessel. Some were identical to Thompson's (1982) categorisation, others combined or even split specific Thompson categories. These 38 vessel types can be reduced to broader vessel groupings used in this paper.

    Southern and Northern Anglia c. 300 to 100 BC
    Settlements   Mean Number of vessel type 5.25

    Southern Anglia c.100 BC to 10 BC
    Settlements   Mean Number of vessel types 14.6
    Cemeteries   Mean Number of vessel types 6.0

    Southern Anglia c. 10 BC to AD 43
    Settlements   Mean Number of vessel types 19.4
    Cemeteries   Mean Number of vessel types 17.2

    Northern Anglia c.10 BC to AD 43
    Settlements Mean Number of vessel types 10.1

4. Assemblages dating to the first century BC lack wheel turned pottery (e.g. Little Thetford – Braddock and Hill 1998; Haddenham V (Hill and Braddock forthcoming) and Coveney phase 1 – Hill 1996). At Greenhouse Farm, Fen Ditton, Cambridge a first century BC handmade assemblage contains a very small number of wheel made sherds (24 out of 3728 sherds) including a pedestalled base (Hill and Braddock unpublished). This is the only excavated settlement site from southern Cambridgeshire or the Fens with wheel made pottery of this date. Wheel turned forms on sites such as West Stow (West 1989), Coveney (Hill 1996), Werrington (Mackreth 1988) and Fengate (Pryor 1984) etc. all date to at least after 10 BC and are probably post-Augustan or later: a date after AD20–30 is most likely on current evidence. On all of these sites this wheel made pottery may also continue in use and manufacture for up to 20–40 years after the Roman Conquest. For example, on the basis of radiocarbon dating Haddenham V could have been abandoned in the first two decades of the first century AD, but lacks any wheel made pottery. The actual proportions of wheel turned vessels are difficult to establish as most reports do not provide quantification of this or other aspects of the assemblage. However, not all sites may have had equal quantities of wheel made pottery.

14   Roman Pottery in Iron Age Britain

Andrew Fitzpatrick and Jane Timby

Introduction

Roman pottery probably first arrived in Britain in the second century BC, but it was only in the final decades of the first century BC that vessels imported from across the Channel began to appear in any quantity. The distribution of imported pottery before the Claudian conquest of southern England was largely restricted to southern England and the east Midlands. The closing years of the first millennium BC also saw great changes in the range of ceramics available in southern England, with indigenous wares displaying a noticeable development in quality, mainly as a result of improved firing techniques and the introduction of the fast wheel.

The appearance of imported Roman pottery has been considered to be of great significance. The imports signal a considerable increase in the archaeological visibility of cross-Channel contact. Their presence provides a valuable chronological indicator, and some of the new forms of the imported vessels had a marked impact on the development of the indigenous ceramic repertoire as they were copied widely. In addition the imported vessels indicate changes in the preparation and consumption of food and drink, and act as one index of the considerable changes in the period preceding the Roman conquest.

Roman Pottery

The imported wares can be divided into three distinct functional groups:

- amphorae, imported for their contents
- food preparation vessels and coarsewares (some of which were possibly also imported for their contents), and
- fine tablewares for use and display.

These imports may also be divided broadly according to their origins; those from the Mediterranean world, for example amphorae and tablewares, and those emanating from non-Mediterranean Gaul. A chronological distinction may also be made between vessels imported in the late Republican period and those of the early Empire. The distinction between these two groups is set at around 20 BC, coincident with the increased 'romanisation' of central and northern Gaul, and the campaigns of the Roman armies into Germany. It would be mistaken to try and draw too fine a distinction between these two periods, which is essentially the same division as that made by Stead for the 'Welwyn' and 'Lexden' phases of 'Aylesford' type burials (Stead 1967, 46–8; 1976, 401–2, 412).

The study of Roman pottery in Iron Age Britain has followed that of Romano-British pottery, traditionally being examined by type of ware, often on the basis of the region of which it is a product of, for example the Gallo-Belgic pottery of northern Gaul (e.g. Rigby 1981). Such wares were the products of professional potters and the conventional description of them forming ceramic 'industries' is used here as convenient shorthand.

Imported Roman pottery is also a valuable chronological indicator in Iron Age Britain. Some wares, notably the fine 'Arretine' or Italian type terra sigillata table wares, are also found on continental European sites such as the Roman forts in Germany. These sites and others such as Amiens in Picardy and the Titelberg in Luxembourg are well dated by their historical context, their archaeological associations and sequences, and sometimes by dendrochronology. Considerable emphasis has been placed on these cross-associations for their chronological value and this relatively precise dating has allowed aspects of the development of individual pottery industries to be explored (e.g. Dannell 1977). This emphasis on chronology represents the same emphasis as that placed on pottery from Romano-British sites (Fulford and Huddlestone 1991, 5–6).

As Roman pottery in Iron Age Britain has frequently been regarded as being exotic, the quality of information about the typology of it and the scale of application of provenancing studies are both high. Studies on aspects of it by scholars such as Hull, Peacock, Rigby, Sealey and Williams have been of international significance.

It is not, however, the purpose of this paper to describe every category of Roman pottery imported into Iron Age Britain, to review the development of individual industries in any detail or to explore the history of potting within Gaul. Instead it seeks to present a brief overview of the principal sorts of pottery imported into Britain in the Late Iron Age and accordingly each of the three functional groups; i) amphorae, imported for their contents, ii) vessels for food preparation and coarsewares, and iii) fine tablewares will be examined briefly according to the types represented and where appropriate their contents, and their chronology. In the case of finewares where similar forms were manufactured in separate regions it is helpful to present this data by region.

Imports of Republican date

Amphorae: Containers for Wines and Foodstuffs

Amphorae represent one of the first identifiable commodities from Italy to be imported into Iron Age Britain. The main difference between the Republican and Imperial groups is the change from a largely Italian group, usually of Dressel 1 wine amphorae, to a more diverse group with a wider range of vessels containing a greater variety of commodities from several regions. All of these amphorae were traded and exchanged for their contents. The literature has been reviewed by Peacock in 1971 and in 1984, by Sealey in 1985, and by Fitzpatrick in 1994 (forthcoming).

The predecessors of the Dressel 1, the Graeco-Italic types are not known certainly from Britain, although some possible transitional types have been noted from a harbour site at Yarmouth Rhodes on the Isle of Wight (Peacock 1984, 38). The Dressel 1 has been subdivided into many varieties, the three most widely recognised being Dressel 1A, 1B and 1C. The principal differences between the 1A and the 1B are that the 1A variety contained less, and was proportionately lighter than the 1B, i.e. it has a smaller volume. All contained something approaching 20–25 litres of red wine. Although Dressel 1A and 1B varieties differ in many respects, these can be difficult to identify in a fragmentary state. In

practice, the varieties are usually distinguished typologically by a single trait; whether the rim is triangular, or vertical. The dominant commodity contained in these amphorae was wine, although foodstuffs such as olives are also known to have been transported in them. Although Dressel 1 were manufactured in Gaul and Iberia, the scale of production was comparatively modest and all the vessels found in England appear to be Italian.

The chronology of the varieties is relatively well established. Dressel 1A is generally thought to appear in the third quarter of the second century BC, overlapping for some decades with the later varieties of Graeco-Italic, and it is found in Gaul in contexts which date to the 50s BC. There was also a period of overlap with the later 1B. This has been claimed to appear from around 100 BC (Hesnard 1990, 51) but it is not found commonly until the 60s BC and it continued to be produced to c.20 BC. By that time, however, it was already being replaced by the Dressel 2–4.

In Britain it remains true that most, if not all Dressel 1A amphorae are found in central southern England. Dressel 1B also occur regularly on settlements over much of central southern and south eastern England. Although Dressel 1B occur in well-furnished 'Welwyn'-type burials in south east England (Fig. 14.1), it is the quantity of wine which they signify to have been consumed in the burial rites which is important. The presence of a single wine amphora is insufficient evidence on which to label a burial as being 'rich'.

The Dressel 1C form, broadly contemporary with Dressel 1A, and found in small numbers in France also seems to have contained wine. However, there are also suggestions that it may have also contained fish-based products such as garum, and occasionally other products such as olives. Their presence in Britain may be anticipated but is not yet conclusively proven. Similarly the Lamboglia 2, probably from south east Italy (Fitzpatrick 1985, 307), and the occasional 'Neo-Punic' vessel from North Africa may have reached Britain. Figs have been found at Hengistbury Head on the Dorset coast in Iron Age contexts and these are likely to have arrived in amphorae, most probably from Italy.

Storage Vessels and Tablewares

Gaulish coarsewares

A range of coarse and fine wares was imported from Armorica at the same time as Dressel 1 amphorae but in both culturally and chronological terms these wares are Iron Age rather than Roman. Three broad classes of ware have been defined; (i) black cordoned, (ii) rilled micaceous, and (iii) graphite-coated. The quality of these vessels is high and the

Fig. 14.1. Reconstruction of the Welwyn Garden City burial. Photograph by courtesy of the British Museum.

surface finishes are distinctive; fine, black and shiny in the case of cordoned ware, glittering in the case of micaceous ware and shining in the case of the graphite coated ware. These vessels were mainly made as jars and bowls and most of them are conventionally thought to have been imported between *c.* 100–50 BC, although the absolute chronology is not yet established precisely. These Armorican wares are best known at Hengistbury Head where large quantities have been found (Cunliffe and Brown 1987, 310–16; Cunliffe and de Jersey 1997). Smaller quantities have been found in Poole Harbour but their distribution beyond this area of central southern England is limited (Cunliffe and de Jersey 1997; Fitzpatrick 1998).

Petrological analysis has indicated a source for the cordoned wares on the gabbro massif of Trégomar, near Lamballe (Morzadec 1991), whilst the rilled micaceous wares and graphite coated wares show an essentially western Armorican distribution (Daire 1992; de Jersey 1993, 330). Other possible imports may also occur at Hengistbury Head and at other sites in less petrologically distinctive sandy wares.

Roman pottery

Throughout the later Republic fine, usually black, 'Campanian' tablewares were manufactured in Italy and, on a lesser scale, its provinces. Campanian ware was superseded by the red-slipped *terra sigillata* (Italian type *terra sigillata* and then samian wares)

during the course of the second half of the first century BC. The distribution of Campanian ware in northern Gaul is sparse (e.g. Metzler 1995, 480–1, Abb. 248) and to date only two sherds have been found in reliable archaeological contexts in England, at Ower on Poole Harbour in Dorset (Timby 1987, 78) and at Silchester, Hampshire (Timby forthcoming). The former was residual in a second century AD context and whilst the latter, part of a pedestalled vessel, came from the fill of a pre-conquest pit, it is uncertain whether either vessel reached Britain before the late first century BC. It is most likely, however, that the vessels arrived alongside the Dressel 1B amphorae.

Some of the earliest products of the increasingly romanised central Gaulish potteries, and which have a distinctive micaceous fabric, copy the forms of these Campanian wares. Two such platters from the Welwyn Garden City burial (Rigby and Freestone 1986, 8) are red (*terra rubra*) rather than black and may date to around 30 BC (Fig. 14.1). Other early products of this industry include white slipped flagons, an example of which was also found in the Welwyn Garden City burial (Fig. 14.1; 14.2,1).

Imports of Early Imperial Date

It was not until the last two decades of the 1st century BC, however, that southern England saw a significant influx of Roman, and Roman inspired, fine tablewares from across the Channel, originating from the pottery industries of Italy and the newly established ones of southern, central and northern Gaul. The range of amphorae also increased dramatically, although the absolute quantities remained broadly constant. Although these imports are found on a wide range of sites, the quantities are usually small, often with only a few vessels represented. Larger groups of imports, often with a variety of types, are found most frequently on the so-called *oppida* (Trow 1990, 104). The larger assemblages come from sites such as Bagendon, Gloucestershire (Clifford 1961; Trow 1990); Braughing, Hertfordshire (Partridge 1981; Potter and Trow 1988); Canterbury (Blockley *et al.* 1995), Chichester, West Sussex (Down 1978; 1981); Colchester, Essex (Hawkes and Hull 1947; Niblett 1985; Sealey 1985; Crummy 1993); Leicester (Jarvis 1986; Clay and Mellor 1984; Clay and Pollard 1994); Silchester, Hampshire (Boon 1969; Fulford with Corney 1984; Fulford and Timby forthcoming); and St Albans, Hertfordshire (Wheeler and Wheeler 1936; Stead and Rigby 1989). Even allowing for the uncertainties as to the exact character of these sites (e.g. Woolf 1993a) and, where occupation continued in the early Roman period, the difficulty in distinguishing between imports of pre- and post-conquest date, the association between theses sites and large quantities of imported pottery appears significant.

Amphorae: Containers for Wines and Foodstuffs

The strong Italian connection represented by the Dressel 1 was not maintained in the Imperial group, which is characterised by dramatic changes from around the 30s BC. A much greater diversity of both commodity and container was introduced including a range of wines, olive oil, fish-based products, liqueur wines and/or olives, and fruits. Italy lost its pre-eminence, not just to products of the western provinces, but also, although to a lesser extent, to those of the eastern ones.

Amongst the better documented types reaching England is the Pascual 1 wine amphora from north east Spain. The type, which was also produced on a small scale in southern France, first appears in the 30's BC, overlapping with and partially superseding the Italian Dressel 1B, and continued to be produced into the second decade AD. The form is known to occur widely in central, and more rarely in south-eastern, England and contained *c*.22 litres of wine.

Both the Dressel 1 and Pascual 1 forms were themselves superseded by the Dressel 2–4 form, another wine amphora made in Italy and several provinces across the Empire. In Italy the type may appear around the mid-first century BC and most finds of Dressel 2–4 from Iron Age Britain are Italian,

containing *c*.26–30 litres of wine. Occasional vessels from the eastern Mediterranean with similar capacities, most notably the Rhodian wine amphora, might occur in Iron Age contexts but these amphorae could equally be of post-conquest date. A small number of flat-bottomed Gauloise wine amphorae from southern Gaul have also been recognised in Iron Age contexts, for example, Braughing-Ermine Street (Potter and Trow 1988, 114, 147, fig. 67,10). These have often been classified as flagons but the earliest types of Gauloise contained about the same quantity of wine, *c*.26 litres, as amphorae with spike shaped bases. Finally, one Italian import occasionally found in Iron Age contexts is the very large single-handled flagon, *Camulodunum* type 139, with a distinctive black sand fabric directly comparable to Dressel 2–4 amphorae. It is possible that these vessels, which could contain *c*.23 litres, may have been used as wine containers.

The early variety of the Dressel 20 south Spanish olive oil amphorae, the Oberaden 83 is also found occasionally in Iron Age Britain, but by the Tiberian period the Dressel 20 superseded it. Olive-oil amphorae contained significantly more liquid than wine amphorae; the average capacity of the Dressel 20 is *c*.60–65 litres. Very occasionally examples of Dressel 6 from north eastern Italy have been identified. It is not known whether these examples contained the famous Istrian olive oil from north east Italy or wine as both commodities were carried in slightly different varieties of the type.

Amphorae containing fish-based commodities derive almost entirely from southern Spain. These types contained a variety of pastes and sauces (akin to a modern brown sauce) made from fish, as well as dried fish on their own, and are usually subsumed within the all embracing category of Beltrán I. This grouping is broadly equivalent to types Dressel 7–11 and although their capacity varies it is slightly higher than those of wine amphorae, at *c*.27–33 litres. The Haltern 70, also from southern Spain, and generally thought to contain *c*.30 litres of a form of liqueur wine and/or olives, is another type well-represented from the Augustan period onwards. As the Haltern 70 was made in the same region as Dressel 20 it is frequently difficult to distinguish between sherds of the two types. A few other types of amphorae such as the Richborough 527, which may have contained dried fruits, and the Dressel 28 which contained wine occur very rarely in Iron Age Britain.

Food Preparation Vessels and Storage Vessels
Mortaria
Mortaria were used for crushing and mixing foodstuffs, being used as a mortar (Fig. 14.2,2). Trituration grits, which provided an abrasive agent and

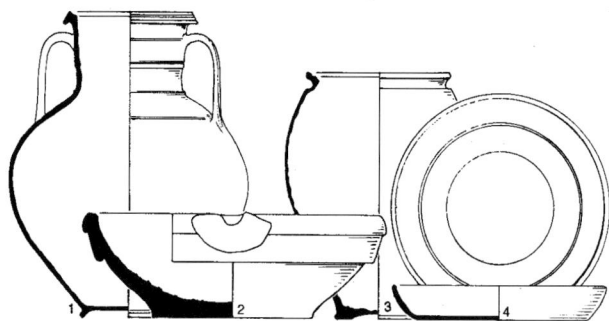

Fig. 14.2. Food storage and preparation vessels., 1. Flagon Camulodunum *type 165, 2. mortarium* Camulodunum *type 191B, 3. Jar* Camulodunum *type 102/ 262, 4. Pompeian Red Ware platter.*

helped to protect the vessel, are not found on the earliest vessels. Production of these vessels in Gaul does not generally seem to have commenced until a 'Romanised' cuisine was adopted and it is possible that the finds from Colchester-Sheepen and Braughing-Gatesbury and Skeleton Green, if they are definitely pre-conquest imports, are from Central Italy and Central Gaul.

Pompeian Red Ware
So called because the colour of the slip on the inside of the dishes is similar to that of wall paintings in Pompeii, Pompeian Red Ware was made exclusively as flat dishes with a matching lid (Fig. 14.2,4). The dishes are large: usually between 350–450 mm in diameter and sometimes up to 950 mm. Although it is often asserted that Pompeian Red Ware dishes from Pompeii contained somewhat overdone loaves, there is no certain evidence that this was the case. Instead it seems more likely that the red slip on the interior of the dishes acted as a non-stick cooking surface, with the lids providing some flexibility as to the method of cooking. Where their fabrics have been examined, finds from Iron Age Britain are from Italy, perhaps around Pompeii and Herculaneum (Peacock 1977, but see Peña 1990). As with mortaria, their presence in Iron Age contexts hints at a Roman style of cuisine: if they were used in the same way as in the classical world.

Flagons
The earliest products of the central Gaulish industries could have reached Britain by around 30 BC. (Fig. 14.1). Some of the most distinctive types from central Gaul are large two-handled flagons covered by a cream or white slip, and unslipped flagons with reeded rims. The flagons are large, with heights of up to 450 mm and girths of up to 350 mm, and thin-walled (Fig. 14.2,1). The Central Gaulish flagons

from Iron Age burial 299 at St Albans-King Harry Lane (Stead and Rigby 1989, 120, 346, fig. 148. 299, 2) weighed 3 kilograms each when empty and could contain nearly 10 litres of liquid, giving a total weight of c.12 kilograms (Rigby and Freestone 1986, 18–19). Although these vessels are distributed quite widely (Rigby and Freestone 1986, fig. 2), on this basis it remains uncertain whether they were exchanged for their contents or as serving and storage vessels in their own right. Comparable fine flagons were also made in white 'pipeclay' fabrics in Northern Gaul which first appear later than the earliest Central Gaulish types but which are still contemporary with the later products of that region. They too are widely distributed.

Jars
In the later first century BC and early first century AD, coarse and fineware jars from Central Gaul (*Camulodunum* forms 262 and 102; cf. Ferdière and Ferdière 1972), are also found in southern England (Fig. 14.2,3). The vessels have a coarsely tempered fabric containing fragments of igneous rock. The smaller jars (*Camulodunum* form 102) often have a thin golden micaceous slip on the rim and shoulder. It is not immediately apparent why such vessels were exchanged unless they came either as part of larger cargoes of pottery from the region or were imported for their contents. The suggestion that they were imported for their contents is supported by the moulding on the rims which provides seating for lids, and by the rare occurrence of lids in the same fabric. The jars share a similar distribution to the flagons from Central Gaul but are less frequent (Rigby and Freestone 1986). A fragmented jar from the Lexden Tumulus, Colchester, Essex (Rigby 1986, 118–20) may be a related type of Central Gaulish derivation.

Finewares
A wide range of finewares appears in Late Iron Age Britain. The fine red-gloss vessels of the Italian type *terra sigillata* industry superseded Campanian wares during the course of the first century BC and these red-gloss wares (or *terra sigillata*) were widely imitated in Gaul either in new industries or in ones developing from existing traditions (Fig. 14.3,4–5). As it is now known that Italian type *terra sigillata* wares were also made in Gaul, the term 'Italian-type terra sigillata' while cumbersome, is more correct (Ettlinger *et al.* 1990).

Italian
Italian type *terra sigillata* was originally named 'Arretine' ware after the pottery at Arrezzo in central Italy, and is a high gloss *terra sigillata*. It was

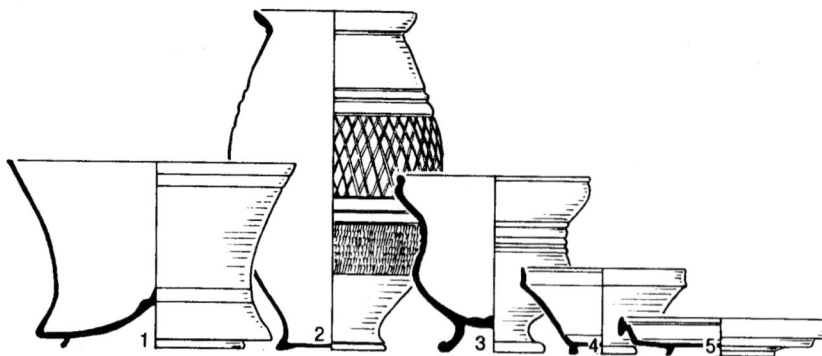

Fig. 14.3. Serving and drinking and eating vessels from Gaul. 1. Bowl Camulodunum *type 51 in* terra nigra, *2. Butt beaker* Camulodunum *type 112 in* terra rubra, *3. Beaker* Camulodunum *type. 76 in* terra rubra, *4. cup* Camulodunum *type 56A cup in* terra rubra, *5. platter* Camulodunum *type 7. The cup and platter copy Italian terra sigillata forms.*

manufactured in a wide range of mould-made forms but those found most frequently are small bowls or cups (Fig. 14.5, front right), and platters. Relief-decorated pedestalled bowls (more properly called a chalice but usually called a *krater* in the older literature) are also found, and these were also drinking vessels. Italian type *terra sigillata* was manufactured over much of Italy and also in Central Gaul and from the evidence of the makers' stamps on the vessels it is clear that some Italian firms set up workshops in Gaul, notably at Lyon where the firm of Ateius directly established a pottery at the site of La Muette shortly after *c*.10 BC.

Italian type *terra sigillata* was never abundant in Iron Age Britain but the earliest assemblage currently known comes from Braughing-Gatesbury and is exclusively Italian in origin. Gradually Gaulish wares became more common but it is frequently impossible to distinguish between Italian and Gaulish products without chemical analyses. Most finds are concentrated in the Essex-Hertfordshire region, for example at Braughing and Colchester, but an important collection has been recovered from the recent excavations on the basilica site at Silchester, including products from both Arezzo and Pisa (Bird forthcoming). A closely similar group has been recovered from excavations at the Canterbury-Marlowe Car Park sites, where it was also associated with Late Iron Age occupation (Bird 1995, 772–3). The wares are again found at sites such as Bagendon, Fishbourne and Chichester (West Sussex), and Leicester.

South and South West Gaul

The earliest products of the south Gaulish samian workshops begin to make an appearance from around AD. 20 at sites such as Silchester, Colchester and Braughing. Early samian is, however, much less frequent that Italian type *terra sigillata* in southern England but it may be noted that the quantity of Gallo-Belgic wares imported from northern Gaul did not diminish at this time.

The Aquitaine, and in particular the region around Saintes, possessed a thriving pottery industry from at least the late La Tène. The repertoire of forms suggests contact and inspiration from the Campanian and early sigillata industries. A small number of fine blackware vessels from Hengistbury Head (Rigby 1987, 279–80, ill. 192) and Ower, Dorset (Timby 1987, 78, fig. 41, 32, 34) may originate from the Aquitanian workshops. Forms made in the Aquitaine include the distinctive carinated bowl (*vase bobine*) with an omphalos base (*Camulodunum* type 51)(Fig. 14.3,1), and platters.

Central Gaulish

The central region of Gaul covering the Auvergne, Allier and the area around Lyons boasts a long history of potting. As well as Italian type *terra sigillata*, flagons and storage jars, a range of central Gaulish finewares appear in the first century BC. Prominent amongst these are the fine micaceous wares, usually cups and platters, in black or red referred to as micaceous *terra nigra* or *terra rubra* respectively. Butt beakers were also made.

Micaceous *terra nigra* has been documented at a number of sites across central and southern Britain, notably Silchester; Colchester-Camulodunum, Canterbury, and Baldock (Stead and Rigby 1986). Micaceous *terra rubra* is less common with examples recorded from the Welwyn Garden City burial (Fig. 14.1), Silchester, Braughing-Puckeridge, and Canterbury. At the Silchester *oppidum* and in the Welwyn Garden City burial, micaceous central Gaulish platters appear before the great influx of wares from the Gallo-Belgic industries of northern Gaul. The earliest platter forms, such as the Welwyn Garden City examples (cf. *Camuldonum* type 1), owe their inspiration directly to the Campanian industry, whilst the slightly later moulded platter forms show more affinity to Italian type *terra sigillata* types. Other types suggest more indigenous prototypes. The industry could, therefore, be regarded as a direct offshoot of the early Gaulish Italian type *terra sigillata* industries. Like the potters who made that ware, those in central Gaul stamped their names on some of the finished products. Many of the names appear to be Gallic rather than Latin and the word *avot* is often used instead of *fecit*, the Latin for 'made by'.

As well as high gloss Italian type *terra sigillata* wares, the workshops established by Italian firms produced other wares such as unslipped thin-walled beakers. These very fine, thin, beakers were also made in Italian type *terra sigillata* but they are less frequent than the unslipped examples. Only a single such beaker is currently known from Iron Age Britain, an unslipped beaker of Aco-Hilarus type (so called after the names of the maker on them) from Silchester (Timby forthcoming). So-called 'Roanne painted bowls' although comparatively common in Gaul are rare in Britain, with just two examples recognised to date: one from Ower (Timby 1987, 76), and a vessel published amongst the Oare group from Wiltshire (cf. Swan 1975, fig. 5.57). Both examples could, however, be imports of either immediately pre- or post-conquest date.

Northern Gaul

The proliferation of workshops producing fine tablewares in black and red wares spread northwards, and a new industry emerged in the last decades of the first century BC. in north east Gaul, in particular in and around Reims, Marne. In addition, various whitewares were made, mainly beakers, and the flagons already mentioned (Fig. 14.4,2–5; 14.5). As with the other non-*terra sigillata* Gallic industries, the Gallo-Belgic wares appear to be a fusion of two very different traditions: Roman and native Gaulish. Loeschcke, who was one of the founding fathers of the study, regarded the ware as a substitute for the barbarians for Italian *terra sigillata* – a Belgic *sigillata* (Loeschke 1909, 258).

Terra nigra and the various forms of *terra rubra* have been found on a large number of sites dating to the first centuries BC–AD in Britain and far outnumber the other types of finewares mentioned above. Rigby (1973) has described the range of fabrics in which they occur. The greatest density of pre-conquest finds is to be found in central southern and south eastern England, and the East Midlands (Fig. 14.4). Again, the majority of finds come from

oppida such as Bagendon, Braughing, Canterbury, Colchester, Leicester and Silchester. Gallo-Belgic wares were also placed as grave goods in cremation burials in south eastern and central England. A few sherds are also known from shrines or temples such as Hayling Island, Hampshire, Lancing Ring, West Sussex, and Great Chesterford, Essex.

Other north Gaulish products include the well-known whiteware butt beakers (*Camulodunum* type 113) which are also known to have been manufactured further to the west of the principal Gallo-Belgic potteries in the Marne at Amiens in Picardy (Roffin and Vaisselle 1966; Ben Redjeb 1987). The form can be traced to the late La Tène and similar forms were undoubtedly made in central and perhaps southern Gaul. At Silchester, whiteware butt beakers are stratigraphically the earliest imports to be recorded to date, being associated with the earliest well beneath the later basilica.

Discussion

The Development and Significance of Cross-Channel Contact

The late Iron Age in central southern and south eastern England was a period of rapid and profound changes. The archaeological evidence for this is well known – an exponential increase in the quantity and complexity in the issue of coinage, the re-adoption of the rite of cremation burial, the appearance of specialist religious sites, the adoption of the fast potter's wheel, the appearance of *oppida*, and the possible extensification and intensification of farming (e.g. Haselgrove 1982; Trow 1990; Woolf 1993b). It needs no rehearsal here. The appearance of Roman pottery is often seen as integral with these changes.

As many of these changes have strong links, either directly or indirectly, with continental Europe a number of assumptions have strongly influenced the interpretation of their significance. Three assumptions have been particularly influential and they have been called the 'current orthodoxy';

– foreign contact equates with change, particularly rapid change
– that Roman goods indicate either a trade with Rome or one which was ultimately inspired by her
– that there must be a 'Balance of Trade'

A critique of these assumptions may be found elsewhere (Fitzpatrick 1989, 39–42; 1993, 235). Here it is sufficient to note the emphasis that these views place on imported goods. As Roman pottery is the category found most frequently in excavated con-

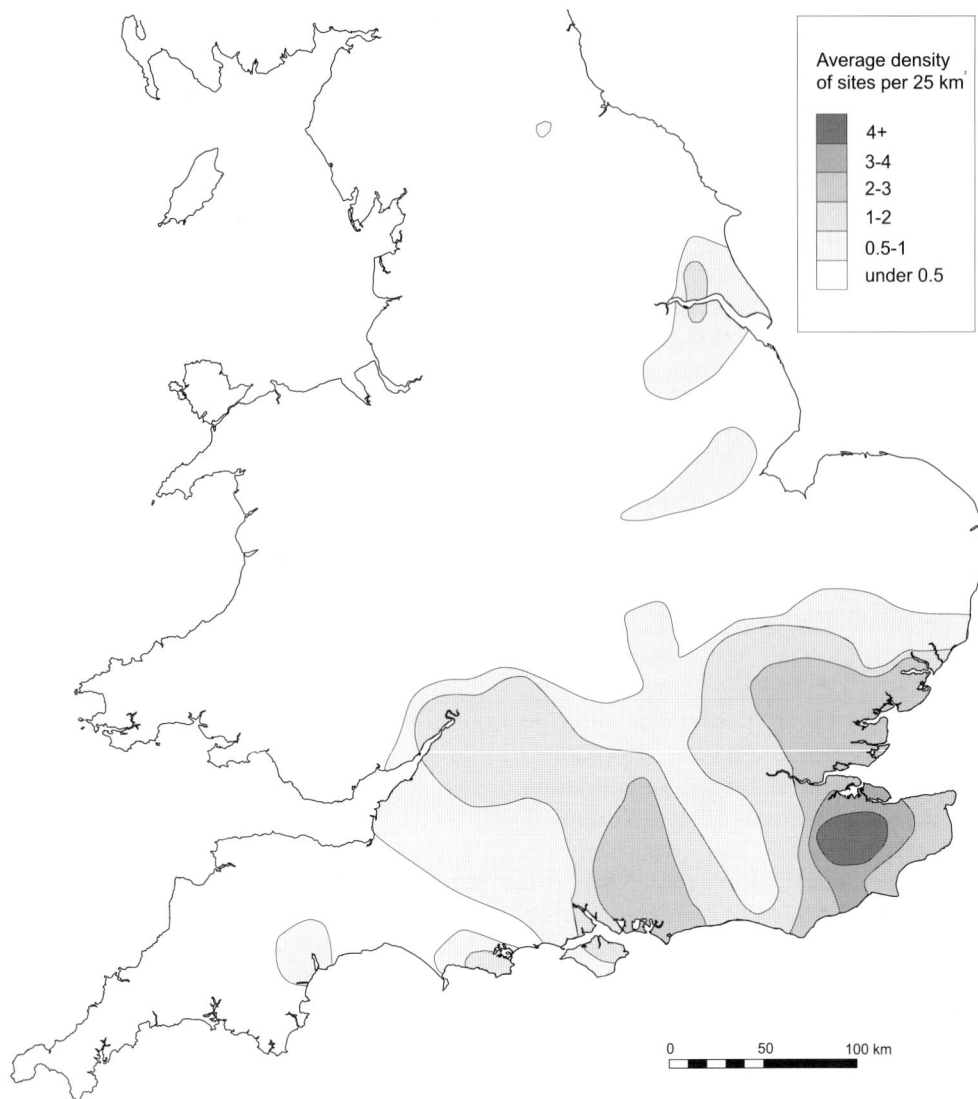

Fig. 14.4. Trend surface map of the distribution of Gallo-Belgic wares in England. Drawn by Jane Timby.

texts considerable emphasis was, and is, often placed on it. This often takes the form of the pottery being assumed to have an 'independent' value, which can be transferred and ascribed to the contexts in which it has been found.

Clearly this is not the case, and it is important to recall the very small proportion which imports comprise in many assemblages and not to conflate evidence both chronologically and spatially for what may have been very different cultural circumstances. Situations at Hengistbury Head on the Dorset coast in 80 BC were very different from those in Braughing in Hertfordshire a hundred years later in AD 20. The earliest Roman pots found in southern England, Dressel 1A wine amphorae, are found most frequently found at settlements in southern England; in some cases alongside Armorican coarse and fine wares. It

seems likely that these amphorae should be seen as arriving in the context of cross-Channel exchanges between Britons and Gauls, and in the wider context of trade and exchange within western and central Europe in the Late Iron Age. The character and extent of any associated contact between Britain and the Roman world is unknown (Fitzpatrick 1989; 1993). The distribution of Dressel 1 amphorae, particularly the later 1B variety, is also heavily weighted to the south-east by its selection as a grave good in that region and discussions of changes in 'trade routes' should be viewed cautiously (cf. Fitzpatrick 1985, 316, fig. 6). It is clear, however, that the emphasis of cross-Channel exchange drifts from west to east through the Late Iron Age.

As central and northern Gaul became increasingly romanised, the range and quantity of goods imported into southern England increased. Figure 14.4 illustrates the relative density of sites with north Gaulish *terra nigra* and/or *terra rubra*. Two spatially exclusive zones are apparent, one straddles the Thames Estuary; the other extends from the South Coast around Chichester Harbour,and northwards towards the River Thames. Minor concentrations of finds occur around the River Exe, Poole Harbour, the Humber Estuary, and in Lincolnshire. These changes in the range and quantity of goods imported should not, however, be construed as representing a period of direct as opposed to indirect contact. The principle change is in the quantity of imported pottery arriving at the Solent and Thames Estuary via the Seine Basin. Contacts with this region are well documented throughout the Later Iron Age, particularly by the distribution of Gallo-Belgic coinage (Fitzpatrick 1992, 3–20). The increased quantities of Roman pottery of early Imperial date which became available appear to continue the trend first seen in the distribution of Dressel 1B amphorae. The most likely cause for this increase in the availability of pottery is the increasing romanisation of central Gaul and the more direct incorporation of northern Gaul within the Empire causing more pottery – and pottery of Roman types – to be made and used in these regions. The changing history of the western Roman provinces directly affected the types of pottery available to the Iron Age peoples in Britain, with the new provinces providing a greater proportion of the imported pottery. The Catalonian wine amphorae and Aquitanian pottery from sites such as Hengistbury Head and Ower suggest that contact along the western seaboards continued.

Contact before the Conquest was also not restricted to contact with continental Europe. Although the quantities are relatively small, Roman pottery has been found at a number of sites in Lincolnshire and Yorkshire (Evans 1995, 53–6; Willis 1996, 185–207; Rigby and Elsdon 1996) and it seems likely that these goods arrived by way of exchanges within Britain. Some of the material at sites such as Redcliff, East Riding of Yorkshire may also have arrived after AD 43, but before the Roman conquest of northern England. The slightly later assemblage from the possible *oppidum* of Stanwick is comparatively large and has an unusually high proportion of samian, which includes a number of rare forms. As with comparable sites in southern England it seems likely that these wares may indicate direct contact with the Roman world (Evans 1995, 53–6; Willis 1996, 202–3).

Changes in Iron Age Potting Traditions

These changes in the quantities and sources of the imported pottery should not obscure the continuing changes within the ceramic traditions of southern England during the Late Iron Age. At an earlier stage Armorican pottery is thought to have influenced the cordoned wares of south-western England (Cunliffe 1987, 343, ill. 219) and some forms chosen as grave goods at the cremation burial cemetery at Westhampnett, West Sussex, clearly copy Armorican forms, even though imported pots themselves do not appear to be present (Mepham 1997, 131). It is difficult to assess the later changes quantitatively. Frequently Roman imports are treated in specialist reports as source specific assemblages such as the Gallo-Belgic wares, and are divorced from their immediate contexts. Reports, which deal with indigenous and imported wares as a single assemblage, such as that from Braughing-Ermine Street (Potter and Trow 1988, 121–33; Trow 1990, 10–6), remain rare.

Hill discusses aspects of these changes in East Anglia in Chapter 13, and one of them is particularly relevant here. This is the diversification in the range of pottery shapes and forms in that region. Middle Iron Age settlement assemblages in south-eastern England were dominated by ubiquitous bowl/jar forms but in the Late Iron Age a much wider range of clearly defined forms appeared (Thompson 1982; Rigby and Freestone 1997). The continental European Iron Age forms copied most widely were the tall forms of the pedestalled urn and the butt beaker (Willis 1994). The Roman forms copied most frequently were platters and cups. For obvious reasons, specialist shipping containers such as amphorae were not copied. The large closed shape of the flagons was harder to imitate and was copied less frequently, or at least less successfully but copying did commence at an early date. However, in other regions such as the Thames Valley, imported wares which appear to have been less frequent in the region, appear to have been copied only rarely.

One of the earliest occasions at which it is possible to see this copying in south-eastern England is in the Welwyn Garden City burial (Fig. 14.1). An imported two-handled flagon was placed in the burial as well as locally made copies which are all orange-coloured, apparently imitating the colour and texture of the imported pots as well as their shapes. The locally made pedestalled drinking cups in the grave presumably copy Campanian wares. However, the technological constraints in copying wheel made or moulded pots which were fired in permanent kilns reaching high temperatures and which were often brightly coloured and with shiny surfaces should not be underestimated. In contrast the manufacture of pedestalled urns and butt beakers did not present significant technological difficulties. These vessels may have been for serving or drinking liquids from and their appearance indicates changes within Iron Age societies in the presentation and, perhaps, the

Fig. 14.5. Imported Roman pottery, mainly from the King Harry Lane cemetery. Other imported objects include a circular mirror and also an unguentarium or perfume bottle (though this is not certainly of Iron Age date) from the same cemetery, a Hellenistic glass bowl from the Hertford Heath, Hertfordshire burial, an Aylesford pan (part of a washing set) from Aylesford, Kent, a silver cup from the Welwyn 'B', Hertfordshire burial, gold jewellery from the Alton, Hampshire hoard, and glass gaming pieces from the Welwyn Garden City burial. Photograph by courtesy of the British Museum.

consumption of food. The Roman cups and platters comprised individual place settings.

Romanised Cuisine, or a Roman Cuisine?

Whilst the presence of wine, olive oil and fish-based commodities can be demonstrated from the evidence of the amphorae which were transport containers, the evidence for other foodstuffs, such as the contents of central Gaulish storage jars is less tangible. The provision of storage or serving vessels such as flagons and tablewares including platters, bowls and dishes also implies other changes. These changes may have been not only in the manners of presenting and serving of food. It is sometimes suggested that imported wine was drunk in the Roman style, by being diluted (Rigby and Freestone 1986, 15–16). In the Welwyn Garden City burial, there are amphorae which contained wine from Italy, a silver drinking goblet also from Italy (Fig. 14.5) and local copies of imported pottery vessels, imported and local flagons which wine could have been mixed in and served from, and a metal strainer and a metal bowl. It is important to remember, though, that the copper alloy jugs and and pans (Fig. 14.5) found in other burials such as Welwyn B and Snailwell were

probably used for washing hands rather than serving wine (Nuber 1971).

In other cases the range of imported pottery raises the question of the ethnicity of the individuals using the pots. The platter is not a form characteristic of the later Iron Age in Britain or non-Mediterranean Gaul. Was it therefore used for serving items not previously part of the British diet, or was it a prestigious display item?, and when it is associated with a range of foodstuffs, food preparation vessels and table wares, were foreigners eating off them?

As noted above the principal collections of Roman pottery come from *oppida*. The difficulties in the interpretation of these sites (Haselgrove 1987, 58–63, 139–49, 163–78) have been alluded to above. None the less, it is clear that at least some of these sites were amongst other thing mints, and probably the seats of royal authority. The composition of the assemblages of imported pottery from these sites is distinctive in their quantity and diversity. At most smaller settlements imported pottery comprises less than 1% of the assemblage with only a handful of vessels present. Given the small proportion of any assemblage which imported pottery comprises on these sites, it is hazardous to use its absence as a chronological indicator. In contrast at a number of *oppida*, for example Braughing, Leicester and Silchester, the proportions of imported pottery form a very high proportion of the assemblage, between 10–30% (Partridge 1981; Clay and Mellor 1985; Clay and Pollard 1994; Timby forthcoming).

In the case of Stanwick, North Yorkshire it has been suggested that the imports may represent diplomatic gifts (Evans 1995, 55). It seems likely that Gauls were present at some of *oppida*, notably at Braughing where the graffiti on some pots, presumably giving the owners names, give Latin names (Partridge 1982). Taken together this evidence poses the question as to whether Gauls or Romans occupied parts of these sites, bringing their own cuisine and its associated material culture with them?

The Inter-site Distribution of Roman Pottery: Silchester and its Environs

This scenario might also explain why, for example, so few of the smaller settlements around the *oppidum* at Silchester appear to have had access to imported goods. Several sites within 20–30 km of the *oppidum* have yielded evidence of pre-conquest occupation, for example, Aldermaston Wharf (Cowell *et al* 1980), Cowdery's Down (Millett and James 1983), Reading Business Park (Moore and Jennings 1992), Risely Farm (Lobb and Morris 1991–3), Ructstalls Hill (Oliver and Applin 1978), Ufton Nervet (Manning 1974), and Viables Farm (Millet and Russell 1984). Many of the coarsewares from the excavations at the *basilica* in Silchester find parallels amongst material from these sites, suggesting that they were occupied at the same time. A recurrent feature of nearly all these sites is the paucity of the imported finewares present. There is, therefore, little evidence to presently suggest that Silchester was redistributing imported wares to sites in its immediate environs or that these wares travelled any further than the objects of local exchanges. It may have been that there was little interest or demand for such, except by those wishing or able to acquire what may have been more prestigious products, with which they were later buried, for example, the burials at Burghfield (Boon and Wymer 1958), Crookhams (an old unpublished find) and Hurstbourne Tarrant (Hawkes and Dunning 1930). It is possible that Silchester was instead exchanging commodities and ideas with larger settlements further afield, for example, Dorchester-on-Thames, Oxfordshire, where a number of imports have been found, or even Bagendon farther to the west in Gloucestershire, from where there is again little evidence for the local redistribution of pottery (Trow 1990, 104). Conversely, there may not have been large enough quantities of pottery to be redistributed.

Whatever the reasons, a similar pattern of a slow acceptance of new ceramic wares can perhaps be seen in the slow adoption of Romanised forms in many rural sites in the Thames Valley and further afield, where it is not until the very late first century AD or early second century that Romanised wheel-made wares appear.

Elsewhere, however, the situation differed. On the basis of the evidence presently available, imported goods appear to have been available more widely in south eastern England. The settlement at Kelvedon, Essex is close to the *oppidum* at Colchester and it appears to have been a larger site than the individual farmsteads around Silchester. It received a wider range of imports (Rodwell 1988), and in many respects appears to be intermediate between *oppida* and farmsteads in size and perhaps importance. The same may be true for Baldock in Hertfordshire (Stead and Rigby 1986).

The Selection of Roman Pottery as Grave Goods

Although the quantities and quality of material at *oppida* may be distinctive, there is little indication that imported Roman pottery was deposited or discarded in particular contexts or locations within them or on other types of settlements. There are, however, clear differences in the ways in which the material was regarded as appropriate for inclusion in burials.

The simple presence of Dressel 1 amphorae in 'Aylesford'-type cremation burials has been taken by many to indicate that the deceased were wealthy and powerful individuals (e.g. Rodwell 1976). There are some difficulties with the ways in which this interpretation has been formulated, notably in establishing whether a single amphora represents sufficient grounds to categorise it as 'rich', but Roman pottery continued to be selected for inclusion in well-furnished burials. In comparison to Dressel 1 amphorae, other types of amphorae appear to have been selected for inclusion in burials much less frequently. Where they are found, however, there appears to be a stronger correlation with well-furnished burials where the sheer size of the grave chamber and the variety and quantity of grave goods would be sufficient to identify these burials as being those of individuals of some status. In the mortuary rites for the man buried under the Lexden Tumulus, Colchester, *c.*450 litres of Italian wine were consumed (Foster 1986). Nearly all the pottery from the Snailwell, Cambridgeshire, burial is Roman in type (14 of 16 vessels; Lethbridge 1953) and considerable quantities of Roman pottery were also present in the poorly recorded burial from Mount Bures, Essex (Smith 1852, 25–8). All the pottery, at least 24 vessels dated between AD 20–30, in the central burial chamber in enclosure 3 of the 'royal graves' at

Colchester-Stanway is Roman (Crummy 1993) and the impression of the grave goods is of a burial of Roman style before the conquest. In view of the sumptuousness of the Lexden Tumulus burial, which is of a client or friendly king of Rome who died in the first century BC, this Roman appearance is hardly surprising.

However, the interpretation of Late Iron Age burials is not simply a matter of searching for the social status or *social persona* of the deceased. Many factors determine the choice of materials for inclusion as grave goods. For example, although some burials in the St Albans-King Harry Lane cremation burial cemetery include a large number of imported Roman pots, red-coloured imported pots are comparatively rare in the cemetery as a whole. This may be due to red being regarded as an inappropriate colour for use in mortuary rituals (Millett 1993, 275). In contrast in Dorset, Roman imports appear not to have been selected at all for incorporation in Durotrigian type inhumation burials.

Clearly then, the presence or absence of Roman pottery as grave goods cannot simply be 'read off' as an index of social status. Also, in all these examples the pottery appears to be used in this stage of the mortuary rituals to symbolise a meal. This meal may have been for the dead, or their spirits, or for the gods, but the underlying significance of this stage of the rituals which included the sacrifice and offering of animals and birds does not appear to alter whether the pottery is imported or indigenous.

Conclusion

In terms of typology, chronology, provenance, and distribution the quality of information about Roman pottery in Iron Age Britain is very high. The techno-logical influence of the pottery with regard to romanisation and technological innovation has been explored thoroughly, although the geographical distribution of this appears to be very variable. The roles the vessels played in prestige good economies, and the status of settlements and burials in which they are found have also received considerable interest.

Yet other areas have seen little work. Reports where Roman pottery is integrated with, and quantified in the same way as, indigenous pottery are rare, and relatively little attention has been paid to the associations and distribution of the material within settlements. The composition of those pottery assemblages by functional type and size, and how they relate to the associated faunal assemblages has barely been considered.

It is important to remember that when Roman pottery first arrived in Iron Age Britain in significant quantities the table wares and flagons represented an exotic range of new shapes and sizes in brilliant colours with different textures and shining finishes (Fig. 14.5). The large, heavy, amphorae and some storage jars contained new foodstuffs with new flavours: wines, olive oils, dried fishes and fish sauces, olives and figs. The people using mortars and non-stick cooking dishes may have brought new styles of cooking, serving and eating. These changes have to be seen in the broader context of southern England and the East Midlands in relation to continental Europe, and in association with other changes which bound Britain into the Roman world both indirectly, such as the adoption of conditional literacy, and directly in the adoption by kings of the status of client or friendly king of Rome. Yet these changes also need to be seen in the context of the prehistoric ceramics alongside which they were used.

Bibliography

Abercromby, J. 1912, *A Study of the Bronze Age Pottery in Great Britain and Ireland and its Associated Grave-goods*. Oxford, Clarendon.

Adkins, L. & Needham, S. 1985, New research on a Late Bronze Age enclosure at Queen Mary's Hospital, Carshalton, *Surrey Archaeological Collections* 76, 11–50.

Aitken, M.J. 1985, *Thermoluminescence Dating*, Academic Press, New York.

Alcock, L. 1980, The Cadbury sequence in the first millennium BC, *Bulletin of the Board of Celtic Studies* 28, 656–718.

Alcock, L. & Foster, I. (ed.) 1963, *Culture and Environment: Essays in Honour of Sir Cyril Fox*, Routledge & Kegan Paul, London.

Allen, C.S.M. 1988, *Bronze Age Pottery of the Second Millennium bc in the East Midlands of England*. Unpublished PhD thesis, University of Nottingham.

Allen, C.S.M., Harman, M. & Wheeler, H. 1987, Bronze Age cremation cemeteries in the East Midlands, *Proceedings of the Prehistoric Society* 53, 187-221.

Allen, C.S.M. & Knight, D. 1995, Breaking the code: a scheme for prehistoric pottery fabric types, *Old Potter's Almanack* 3, 1–4.

Allen, M.J. 1997, Landscape, land-use, and farming. In Smith *et al.* 1997, 277–83.

Allen, T.G. & Robinson, M. 1993, *The Prehistoric Landscape and Iron Age enclosed settlement at Mingies Ditich, Hardwick-with-Yelford. Oxon.*, Oxford University Committee for Archaeology/Oxford Archaeological Unit, Oxford.

Allen, T.G. 1990, *An Iron Age and Romano-British Enclosed Settlement at Watkins Farm, Northmoor, Oxon*, Oxford University Committee for Archaeology, Oxford.

Armit, I. (ed.) 1990, *Beyond the Brochs: Changing Perspectives on the Later Iron Age in Atlantic Scotland*, Edinburgh University Press, Edinburgh.

Armit, I. 1991, The Atlantic Scottish Iron Age: five levels of chronology, *Proceedings of the Society of Antiquaries of Scotland*, 121, 181–214.

Armit, I. 1992, The Hebridean Neolithic. In Sharples & Sheridan (eds) 1992, 307–321.

Armit, I., Dunwell, A.J., & Campbell, E. Forthcoming, Excavation of an Iron Age, Early Historic and Medieval settlement and metalworking site at Eilean Oblabhat, North Uist.

Arnold, D.E. 1981, A model for identification of non-local ceramic distribution: A view from the present. In Howard & Morris (eds) 1981, 31–44.

Arnold, D.E. 1984, Social interaction and ceramic design. In Rice (ed.) 1984, 133–61.

Arnold, D.E. 1985, *Ceramic Theory and Cultural Process*, Cambridge University Press, Cambridge.

Arnold, D.E. 1993, *Ecology and Ceramic Production in an Andean Community*, The University Press, Cambridge.

Ashbee, P. 1960, *The Bronze Age Round Barrow in Britain*, London.

Ashbee, P. 1966, The Fussell's Lodge long barrow excavations 1957, *Archaeologia* 100, 1–80.

Atkinson, R.J.C., Piggott, C.M. & Sandars, N.K. 1951, *Excavations at Dorchester, Oxon*, Department of Antiquities Ashmolean Museum, Oxford.

Avery, D.M.E. 1973, British La Tène decorated pottery – an outline, *Etudes Celtiques* 13, 522–51.

Avery, D.M.E. 1981, Furrowed bowls and carinated Hawkes A pottery. In Guilbert (ed.) 1981, 28–64.

Avery, D.M.E, 1982, The Neolithic causewayed enclosure, Abingdon, In Case & Whittle (eds) 1982, 10–50, London

Avery, D.M.E. 1993, *Hillfort Defences of Southern Britain*, British Archaeological Reports 231, Oxford.

Avery, D.M.E., Sutton, J.E.G. & Banks, J.W. 1967, Rainsborough, Northants: excavations 1961–65, *Proceedings of the Prehistoric Society* 33, 207-306.

Bailiff, I.K. 1987, The thermoluminescent dating of the Iron Age pottery. In Heslop 1987, 71–2.

Bailiff, I.K. 1988, *Ancient TL Supplement, Date List 2*.

Bailiff, I.K. & Larsen, P. 1989, Thermoluminescence dating of ceramic samples. In Vyner & Daniels (eds) 1989, 27.

Baillie, M.G.L. & Pilcher, J.R. 1983, Some observations on the high-precision calibration of routine dates. In Ottaway (ed.) 1983, 51–63.

Balfet, H. 1965, Ethnographical observations in North Africa and archaeological interpretation: The pottery of the Mahgreb. In Matson (ed.) 1965, 161–77.

Balfet, H. 1984, Methods of formation and the shape of pottery. In van der Leeuw & Pritchard (eds) 1984, 171–197.

Barclay, A.J. 1995, Cremains of the clay: Unpublished paper presented at the TAG Conference, University of Reading.

Barclay, A.J. 1997, The prehistoric pottery and fired clay. In Bradley, Parsons & Tyler 1997, 68–73.

Barclay, A.J. 1998, A note on the analysis of white inlay in Beaker and Early Iron Age pottery, *Old Potter's Almanack* 6.3, 3–4.

Barclay, A.J. 1999a, The monument complex. In Barclay & Halpin (eds) 1999, 309–20.

Barclay, A.J. 1999b, Grooved Ware from the Upper Thames region. In Cleal & MacSween (eds) 1999, 9–22.

Barclay, A.J. in prep a, The earlier prehistoric pottery. In *Yarnton: The Neolithic and Bronze Age settlement and landscape*, G. Hey (ed.), Oxford Archaeology Unit Thames Valley Monograph.

Barclay, A.J. in prep b, The Neolithic pottery. In Prehistoric and Roman settlement near Heyford Road, Steeple Aston, *Oxoniensia*.

Barclay, A.J. in prep c, Cups, dishes and a flask: orphans and cousins of the Peterborough Ware tradition.

Barclay, A.J. & Halpin, C. (eds) 1999, *Excavations at Barrow Hills, Radley, Oxfordshire. Volume I: the Neolithic and Bronze Age Monument Complex*, Oxford Archaeological Unit Thames Valley Landscapes Mono 11, Oxford.

Barclay, A.J., Lambrick, G., Moore, J. & Robinson, M. (eds) Forthcoming, *Cursus monuments in the Upper Thames Valley: the excavations at Drayton and Lechlade*, Oxford Archaeological Unit Thames Valley Landscapes Monograph.

Barclay, G. & Russell-White, C.J. 1993, Excavations in the ceremonial complex of the fourth to second millennium BC at Balfarg/Balbrinie, Glenrothes, Fife, *Proceedings of the Society of Antiquaries of Scotland* 123, 43–210.

Barker, G. & Gamble, C. (eds) 1985, *Beyond Domestication in Prehistoric Europe*, Academic Press, London.

Baring-Gould, S. 1896, Third report of the Dartmoor Exploration Society, *Transactions of the Devonshire Association* 28, 174–99.

Barley, N. 1994, *Smashing Pots: Feats of Clay from Africa*, British Museum Press, London.

Barley, N. 1995, *Dancing on the Grave: Encounters with death*, John Murray Ltd, London

Barnatt, J. 1994, Excavation of a Bronze Age unenclosed cemetery, cairns, and field boundaries at Eaglestone Flat, Curbar, Derbyshire, 1984, 1989–1990, *Proceedings of the Prehistoric Society* 60, 287–370.

Barnett, S.M. 1996, Luminescence dating of British ceramics from the Late Bronze and Iron Age, *The Old Potter's Almanack*, 4/2, 6–8.

Barnett, S.M. 1998, Luminescence dating of first millennium BC ceramics. In Sinclair *et al.* (eds) 1998, 155–8.

Barnett, S.M. 2000, Luminescence dating of pottery from later Prehistoric Britain, *Archaeometry*, 42/2, 431–57.

Barnett, S.M. In Press, Thermally and optically stimulated luminescence dating of later prehistoric pottery, *Archaeological Sciences 1997*.

Barnett, S.M. & Bailiff, I.K. 1993, Feasibility study: Luminescence dating of ceramics from Wanlip (SK 597 111), Unpublished experimental report, Luminescence Dating Laboratory, University of Durham.

Barnett, W.K. & Hoopes, J.W. (eds) 1995, *The Emergence of Pottery: Technology and Innovation in Ancient Societies*, Smithsonian Institution Press, Washington DC.

Barrett, J.C. 1975, The later pottery: types, affinities, chronology and significance. In Bradley & Ellison (eds) 1975, 101–18.

Barrett, J.C. 1976, Deverel-Rimbury: problems of chronology and interpretation. In Burgess & Miket (eds) 1976, 289–307.

Barrett, J.C. 1978, The EPRIA prehistoric pottery. In Hedges & Buckley 1978, 268–88.

Barrett, J.C. 1979, The pottery – discussion. In Coombs & Thompson 1979, 44–7.

Barrett, J. 1980, The pottery of the later Bronze Age in lowland England, *Proceedings of the Prehistoric Society* 46, 297–330.

Barrett, J.C. 1987, The Glastonbury lake village: models and source criticism, *Archaeological Journal* 144, 409–23.

Barrett, J.C. 1988, The living, the dead and the ancestors: Neolithic and Early Bronze Age mortuary practices. In Barrett & Kinnes (eds), 30–41.

Barrett, J.C. 1989, Food, gender and metal: questions of social reproduction. In Sørensen & Thomas (eds), 1989, 304–320.

Barrett, J.C. 1991a, Bronze Age pottery and the problem of classification. In Barrett, Bradley & Hall (eds), 1991, 201–230.

Barrett, J.C. 1991b, Review of R. Bradley, Passage of Arms, *Antiquity* 65, 743–744.

Barrett, J.C. 1994, *Fragments from Antiquity: An Archaeology of Social Life in Britain, 2900–1200 BC*, Blackwells, Oxford.

Barrett, J.C. & Bradley, R. 1980, *Settlement and Society in the British Later Bronze Age*, British Archaeological Reports British Series 83, Oxford.

Barrett, J.C., Bradley, R. & Green, M. 1991, *Landscape, Monuments and Society: The Prehistory of Cranborne Chase*, Cambridge.

Barrett, J.C., Bradley, R. & Hall, M. (eds), 1991, *Papers on the Prehistoric Archaeology of Cranborne Chase*, Oxbow Monograph 11, Oxford.

Barrett, J.C., Fitzpatrick, A. & Macinnes, I.(eds) 1989, *Barbarians and Romans in North-West Europe*, British Archaeological Reports International Series 471, Oxford.

Barrett, J., Freeman, P. & Woodward, A. 2000, *Cadbury Castle, Somerset: Excavations by Leslie Alcock*, English Heritage Archaeological Report, London.

Barrett, J.C. & Kinnes, I. (eds), 1988, *The Archaeology of Context in the Neolithic and Bronze Age: Recent Trends*, Sheffield.

Barrett, J.C. & Needham, S.P. 1988, Production, circulation and exchange: problems in the interpretation of Bronze Age bronzework. In Barrett & Kinnes (eds) 1988, 127–40.

Bateman, T. 1848, *Vestiges of the Antiquities of Derbyshire*, London, John Russell Smith.

Baxandall, M. 1985, *Patterns of Intention: On the Historical Explanation of Pictures*, Yale University Press, New Haven.

Beadsworth, A. & Keil, T. 1997. *Sociology on the Menu*, London, Routledge.

Beamish, M. 1994, Wanlip, A46 Leicester western bypass (SK 597 111), *Transactions of the Leicestershire Archaeological and Historical Society*, 68, 172–3.

Beamish. M. 1998. A Middle Iron Age site at Wanlip, Leicestershire, *Transactions of the Leicestershire Archaeological and Historical Society* 72, 1–91.

Beaudry, M., Cook, L. & Mrozowski, S. 1991, Artifacts and active voices: material culture as social discourse. In McGuire & Paynter (eds) 1991, 150–191.

Bedwin, O. 1978, Excavations inside Harting Beacon hillfort, 1976, *Sussex Archaeological Collections* 116, 231–239.

Bedwin, O. 1979, Excavations at Harting Beacon, West Sussex; second season 1977, *Sussex Archaeological Collections* 117, 21–36.

Bedwin, O. 1980, Excavations at Chanctonbury Ring, Wiston, West Sussex 1977, *Britannia* 11, 196–203.

Bedwin, O. (ed.) 1997, *The Archaeology of Essex*, Essex County Council, Chelmsford.

Bedwin, O. & Holgate, R. 1979, Excavations at Copse Farm, Oving, West Sussex, *Proceedings of the Prehistoric Society* 51, 220–228.

Bedwin, O. & Pitts, M. 1978, The excavation of an Iron Age settlement at North Bersted, Bognor Regis, West Sussex, 1975–76, *Sussex Archaeological Collections* 116, 315–339.

Bell, M. 1977, Excavations at Bishopstone, *Sussex Archaeological Collections* 115, 1–299.

Bell, M. 1990, *Brean Down Excavations 1983-1987*, English Heritage Archaeological Report 15, London.

Bell, M. 1996, Environment in the first millennium BC. In Champion & Collis (eds) 1996, 5–16.

Bender, B. (ed.) 1993, *Landscape: Politics and Perspectives*, Oxford.

Ben Redjeb, T. 1987, La commercialisation de la céramique Gallo-Belge à Amiens. In Bélmont *et al.* 93–100.

Benson, D.G., Evans, J.G. & Williams, G.H. 1990, Excavations at Stackpole Warren, Dyfed, *Proceedings of the Prehistoric Society* 56, 179–246.

Bélmont, C., Demarolle, J-M., Heckenbenner, D. & Massy, J-L. (eds) 1987, *Mélanges offerts à Marcel Lutz*, Revue Archéologique de l'Est et du Centre 38, Paris.

Bersu, G. 1940, Excavations at Little Woodbury, Wiltshire, part I, *Proceedings of the Prehistoric Society* 6, 30–111.

Beswick, P. 1994, Prehistoric pottery, In Barnatt 1994, 314–324.

Bevan, W. (ed.) 1999, *Northern Exposure: Interpretative Devolution and the Iron Age of the British Isles*, Leicester University Press, Leicester.

Bewley, R.H., Longworth, I.H., Browne, S., Huntley, J.P. & Varndell, G. 1992, Excavation of a Bronze Age cemetery at Ewanrigg, Maryport, Cumbria, *Proceedings of the Prehistoric Society* 58, 325–354.

Bey, G. & Pool, C. (eds) 1992, *Ceramic Production and Distribution: An Integrated Approach*, Westview Press, Boulder.

Bidwell, P.T. & Silvester, R.J. 1981, The Durotrigian pottery. In Silvester 1981, 63–7.

Binford, L. 1983, *In Pursuit of the Past: Decoding the Archaeological Record*, London.

Birchall, A. 1965, The Aylesford-Swarling culture: the problem of the Belgae reconsidered, *Proceedings of the Prehistoric Society* 31, 241–367.

Bird, J. 1995, Summary [of the samian and other imported red-slipped fine wares]. In Blockley *et al.* 1995, 772–5.

Bird, J. 2001, The sigillata. In Fulford & Timby 2001.

Blackmore, C., Braithwaite, M. & Hodder, I. 1979, Social and cultural patterning in the Late Iron Age in southern England. In Burnham & Kingsbury (eds) 1979, 93–117.

Blagg, T. & Millett, M. (eds) 1989, *The Early Roman Empire in the West*, Oxbow monographs, Oxford.

Blitz, J. 1993, Big pots for big shots: feasting and storage in a Mississippian community, *American Antiquity* 58, 80–96.

Blockley, K., Blockley, M., Blockley, P., Frere, S. & Stow, S. 1995, *Excavations in Marlowe Car Park and Surrounding Areas*, Archaeology of Canterbury 5, Canterbury.

Boast, R. 1990, *The Categorisation and Design Systematics of British Beakers: A Re-examination*, Cambridge University, Unpublished PhD.

Boast, R. 1995, Fine pots, pure pots, Beaker pots. In Kinnes & Varndell (eds) 1995, 69–80.

Bond, D. 1988, *Excavation at the North Ring, Mucking, Essex*, East Anglian Archaeology 43, Chelmsford.

Boon, G.C. 1969, Belgic and Roman Silchester: the excavations of 1954–8: with an excursus on the early history of Calleva, *Archaeologica* 102, 1–81.

Boon, G.C. & Wymer, J. 1958, A Belgic cremation burial from Burghfield, *Berkshire Archaeological Journal* 66, 46–53.

Bowman, S. 1990, *Radiocarbon Dating*. The British Museum, London.

Boyle, A.M. 1999, Human Remains. In Barclay & Halpin (eds) 1999, 171–82.

Bradley, P., Parsons, M. & Tyler, R. 1997, The Excavation of two Barrows at Merton, Oxfordshire, *Oxoniensia* 62, 51–86.

Bradley, R. 1978, *The Prehistoric Settlement of Britain*. Routledge & Kegan Paul, London.

Bradley, R. 1984, *The Social Foundations of Prehistoric Britain*, Longmans, Harlow.

Bradley, R. 1990a, *The Passage of Arms; An archaeological Analysis of Prehistoric Hoards and Votive Deposits*, The University Press, Cambridge.

Bradley, R. 1990b, Perforated stone axe-heads in the British Neolithic: their distribution and significance, *Oxford Journal of Archaeology* 9, 299–304.

Bradley, R. 1992, The excavation of an oval barrow beside the Abingdon causewayed enclosure, Oxfordshire, *Proceedings of the Prehistoric Society* 58, 127–42.

Bradley, R. 1993, *Altering the Earth*, Society of Antiquaries for Scotland, Edinburgh.

Bradley, R. & Edmonds, M. 1993, *Interpreting the Axe Trade*, The University Press, Cambridge.

Bradley, R. & Ellison, A.B. 1975, *Rams Hill: a Bronze Age Defended Enclosure and its Landscape*, British Archaeological Reports 19, Oxford.

Bradley, R., Entwhistle, R. & Raymond, F. 1994, *Prehistoric Land Divisions on Salisbury Plain*, English Heritage Archaeological Report 2, London.

Bradley, R. & Fulford, M. 1980, Sherd size in the analysis of occupation debris, *Bulletin of the Institute of Archaeology* 17, 85–94.

Bradley, R. & Gardiner, J. (eds) 1984, *Neolithic Studies: A Review of Some Current Research*, British Archaeological Reports British Series 133, Oxford.

Bradley, R. & Gordon, K. 1988, Human skulls from the river Thames, their dating and significance, *Antiquity* 62 (236), 503–9.

Bradley, R., Lobb, S., Richards, J. & Robinson, M. 1980, Two Late Bronze Age Settlements on the Kennet gravels: excavations at Aldermaston Wharf and Knights' Farm, Burghfield, Berkshire, *Proceedings of the Prehistoric Society* 46, 217–95.

Brailsford, J. 1948, Excavations at Little Woodbury, part II, *Proceedings of the Prehistoric Society* 14, 1–23.

Brailsford, J.W. 1957, The Durotrigian culture, *Proceedings of the Dorset Natural History and Archaeological Society* 79, 118–121.

Brailsford, J.W. 1958, Early Iron Age 'C' in Wessex, *Proceedings of the Prehistoric Society* 24, 101–119.

Braithwaite, M. 1982, Decoration as ritual symbol: a theoretical proposal and an ethnographic study in southern Sudan. In I. Hodder (ed.) 1982, 80–88.

Braithwaite, M. 1984, Ritual and prestige in the prehistory of Wessex c. 2200–1400 BC: a new dimension to the archaeological evidence. In Miller & Tilley (eds) 1984, 93–110.

Brannigan, K. & Foster, S. 1995, *Barra. Archaeological Research on Ben Tangaval*, Academic Press, Sheffied.

Braun, D. 1983, Pots as tools. In J.A. Moore & A.S. Keene (eds) 1983, 107–134.

Braun, D. 1991, Why decorate a pot? Midwestern household pottery, 200BC – AD600, *Journal of Anthropological Archaeology* 10, 367–397.

Briggs, C.S., Britnell, W.J. & Gibson, A.M. 1990, Two cordoned urns from Fan y Big, Brecon Beacons, Powys, *Proceedings of the Prehistoric Society* 56, 173–178.

Bronitsky, G. & Hamer, R. 1986, Experiments in ceramic technology; the effects of various tempering materials on impact and thermal-shock resistance, *American Antiquity* 51, 89–101.

Brown, A. 1991, Structured deposition and technological change among the flaked stone artefacts from Cranborne Chase. In Barrett, Bradley & Hall (eds) 1991, 101–33,

Brown, G., Field, D. & McOmish D. 1994, East Chisenbury midden complex. In Fitzpatrick & Morris (eds) 1994, 46–9.

Brown, L. 1987, The later prehistoric pottery. In Cunliffe 1987, 207–66.

Brown, L. 1991a, Later prehistoric pottery. In Sharples 1991, 185–205.

Brown, L. 1991b, Iron Age pottery. In Cunliffe & Poole 1991b, 277–319.

Brown, L. 1997, Marketing and commerce in late Iron Age Dorset: the Wareham/Poole harbour pottery industry. In Gwilt & Haselgrove (eds) 40–45.

Brown, N. 1988, A Late Bronze Age enclosure at Lofts Farm, Essex, *Proceedings of the Prehistoric Society* 54, 249–302.

Brown, N. 1992, Prehistoric pottery, In Early Iron Age settlement at Maldon and the Maldon 'burh': excavations at Beacon Green 1987, *Essex Archaeology and History* 23, 10–24.

Brown, N. 1995, Ardleigh reconsidered: Deverel-Rimbury pottery in Essex. In Kinnes & Varndell (eds), 123–144.

Brown, N. 1997, The Archaeology of Essex 1500-500 BC, In Bedwin 1997, 26–37.

Bryant, S. 1995, The late Bronze Age to the Middle Iron Age in the Chilterns. In Holgate (ed.) 1995, 17–27.

Bryant, S. 1997, Iron Age. In Glazebrook (ed.) 1997 23–34.

Budd, P., Chapman, B., Jackson, C., Janaway, R. & Ottaway, B. (eds), 1989, *Archaeological Sciences 1989*, Oxbow Monographs 9, Oxford.

Bulleid, A. & Gray, H. St. George 1911, *The Glastonbury Lake Village Volume 1*, Glastonbury.

Bulleid, A. & Gray, H. St. George 1917, *The Glastonbury Lake Village Volume 2*, Glastonbury.

Burgess, C.B. 1980, *The Age of Stonehenge*. Dent, London.

Burgess, C.B. 1986, 'Urns of no small variety': Collared Urns reviewed, *Proceedings of the Prehistoric Society* 52, 339–51.

Burgess, C.B. & Miket, R. (eds) 1976, *Settlement and Economy in the Third and Second Millennia B.C.* British Archaeological Reports British Series 33, Oxford.

Burnham, B.C. & Johnson, H.B. (eds) 1979, *Invasion and Response. The Case of Roman Britain*. British Archaeological Reports British Series 73, Oxford.

Burnham, B.C. & Kingsbury, J. (eds) 1979, *Space, Hierarchy and Society*, British Archaeological Reports International Series 59, Oxford.

Burl, H.A.W. 1976, *Stone Circles of the British Isles*, Yale University Press, Yale & London.

Burstow, G.P. & Holleyman, G.A. 1957, Late Bronze Age settlement on Itford Hill, Sussex, *Proceedings of the Prehistoric Society* 23, 167–212.

Bushe-Fox, J.P. 1925, *Excavation of the Late-Celtic Urn-field at Swarling, Kent*, Reports of the Research Committee of the Society of Antiquaries of London, 5, Oxford.

Campbell, E. 1991, Excavations of a wheelhouse and other Iron Age structures at Sollas, North Uist by R.J.C. Atkinson in 1957, *Proceedings of the Society of Antiquaries of Scotland*, 121, 117–73.

Carney, J. 1998a, *Petrographic Examination of Pottery Sherds from Sites at Swarkestone Lowes and Gamston*, British Geological Survey (report 141/98/10/JNC).

Carney, J. 1998b, *Petrographic Examination of Pottery sherds from Gamston*, British Geological Survey (report 126/98/34/JNC).

Case, H.J. 1956a, The Neolithic causewayed camp at Abingdon, Berks, *Antiquaries Journal*, 36, 11–30.

Case, H.J. 1956b, Beaker pottery from the Oxford region, *Oxoniensia* 21, 1–21.

Case, H.J. 1977, The Beaker culture in Britain and Ireland. In Mercer (ed.) 1977, 71–101.

Case, H.J. 1995a, Beakers: loosening a stereotype. In Kinnes & Varndell (eds) 1995, 55–67.

Case, H.J. 1995b Some Wiltshire Beakers and their contexts, *Wiltshire Archaeological Magazine* 88, 1–17.

Case, H.J., Bayne, N., Steele, S., Avery, M. & Sutermeister, H. 1964–5, Excavations at City Farm, Hanborough, Oxon, *Oxoniensia* 29–30, 1–98.

Case, H.J. & Sturdy, D. 1959, Archaeological notes, *Oxoniensia* 24, 98–102.

Case, H.J. & Whittle, A.W.R. 1982, *Settlement Patterns in the Oxford Region: Excavations at the Abingdon Causewayed Enclosure and Other Sites*, Council for British Archaeology Research Report No. 44, London.

Challis, A.J. & Harding, D.W. 1975, *Later Prehistory from the Trent to the Tyne*, British Archaeological Reports British Series 20, Oxford.

Chappel, T. 1977, *Decorated Gourds in North-eastern Nigeria*, Ethnographica, London.

Charters, S., Evershed, R.P., Quye, A., Blinkhorn, P.W. & Reeves, V. 1997, Simulation experiments for determining the use of ancient pottery vessels: the behaviour of epicuticular leaf wax during boiling of a leafy vegetable, *Journal of Archaeological Science* 24, 1–7.

Champion, S. 1994, Regional studies: a question of scale. In Kristiansen & Jensen (eds) 1994, 145–150.

Champion, T.C. 1975, Britain in the European Iron Age, *Archaeologia Atlantica* 1, 127–45,

Champion, T.C. 1994, Socio-economic development in Eastern England in the first Millennium B.C. In Kristiansen & Jensen (eds) 1994, 125–144.

Champion, T.C. & Collis, J. (eds) 1996, *Recent Trends in the Archaeology of Iron Age Britain*, JR Collis publications, Sheffield.

Champion, T., Gamble, C., Shennan, S. & Whittle, A. 1984, *Prehistoric Europe*, Academic Press, London and New York.

Childe, V.G. 1931, *Skara Brae: a Pictish village in Orkney*, London.

Christie, P.M.L. 1978, The excavation of an Iron Age souterrain and settlement at Carn Euny, Sancreed, Cornwall, *Proceedings of the Prehistoric Society*, 44, 309–433.

Chowne, P. 1978, Billingborough Bronze Age settlement: an interim note, *Lincolnshire History and Archaeology* 13, 15–21.

Chowne, P. 1980, Bronze Age settlement in south Lincolnshire. In Barrett & Bradley (eds) 1980, 295–305,

Chowne, P. 1988, *Aspects of Late Prehistoric Settlement in Lincolnshire: a study of the Western Fen Margin and Bain Valley*, Unpublished PhD thesis, University of Nottingham.

Chowne, P., Cleal, R.M., & Fitzpatrick, A.P. with Andrews, P. 2001, *Excavations at Billingborough, Lincolnshire, 1975–8. A Bronze-Iron Age Settlement and Salt-working Site*, East Anglian Archaeology 94.

Chowne, P. & Lane, T. 1987, Bronze Age cremation cemeteries at Old Somerby and Ropsley and Humby, *Lincolnshire History and Archaeology* 22, 35–40.

Clark, A. 1991, Archaeomagnetic dating. In Sharples 1991, 105 and fiche for chapter 4.

Clark, J.G.D. 1952, *Prehistoric Europe: The Economic Basis*, Methuen, London.

Clark, J.G.D, Higgs, E.S. & Longworth, I.H. 1960, Excavations at the Neolithic site at Hurst Fen, Mildenhall, Suffolk, *Proceedings of the Prehistoric Society* 26, 202–45.

Clarke, D.L. 1968, *Analytical Archaeology*, Methuen, London.

Clarke, D.L. 1970, *Beaker Pottery of Great Britain and Ireland*, Cambridge University Press, Cambridge.

Clarke, D.L. 1972, A provisional model of an Iron Age society and its settlement system. In D. Clarke (ed.) 1972, 801–869.

Clarke, D.L. (ed.) 1972, *Models in Archaeology*, Methuen, London.

Clarke, D.L. 1976, The Beaker network. In Lanting & van der Waals (eds) 1976, 5–54.

Clarke, D.L. (ed.) 1977, *Spatial Archaeology*, Academic Press, London.

Clarke, D.V. 1971, Small finds in the Atlantic province: problems of approach, *Scottish Archaeological Forum*, 3, 22–54.

Clarke, D.V. 1978, Excavation and volunteers: a cautionary tale, *World Archaeology* 10, 63–70.

Clarke, D.V., Cowie, T.G. & Foxon, A. 1985, *Symbols of Power at the Time of Stonehenge*, National Museum of Antiquities of Scotland, Edinburgh.

Claassen, C. (ed.) 1992, *Exploring Women through Archaeology*, Prehistory Press, Michigan.

Clay, P. 1992, An Iron Age farmstead at Grove Farm, Enderby, Leicestershire, *Transactions of the Leicestershire Archaeological and Historical Society* 66, 1–82.

Clay, P. & Mellor, J. 1985, *Excavations in Bath Lane, Leicester*, Leicestershire County Council Museums, Arts and Record Services 10, Leicester.

Clay, P. & Pollard, R. 1994, *Iron Age and Roman Occupation in the West Bridge Area, Leicester. Excavations 1962–1971*, Leicestershire County Council Museums, Arts and Record Services.

Clay, R.C.C. 1925, An inhabited site of La Tene 1 date on Swallowcliffe Down, *Wiltshire Archaeological Magazine* 42, 457–96.

Cleal, R.M. 1988, The occurrence of drilled holes in later Neolithic pottery, *Oxford Journal of Archaeology* 7 (2), 139–45.

Cleal, R.M. 1991a, The earlier prehistoric pottery. In Sharples 1991, 171–185.

Cleal, R.M. 1991b, Cranborne Chase – the earlier prehistoric pottery. In Barrett, Bradley & Hall (eds) 1991, 134–200.

Cleal, R.M. 1992, Significant form: ceramic styles in the Earlier Neolithic of southern England. In Sharples & Sheridan (eds) 1992, 286–304.

Cleal, R.M. 1995, Pottery fabrics in Wessex in the fourth to second millennia BC. In Kinnes & Varndell (eds) 1995, 185–194.

Cleal, R.M., Cooper, J. & Williams, D. 1994, Shells and sherds: identification of inclusions in Grooved Ware, with associated Radiocarbon Dates, from Amesbury, Wiltshire, *Proceedings of the Prehistoric Society* 60, 445–8.

Cleal, R.M. & MacSween, A. 1999, *Grooved Ware in Britain and Ireland*, Oxbow Monographs, Oxford.

Cleary, R.M. 1995, Irish later Bronze Age pottery: a preliminary technological assessment. In Linhal & Stilborg (eds) 1995, 77–90.

Clifford, E.M. 1961, *Bagendon: A Belgic Oppida*, Heffers, Cambridge.

Coles, J.M. & Coles, B.J. 1986, *Sweet Track to Glastonbury. The Somerset Levels in Prehistory*, Thames & Hudson, London.

Coles, J.M., Coles, B.J. & Morgan R.A. 1988, Excavations at the Glastonbury Lake Village 1984, *Somerset Levels Papers*, 14, 57–62.

Coles, J.M., Hibbert, F.A. & Orme, B.J. 1973, Prehistoric Roads and Tracks in Somerset: 3. The Sweet Track, *Proceedings of the Prehistoric Society* 39, 256–93.

Coles, J.M. & Minnitt, S. 1995, *'Industrious and Fairly Civilized'. The Glastonbury Lake Village*, Somerset Levels Project and the Somerset County Council Museums Service, Taunton.

Coles J.M., Orme, B.J., May, J. & Moore, C.N. 1979, Excavations of Late Bronze Age or Iron Age date at Washingborough Fen, *Lincolnshire History and Archaeology* 14, 5–10.

Coles J.M & Simpson, M. (eds) 1968, *Studies in Ancient Europe. Essays presented to Stuart Piggott*, Leicester University Press.

Collis, J.R. 1977a, The proper study of mankind is pots. In Collis (ed) 1971, 29–37.

Collis, J.R. 1977b, Iron Age henges?, *Archaeologica Atlantica* 2, 55–63.

Collis, J.R. (ed.) 1977c, *The Iron Age in Britain: A Review*, Department of Archaeology and Prehistory, University of Sheffield.

Collis, J.R.1984, *The European Iron Age*, Batsford, Iron Age.

Collis, J. 1985, Review of *Danebury: An Iron Age Hillfort in Hampshire, Vols 1 and 2*, by B.W. Cunliffe, *Proceedings of the Prehistoric Society* 51, 348–9.

Collis, J.R. Forthcoming, *Actes du 18ème Colloque de l'Association Française pour l'Étude de l'Age du Fer, Winchester, Mai 1994*, University of Sheffield Publications, Sheffield.

Colston, B.J. 1996, Neutron activation analysis of pottery from Dragonby and Ancaster, In May 1996, 422–428.

Conkey, M. & Hastorf, C. (eds) 1990, *The Uses of Style in Archaeology*, The University Press, Cambridge.

Coombs, D.G. & Thompson, F.H. 1979, Excavation of the hillfort of Mam Tor, Derbyshire, 1965–69, *Derbyshire Archaeological Journal* 99, 7–51.

Counihan, C. & Van Esterik, P. (eds) 1997, *Food and Culture: A Reader*, Routledge, London.

Costin, C. 1991, Craft specialization: Issues in defining, documenting and explaining the organisation of production, *Archaeological Method and Theory* 3, 1–56.

Cottam, S., Dungworth, D., Scott, S. & Taylor, J. (eds) 1994, *TRAC 94: Proceedings of the Fourth Theoretical Roman Archaeology Conference, Durham 1994*, Oxbow Books, Oxford.

Cotton, J. & Wood, B. 1996, Recent prehistoric finds from the Thames foreshore and beyond in Greater London, *Transactions of the London & Middlesex Archaeological Society* 47, 1–34.

Cowell, R.W., Fulford, M.G. & Lobb, S.J. 1978, Excavations of prehistoric and Roman settlement at Aldermaston Wharf 1976–77, *Berkshire Archaeological Journal* 69, 1–35.

Cowgill, G. 1972, Models, methods and techniques for seriation. In Clarke 1972, 381–424.

Cra'aster, M, 1961, The Aldwick Iron Age settlement, Barley, Hertfordshire, *Proceedings of the Cambridge Antiquarian Society* 54, 22–46.

Cra'aster, M, 1969, The New Addenbrokes Iron Age site, Long Road, Cambridge, *Proceedings of the Cambridge Antiquarian Society* 62, 21–28.

Crown, P. & Wills, 1995, Economic intensification and the origins of ceramic containers in the American Southwest. In Barnett & Hoopes (eds) 1995, 241–254.

Crummy, P. 1993, Aristocratic graves at Colchester, *Current Archaeology* 11, 492–7.

Cumberpatch, C. & Blinkhorn, P. (eds) 1997, *Not so Much a Pot, More a Way of Life*, Oxbow Monograph 83, Oxford.

Cunliffe, B.W. 1966, *Regional Groupings within the Iron Age of Southern Britain*, PhD thesis, Cambridge.

Cunliffe, B.W. 1968, Early pre-Roman Iron Age communities in eastern England. *Antiquaries Journal* 47, 1–44.

Cunliffe, B.W. 1974, *Iron Age Communities in Britain* (1st edition), Routledge & Kegan Paul Ltd, London.

Cunliffe, B.W. 1976, *Iron Age Sites in Central Southern England*, Council of British Archaeology Res. Rep. 16, London.

Cunliffe, B.W. 1978, *Iron Age Communities in Britain* (2nd edition), Routledge & Kegan Paul Ltd, London.

Cunliffe, B.W. 1984a, *Danebury: An Iron Age Hillfort in Hampshire. Vol. 1: The Excavations, 1969–1978: The Site*, Council for British Archaeology Research Report 52, London.

Cunliffe, B.W. 1984b, *Danebury: An Iron Age Hillfort in Hampshire. Vol. 2: The Excavations, 1969–1978: The Finds*, Council for British Archaeology Research Report 52, London.

Cunliffe, B.W. 1984c, Iron Age Wessex: continuity and change. In Cunliffe & Miles (eds) 1984, 12–45,

Cunliffe, B.W. 1987, *Hengistbury Head, Dorset, Vol. 1: The Prehistoric and Roman Settlement, 3500 B.C. – A.D. 500*, Oxford University Committee for Archaeology Monograph 13. Oxford University, Oxford.

Cunliffe, B.W. 1991, *Iron Age Communities in Britain* (3rd edition), Routledge, London.

Cunliffe, B.W. 1993, *Fertility, Propitiation and the Gods in the British Iron Age*, Amsterdam.

Cunliffe, B.W. 1995, *Danebury: An Iron Age Hillfort in Hampshire. Vol. 6: A Hillfort Community in Perspective*, Council for British Archaeology Research Report 102, York.

Cunliffe, B.W. & Brown, L. 1987, The later prehistoric and Roman pottery. In Cunliffe 1987, 205–321.

Cunliffe, B.W. & Jersey, P. de, 1997, *Armorica and Britain: Cross-Channel Relationships in the Late First Millennium BC*, Studies in Celtic Coinage 3, Oxford University Committee for Archaeology Monagraph 45, Oxford.

Cunliffe, B.W. & Miles, D. (eds) 1984, *Aspects of the Iron Age in Central Southern Britain*, Oxford University Committee for Archaeology Monograph 2, Oxford University, Oxford.

Cunliffe, B.W. & Orton, C. 1984, Radiocarbon age assessment. In Cunliffe 1984a, 190–8.

Cunliffe, B.W. & Poole, C. 1991a, *Danebury. An Iron Age Hillfort in Hampshire. Vol. 4. The Excavations, 1979–88: The Site*, Council for British Archaeology Research Report 73, London.

Cunliffe, B.W. & Poole, C. 1991b, *Danebury. An Iron Age Hillfort in Hampshire. Vol. 5. The Excavations, 1979–88: The Finds*, Council for British Archaeology Research Report 73, London.

Cunliffe, B. & Rowley, T. (eds) 1976, *Oppida: The Beginnings of Urbanisation in Barbarian Europe*, British Archaeological Reports International Series 11, Oxford.

Cunnington, M.E. 1923, *The Early Iron Age Inhabited Site at All Cannings Cross Farm, Wiltshire*, Devizes.

Curle, A.O. 1924, Two Late Neolithic vessels from the Thames, *Antiquaries Journal* 6, 129–50.

Curwen, E.C. 1929, Excavations in the Trundle, Goodwood 1928, *Sussex Archaeological Collections* 70, 33–85.

Curwen, E.C. 1941, Burnishing stones for pottery, *Antiquity* 15, 200–201.

Curwen, E. and E.C. 1927, Excavations in the Caburn near Lewes, *Sussex Archaeological Collections* 68, 1–56.

Dacre, M. & Ellison, A.B. 1981, A Bronze Age urn cemetery at Kimpton, Hampshire, *Proceedings of the Prehistoric Society* 47, 147–203.

Daire, M-Y. 1992, *Les Céramiques Armoricaines de la Fin de l'Age du Fer*, Travaux du Laboratoire d'Anthropologie et la Préhistoires Armoricaines 39, Rennes.

Dannell, G.B. 1977, The samian from Bagendon. In Dore & Greene (eds) 1977, 29–34.

Darling, M.J. 1988, The pottery. In Darling & Jones 1988, 9–37.

Darling, M.J. & Jones, M.J. 1988, Early settlement at Lincoln, *Britannia*, 19, 1–57.

Davidson, J.L. & Henshall, A.S. 1989, *The Chambered Cairns of Orkney*, Edinburgh.

Davies, J.A. 1996, Where eagles dare: the Iron Age of Norfolk, *Proceedings of the Prehistoric Society*, 62, 63–92.

Davies, J.A. & Williamson, T, (eds) Forthcoming, *The Land of the Iceni*, Norwich, Centre for East Anglian Studies.

Davies, S.M. 1981, Excavations at Old Down Farm, Andover. Part II Prehistoric and Roman, *Proceedings of the Hampshire Field Club*, 37, 81–163.

David, N., Sterner, J. & Gavua, K. 1988, Why pots are decorated? *Current Anthropology* 29(3), 365–389.

Deetz, J.F. 1965, *The Dynamics of Stylistic Change in Arikara Ceramics*, University of Illinois Press, Urbana.

Deetz, J.F. 1978, *In Small Things Forgotten*, Double Day, New York.

Detsicas, A.P. (ed.) 1973, *Current Research on Romano-British Coarse Pottery*, Council for British Archaeology Research Report, London.

Didsbury, P. & Steedman, K. 1992, Bronze Age and Early Iron Age pottery from pits at Barnetby Wold Farm, *Lincolnshire History and Archaeology* 27, 5–11.

Dietler, M. 1990, Driven by drink: The role of drinking in the political economy and the case of Early Iron Age France, *Journal of Anthropological Archaeology* 9, 352–406.

Dobres, M. 1995, Gender and prehistoric technology: on the social agency of technical strategies, *World Archaeology* 27(1), 25–49.

Doran, J.E. & Hodson, F.R. 1975, *Mathematics and Computers in Archaeology*, Edinburgh.

Dore, J. & Greene, K.T. (eds) 1977, *Roman Pottery Studies in Britain and Beyond*, British Archaeological Reports Supplementary Series 30, Oxford.

Douglas, M. 1966, *Purity and Danger*, London.

Douglas, M. 1975, Deciphering a meal, *Daedalus* 101, 61–81.

Down, A. 1978, *Chichester Excavations* III, Chicester Excavations Committee, Chichester.

Down, A. 1981, *Chichester Excavations* V, Chicester Excavations Committee, Chichester.

Drewett, P. (ed.) 1978, *Archaeology in Sussex to AD 1500*, Council for British Archaeology Research Report, London.

Drewett, P. 1979, New evidence for the structure and function of Middle Bronze Age roundhouses, *The Archaeological Journal* 136, 3–11.

Drewett, P. 1982a, Later Bronze Age Downland Economy and Excavations at Black Patch, East Sussex, *Proceedings of the Prehistoric Society* 48, 321–400.

Drewett, P. 1982b, *The Archaeology of Bullock Down, Eastbourne, East Sussex*, Sussex Archaeological Society Monograph.

Drewett, P. & Hamilton, S. 1999, Marking time and making space: excavations and landscape studies at the Caburn

hillfort, East Sussex 1996–98, *Sussex Archaeological Collections* 137.

Drury, P. 1978, *Excavations at Little Waltham, Essex*, Council for British Archaeology Research Report 26, London.

Dudd, S.N. & Evershed, R.P. 1998, Direct demonstration of milk as an element of archaeological economies, *Science* 282, 1478–1481.

Dudd, S.N & Evershed R.P. 1999, The organic residue analysis of the Neolithic pottery from Upper Ninepiece. In Gibson 1999, 112–120.

Dumont, L. 1952, A remarkable feature of south Indian pot-making, *Man* 52, 81–3.

Duval, A., Morel, J-P. & Roman, Y, (eds) 1990, *Gaule interne et Gaule méditerranéenne au IIème et Ier siècles avant J.C.: confrontations chronogiques*, Revue Archéologique de Narbonnaise Supplément 21, Paris.

Dyer, G. 1995, *The Missing of The Somme*, Penguin Books, London.

Earle, T. & Ericson, J.K. (eds) 1977, *Exchange Systems in Prehistory*, New York, Academic Press.

Earwood, C, 1993, *Domestic Wooden Artefacts in Britain and Ireland from Neolithic to Viking times*, University of Exter Press, Exeter.

Edmonds, M. 1990, Description, understanding and the Chain Operatoire, *Archaeological Review from Cambridge* 9(1), 55–70.

Edmonds, M. 1992, Their use is wholly unknown. In Sharples & Sheridan (eds) 1992, 179–93.

Edmonds, M, 1993, Interpreting causewayed enclosures in the past and the present. In Tilley (ed.) 1993, 99–142.

Edmonds, M. 1995, *Stone Tools and Society*, Batsford, London.

Elliott, L. & Knight, D. 1999, An Early Mesolithic site and first millennium BC settlement and pit alignments at Swarkestone Lowes, Derbyshire, *Derbyshire Archaeological Journal* 119, 79–153.

Ellis, P. (ed.) 1987, *Beeston Castle, Cheshire, Excavations by Laurence Keen and Peter Hough, 1968-85*, English Heritage Archaeological Report 23, London.

Ellis, S. & Crowther, D. (eds) 1990, *The Humber Region: A Region Through Time*, Hull University Press, Hull.

Ellison, A.B. 1972, The Bronze Age pottery. In Holden 1972, 104–113.

Ellison, A.B. 1975, *Pottery and settlements of the later Bronze Age in southern England*, unpublished PhD thesis: University of Cambridge.

Ellison, A.B. 1976–77, A petrological study of samples of Bronze Age pottery. In J. Bateman, A Late Bronze Age cremation cemetery and Iron Age/Romano-British enclosures in the parish of Ryton-on-Dunsmore, Warwickshire, *Trans. Birmingham Warwickshire Archaeological Society* 88, 19–20.

Ellison, A.B. 1978, The Bronze Age of Sussex. In Drewett (ed.) 1978, 30–37.

Ellison, A.B. 1980a, Deverel-Rimbury urn cemeteries: the evidence for social organisation. In Barrett & Bradley (eds) 1980, 115–126.

Ellison, A.B. 1980b, Settlements and regional exchange: a case study. In Barrett & Bradley (eds) 1980, 127–140.

Ellison, A.B 1981a, Towards a socio-economic model for the Middle Bronze Age in southern England. In Hodder, Isaac & Hammond (eds) 1981, 413–438.

Ellison, A.B. 1981b, Pottery and socio-economic change in British prehistory. In Howard & Morris (eds) 1981, 25–55.

Ellison, A.B. 1987, The Bronze Age Settlement at Thorny Down: pots, post-holes and patterning, *Proceedings of the Prehistoric Society* 53, 385–92.

Elsdon, S.M. 1975, *Stamp and Roulette Decorated Pottery of the La Tene Period in Eastern England*, British Archaeological Reports British Series 10, Oxford.

Elsdon, S.M. 1976, Note: The influence of Iron Age metalworking techniques as seen on the decoration of a pottery bowl from Hunsbury, Northants, *Northamptonshire Archaeology* 11, 163–165.

Elsdon, S.M. 1978, The pottery. In Christie 1978, 396–424.

Elsdon, S.M. 1979, The Iron Age pottery. In Wheeler 1979, 162–78.

Elsdon, S.M. 1982, Iron Age and Roman sites at Red Hill, Ratcliffe-on-Soar, Nottinghamshire: excavations of E. Greenfield, 1963 and previous finds, *Transactions of the Thoroton Society of Nottinghamshire* 89, 14–82.

Elsdon, S.M. 1989, *Later Prehistoric Pottery in England and Wales*, Shire Archaeology, Aylesbury.

Elsdon, S.M. 1992a, East Midlands Scored Ware, *Transactions of the Leicestershire Archaeological and Historical Society*, 66, 83–91.

Elsdon, S.M. 1992b, The Iron Age pottery. In Clay 1992, 38–52.

Elsdon, S.M. 1996a, *Iron Age Pottery in the East Midlands. A Handbook*. Department of Classics and Archaeology, University of Nottingham (second edition).

Elsdon, S.M. 1996b, Decoration and surface treatment. In May 1996, 428–36.

Elsdon, S.M. 1996c, Iron Age pottery from Salmonby, *Lincs. History and Archaeology* 31, 5–9.

Elsdon, S.M. 1997, *Old Sleaford Revealed*, Oxford.

Elsdon, S.M. (undated), *Late Iron Age Stamp and Roulette Decorated Pot from Odell, Beds. SP956568*, Unpublished report (Beds SMR).

Elsdon, S.M. & May, J. 1996, The Iron Age pottery. In May 1996, 397–512.

Ettlinger, E., Hedinger, B., Hoffmann, B., Kenrick, P.M., Pucci, G. Roth-Rubi, K., Schneider, G., Schnurbein, S., Wells, C.M., & Zabehlicky-Scheffenegger, S. 1990, *Conspectus Formae Terrae Sigillatae Italico Modo Confectae*, Materialien zur Römisch-Germanischen Keramik 10, Frankfurt.

Evans, C. 1989a, Archaeology and modern times: Bersu's Woodbury 1938 & 1939, *Antiquity* 63, 436–50.

Evans, C. 1989b, Perishables and worldly goods – artefact decoration and classification in the light of wetlands research, *Oxford Journal of Archaeology* 8, 179–202.

Evans, C. 1997, Hydraulic communities: Iron Age enclosure in the East Anglia fenlands. In Gwilt & Haselgrove (eds) 1997, 216–27.

Evans, C. Forthcoming, *The Later Iron Age and Conquest Period enclosure at Wardy Hill, Coveney*.

Evans, C. & Hodder, I. Forthcoming, *The Haddenham Project: Vol 2 Iron Age and Roman Fenland Landscapes*, MacDonald Institute, Cambridge.

Evans, C. & Serjeantson, D. 1988, The backwater economy and excavation of a Fen-edge community in the Iron Age: the Upper Delphs, Haddenham, *Antiquity* 62, 381–400.

Evans, A.J. 1890, On a late-Celtic urn-field at Aylesford, Kent ..., *Archaeologia*, 2nd Series, 52, Part 2, 315–88.

Evans, J. 1995, Later Iron Age and 'native' pottery in the north-east. In Vyner (ed.) 1995, 46–68.

Evans, J. & Millett, M.J. 1992, Residuality revisited, *Oxford Journal of Archaeology*, 11/2, 225–40.

Evans, J.G. 1990, Notes on some Late Neolithic and Bronze Age events in long barrow ditches in Southern and Eastern England, *Proceedings of the Prehistoric Society* 56, 111–6.

Evershed, R.P., Heron, C. & Goad, L.J. 1991, Epicuticular wax components preserved in potsherds as chemical indicators of leafy vegetables in ancient diets, *Antiquity* 65, 540–544.

Evershed, R.P., Heron, C., Charters, S. & Goad, L.J. 1992, The survival of food residues: new methods of analysis, interpretation and application. In Pollard (ed.) 187–208.

Fasham, P.J. 1985, *The Prehistoric Settlement at Winnall Down, Winchester*, Hampshire Field Club and Archaeological Society, Monograph 2.

Feinman, G.M., Upham, S. & Lightfoot, K.G., 1981, The production step measure: an ordinal index of labor input in ceramic manufacture, *American Antiquity* 46, 871–884.

Fell, C.I. 1936, The Hunsbury hillfort, Northants: a new survey of the material, *Archaeological Journal* 93, 57–100.

Ferdière, A., & Ferdière, M. 1972, Introduction à l'étude d'un type céramique: les urnes à bord mouluré gallo-romaines précoces, *Revue Archéologique de l'Est et du Centre-Est* 23, 77–88.

Ferrell, G. 1995, Space and society: new perspectives on the Iron Age of north-east England. In Hill & Cumberpatch (eds) 1995, 129–48.

Ferguson, L. 1989, Struggling with pots in colonial South Carolina. In McQuire & Paynter (eds) 1989, 28–39.

Fiddes, N. 1991, *Meat: A Natural Symbol*, Routledge, London.

Field, N. 1985–6, An Iron Age timber causeway at Fiskerton, Lincolnshire, *Fenland Research* 3, 49–53.

Field, N. & Knight, D. 1992, A later Bronze Age site at Kirmond le Mire, *Lincolnshire History and Archaeology* 27, 43–5,

Field, N. & White, A. (eds) 1984, *A Prospect of Lincolnshire*, F.N. Field & A.J. White, Lincoln.

Fisher, A.R. 1985, Winklebury hill-fort: a study of artefact distributions from subsoil features, *Proceedings of the Prehistoric Society* 51, 167–180.

Fitts, R.L., Haselgrove, C.C., Lowther, P.C, & Turnbull, P. 1994, An Iron Age farmstead at Rock Castle, Gilling West, North Yorkshire, *Durham Archaeological Journal*, 10, 13–42.

Fitzpatrick, A.P. 1984, The deposition of La Tène Iron Age metal work in watery contexts in Southern England. In Cunliffe & Miles (eds) 1984, 178–190.

Fitzpatrick, A.P. 1985, The distribution of Dressel I amphorae in north-west Europe, *Oxford Archaeological Journal* 4, 305–40.

Fitzpatrick, A.P. 1989, The uses of Roman imperialism by the Celtic barbarians in the later Republic. In Barrett, Fitzpatrick & Macinnes (eds) 1989, 27–54.

Fitzpatrick, A.P. 1992a, The Snettisham, Norfolk, hoards of Iron Age torques: sacred or profane, *Antiquity* 66, 395–398.

Fitzpatrick, A.P. 1992b, The roles of celtic coinage in southeast England. In Mays (ed.), 1992, 1–32.

Fitzpatrick, A.P. 1993, Ethnicity and exchange: Germans, Celts and Romans in the Late Iron Age. In Scarre & Healy (eds) 1993, 233–44.

Fitzpatrick, A.P. 1994, Outside in: the Structure of an Early Iron Age House at Dunston Park, Thatcham, Berkshire. In Fitzpatrick & Morris (eds), 68–72.

Fitzpatrick, A.P. 1997a, *Archaeological Excavations on the Route of the A27 Westhampnett Bypass, West Sussex, 1992. Vol.2 The Late Iron Age, Romano-British and Anglo-Saxon Cemeteries*, The Trust for Wessex Archaeology, Salisbury.

Fitzpatrick, A.P. 1997b, Everyday life in Iron Age Wessex. In Gwilt & Haselgrove 1997, 73–86.

Fitzpatrick, A.P. Forthcoming, Cross-Channel exchange, Hengistbury Head and the end of hillforts. In Collis (ed.) Forthcoming.

Fitzpatrick, A.P. Forthcoming, Roman amphorae in later Iron Age Britain. In Grew & Symonds (eds).

Fitzpatrick, A.P. Forthcoming, Iron Age brooch from Market Deeping. In Lane, Forthcoming.

Fitzpatrick, A.P. & Morris, E.L. (eds) 1994, *The Iron Age in Wessex: Recent Work*, Salisbury, Association Française d'Etude de l'Age du Fer and Wessex Archaeology.

Fletcher, R. 1977, Settlement studies (micro and semi-micro). In D. Clarke (ed.) 1977, 47–162.

Forcey, C., Hawthorne, J. & Witcher, R. (eds) 1998, *TRAC 97 Proceedings of the Seventh Annual Theoretical Roman Archaeology Conference*, Oxford, Oxbow Books, 1998.

Foster, J. 1986, *The Lexden Tumulus: A re-appraisal of an Iron Age Burial from Colchester, Essex*, British Archaeological Reports, British Series, Oxford.

Foster, S. 1992, Dating and the development of the Atlantic Iron Age: the impact of Carbon 14 on dating change in later prehistory. Paper presented at the New Approaches to the British Iron Age Seminar, University of Edinburgh, October 1992.

Fowler, E. 1960, The origins and development of the pennanular brooch in Europe, *Proceedings of the Prehistoric Society* 26, 149–77.

Fox, C.F. 1923, *The Archaeology of the Cambridge Region*, Cambridge.

Fox, C.F. 1958, *Pattern and Purpose: A Survey of Early Celtic Art in Britain*, National Museum of Wales, Cardiff.

Fox, C. 1959, *Life and Death in the Bronze Age: An Archaeologist's Fieldwork*, London.

Freestone, I. 1992, Petrology of the Bronze Age pottery. In Bewley *et al.* 1992, 340.

Freestone, I. & Rigby, V. 1988, The introduction of Roman ceramic styles and techniques into Roman Britain: a case study from the King Harry Lane cemetery, St Albans, Hertfordshire. In Sayre, E. *et al* (eds) 1988, 109–15.

Freestone, I. & Gaimster, D. (eds) 1997, *Pottery in the Making*, London, British Museum.

Frere, S.S. (ed.), 1961, *Problems of the Iron Age in Southern Britain*. London.

Friendship-Taylor, R.M. 1998, *Aspects of Late La Tène Pottery of the Nene and Welland Valleys of Northamptonshire: with Particular Reference to Channel-Rim Jars*, Unpublished M.Phil. thesis, University of Nottingham.

Friendship-Taylor, R.M. 2000, *Late La Tène Pottery of the Nene and Welland Valleys of Northamptonshire*, British Archaeological Reports British series 280, Oxford.

Fulford, M.G. & Huddlestone, K. 1991, *The Current State of Romano-British Pottery Studies. A Review for English Heritage*, English Heritage Occasional Paper 1, London.

Fulford, M.G. & Timby, J.R. 2001, *Excavations on the Site of the Forum-Basilica, Silchester*, Britannia Monograph, London.

Gale, F. 1979, The ceramics. In Wainwright 1979, 49–56.

Garton, D. 1987, Dunston's Clump and the brickwork plan field systems at Babworth, Nottinghamshire: excavations 1981, *Transactions of the Thoroton Society of Nottinghamshire* 91, 16–73.

Garwood, P., Jennings, D., Skeates, R. & Toms, R. (eds), 1991, *Sacred and Profane: Proceedings of a Conference on Archaeology, Ritual and Religion, Oxford, 1989*, Oxford University Committee for Archaeology, Monograph 32, Oxford.

Gell, A.S.R. 1949, An Early Iron Age site at Lakenheath, Suffolk, *Proceedings of the Cambridge Antiquarian Society* 42, 112–116.

Gent, H. 1983, Centralized storage in later prehistoric Britain, *Proceedings of the Prehistoric Society* 49, 243–268.

Gerrish, E.J.S. 1983, The prehistoric pottery from Mam Tor: further considerations, *Derbyshire Archaeological Journal* 103, 43–6.

Gero, J.M. 1992, Feasts and females: gender ideology and political meals in the Andes, *Norwegian Archaeological Review* 25(1), 15–30.

Gero, J.M. & Conkey, M.W. (eds) 1991, *Engendering Archaeology*, Oxford, Blackwell.

Gibson, A.M. 1978, *Bronze Age Pottery in the North-East of England*, British Archaeological Reports British Series 56, Oxford.

Gibson, A.M. 1986, The excavation of an experimental firing area at Stamford Hall, Leicester, 1985, *Bulletin of the Experimental Firing Group* 4, 5–14.

Gibson, A.M. 1995a, First impressions: a review of Peterborough Ware in Wales. In Kinnes & Varndell (eds) 1995, 23–40.

Gibson, A.M. 1995b, The neolithic pottery from Allt Chrisal. In Branningen & Foster 1995, 100–115.

Gibson, A.M. 1997, The Pottery. In W.J. Britnell *et al.* Excavations at Glanfeinion, Powys, *Proceedings of the Prehistoric Society* 63, 178–198.

Gibson, A.M. 1999, The Walton Basin Project: Excavation and survey in a prehistoric landscape 1993–7, Council for British Archaeology Research Report 118, York.

Gibson, A.M. & Kinnes, I.A. 1997, On the Urns of a Dilemma: Radiocarbon and the Peterborough Problem, *Oxford Journal of Archaeology* 16(1), 65–72.

Gibson, A.M. & Woods, A.J. 1997, *Prehistoric Pottery for the Archaeologist* (2nd Edition), Leicester University Press, Leicester.

Gilman, P.A., Canouts, V. & Bishop, R.L. 1994, The production and distribution of Classic Mimbres Black-on-White pottery, *American Antiquity* 59(4), 695–709.

Gingell, C. 1992, *The Marlborough Downs: A Later Bronze Age Landscape and its Origins*, Devizes.

Gingell, C. & Lawson, A. 1984, The Potterne project: excavation and research at a major settlement of the Late Bronze Age, *Wiltshire Archaeological and Natural History Magazine* 78, 31–4.

Glazebrook, J. (ed.) 1997, *Research and Archaeology: A Framework for the Eastern Counties*, East Anglian Archaeology Occasional Paper 3, Norwich.

Going, C.J. 1987, *The Mansio and Other Sites in the South-Eastern Sector of Caesaromagnus: The Roman Pottery*, Chelmsford Archaeological Trust Report 3.2, Council for British Archaeology Research Report 62, London.

Goody, J. 1982, *Cooking, Cuisine and Class*, Cambridge, The University Press.

Gosden, C. 1989, Debt, production and prehistory, *Journal of Anthropological Archaeology* 8, 355–387.

Gosselain, O. 1992, Technology and style: potters and pottery among Bafia of Cameroon, *Man* (N.S.), 27: 559–586.

Gosselain, O. & Livingstone-Smith, A. 1995, The ceramics and society project: An ethnographic and experimental approach to teachnological choices. In Linhal & Stilborg (eds) 1995, 147–160.

Graham, I., Galloway, P. & Scollar, J. 1976, Model studies in computer seriation, *Journal of Archaeological Science* 3, 1–30.

Gray, H. St George & Cotton, M.A. 1966, *The Meare Lake Village Volume III*. Taunton.

Grimes, W.F. 1953, Art on British Iron Age pottery, *Proceedings of the Prehistoric Society* 18, 160–75.

Green, C. 1980, Handmade pottery and society in Late Iron Age and Roman East Sussex, *Sussex Archaeological Collections*, 118, 69–86.

Green, M. 1986, *The Gods of the Celts*, Alan Sutton, Gloucester.

Greig, I. 1997, Excavation of a Bronze Age settlement at Varley Halls, Coldean Lane, Brighton, East Sussex, *Sussex Archaeological Collections* 135, 31–47.

Gregory, T. 1991, *Excavations in Thetford, 1980–1982: Fison Way*, East Anglian Archaeology 53, Norwich.

Grimes, W.F. 1960, *Excavations on defence sites, 1939–1945, 1: mainly Neolithic-Bronze Age*, Ministry of Works Archaeological Reports 3, HMSO London.

Grew, F. & Symonds R.P. Forthcoming, *Roman Amphorae: Recent Work*, Journal of Roman Pottery Studies, Special Edition, Oxbow, Oxford.

Guido, M. 1974, A Scottish crannog redated, *Antiquity*, 48, 54–6.

Guilbert, G. (ed.) 1981, *Hill-fort Studies: Essays for A.H.A. Hogg*, Leicester University Press.

Guilbert, G. & Vince, A. 1996, Petrology of some prehistoric pottery from Mam Tor, *Derbyshire Archaeological Journal* 116, 49–59.

Gurney, F.G. & Hawkes, C.F.C. 1940, An Early Iron Age inhumation burial at Egginton, Bedfordshire, *Antiquaries Journal* 20, 230–44.

Gwilt, A. 1995, Specialised cultural contact and innovation at a border? The context for the deposition of decorated bowls within a late Iron Age enclosure in Northamptonshire, Paper presented at the PCRG session at TAG'95, Reading, December 1995.

Gwilt, A. 1997, Popular practices from material culture: a case study of the Iron Age settlement at Wakerley, Northamptonshire. In Gwilt & Haselgrove (eds) 1997, 153–166.

Gwilt, A. & Haselgrove, C.C. (eds) 1997, *Reconstructing Iron Age Societies*, Oxbow Monograph 71, Oxbow, Oxford.

Haffner, A. & Miron, A. (eds) 1991, *Studien zur Eisenzeit im Hunsrück-Hahe-Raum*, Trierer Zeitschrift Beiheft 13.

Hains, B.A. & Horton, A. 1969, *Central England*, HMSO, London.

Hall. D.N. & Coles, J. 1994, *Fenland Survey: An Essay in Landscape and Persistence*, English Heritage, London.

Hall, D.N. & Nickerson, N. 1967, Excavations at Irchester, 1962–3, *Archaeological Journal* 129, 65–99.

Hally, D.J. 1983, Use alteration of pottery vessel surfaces: an important source of evidence for the identification of vessel function, *North American Archaeologist* 4, 1–25.

Hally, D.J. 1986, The identification of vessel function: a case study from northwest Georgia, *American Antiquity* 51 (2), 267–295.

Halstead, P., Hodder, I. & Jones, M. 1978, Behavioural archaeology and refuse patterns: a case study, *Norwegian Archaeological Review* 11, 118–31.

Hamilton, S. 1977, The Iron Age pottery. In Bell 1977, 83–117.

Hamilton, S. 1979, The Iron Age pottery. In Bedwin 1979, 27–30.

Hamilton, S. 1980, The Iron Age pottery, In Bedwin 1980, 196-203.

Hamilton, S. 1982, The Iron Age pottery. In Drewett 1982b, 81–89.

Hamilton, S. 1984, Earlier first millennium BC pottery from the excavations at Hollingbury Camp, Sussex, 1967–9, *Sussex Archaeological Collections* 122, 55–61.

Hamilton, S. 1985, Iron Age pottery. In Bedwin & Holgate 1985, 220–228.

Hamilton, S. 1987, The Late Bronze Age pottery. In Rudling 1987, 59–61.

Hamilton, S. 1988, Earlier first millennium BC pottery from Rectory Road and Baker Street. In Wilkinson 1988, 75–80.

Hamilton, S. 1993, *First Millennium BC Pottery Traditions in Southern Britain*, University of London unpublished Ph.D. thesis.

Hamilton, S. 1994, Bronze Age pottery, In Priesley-Bell 1994, 42-44.

Hamilton, S. 1997, East Sussex later Bronze Age pottery traditions: the assemblage from Varley Halls. In Greig 1997, 31–47.

Hamilton, S. & Manley, J. 1997, Points of view: prominent enclosures in 1st millennium BC Sussex, *Sussex Archaeological Collections* 134, 93–112.

Harding, D.W. 1966, An Iron Age site at Kirtlington, Oxon., *Oxoniensia* 31, 157–61.

Harding, D.W. 1972, *The Iron Age in the Upper Thames Basin*, Clarendon Press, Oxford.

Harding, D.W. 1974, *The Iron Age in Lowland Britain*, Routledge and Kegan Paul, London.

Harding, D.W. (ed.) 1982, *Later Prehistoric Settlement in South-East Scotland*, University of Edinburgh Department of Archaeology Occasional Paper 8, Edinburgh.

Hardy, H.R. & Curwen, E.C. 1937, An Iron Age pottery site near Horsted Keynes, *Sussex Archaeological Collections* 78, 252–265.

Haselgrove, C.C. 1976, External trade ad a stimulus to urbanization. In Cunliffe & Rowley, (eds) 1976, 25–50.

Haselgrove, C.C. 1982, Wealth, prestige and power: The dynamics of Late Iron Age centralization in South Eastern England. In Renfrew & Shennan (eds) 1982, 79–88.

Haselgrove, C.C. 1984, The later pre-Roman Iron Age between the Humber and the Tyne. In Wilson, Jones & Evans (eds) 1984, 9–25,

Haselgrove, C.C. 1986, An Iron Age community and its hillfort: the excavations at Danebury, Hampshire, 1969–78, *The Archaeological Journal*, 143, 363–9.

Haselgrove, C.C. 1987, *Iron Age Coinage in South-East England: The Archaeological Context*, British Archaeological Reports British Series 174, Oxford.

Haselgrove, C.C. 1988, The archaeology of British potin coinage, *The Archaeological Journal*, 145, 99–122.

Haselgrove, C.C. 1989, The later Iron Age in southern Britain and beyond. In Todd (ed.) 1989, 1–18.

Haselgrove, C.C. 1992, Warfare, ritual and society in Iron Age Wessex, *The Archaeological Journal*, 149, 407–15.

Haselgrove, C.C. 1995, Potin coinage in Iron Age Britain: archaeology and chronology, *Gallia*, 52, 117–27.

Haselgrove, C.C. 1996, Roman impact on rural settlement and society in southern Picardy. In Roymans (ed.) 1996, 127–187.

Haselgrove, C.C. 1997, Iron Age brooch deposition and chronology. In Gwilt & Haselgrove (eds) 1997, 51–72.

Haselgrove, C.C., Armit, I., Champion, T.C., Creighton, J.D., Gwilt, A., Hill, J.D., Hunter, F., & Woodward, A. 2001, *Understanding the British Iron Age: An Agenda for Action*, Iron Age Research Seminar & Prehistoric Society, Wessex Archaeology, Salisbury.

Haselgrove, C.C., Fitts, R.L., Willis, S.H. & Turnbull, P. Forthcoming, Excavations in Tofts Field, Stanwick, North Yorkshire.

Haselgrove, C.C., Turnbull, P., & Fitt, R. 1990, Stanwick, North Yrokshire: Recent research. *Archaeological Journal* 147, 1–15.

Hawkes, C.F.C. 1939, The Caburn pottery and its implications, *Sussex Archaeological Collections* 80, 217–262.

Hawkes, C.F.C. 1959, The ABC of the British Iron Age, *Antiquity* 33, 170–182.

Hawkes, C.F.C. 1995, Camulodunum. In Hawkes & Crummy 1995, 3–69.

Hawkes, C.F.C. & Crummy, P. 1995, *Camulodunum 2*. Colchester Archaeological Report 11, Colchester Archaeological Trust, Colchester.

Hawkes, C.F.C. & Dunning, G.C. 1931, The Belgae of Gaul and Britain, *Archaeological Journal* 87, 150–335.

Hawkes, C.F.C. & Fell, C.I. 1943, The Early Iron Age settlement at Fengate, Peterborough, *Archaeological Journal* 100, 188–223.

Hawkes, C.F.C. & Hull, M.R. 1947, *Camulodunum. First Report on the Excavations at Colchester 1930–1939*, Reports of the Research Committee of the Society of Antiquaries of London 14, Oxford.

Hawkes, S.C. 1969, Finds from two Middle Bronze Age pits at Winnall, Winchester, Hants., *Proceedings of the Hampshire Field Club* 26, 5–18.

Hawkes, S.C. 1994, Longbridge Deverill Cow Down, Wiltshire, House 3: a major round house of the Early Iron Age, *Oxford Journal of Archaeology* 13, 49–69.

Hawkes, J. 1985, The prehistoric pottery. In Fasham 1985, 60–69.

Hayden, B, & Cannon, A. 1983, Where all the garbage goes: refuse disposal in the Maya highlands, *Journal of Anthropological Archaeology* 2, 117–163.

Hayes, P.P. & Lane, T.W. 1992, *The Fenland Project Number 5: Lincolnshire Survey, the South-West Fens*, East Anglian Archaeology Report No.55, Heritage Trust of Lincolnshire.

Healy, F. 1995, Pots, pits and peat: ceramics and settlement in East Anglia. In Kinnes & Varndell (eds) 1995, 173–184.

Henderson, J. 1991, Industrial specialization in late Iron Age Britain and Europe, *Archaological Journal* 148, 104–148.

Hearne, C.M. & Cox, P. 1994, The development of settlement, Industry and trade on the Purbeck Heath and southern shore of Poole Harbour, Dorset. In Fitzpatrick & Morris (eds) 1994, 102–106.

Hearne, C.M. & Heaton, M.J. 1994, Excavations at a Late Bronze Age settlement in the Upper Thames Valley at Shorncote Quarry near Cirencester, 1992, *Trans. Bristol and Gloucestershire Archaeological Society* 112, 34–43.

Hedges, J. & Buckley, D. 1978, Excavations at a Neolithic causewayed enclosure, Orsett, Essex, 1975, *Proceedings of the Prehistoric Society* 44, 219–308.

Herbich, I. 1987, Learning patterns, potter interaction and ceramic style among the Luo of Kenya, *African Archaeological Review* 5, 193–204.

Heslop, D.H. 1987, *The Excavation of an Iron Age Settlement at Thorpe Thewles, Cleveland, 1980–1982*, Council for British Archaeology Research Report 65, London.

Hesnard, A. 1990, Les amphores. In Duval *et al* 1990, 47–54.

Henrickson, E.F. & McDonald, M.A. 1983, Ceramic form and function: an ethnographic search and an archaeological application, *American Anthropologist* 85, 630–643.

Herne, A. 1988, A time and a place for the Grimston Bowl. In Barrett & Kinnes (eds) 1995, 9–29.

Heron, C., Evershed, R.P. & Goad, L.J. 1991b, Effects of migration of soil lipids associated with buried potsherds, *Journal of Archaeological Science* 18, 641–659.

Heron, C., Evershed, R.P. Goad, L.J. & Denham, V. 1991a, New approaches to the analyses of organic residues from archaeological ceramics. In Budd, B. *et al* (eds) 1991, 332–339.

Heslop, D.H. 1987, *The Excavation of the Iron Age Settlement at Thorpe Thewles, Cleveland, 1980–82*, Council for British Archaeology Research Report 65, London.

Hill, J.D. 1989, Re-thinking the Iron Age, *Scottish Archaeological Review* 6, 16–24.

Hill, J.D. 1993, Can we recognise a different European past? A contrastive archaeology of later prehistoric settlement in southern England, *Journal of European Archaeology* 1(1), 57–76.

Hill, J.D. 1994, Why we should not take the data from Iron Age settlements for granted: recent studies of intra-settlement patterning. In Fitzpatrick & Morris (eds) 1994, 4–8.

Hill, J.D. 1995a, *Ritual and Rubbish in the Iron Age of Wessex*, British Archaeological Reports British Series 242, Oxford.

Hill, J.D. 1995b, The pre-Roman Iron Age in Britain and Ireland: an overview, *The Journal of World Prehistory* 9(1), 47–98.

Hill, J.D. 1995c, How should we study Iron Age societies and hillforts? A contextual study from Southern England. In Hill & Cumberpatch (eds), 1995, 45–66.

Hill, J.D. 1996, Report on the papers presented at the *Chronology and contact at the turn of the millennium* session at the AGM of the Prehistoric Ceramics Research Group, Oxford 1996, *The Old Potter's Almanack*, 4(2), 2–6.

Hill, J.D. 1997, 'The end of one kind of body and the beginning of another kind of body'? Toilet instruments and 'Romanization' in southern England during the first century AD. In Gwilt & Haselgrove (eds) 1997, *Reconstructing Iron Age Societies*, (Oxbow Monograph 71, Oxbow, Oxford), 96–107.

Hill, J.D. & Braddock, P. Forthcoming, The Iron Age pottery from Haddenham V. In Evans & Hodder Forthcoming.

Hill, J.D. & Cumberpatch, C. (eds), 1995, *Different Iron Ages: Studies on the Iron Age in Temperate Europe*, British Archaeological Reports International Series 602, Oxford.

Hill, J.D., Evans, C. & Alexander, M. 1999, Hinxton Rings, A late Iron Age cemetery at Hinxton, Cambridgeshire, with a reconsideration of northern Aylesford-Swarling distributions, *Proceedings of the Prehistoric Society* 65, 23–275.

Hill, J.D. & Horne, L. Forthcoming, The Later Iron Age and Conquest period pottery from Wardy Hill, Coveney. In Evans Forthcoming.

Hill, J.N. 1970, *Broken K Peublo: prehistoric social organization in the American southwest*, University of Arizona Press, Tucson.

Hill, P.H. 1982, Settlement and chronology, In Harding 1982, 4-43.

Hills, C. 1984, *The Blood of the British*, Channel 4, London.

Hillam, J. 1985, Recent tree-ring work in Sheffield, *Current Archaeology* 96, 21–26.

Hillman, G. 1981, Reconstructing crop husbandry practices from charred remains of crops. In Mercer (ed.) 1981, 123–62.

Hingley, R. 1990a, Boundaries surrounding Iron Age and Romano-British settlements, *Scottish Archaeological Review* 7, 96–103.

Hingley, R. 1990b, Domestic organisation and gender relations in Iron Age and Romano-British households. In Samson (ed.) 1990, 125–149.

Hingley, R. 1990c, Iron Age 'currency bars': The archaeological and social context, *Archaeological Journal* 147, 91–117.

Hingley, R. 1992, Society in Scotland from 700 BC to AD 200, *Proceedings of the Society of Antiquaries of Scotland* 122, 7–53.

Hodder, I, 1978, *The archaeology of the M11: Excavations at Wendons Ambo*, London.

Hodder, I. 1979, Social and economic stress and material culture patterning, *American Antiquity* 44, 446–54.

Hodder, I. 1982a, *Symbols in Action*, Cambridge University Press, Cambridge.

Hodder, I. (ed.) 1982b, *Symbolic and Structural Archaeology*, Cambridge, The University Press.

Hodder, I. 1982c, Sequences of structural change in the Dutch Neolithic. In Hodder (ed.) 1982b, 162–177.

Hodder, I. 1990a, *The Domestication of Europe*, Blackwell, Oxford.

Hodder, I. 1990b, Style as historical quality. In Conkey & Hastorf (eds) 1990, 44–51.

Hodder, I. 1991, The decoration of containers: An ethnographic and historical study. In Longacre (ed.) 1991, 71–95.

Hodder, I., Isaac, G. & Hammond, N. (eds) 1981, *Pattern of the Past: Studies in Honour of David Clarke*, The University Press, Cambridge.

Hodson, F.R. 1962, Some pottery from Eastbourne, the 'Marnians' and the pre-Roman Iron Age in southern England, *Proceedings of the Prehistoric Society* 28, 140–155.

Hodson, F. 1964, Cultural groupings within the British pre-Roman Iron Age, *Proceedings of the Prehistoric Society* 30, 99–110.

Hodson, F.R. 1980, Cultures as types? Some elements of classification theory, *Bulletin of the Institute of Archaeology*, University of London 17, 1–10.

Hodson, F., Kendall, D. & Tautu, P. (eds) 1971, *Mathematics in the Archaeological and Historical Sciences*, Edinburgh University Press, Edinburgh.

Holden, E.W. 1972, A Bronze Age Cemetery-Barrow on Itford Hill, Beddingham, Sussex, *Sussex Archaeological Collections* 110, 70–117.

Holgate, R. 1988, *Neolithic Settlement of the Thames Basin*, British Archaeological Reports British Series 194, Oxford.

Holgate, R. (ed.) 1995, *Chiltern Archaeology: Recent Work*, Dunstable, The Book Castle.

Hope, M. 1971, Iron Age Pottery in Leicestershire, BA thesis, University of Leicester.

Hope-Taylor, B. 1977, *Yeavering: an Anglo-British centre of early Northumbria*, London.

Howard, H. 1981, In the wake of distribution: towards an integrated approach to ceramic studies in prehistoric Britain. In Howard & Morris (eds) 1981, 1–30.

Howard, H. & Morris, E.L. (eds) 1981, *Production and Distribution: a Ceramic Viewpoint*, British Archaeological Reports International Series 120, Oxford.

Huntley, J.P. & Stallibrass, S. (eds) 1995, *Plant and Vertebrate Remains from Archaeological Sites in Northern England: Data Reviews and Future Directions*, Architectural and Archaeological Society of Durham and Northumberland Research Report 4, Durham.

Hughes, G. 1999, The excavation of an Iron Age cropmark site at Foxcovert Farm, Aston-on-Trent 1994, *Derbyshire Archaeological Journal* 119, 176–188.

Hull, G. 1998, The Excavation of a Late Bronze Age ringwork and pits and Late Iron Age Pits on land off Huntingdon Road, Thrapston, Northamptonshire', Unpublished report for David Wilson Homes Ltd., Thames Valley Archaeological Services.

Hunn, J.R. 1992, The Verulamium oppidum and its landscape in the late Iron Age, *Archaeological Journal* 149, 39–68.

Hunn, J.R. & Rackham, J. Forthcoming, *The Rectory Farm Project*. British Archaeological Reports British Series, Oxford.

Jackson, D. 1995, *When were 'middle Iron Age' ceramic assemblages in use in southern and eastern England?* University of Durham M.A. project, unpublished.

Jackson, D.A. 1974, Two new pit alignments and a hoard of currency bars from Northamptonshire, *Northamptonshire Archaeology* 9, 13–45,

Jackson, D.A. 1975, An Iron Age site at Twywell, Northamptonshire, *Northamptonshire Archaeology* 10, 31–93.

Jackson, D.A. 1977, Further excavations at Aldwincle, Northamptonshire, 1969–71, *Northamptonshire Archaeology* 12, 9–54.

Jackson, D.A. 1980, Roman buildings at Ringstead, Northants., *Northamptonshire Archaeology* 15, 12–34.

Jackson, D.A. 1981, Archaeology at an ironstone quarry in the Harringworth-Wakerley area 1968–79, *Northamptonshire Archaeology* 16, 14–33.

Jackson, D.A. & Ambrose, T. 1978, Excavations at Wakerley, Northamptonshire. 1972–5, *Britannia* 9, 115–242.

Jackson, D.A. & Dix, B. 1988, Late Iron Age and Roman settlement at Weekley, Northants, *Northamptonshire Archaeology*, 21, for 1986–7, 41–93.

Jackson, D.A, & Knight, D. 1985, An early Iron Age and Beaker site near Gretton, Northants, *Northamptonshire Archaeology* 20, 67–85.

Jacobsthal, P. 1944, *Early Celtic Art*, Oxford.

James, S. & Rigby, V. 1997, *Britain in the Celtic Iron Age*, London, British Museum.

Jarvis, P. 1986, The early pits of the Jewry Wall site, Leicester, *Leicestershire Archaeological and Historical Society Transactions* 60, 7–15,

Jersey, P. de, 1993, The early chronology of Alet, and its implications for Hengistbury Head and cross-channel trade in the Late Iron Age, *Oxford Journal of Archaeology* 12, 321–35.

Jesson, M. and Hill, D. (eds), *The Iron Age and its Hillforts* Southampton University Monograph Series 1, Southampton.

Jobey, G. 1959, Excavations at the native settlement at Huckhoe, Northumberland, 1955–57, *Archaeologia Aeliana*, 4th Series, 37, 217–78.

Jobey, G. 1968, A radiocarbon date for the palisaded settlement at Huckhoe, *Archaeologia Aeliana*, 4th Series, 46, 293–5.

Jobey, G. 1970, An Iron Age settlement and homestead at Burradon, Northumberland, *Archaeologia Aeliana*, 4th Series, 48, 51–95.

Jobey, I. & Jobey, G. 1987, Prehistoric, Romano-British and later remains on Murton High Crags, Northumberland, *Archaeologia Aeliana*, 5th Series, 15, 151–98.

Jones, M. 1986, *England Before Domesday*, Batsford, London.

Jones, M. 1992, Food remains, food webs and ecosystems. In Pollard (ed.) 1992, 209–219.

Jones, M. 1996, Plant exploitation. In Champion & Collis (eds) 1996, 29–40.

Jones, M. & Dimbleby, G. (eds), 1981, *The Environment of Man: the Iron Age to the Anglo-Saxon Period*, British Archaeological Reports British Series 87, Oxford.

Jones, M.U. 1975, A potter's tournette of the early Iron Age from Mucking, Essex, *Antiquaries Journal* 55, 408–9.

Jope, E.M. 1961a, The beginnings of the La Tène ornamental style in the British Isles. In Frere (ed.) 1961, 69–83.

Jope, E.M. 1961b, Daggers of the Early Iron Age in Britain, *Proceedings of the Prehistoric Society* 27, 307–43.

Jordan, D., Haddon-Reece, D. & Bayliss, A. 1994, *Radiocarbon Dates from Samples funded by English Heritage and Dated before 1981*, English Heritage, London.

Jundi, S. & Hill, J.D. 1998, Brooches and identities in first century AD Britain: More than meets the eye? In Forcey et al (eds) 1998, 125–137.

Kaenel, G. 1990, La dendrochronologie appliquée au Ile et ler siècle avant J.C. In Duval et al (eds) 1990, 321–6.

Keiller, A. & Piggott, S. 1939, Badshot long barrow, Oakley et al (eds) 1939, 133–49.

Kempton, W. 1981, *The Folk Classification of Ceramics*, Academic Press, New York.

Kendall, D.G. 1971, Seriation from abundance matrices. In Hodson et al (eds) 1971, 215–52.

Kenward, R. 1982, A Neolithic burial at New Wintles Farm, Eynsham. In Case & Whittle (eds) 1982, 10–50.

Kenyon, K.M. 1948, *Excavations at the Jewry Wall Site, Leicester*, Society Antiquaries London Research Report 15,

Kenyon, K.M. 1950, Excavations at Breedon-on-the-Hill, *Leicestershire Archaeological and Historical Society Transactions* 26, 37–82.

Kenyon, K.M. 1952, A Survey of the evidence concerning the chronology and origins of Iron Age 'A' in southern and midland Britain, *Bulletin of the Institute of Archaeology, University of London* 8, 29–78.

King, A. 1984, Animal bones and dietary identity of military and civilian groups in Roman Britain, Germany and Gaul. In Blagg & King (eds) 1984, 187–217.

Kingery, W. (ed.) 1986, *Technology and Style*, The American Ceramics Society, Inc., Columbus, Ohio.

Kingery, W. (ed.) 1993, *The Social and Cultural Contexts of New Ceramic Technologies*, Westerville, The American Ceramic Society.

Kinnes, I, 1978, The earlier prehistoric pottery. In Excavations at A Neolithic causewayed enclosure, Orsett, Essex 1975. *Proceedings of Prehistoric Society* 44, 259–68.

Kinnes, I. 1979, *Round Barrows and Ring-ditches in the British Neolithic*, British Museum Occasional Paper 7, London.

Kinnes, I, 1991, The Neolithic pottery. In Needham 1991, 57–61.

Kinnes, I. 1992, *Non-Megalithic Long Barrows and Allied Structures in the British Neolithic*, British Museum Occasional Paper 52, London.

Kinnes, I., Gibson, A., Ambers, J., Bowman, S., Leese, M. & Boast, R. 1991, Radiocarbon dating and British Beakers: the British Museum programme, *Scottish Archaeological Review* 8, 35–78.

Kinnes, I. & Longworth, I. 1985, *Catalogue of the Excavated Prehistoric and Romano-British Material in the Greenwell Collection*, London, British Museum Publications, London.

Kinnes, I. & Varndell, G. (eds) 1995, *'Unbaked Urns of Rudely Shape'*, Oxbow Monographs 55, Oxford.

Knight, D, 1984, *Late Bronze Age and Iron Age Settlement in the Nene and Great Ouse Basins*, British Archaeological Reports British Series 130, Oxford.

Knight, D, 1992, Excavations of an Iron Age settlement at Gamston, Nottinghamshire, *Transactions of the Thornton Society of Nottinghamshire* 96, 16–90.

Knight, D. 1997a, Iron Age Pottery from Sites Located during Archaeological Monitoring of the Eagle to Harby Water Main Pipeline, Unpublished report for Lindsey Archaeological Services, Trent & Peak Archaeological Trust, Nottingham.

Knight, D. 1997b, Revised guidelines for the analysis of later prehistoric pottery fabrics, *Old Potter's Almanack* 5 no. 2, 1–2.

Knight, D. 1999, Prehistoric Pottery and Fired Clay from Baston No.2 Quarry, Langtoft, Lincolnshire: Assessment Report, Unpublished report for Cambridge Archaeological Unit, Trent & Peak Archaeological Trust, Nottingham.

Knight, D. Forthcoming (a), The Late Bronze Age pottery from Stickford. In Lane Forthcoming.

Knight, D. Forthcoming (b), The Iron Age pottery from Cowbit. In Lane & Morris Forthcoming.

Knight D. Forthcoming (c), The Iron Age pottery from Market Deeping. In Lane Forthcoming.

Knight, D., Allen, C.S.M. & Appleton, E.M. Forthcoming, The prehistoric pottery. In Hunn & Rackham Forthcoming.

Knight, T.W. 1983, Transformations of languages of design: parts 1–3, *Planning and Design* 10:125–177.

Kolb, C.C. (ed.) 1987, *Ceramic Ecology Revisited*, British Archaeological Reports International Series 436, Oxford.

Kolb, C.C. & Lackey, L.M. (eds) 1988, *A Pot for All Reasons: Ceramic Ecology Revisited*, Philadelphia, Temple University.

Kramer, C. 1985, Ceramic ethnoarchaeology, *Annual Review of Anthropology* 14, 77–102.

Kristiansen, K. & Jensen, J. (eds) 1994, *Europe in the First Millennium B.C.* , J.R. Collis, Sheffield.

Lambrick, G.H. 1984, Pitfalls and possibilities in Iron Age pottery studies – experiences in the Upper Thames Valley. In Cunliffe & Miles (eds) 1984, 162–77.

Lambrick, G.H. 1994, Comments upon the calibration of C14 samples from Abingdon: Ashville Trading Estate, Oxfordshire. In Jordan, *et al.* 1994, 1.

Lane, A. 1990, Hebridean pottery: problems of definition, chronology, presence and absence. In Armit (ed.) 1990, 108–30.

Lane, T.W. 1992a, Iron Age and Roman salterns in the south-western Fens. In Hayes & Lane 1992, 218–229.

Lane, T.W. 1992b, Prehistoric ceramics. In Hayes & Lane 1992, 230–233.

Lane, T.W. Forthcoming, *Prehistoric Sites from the Fenland Management Project in Lincolnshire*, Lincolnshire Archaeology Heritage Report Series

Lane, T.W. & Morris, E.L. 2001, *A Millennium of Salt Making: Prehistoric and Romano-British Salt Production in the Fenland,* Lincolnshire Archaeology Heritage Report Series 4, Lincoln

Latour, B. & Woolgar, S. 1986, *Laboratory life: the con-struction of scientific facts*, Princeton University Press, Princeton, New Jersey.

Lawson, A.J. 1994, Potterne. In Fitzpatrick & Morris (eds) 1994, 42–46.

Leary, R.S. 1987, The pottery. In Garton 1987, 43–52.

Leeds, E.T. 1928, A Neolithic site at Abingdon, Berkshire (second report), *Antiquaries Journal* 8, 461–77.

Legge, A.J. 1991, The animal remains from six sites at Down farm, Woodcutts. In Barrett, Bradley & Hall (eds) 1991, 54–100.

Lemonnier, P. 1986, The study of material culture today: towards an anthropology of technical systems, *Journal of Anthropological Archaeology* 5.

Lemonnier, P. 1990, Topsy, turvy techniques: remarks on the social representation of techniques, *Archaeological Review from Cambridge* 9(1), 27–37.

Lemonnier, P. (ed.) 1993, *Technological Choices; Trans-formations in Material Culture Since the Neolithic*, London & New York.

Lethbridge, T.C. 1953, Burial of an Iron Age warrior at Snailwell, *Proceedings of the Cambridge Antiquarian Society* 47, 25–37.

Liddell, D. 1929, New light on an old problem, *Antiquity* 3, 283–91.

Liddle, P. 1982, *Leicestershire Archaeology – the Present State of Knowledge. Vol.1: to the end of the Roman Period*, Archaeological Reports no.4, Leicestershire Museums, Art Galleries and Records Service.

Lindhal, A. & Stilborg, O. (eds) 1995, *The Aim of Laboratory Analyses of Ceramics in Archaeology*, Stockholm, Royal Academy of Letters, History and Literature.

Lock, G. 1984a, Tests 3–5: Fabric change according to ceramic phase. In Cunliffe 1984b, 237–40.

Lock, G. 1984b, Test 9: Fine phasing by seriation within CP 7–8. In Cunliffe 1984b, 242–4.

Lock, G. 1991, Quantifying problem areas. In Cunliffe & Poole 1991b, 278–84.

Lock, G. 1995, Study 2: phasing the pits. In Cunliffe 1995, 118–23.

Lobb, S.J. & Morris, E.L. 1991–3, Investigation of Bronze and Iron Age features at Riseley Farm, Swallowfield, *Berkshire Archaeological Journal* 74, 37–68.

Loeschcke, S. 1909, Keramische funde in Haltern: ein beitrag zur geschichte der augusteischen kultur in Deutschland, *Mitteilungen der Altertumskommission für Westfalen* 5, 103–322.

Longacre, W.A. (ed.) 1991, *Ceramic Ethnoarchaeology*, University of Arizona Press, Tucson.

Longacre, W.A. 1970, *Archaeology as Anthropology: A case study*, University of Arizona Press, Tucson.

Longley, D. 1980, *Runnymede Bridge 1976: Excavations on the site of a Late Bronze Age Settlement*, Research Volume 6, Surrey Archaeological Society, Guildford.

Longworth, I.H. 1984, *Collared Urns of the Bronze Age in Great Britain and Ireland*, The University Press, Cambridge.

Longworth, I.H. 1990, Neolithic pottery: time to take another look, *Scottish Archaeological Review* 7, 77–9.

Mackreth, D.F. 1988, Excavation of an Iron Age and Roman enclosure at Werrington, Cambridgeshire, *Britannia* 19, 59–151.

Mackie, D. 1993, Prehistoric ditch systems at Ketton and

Tixover, Rutland, *Leicestershire Archaeological and Historical Society Transactions* 67, 1–14.

Macready, S. & Thompson, F. (eds) 1984, *Cross-Channel Trade between Gaul and Britain in the Pre-Roman Iron Age*, Society of Antiquaries, London.

MacSween, A. 1995, Grooved Ware from Scotland: aspects of decoration. In Kinnes & Varndell (eds) 1995, 41–48.

Mahias, M-C. 1993. Pottery techniques in India. In Lemonnier (ed.) 1993, 157–180.

Maltby, M. 1985, Patterns in faunal assemblage variability. In Barker & Gamble (eds) 1985, 33–74.

Maltby, M. 1994, Animal exploitation in Iron Age Wessex. In Fitzpatrick & Morris (eds) 1994, 9–10.

Maltby, M. 1996, The exploitation of animals in the Iron Age: the archaeo-zoological evidence. In Champion & Collis (eds) 1996, 17–27.

Manning, W.H. 1974, Excavations on Late Bronze Age, Roman and Saxon sites at Ufton Nervet, Berkshire in 1961–1963, *Berkshire Archaeological Journal* 67, 1–61.

Marsden, P. 1998, The prehistoric pottery. In Beamish 1998, 45–62.

Marshall, Y. 1985, Who made Lapita pots, *Journal of Polynesian Prehistory* 94(3).

Marshall, Y. & Maas, A. 1997, Dashing dishes, *World Archaeology* 28 (3), 275–290.

Matson, F.R. (ed.) 1965a, *Ceramics and Man*, Aldine, Chicago.

Matson, F.R. 1965b, Ceramic ecology: an approach to the study of the early cultures of the Near East. In Matson (ed.) 1965, 202–17.

Matthews, C.L. 1976, *Occupation Sites on a Chiltern Ridge; part 1: Neolithic, Bronze Age and Early Iron Age*, British Archaeological Reports British Series 29, Oxford.

May, J. 1976a, *Prehistoric Lincolnshire*, Lincoln.

May, J. 1976b, The growth of settlements in the later Iron Age in Lincolnshire. In Cunliffe & Rowley (eds) 1976, 163–80.

May, J. 1984, The major settlements of the later Iron Age in Lincolnshire. In Field & White (eds) 1984, 18–22.

May, J. 1996, *Dragonby. Report on Excavations at an Iron Age and Romano-British Settlement in North Lincolnshire, Vol.1 and 2*, Oxbow Monograph 61, Oxford.

Mays, M. 1992, *Celtic Coinage: Britain and Beyond*, British Archaeological Reports British Series 222, Oxford.

McKinley, J.I. 1994a, *The Anglo-Saxon Cemetery at Spong Hill, North Elmham Part VIII: The Cremations*, East Anglian Archaeology No 64, Norwich.

McKinley, J.I. 1994b, A pyre and grave goods in British cremation burials; have we missed something? *Antiquity* 68, 132–4.

McOmish, D. 1996, East Chisenbury: ritual and rubbish at the British Bronze Age-Iron Age transition, *Antiquity* 70, 68–76.

McGuire, R. & Paynter, R. (eds) 1989, *The Archaeology of Inequality*, Blackwell, Oxford.

Medlycott, M. 1994, Iron Age and Roman material from Birchanger, near Bishops Stortford; excavations at Woodside Industrial Park, 1992, *Essex Archaeology and History* 25, 28–45.

Mepham, L.N. 1997, Pottery. In Fitzpatrick 1997a, 114–38.

Mercer, R. (ed.) 1977, *Beakers in Britain and Europe*, British Archaeological Reports British Series 26, Oxford.

Mercer, R. (ed.) 1981, *Farming Practice in British Prehistory*, Edinburgh University Press.

Metzler, J. 1995, *Da Treverische Oppidum auf dem Titelberg*, Dossiers d'Archéologie du Musée Nationale d'Historie et d'Art 3. Luxembourg.

Middleton, A. 1996, Petrography. In May 1996, 419–21.

Middleton, A. & Freestone. I (eds), 1991, *Recent Developments in Ceramic Petrology*, British Museum Occasional Paper 81, London.

Miller, D. 1982, Structures and strategies: an aspect of the relationship between social heirarchy and cultural change. In I. Hodder 1982 (eds), 89–99.

Miller, D. 1985, *Artefacts as Categories*, Cambridge University Press, Cambridge.

Miller, D. & Tilley, C. 1984, *Ideology, Power and Prehistory*, Cambridge University Press, Cambridge.

Millett, M.J. 1979a, *Pottery and the Archaeologist*, London, Institute of Archaeology.

Millett, M.J. 1979b, The dating of Farnham (Alice Holt) pottery, *Britannia*, 10, 121–37.

Millett, M.J. 1987, A question of time? Aspects of the future of pottery studies, *Bulletin of the Institute of Archaeology*, 24, 99–108.

Millett, M.J. 1990a, *The Romanization of Britain*, The University Press, Cambridge.

Millett, M.J. 1990b, Iron Age and Roman settlement in the southern Vale of York and beyond. In Ellis & Crowther (eds) 1990, 347–356.

Millett, M.J. 1993, A cemetery in an age of transition: King Harry Lane reconsidered. In Struck (ed.) 1993, 255–82.

Millett, M.J. & Graham, D. 1986, *Excavations on the Romano-British Small Town at Neatham, Hampshire, 1969–1979*, The Hampshire Field Club with the Farnham and District Museum Society, Gloucester.

Millett, M.J & James, S. 1983, Excavations at Cowdery's Down, Basingstoke, Hampshire, 1978–81, *Archaeological Journal* 140, 151–279.

Millett, M.J. & McGrail, S. 1987, The archaeology of the Hasholme Logboat, *The Archaeological Journal*, 144, 69–155.

Millett, M.J. & Russell, D. 1984, An Iron Age and Romano-British site at Viables farm, Basingstoke, *Proceedings of the Hampshire Field Club* 40, 49–60.

Miron, A. 1986, Das gräberfeld von Horath: unter-surchumgen zur Mittel- und Spätlatènezeit im Saar-Mosel-Raum, *Trierer Zeitschrift*, 49, 7–198.

Miron, A. 1991, Die Späte Eisenzeit im Hunsrück-Nahe-Raum: mittel und spätlatènezeitliche Gräberfelder. In Haffner & Miron (eds) 1991, 151–69.

Mitchell, M. 1934, A new analysis of the Early Bronze Age potter of Scotland, *Proceedings of the Society of Antiquaries, Scotland* 68, 132–189.

Mizoguchi, K. 1995, The 'materiality' of Wessex Beakers, *Scottish Archaeological Review* 9/10, 175–85.

Moore, H.L. 1982, The interpretation of spatial patterning in settlement residues. In I. Hodder (ed.) 1982, 74–9.

Moore, H.L. 1986, *Space, Text and Gender*, The University Press, Cambridge.

Moore, J. & Jennings, D. 1992, *Reading Business Park: A Bronze Age Landscape*, Oxford University Committee for Archaeology, Oxford.

Moore, J.A. & Keene, A.S. (eds) 1983, *Archaeological*

Hammers and Theories, Academic Press, New York and London.

Moore, W.R.G. 1971, Chapel Brampton (SP 722664), Brampton Hill Farm, Interim report on the excavation of a middle or late Bronze Age cremation cemetery, *Bulletin of the Northamptonshire Federation of Archaeological Societies* 5, 1–2.

Moorhouse, S. 1986, Non-dating uses of Medieval pottery, *Medieval Ceramics* 10, 85–123.

Morgan, R.A. 1988, Tree-ring studies at Glastonbury and Meare. In Coles *et al.* 1988, 61–2.

Morris, E.L. 1978a, The Iron Age pottery. In Bedwin & Pitts 1978, 315–339.

Morris, E.L. 1978b, The pottery. In Bedwin 1978, 231–239.

Morris, E.L. 1983, Seriation analysis by fabric type of the Iron Age pottery. In Saville 1983, 18–9.

Morris, E.L. 1985, Prehistoric salt distributions: two case studies from Western Britain, *Bulletin Board Celtic Studies* 32, 336–379.

Morris, E.L. 1988, The Iron Age occupation at Dibble's Farm, Christon, *Proceedings of the Somerset Archaeological and Natural History Society*, 132, 23–81.

Morris, E.L. 1991, Ceramic analysis and the pottery from Potterne: a summary. In Middleton & Freestone (eds) 1991, 277–287.

Morris, E.L. 1993, How Much Copper Does It Take to Make a Pot? And Are Piggy Back Rides Allowed? Exchange Systems in Western Britain During the Iron Age, paper presented at the 1993 Theoretical Archaeology Group conference, Durham.

Morris, E.L. 1994a, Pottery. In C.M. Hearne & M.J. Heaton, 1994, 34–43.

Morris, E.L. 1994b, Production and distribution of pottery and salt in Iron Age Britain; a review, *Proceedings of the Prehistoric Society* 60, 371–93.

Morris, E.L. 1996, Iron Age artefact production and exchange. In Champion & Collis (eds) 1996, 41–65,

Morris, E.L. 1997a, Where is the Danebury Ware? In Gwilt & Haselgrove (eds) 1997, 36–39.

Morris, E.L. 1997b, Review of 'New Approaches to the Study of Organic Residues in Archaeological Ceramics' by Dr. R. Evershed, *The Old Potter's Almanack* 5 (1), 7–8.

Morris, E.L., Earl, G., Poppy, S., Westcott, K. & Champion, T.C. 1998, *The Later Prehistoric Pottery Collections Register and Bibliography for England: a Gazetteer*, Report for English Heritage on behalf of the Prehistoric Ceramics Research Group, University of Southampton.

Morris, E.L. & Gelling, P.S. 1991, A note on the Berth, *Transactions of the Shropshire Archaeological and Historical Society* 67, 58–62.

Morzadec, H. 1991, Les poteries fines à cordons: synthèse pétro-archéologique à partir de l'étude de celles du site de Hengistbury Head, *Oxford Journal of Archaeology* 10, 75–94.

Murcott, A. 1982, On the social significance of the 'cooked dinner' in South Wales, *Social Science Information* 21, 677–96.

Murray, P. 1988, Discard location: The ethnographic data, *American Antiquity* 45, 490–502.

Needham, S.P. 1988, Selective deposition in the British Early Bronze Age, *World Archaeology* 20(2), 229–49.

Needham, S.P. 1991, *Excavation and Salvage at Runnymede Bridge, 1978: The Late Bronze Age Waterfront Site*, British Museum, London.

Needham, S.P. 1995, A bowl from Maidscross, Suffolk; burials with pottery in the Post Deverel-Rimbury period. In Kinnes & Varndell (eds) 1995, 159–71.

Needham, S.P. 1996, Chronology and periodisation in the British Bronze Age, *Acta Archaeologica* 67, 121–140.

Needham, S.P. 1997, An independent chronology for British Bronze Age metalwork: the results of the Oxford radiocarbon accelerator programme, *Archaeological Journal* 154, 55–107.

Needham, S.P. & Ambers, J. 1994, Redating Rams Hill and reconsidering Bronze Age enclosure, *Proceedings of the Prehistoric Society*, 60, 225–44.

Needham, S.P. & Evans J. 1987, Honey and dripping: Neolithic food residues from Runnymede Bridge, *Oxford Journal of Archaeology* 6 (1), 21–28.

Needham, S.P. & Spence, T. 1997, Refuse and the formation of middens, *Antiquity* 71, 77–90.

Needham, S.P. & Sørensen, M.L.S. 1988, Runnymede refuse tip: A consideration of midden deposits and their formation. In Barrett & Kinnes (eds) 1988, 113–26.

Nelson, B.A. 1985a, Reconstructing ceramic vessels and their systemic contexts. In Nelson (ed.) 1985, 310–329.

Nelson, B.A. (ed.) 1985b, *Decoding Prehistoric Ceramics*, Southern Illinois University, Carbondale.

Nelson, B.A. 1991, Ceramic Frequency and use-life: A highlands Mayan case in cross-cultural perspective. In Longacre (ed.) 1991, 162–181.

Niblett, B.R.K. 1985, *Sheepen: An Early Industrial Site at Camulodunum*, Council for British Archaeology Research Report 57, London.

Nowakowski, J. 1993, Trethellan Farm, Newquay: the excavation of a lowland Bronze Age settlement and Iron Age cemetery, *Cornish Archaeology* 30, 5–242.

Nuber, H-U. 1972, Kanne und griffschale. Ihr gerbrauch im täglischen leben und die beigabe in gräben der römischen kaiserzeit, *Jahrbuch der Römische-Germanishes Zentralmuseum Mainz* 53, 1–232.

O'Brien, C. 1979, Iron Age and Romano-British settlement in the Trent basin. In Burnham and Johnson (eds) 1979, 299–313.

O'Connell, M. 1986, *Petters Sports Field, Egham. Excavation of a Late Bronze Age/Early Iron Age Site*, Research Volume 10, Surrey Archaeological Society, Guildford.

O'Connor, B.J. 1980, *Cross-Channel Relations in the Later Bronze Age*, British Archaeological Reports International Series 91, Oxford.

Oakley, K.P., Rankine, W.F. & Lowther, A.W.G. (eds) 1939, *A Survey of the Prehistory of the Farnham District*, Guilford.

Okpoko, A.I. 1987, Pottery-making in Igboland, Eastern Nigeria: an ethno-archaeological study, *Proceedings of the Prehistoric Society* 53, 445–456.

Okun, M.L. 1989, An Example of the Process of Acculturation in the Early Roman Frontier, *Oxford Journal of Archaeology* 8(1), 41–54.

Olivier, A.C.H. 1987, Excavation of a Bronze Age funerary cairn at Manor Farm, near Borwick, North Lancashire, *Proceedings of the Prehistoric Society* 53, 129–186.

Olivier, M. & Applin, B. 1978, Excavation of an Iron Age and Romano-British settlement at Ruckstalls Hill, *Proceedings of the Hampshire Field Club* 35, 41–92.

Orton, C, 1995, The radiocarbon dates revisited. In Cunliffe 1995, 129–30.

Ottaway, B.S. (ed.) 1983, *Archaeology, Dendrochronology and the Radiocarbon Curve*, University of Edinburgh Department of Archaeology Occasional Paper 9, Edinburgh.

Orton, C., Tyers, P. & Vince, A. 1993, *Pottery in Archaeology*, The University Press, Cambridge.

PCRG 1991, *The Study of Later Prehistoric Pottery: General Policies*, Prehistoric Ceramics Research Group Occasional Paper 1, Oxford.

PCRG 1995, *The Study of Later Prehistoric Pottery: General Policies and Guidelines for Analysis and Publication*, reprint, Prehistoric Ceramics Research Group Occasional Papers 1 and 2, Oxford.

PCRG 1997, *The Study of Later Prehistoric Pottery: General Policies and Guidelines for Analysis and Publication*, reprint, Prehistoric Ceramics Research Group Occasional Papers 1 and 2, revised edition, Oxford.

Palmer, R. 1976, Interrupted ditch enclosures in Britain: the use of aerial photography for comparative studies, *Proceedings of the Prehistoric Society* 42, 161–86.

Palmer-Brown, C.P.H. & Knight, D. (in prep.), Excavations of an Iron Age and Romano-British settlement near Aslockton, Nottinghamshire, *Transactions of the Thoroton Society of Nottinghamshire*.

Parker Pearson, M. 1990, The production and distribution of Bronze Age pottery in south-west Britain, *Cornish Archaeology* 32, 146-152.

Parker Pearson, M. 1995, Southwestern Bronze Age pottery. In Kinnes & Varndell (eds), 89–100.

Parker Pearson, M. 1996, Food, fertility and front doors in the first millennium BC. In Champion & Collis (eds) 1996, 117–132.

Parker Pearson, M. & Richards, C. 1994a, Architecture and order: spatial representation and archaeology. In Parker Pearson & Richards (eds), 38–72.

Parker Pearson. M. & Richards, C. (eds) 1994b, *Architecture and Order: Approaches to Social Space*, Routledge, London.

Parker Pearson, M. & Sharples, N. 1999, *Between Land and Sea: Excavations at Dun Vulan, South Uist*, Sheffield, Sheffield Academic Press.

Parrington, M. 1978, *The Excavation of an Iron Age Settlement, Bronze Age Ring-Ditches and Roman Features at Ashville Trading Estate, Abingdon (Oxfordshire), 1974–76*, Council for British Archaeology Research Report 28, London.

Partridge, C. 1978, Excavations and field work at Braughing, 1968–73, *Hertfordshire Archaeology* 5.

Partridge, C. 1981, *Skeleton Green: A Late Iron Age and Romano-British Site*, Britannia Monograph 2, London.

Partridge, C. 1982, Graffiti from Skeleton Green, *Britannia* 13, 325–6.

Patton, M. 1991, An Early Neolithic axe factory at Le Pinacle, Jersey, Channel Islands, *Proceedings of the Prehistoric Society* 57(2), 51–60.

Pauketat, T.R. & Emerson, T.E. 1991, The ideology of authority and the power of the pot, *American Anthropologist* 93, 919–941.

Peacock, D.P.S. 1968, A petrological study of certain Iron Age pottery from western England, *Proceedings of the Prehistoric Society* 34, 414–27.

Peacock, D.P.S. 1969a, A contribution to the study of Glastonbury ware from south western England, *Antiquaries Journal* 49, 41–61.

Peacock, D.P.S. 1969b, Neolithic pottery production in Cornwall, *Antiquity* 49, 145–149.

Peacock, D.P.S. 1971. Roman amphorae in pre-Roman Britain. In Jesson and Hill (eds) 1971, 161–88.

Peacock, D.P.S. 1977, *Pottery and Early Commerce*, London, Academic Press.

Peacock, D.P.S. 1979, Glastonbury ware: an alternative view. In Burnham & Kingsbury (eds) 1979, 113–118.

Peacock, D.P.S. 1982, *Pottery in the Roman World*, Longman, London.

Peacock, D.P.S. 1984, Amphorae in Iron Age Britain: a reassessment. In Macready & Thompson (eds) 1984, 37–42.

Peacock, D.P.S. 1988, The gabbroic pottery of Cornwall, *Antiquity* 62, 302–4.

Peacock, D.P.S. & Williams, D.F. 1986, *Amphorae and the Roman Economy*, Longmans, London.

Pearce, S.M. 1970–1, A Late Bronze Age hoard from Glentanar, Aberdeenshire, *Proceedings Society of Antiquaries Scotland* 103, 57–64.

Pearson, G.W. 1987, How to cope with calibration, *Antiquity* 61, 98–103.

Peña, J.T. 1990, Internal red-slip cookware (Pompeian Red Ware) from Cetamura del Chianti, Italy: mineralogical composition and provenance, *American Journal of Archaeology* 4, 647–61.

Pfaffenburger, P. 1988, Fetished objects and human nature: towards an anthropology of technology, *Man* (NS) 23, 236–52.

Phillips, P. & Thomas, J. 1987, A Late Neolithic pottery deposit at Ash Hill long barrow, Swinhope, Lincs., *Proceedings of the Prehistoric Society* 53, 485–8.

Pierpoint, S. 1980, *Social Patterns in Yorkshire Prehistory 3500–750 BC*, British Archaeological Reports British Series 74.

Piggott, S. 1928, Neolithic pottery and other remains from Pangbourne, Berks and Caversham, Oxon., *Proceedings of the Prehistoric Society of East Anglia* 6, 30–9.

Piggott, S. 1931, The Neolithic pottery of the British Isles, *Archaeological Journal* 88, 67–158.

Piggott, S. 1954, *Neolithic Cultures of the British Isles*, Cambridge University Press, Cambridge.

Piggott, S. 1958, Native economies and the Roman occupation of north Britain. In Richmond (ed.) 1958, 1–27.

Piggott, S. 1962, *The West Kennet Long Barrow*, HMSO, London.

Piggott, S. 1963, Abercromby and after: the Beaker cultures in Britain re-examined. In Alcock & Foster (eds) 1963, 53–91.

Plog, S. 1980, *Stylistic Variation in Prehistoric Ceramics*, The University Press, Cambridge.

Pollard, A.M. (ed.) 1990, *New Developments in Archaeological Science*, Oxford University Press, Oxford.

Pollard, J. 1992, The Sanctuary, Overton Hill, Wiltshire: a re-examination, *Proceedings of the Prehistoric Society* 58, 213–226.

Pollard, J. 1995, Inscribing Space: formal deposition at the later Neolithic monument of Woodhenge, Wiltshire, *Proceedings of the Prehistoric Society* 61, 137–56.

Pollard, R.J. 1988, *The Roman Pottery of Kent*, Kent Archaeological Society Monograph 5, Kent Archaeological Society, Maidstone.

Potter, T.W. & Trow, S.D. 1988, Puckeridge-Braughing, Herts: The Ermine Street excavations, 1971–1972, *Hertfordshire Archaeology* 10.

Powell, T.G.E. 1948, The Late Bronze Age hoard from Welby, Leicestershire, *Archaeological Journal* 105, 27–40.

Price, S. 1989, *Primitive Art in Civilised Places*, University of Chicago Press, Chicago.

Priesley-Bell, G. 1994, Archaeological excavations at America Wood, Ashington, West Sussex, *Sussex Archaeological Collections* 132.

Pryor, F.M.M. 1974, *Excavations at Fengate, Peterborough, England: the First Report*, Royal Ontario Museum Archaeology Monograph 3, Toronto.

Pryor, F.M.M. 1980, *Excavations at Fengate, Peterborough, England: The Third Report*, Northamptonshire Archaeological Society Monograph 1/Royal Ontario Museum Archaeology Monograph 6, Toronto.

Pryor, F.M.M. 1984, *Excavations at Fengate, Peterborough, England: the Fourth Report*, Northamptonshire Archaeological Society Monograph 2/Royal Ontario Museum Archaeology Monograph 7, Toronto.

Pryor, F.M.M. 1992, Discussion: the Fengate/Northey landscape, *Antiquity* 66, 518–31.

Pryor, F.M.M. 1998, Welland Bank Quarry, South Lincolnshire, *Current Archaeology* 160, 139-45,

Pryor, F.M.M. 2001, *Archaeology and Environment of the Flag Fen Basin, Peterborough*, English Heritage Archaeology Report.

Pryor, F.M.M., French, C. & Taylor, M. 1985, An interim report on excavations at Etton. Maxay, Cambridgeshire, 1982–1984, *Antiquaries Journal* 65, 275–311.

Quinnell, H. 1986, Cornwall during the Iron Age and the Roman Period, *Cornish Archaeology* 25, 111–34.

Quinnell, H. 1987, Cornish gabbroic pottery: the development of a hypothesis, *Cornish Archaeology* 26, 7–12.

Radford, C.A.R. 1951, Report on the excavations at Castle Dore, *Journal of the Royal Institution of Cornwall* new series 1, 1–119.

Raftery, B. 1994, *Pagan Celtic Ireland*, Thames & Hudson, London.

Raftery, B. (ed.) 1995a, *Sites and Sights of the Iron Age*, Oxbow Monograph 56, Oxford.

Raftery, B. 1995b, The conundrum of Irish Iron Age pottery. In Raftery 1995a (ed.), 149–156.

Rawlings, M. & Fitzpatrick, A.P. 1996, Prehistoric Sites and a Romano-British settlement at Butterfield Down, Amesbury, *Wiltshire Archaeological and Natural History Magazine* 89, 1–43.

Raymond, F. 1994, The Pottery. In Bradley *et al* (eds) 1994, 69–90.

Reimer, H. 1997, Form and Function. A contribution to the systematic recording and comparative analysis of prehistoric pottery vessels, *Archäologische Informationen* 20(1), 117–131.

Reina, R.E. & Hill, R.M. 1978, *The Traditional Pottery of Guatemala*, University of Texas Press, Austin.

Renfrew, A.C. (ed.) 1974, *British Prehistory. A New Outline*, London.

Renfrew, A.C. 1977, Alternative models for exchange and spatial distribution. In Earle & Ericson (eds) 1977, 71–90.

Renfrew, A.C. & Bahn, P. 1996, *Archaeology: Theories, Methods and Practice*, Thames & Hudson, London.

Renfrew, A.C. & Shennan, S. (eds) 1982, *Ranking, Resource and Exchange*, The University Press, Cambridge.

Rice, P.R. 1981, Evolution of specialised pottery production: a trail model, *Current Anthropology* 22, 219–240.

Rice, P.R. (ed.) 1984, *Pots and Potters: Current Approaches in Ceramic Archaeology*, University of California Press, Los Angeles.

Rice, P.R. 1987, *Pottery Analysis; A Sourcebook*, The University of Chicago Press, Chicago.

Rice, P.R. 1991, Women and prehistoric pottery production. In Walde & Williams (eds) 1991, 436–444.

Rice, P.R. 1996, Recent ceramic analysis: 1. Function, style and origins, *Journal of Archaeological Research* 4(2), 133–163.

Richards, C. & Thomas, J. 1984, Ritual activity and structured deposition in Later Neolithic Wessex. In Bradley & Gardiner (eds) 1984, 189–218.

Richards, C. 1993, Contextual analysis of the Grooved Ware at Balfarg. In Barclay & Russell-White, 1993, 43–210.

Richards, J. 1990, *The Stonehenge Environs Project*, London.

Richmond, I.A. (ed.) 1958, *Roman and Native in North Britain*, Nelson, London.

Rieckhoff, S. 1995, *Süddeutschland im Spannungsfeld von Kelten, Germanen und Römern. Studien zur Chronologie der Spätlatènezeit im Südlichen Mitteleuropa*, Trierer Zeitschrift 19.

Rigby, V. 1973, Potters stamps on *terra nigra* and *terra rubra* found in Britain. In Detsicas (ed.) 1973, 7–24.

Rigby, V. 1981, The Gallo-Belgic ware. In Partridge 1981, 159–95.

Rigby, V. 1986, The pottery. In Foster 1986, 110–23.

Rigby, V. 1987, Early Gaulish imported table wares. In Cunliffe 1987, 276–80.

Rigby, V. 1997, Gaulish imports. In Elsdon 1997, 95–100.

Rigby, V. & Elsdon, S.M. 1996, Gallo-Belgic and other imported pottery. In May 1996, 587–591.

Rigby, V. & Freestone, I. 1986, The petrology and typology of the earliest identified central Gaulish imports, *Journal of Roman Pottery Studies* 1, 6–16.

Rigby, V. & Freestone, I. 1997, Ceramic changes in Late Iron Age Britain. In Freestone & Gaimster (eds) 1997, 56–61.

Robertson-Mackay, R.E. 1980, A 'head and hoofs' burial beneath a round barrow, with other Neolithic and Bronze Age sites, on Hemp Knoll, near Avebury, Wiltshire, *Proceedings of the Prehistoric Society* 46, 123–76.

Robertson-Mackay, R.E. 1987, The Neolithic causewayed enclosure at Staines, Surrey: excavations 1961–63, *Proceedings of the Prehistoric Society* 53, 23–128.

Robinson, W. 1951, A method for chronologically ordering archaeological deposits, *American Antiquity*, 16(4), 293–301.

Robinson, W. & Brainerd, G. 1952, Robinson's co-efficient of agreement – a rejoinder, *American Antiquity*, 18 (1) 60–1.

Rodwell, K.A. 1988, *The Prehistoric and Roman Settlement at*

Kelvedon, Essex, Chelmsford Archaeological Trust 6, Council for British Archaeology Research Report 63, Chelmsford & London.

Rodwell, W.J. 1976, Coinage, oppida and the rise of Belgic power in south-eastern Britain. In Cunliffe & Rowley (eds) 1976, 181–367.

Roe, F.E.S. 1966, The battle-axe series in Britain, *Proceedings of the Prehistoric Society* 32, 199–245.

Roe, F.E.S. 1968, Stone mace-heads and the latest Neolithic cultures of the British Isles. In Coles & Simpson (eds), 145–72.

Roffin, R. & Vaisselle, F. 1966, Habitat gallo-romain au nord-ouest d'Amiens: inventaire du material Gallo-Romaine, *Revue du Nord* 48, 605–25.

Rollo, L. 1988, The shell-gritted wares. In Mackreth 1988, 107–20.

Roux, V. & Corbetta, D. 1989, *The Potter's Wheel: Craft Specialism and Technical Competence*, Oxford University Press, New Delhi/Oxford.

Rowlands, M.J. 1971, A group of incised decorated armrings and their significance for the Middle Bronze Age of southern Britain. In Sieveking (ed.) 1971, 51–74.

Rowlands, M.J. 1976, *The Production and Distribution of Metalwork in the Middle Bronze Age of Southern Britain*, British Archaeological Reports Brit. Ser. 31, Oxford.

Rowlands, M.J. 1980, Kinship, alliance and exchange in the European Bronze Age. In Barrett & Bradley (eds) 1980, 15–55.

Royle, C. & Woodward, A. 1993, The prehistoric pottery. In Ellis (ed.) 1993, 63–78.

Roymans, N. 1996, *From the Sword to the Plough*, Amsterdam Archaeological Studies 1, Amsterdam.

Russell, M. 1996, Problems of phasing: a reconsideration of the Black Patch Middle Bronze Age 'nucleated village', *Oxford Journal of Archaeology* 15, 33–38.

Russell-White, C.E., Lowe, C.E. & McCullagh, R.P.J. 1992, Excavations at three Early Bronze Age burial monuments in Scotland, *Proceedings of the Prehistoric Society* 58, 285–324.

Rye, O.S. 1976, Keeping your temper under control: materials and the manufacture of Papuan pottery, *Archaeology and Physical Anthropology in Oceania* 11 (2), 106–137.

Rye, O.S. 1981, *Pottery Technology: Principles and Reconstruction*, Taraxacum, Washington DC.

Sackett, J.R. 1985, Style and ethnicity in the Kalahari: a reply to Wiessner, *American Antiquity* 50:154–159.

Samson, R. (ed.) 1990, *The Social Archaeology of Houses*, Edinburgh University Press, Edinburgh.

Sassaman, K.E. 1992, Gender and technology at the Archaic-Woodland 'transition'. In Claassen (ed.) 1992.

Saunders, A. & Harris, D. 1982, Excavation at Castle Gotha, St. Austell, *Cornish Archaeology*, 21, 109–53.

Saunders, C, 1972, The pre-Belgic Iron Age in the central and western Chilterns, *Archaeological Journal* 128, 1–30.

Saville, A. 1983, *Uley Bury and Norbury Hillforts: Rescue Excavations at two Gloucestershire Iron Age sites*, Western Archaeological Trust Excavation Monograph 5, Western Archaeological Trust.

Sayre, E., Vandiver, P., Druzik, J. & Stevenson, C. (eds) 1988, *Material Issues in Art and Archaeology*, London.

Scarre, C. & Healy, F. (eds) 1993, *Trade and Exchange in Prehistoric Europe*, Oxbow Books, Oxford.

Schiffer, M.B. 1976, *Behavioural Archaeology*, Academic Press, New York.

Schiffer, M.B. 1987, *Formation Processes of the Archaeological Record*, Albuquerque.

Schiffer, M.B. 1990, The influence of surface treatment on heating effectiveness of ceramic vessels, *Journal of Archaeological Science* 17, 373–381.

Schiffer, M.B. & Skibo, J.M. 1987, Theory and experiment in the study of technological change, *Current Anthropology* 28, 595–622.

Schiffer, M.B, Skibo, J.M., Boelke, T.C., Neupert, M.A. & Aronson, M. 1994, New perspectives on experimental archaeology: surface treatments and thermal response of the clay cooking pot, *American Antiquity* 59 (2), 197–217.

Schofield, A.J. 1989, Understanding early medieval pottery distributions: cautionary tales and their implications for further research, *Antiquity* 63, 460–70

Schofield, A.J. (ed.) 1995, *Lithics in Context: Suggestions for the Future Direction of Lithics Studies*. Lithic Studies Society Occasional Paper 5.

Sealey, P. 1985, *Amphoras from the 1970 Excavations at Colchester Sheepen*, British Archaeological Report, British Series 142, Oxford.

Sealey, P. 1997, The Iron Age. In Bedwin (eds) 1997, 26–68.

Seager-Smith, R. & Woodward, A. 2001, The prehistoric pottery. In D. Farwell & R. Whinney, *Excavations on Twyford Down, Hampshire.*

Sergeantson, D., Wales, S. & Evans, J. 1994, Fish in later prehistoric Britain, *Offa* 51, 332–339.

Shand, P. & Henderson, R. Forthcoming, Corporation Farm. In Barclay *et al* (eds.).

Shanks, M. & Tilley, C. 1987a, *Social Theory and Archaeology*, Polity Press, London.

Shanks. M. & Tilley, C. 1987b, *Reconstructing Archaeology*, The University Press, Cambridge.

Sharples, N. 1991, *Maiden Castle, Excavations and Field Survey 1985–6*, English Heritage Archaeological Report 19, Historic Buildings and Monuments Commission for England, London.

Sharples, N. & A. Sheridan (eds) 1992, *Vessels for the Ancestors*, Edinburgh University Press, Edinburgh.

Shennan, S. 1981, Appendix 1. A multidimensional scaling analysis of the Old Down Farm pits. In Davies 1981, 158–60.

Shennan, S. 1982, Ideology, change and the European Bronze Age. In Hodder (ed.) 1982b, 133–161.

Shennan, S., Healy, F. & Smith, I.F. 1985, The excavation of a ring ditch at Tye Field, Lawford, Essex, *Archaeological Journal* 142, 150–215.

Shepard, A.O. 1956, *Ceramics for the Archaeologist*, Washington, DC.

Shepard, A.O. 1985, *Ceramics for the Archaeologist*, Washington D.C.

Sheridan, A. 1995, Irish Neolithic pottery: the story in 1995. In Kinnes & Varndell (eds), 3–21.

Sherratt, A.G. 1987, Cups that cheered. In Waldren & Kennard (eds) 1987. 81–114.

Sherratt, A. 1991, Sacred and profane substances: the ritual use of narcotics in later Neolithic Europe, In Garwood *et al* (eds) 1991, 50-64.

Shot, M. 1996, Mortal pots: on use life and vessel size in the formation of ceramic assemblages, *American Antiquity* 61(3), 463–482

Sieveking, G. de G. (ed.) 1971, *Prehistoric and Roman Studies*, The British Museum, London.

Sieveking, G. de G., Longworth, I. & Wilson, K. (eds) 1976, *Problems in Economic and Social Archaeology*, Duckworth, London.

Silvester, R.J. 1981, Excavations at Honeyditches Roman villa, Seaton, in 1978, *Proceedings of the Devon Archaeological Society*, 39, 37–87.

Simmel, G. (ed. D.N. Levine) 1971, *On Individuality and Social Forms: Selected Works*, University of Chicago Press, Chicago & London.

Sillar, B. 1996, The dead and the drying: Techniques for transforming people and things in the Andes, *Journal of Material Culture* 1(3), 259–289.

Simpson, D.D.A. 1996, Crown antler maceheads and the later Neolithic in Britain, *Proceedings of the Prehistoric Society* 62, 293–311.

Simoons, F.J. 1967, *Eat Not of This Flesh*, Wisconsin.

Sinclair, A., Slater, E. & Gowlett, J. (eds) 1998, *Archaeological Sciences 1995*, Oxbow Monograph 64, Oxford.

Sinopoli, C.M. 1991, *Approaches to Archaeological Ceramics*, Plenum Press, New York.

Skeates, R. 1995, Animate objects: a biography of prehistoric 'axe-amulets' in the central Mediterranean region, *Proceedings of the Prehistoric Society* 61, 279–302.

Skibo, J.M. 1992, *Pottery Function: a Use-Alteration Perspective*, Plenum Press, New York.

Skibo, J.M. & Schiffer, M.B. 1987, The effects of water on processes of ceramic abrasion, *Journal of Archaeological Science* 14, 83–96

Skibo, J.M., Butts, T.C. & Schiffer, M.B. 1997, Ceramic surface treatment and abrasion resistance: an experimental study, *Journal of Archaeological Science* 24, 311–317.

Smith, A.H. 1995, A Late Iron Age settlement in the Winestead Drain (Holderness), *First Annual Report of the Humber Wetlands Survey (1994–95)*, The Humber Wetlands Project, University of Hull, Hull, 18–9.

Smith, C.A. 1978, The landscape and natural history of Iron Age settlement on the Trent gravels. In Cunliffe & Rowley (eds) 1978, 91–101.

Smith, C.A. (ed.) 1979, *Fisherwick: the Reconstruction of an Iron Age Landscape*, British Archaeological Reports 61, Oxford.

Smith, C.R. 1852, Roman remains found at Mount Bures, near Colchester, *Collectanea Antiqua* 2, 25–36.

Smith, I.F. 1965, *Windmill Hill and Avebury. Excavations by Alexander Keiller 1925–1939*, Oxford University Press, Oxford.

Smith, I.F. 1974, The Neolithic. In Renfrew (ed.) 1974, 100–36.

Smith, I.M. (ed. J. Taylor) 2000, Excavations on Iron Age and Medieval earthworks at The Dod, Borders Region, 1979–81, *The Archaeological Journal* 157, 229–353.

Smith, M.A. 1959, Some Somerset hoards and their place in the Bronze Age of southern Britain, *Proceedings of the Prehistoric Society* 25, 144–87.

Smith, M.F. 1988, Function from whole vessel shape: a method and an application to Anasazi Black Mesa, Arizona, *American Anthropologist* 90, 912–923.

Smith, R.A. 1924, Two prehistoric vessels, *Antiquaries Journal* 4, 127–30

Smith, R., Healy, F., Allen, M., Morris, E., Barnes, I. & Woodward, P. 1997, *Excavations Along the Route of the Dorchester By-pass, Dorset, 1986–8*, Wessex Archaeology Report no. 11, Salisbury.

Sørensen, M.L. & Thomas, R. (eds) 1989, *The Bronze Age-Iron Age Transition in Europe*, British Archaeological Reports International Series 483, Oxford.

Standford, S.C. 1974, *Croft Ambrey*, Hereford.

Stanford, S.C. 1982, Bromfield, Shropshire – Neolithic, Beaker and Bronze Age sites 1966–79, *Proceedings of the Prehistoric Society* 48, 279–320.

Stanley, J. 1954, An Iron Age fort at Ball Cross Farm, Bakewell, *Derbyshire Archaeological Journal* 74, 85–99.

Stead, I.M. 1967, A La Tène III burial at Welwyn Garden City, *Archaeologia* 101, 1–62.

Stead, I.M. 1976, The earliest burials of the Aylesford culture. In Sieveking, Longworth & Wilson (eds) 1976, 401–16.

Stead, I.M. 1991a, *Iron Age cemeteries in East Yorkshire: excavations at Burton Fleming, Rudston, Garton-on-the-Wolds, and Kirkburn*, English Heritage Archaeological Report 22, English Heritage in association with British Museum Press.

Stead, I.M. 1991b, The Snettisham treasure: excavations in 1990, *Antiquity* 65, 447–65.

Stead, I.M. & Rigby, V. 1986, *Baldock: The Excavation of a Roman and Pre-Roman Settlement, 1968–72*, Britannia Monograph Series 7, London.

Stead, I.M. & Rigby, V. 1989, *Verulamium: The King Harry Lane site*, English Heritage Archaeological Report 12, London.

Steponaitis, V.P. 1984, Technological studies of prehistoric pottery from Alabama: physical properties and vessel function. In van der Leeuw & Pritchard (eds), 79–127.

Sterner, J. 1989, Who is signalling whom? Ceramic style, ethnicity and taphonomy among the Sirak Bulahey, *Antiquity* 63, 451–460.

Stoneham, D., Tite, M.S. & May, J. 1996, The analysis of 1992. In May 1996, 438–443.

Struck, M. (ed.) 1993, *Römerzeitlicher Gräber als Quellen zu Religion, Bevölkersungsstruktur und Sozialgeschichte*, Archäologische Schriften Institutes für Vor- und Frügeschichte der Johannes Gutenberg Universität Mainz 3, Mainz.

Sullivan, A.P. 1989, The technology of ceramic reuse: formation processes and archaeological evidence, *World Archaeology* 21, 101–114.

Sunter, N. & Woodward, P.J. 1987, *Romano-British Industries in Purbeck*, Dorset Natural History and Archaeological Society Monograph 6, Dorchester.

Swan, V.G. 1975, Oare reconsidered and the origins of Savernake ware in Wiltshire, *Britannia* 6, 37–61.

Swan, V.G. 1984, *The Pottery Kilns of Roman Britain*, London, Royal Commission on Historical Monuments.

Sylvester-Bradley, P.C. & Ford, T.D. 1968, *The Geology of the East Midlands*, Leicester University Press.

Tait, J.G. 1965, *Beakers from Northumberland*, Newcastle-upon-Tyne.

Thomas, J. 1988, Neolithic explanations revisited: the Mesolithic-Neolithic transition in Britain and South Scandinavia, *Proceedings of the Prehistoric Society* 54, 59–66.

Swain, H.P. 1987, The Iron Age pottery. In Heslop 1987, 57–71.

Thomas, J. 1990, A long, cold look: reply to Ian Longworth, *Scottish Archaeological Review* 7, 81–3.

Thomas, J. 1991a, *Rethinking the Neolithic*, The University Press, Cambridge.

Thomas, J. 1991b, Reading the body: Beaker funerary practice in Britain. In Garwood *et al* 1991, 33–42.

Thomas, J. 1993, The politics of vision and the archaeologies of landscape. In B.Bender (ed.) 1993, 19–48.

Thomas, J. 1996, *Time, Culture and Identity: An Interpretative Archaeology*, Routledge, London & New York.

Thomas, J. & Tilley, C. 1993, The axe and the torso: symbolic structures in the Neolithic of Brittany. In Tilley (ed.) 1993, 225–326.

Thomas, J. & Whittle, A. 1986, Anatomy of a tomb – West Kennet revisited, *Oxford Journal of Archaeology* 5(2), 129–56.

Thompson, I. 1979, Wheathampstead revisited, *Bulletin of the Institute of Archaeology, University of London* 16, 159–85,

Thompson, I. 1982, *Grog-tempered 'Belgic' Pottery of South-eastern England*, British Archaeological Reports British Series 108, Oxford

Thorpe, N. 1984, Ritual, power and ideology: a reconsideration of earlier Neolithic rituals in Wessex. In Bradley & Gardiner (eds) 1984, 41–60.

Thorpe, N. & Richards. C. 1984, The decline of ritual authority and the introduction of the Beaker in Britain. In Bradley & Gardiner (eds) 1984, 67–84.

Thurnam, J. 1871, On British barrows, especially those of Wiltshire and the adjoining counties, *Archaeologia*, 43, 285–552.

Tilley, C. (ed.) 1993, *Interpretative Archaeology*, Berg, Oxford and Providence.

Timby, J.R. 1987, First century imports and native fine wares. In Woodward 1987, 73–9.

Timby, J.R. 2001, The pottery. In Fulford & Timby 2001.

Tobert, N. 1984, Ethno-archaeology of pottery firing in Darfur, Sudan: implications for ceramic technology studies, *Oxford Journal of Archaeology* 3(2), 141–56.

Todd, M. (ed.) 1978. *Studies in the Romano-British Villa*, Leicester University Press.

Todd, M. (ed.) 1989, *Research on Roman Britain: 1960–89*, Britannia Monograph 11, London.

Tomalin, D.J. 1983, *British Biconical Urns, their Character and Chronology and the Relationship with Indigenous Early Bronze Age Ceramics*, unpublished PhD thesis: University of Southampton.

Tomalin, D.J. 1988, Armorican Vases à Anses and their occurrence in southern Britain, *Proceedings of the Prehistoric Society* 54, 203–21.

Tomalin, D.J. 1995, Cognition, ethnicity and some implications for linguistics in the perception and perpetation of 'Collared Urn' art. In Kinnes & Varndell (eds) 1985, 101–112.

Topping, P.G. 1987, Typology and chronology in later prehistoric pottery assemblages of the Western Isles, *Proceedings of the Society of Antiquaries of Scotland*, 117, 67–84.

Torday, E. & Joyce, T. 1910, *Notes Ethnographiques sur les Peuples communment appels Bukuba ainsi que sur les Peuplades Apparentes*. Les Bushongo, Documentes Ethnographiques concernant les Populations du Congo Belge, Tome II, Fasc. I, Brussels.

Torrence, R. & van der Leeuw, S.E. 1989, Introduction: what's new about innovation? In Van der Leeuw & Torrence (eds) 1989, 1–15.

Tringham, R. 1991, Households with faces: the challenge of gender in architectural remains. In Gero & Conkey (eds) 1991, 93–131.

Trow, S.D. 1990, By the northern shores of Ocean: Some observations on acculturation processes at the edge of the Roman world. In Blagg & Millett (eds) 1989, 35–41.

Tucker, M.E. 1981, *Sedimentary Petrology: an Introduction*, Blackwell Scientific, Oxford.

Turner, J. & Turner, C. 1997, *Dorket Head, Nottinghamshire*, Sherwood Archaeological Society, Mansfield.

Tyers, P.A. 1996, *Roman Pottery in Britain*, Batsford, London.

Van de Noort, R. & Ellis, S. (eds) 1995, *Wetland Heritage of Holderness: An Archaeological Survey*, The Humber Wetlands Project, University of Hull, Hull.

Van de Noort, R. & Ellis, S. (eds) 1995, *Wetland Heritage of Holderness*, Humber Wetlands Project, School of Geography and Earth Resources, University of Hull.

Van de Noort, R. & Ellis, S. (eds) 1997, *Wetland Heritage of the Humberhead Levels*, Humber Wetlands Project, School of Geography and Earth Resources, University of Hull.

Van de Noort, R. & Ellis, S. (eds) 1998, *Wetland Heritage of the Ancholme and Lower Trent*, Humber Wetlands Project, School of Geography and Earth Resources, University of Hull.

Van der Leeuw, S.E. 1977, Towards a study of the economics of pottery making, *Ex Horro* 4, 68–76.

Van der Leeuw, S.E. 1989, Giving the pottery a choice; conceptual aspects of pottery techniques. In van der Leeuw & Torrence (eds) 1989, 238–288.

Van der Leeuw, S.E. & Pritchard, A.C. (eds) 1984, *The Many Dimensions of Pottery*, Universiteit van Amsterdam, Amsterdam.

Van der Leeuw, S.E & Torrence, R. (eds) 1989, *What's New? A Closer Look at the Process of Innovation*, Routledge, London.

Van der Veen, M. 1992, *Crop Husbandry Regimes: An Archaeological Study of Farming in Northern England 100 BC – AD 500*, Sheffield Archaeological Monograph 3, Sheffield.

Vencl, S. 1994, The archaeology of thirst, *Journal of European Archaeology* 2(2), 299–326.

Vyner, B.E. 1988, The hill-fort at Eston Nab, Eston, Cleveland, *The Archaeological Journal*, 145, 60–98.

Vyner, B.E. (ed.) 1995, *Moorland Monuments: Studies in the Archaeology of North-East Yorkshire in honour of Raymond Hayes and Don Spratt*, Council for British Archaeology Research Report 101, London.

Vyner, B.E. & Daniels, R. 1989, Further investigation of the Iron Age and Romano-British settlement site at Catcote, Hartlepool, Cleveland, 1987, *Durham Archaeological Journal*, 5, 11–34.

Wacher, J.S. 1977, Excavations at Breedon-on-the-Hill, *Leicestershire Archaeological and Historical Society Transactions* 52, 1–35,

Wainwright, G.J. 1967, *Coygan Camp: a Prehistoric, Romano-British and Dark Age settlement in Carmarthenshire,* Cambrian Archaeological Association, Cardiff.

Wainwright, G.J. 1993, *English Heritage Archaeological Review 1992–93,* English Heritage.

Wainwright, G.J. & Longworth, I. 1971, *Durrington Walls Excavations: 1966–68,* Research Report No. 29, London: Society of Antiquaries.

Walde, D. & Willows, N. (eds) 1991, *The Archaeology of Gender,* Calgary.

Wallaert, H. 1997, Manual Laterality Apprenticeship as First Learning Rule Prescribed to Potters: A Case Study in Handmade Pottery from Northern Cameroon. Paper presented at the Ethno-Analogy and the Reconstruction of Prehistoric Artefact Use and Production Conference, Institute of Prehistory, University of Tübingen Germany.

Waldren, W.H. & Kennard. R.C. (eds) 1987, *Bell-Beakers of the Western Mediterranean,* British Archaeological Reports International Series 331, Oxford.

Wardle, P. 1992, *Earlier Prehistoric Pottery Production and Ceramic Petrology in Britain,* British Archaeological Reports British Series 225, Oxford.

Walker, J. 1978. Anglo-Saxon traded pottery. In Todd (ed.) 1978, 224–8.

Ward, J. 1890, On some diggings near Brassington, Derbyshire, *Derbyshire Archaeological Journal* 12, 108–38.

Washburn, D. 1983, *Structure and Cognition in Art,* Cambridge University Press, Cambridge.

Welbourn, A. 1984, Endo ceramics and power strategies. In Miller & Tilley (eds) 1984, 17–24

West, S. 1990, *West Stow: The Prehistoric and Roman-British Occupations,* East Anglian Archaeology 48, Ipswich.

Wheeler, R.E.M. & Wheeler, T. 1936, *Verulamium: A Belgic and Two Roman Cities,* Research Report of the Society of Antiquities of London 11, London.

Wheeler, R.E.M. 1954, *The Stanwick Fortifications,* Reports of the Research Committee of the Society of Antiquaries of London, 17, London.

Wheeler, H. 1979, Excavations at Willington, Derbyshire, 1970–2, *Derbyshire Archaeological Journal* 99, 58–220.

White, D.A. 1982, *The Bronze Age Cremation Cemeteries at Simons Ground, Dorset,* Dorset Natural History and Archaeological Society Monograph 3, Dorchester.

Whittle, A. 1977, *The Earlier Neolithic of Southern Britain and its Continental Background,* British Archaeological Reports S35, Oxford.

Wiessner, P. 1984, Reconsidering the behavioural basis of style, *Journal of Anthropological Archaeology* 3:190–234.

Wiessner, P. 1985, Style or isochrestic variation? a reply to Sackett, *American Antiquity* 50, 160–166.

Wiessner, P. 1990, Is there a unity to style. In M. Conkey & C. Hastorf (eds), 105–112.

Wilkinson, T.J. 1988, *Archaeology and Environment in South Essex,* 75–80, East Anglian Archaeology 42, Chelmsford.

Williams, J.H. (ed.) 1974, *Two Iron Age Sites in Northampton,* Northampton.

Williams, D.F. 1977, Petrology of Iron Age pottery from Weekley, *Northamptonshire Archaeology* 12, 183–4.

Williams, D.F. 1984, A fabric analysis of some Iron Age pottery from Fengate. In Pryor 1984, 134.

Williams, D.F. 1986–7, Weekley, Northamptonshire: petrological examination of Iron Age pottery. In Jackson & Dix, 1986–7, microfiche 124–126.

Williams, D.F. 1992, *A Note on the Petrology of some Late Iron Age Sherds from Gamston, Nottinghamshire,* Ancient Monuments Laboratory Report 14/92.

Williams, D.F. 1997, *A Petrological Note on Iron Age Pottery from Swarkestone, Derby Southern By-Pass,* English Heritage Ceramic and Lithic Petrology Project, Dept. of Archaeology, University of Southampton.

Williams, D.F. & Vince, A. 1997, The characterisation and interpretation of early to middle Saxon granitic tempered pottery in England, *Medieval Archaeology* 61, 214–20.

Willis, S.H. 1994, Roman imports into Late Iron Age British societies: Towards a critique of existing models. In Cottam, Dungworth, Scott & Taylor (eds), 141–150.

Willis, S.H. 1996, The Romanization of pottery assemblages in the east and north-east of England during the first century AD: a comparative analysis, *Britannia,* 27, 179–221.

Willis, S.H. 1997, Settlement, materiality and landscape in the Iron Age of the East Midlands; evidence, Interpretation and wider resonance. In Gwilt & Haselgrove (eds) 1997, 205–15.

Willis, S.H. 1999, Without and within: Culture and community in the Iron Age of North-Eastern England: regional identity and continuity. In Bevan 1999, 81–110.

Willis, S.H. 2000, The later prehistoric pottery. In Smith 2000, 320–23.

Wilson, A.E. 1940, Excavations at the Caburn 1938, *Sussex Archaeological Collections* 80, 193–213.

Wilson, P.R., Jones, R.J.F. & Evans, D.M. (eds) 1984, *Settlement and Society in the Roman North.* School of Archaeological Sciences, University of Bradford.

Woolf, A. & Eldridge, R. 1994, Sharing a drink with Marcel Mauss, *Journal of European Archaeology* 2(2) 327–340.

Woolf, G. 1993a, Rethinking the oppida, *Oxford Journal of Archaeology* 12(2), 223–233.

Woolf, G. 1993b, The social significance of trade in Late Iron Age Europe. In Scarre & Healy (eds) 1993, 211–218.

Woods, A.J. 1984, Methods of pottery manufacture in the Kavango region of South West Africa/Namibia: two case studies. *Colloquies of Art and Archaeology in Asia* 12, 303–25: Percival David Foundation.

Woods, A.J. 1986, Form, fabric and function: some observations on the cooking pot in antiquity. In Kingery (ed.) 1986, 157–172.

Woods, P.J. 1969, *Excavations at Hardingstone, Northants, 1967–8,* Northamptonshire County Council, Northampton.

Woodward, A.B. 1990, The Bronze Age Pottery. In M. Bell, *Brean Down Excavations 1983–1987,* 121–145, English Heritage Archaeological Report 15, London.

Woodward, A.B. 1995, Vessel Size and Social Identity in the Bronze Age of Southern Britain. In Kinnes & Varndell (eds), 195–202.

Woodward, A.B. 1997, Size and style: an alternative study

of some Iron Age pottery in southern England. In Gwilt & Haselgrove (eds), 26–35.

Woodward, A.B. 2000a, The prehistoric pottery. In Barrett, Freeman & Woodward 2000.

Woodward, A.B. 2000b, The prehistoric pottery. In Hughes, *Excavations at the Early Bronze Age barrow cemetery at Lockington, Leicestershire.*

Woodward, A.B. & Blinkhorn, P. 1997, Size is important: Iron Age vessel capacities in central and southern England. In Cumberpatch & Blinkhorn, (eds) 1997, 153–162.

Woodward, A.B. & Candy, J. Forthcoming, The Iron Age pottery from Wasperton, Warks.

Woodward, A.B. & Cane. C. 1991, The Bronze Age pottery. In Nowakowski, 1991, 103–31.

Woodward, P.J. 1987, The excavation of a Late-Iron Age trading settlement and Romano-British BB1 production site at Ower, Dorset, In Sunter & Woodward 1987.

Wolseley, G.R., Smith, R.A. & Hawley, W. 1927, Prehistoric settlements on Park Brow, *Archaeologia* 76, 1–40.

Wright, R.P. 1991, Women's labour and pottery production in prehistory. In Gero & Conkey (eds) 1991, 194–223.

Yentsch, A. 1991, The symbolic divisions of pottery: Sex-related attributes of English and Anglo-American household pots. In McGuire & Paynter (eds) 1991,192–230.

Contributors

Alistair Barclay
Oxford Archaeological Unit
Janus House
Osney Mead
Oxford
OX2 0ES

Robin Boast
The Museum of Archaeology and Anthropology
University of Cambridge
Cambridge
CB2 3DZ

Andrew Fitzpatrick
Wessex Archaeology
Portway House
South Portway Estate
Old Sarum
Salisbury
SP4 6EB

Alex Gibson
Department of Archaeological Sciences
University of Bradford
Bradford
BD7 1DP

Sue Hamilton
The Institute of Archaeology
University College London
31–4 Gordon Square
London
WC1H 0PY

J. D. Hill
The Department of Prehistory and Early Europe
The British Museum
London
WC1B 3DG

David Knight
Trent and Peak Archaeological Trust
University Park
Nottingham
NG7 2RD

Elaine L. Morris
The Department of Archaeology
University of Southampton
Southampton
SO17 2BJ

Joshua Pollard
SCARAB
University College
Caerleon Campus
Newport
NP6 1YG

Jane Timby
Burleigh Heights
Burleigh
Stroud
GL5 2PL

Steven Willis
Department of Archaeology
University of Durham
Durham
DH1 3LE

Ann Woodward
Department of Ancient History and Archaeology
University of Birmingham
Birmingham
B15 2TT